CITIZENSHIP AND CIVIL SOCIETY

A FRAMEWORK OF RIGHTS AND OBLIGATIONS IN LIBERAL, TRADITIONAL, AND SOCIAL DEMOCRATIC REGIMES

THOMAS JANOSKI
University of Kentucky

CAMBRIDGE
UNIVERSITY PRESS

PUBLISHED BY THE PRESS SYNDICATE OF THE UNIVERSITY OF CAMBRIDGE
The Pitt Building, Trumpington Street, Cambridge CB2 1RP, United Kingdom

CAMBRIDGE UNIVERSITY PRESS
The Edinburgh Building, Cambridge CB2 2RU, United Kingdom
40 West 20th Street, New York, NY 10011-4211, USA
10 Stamford Road, Oakleigh, Melbourne 3166, Australia

First published 1998

Printed in the United States of America

Typeset in Sabon

Library of Congress Cataloging-in-Publication Data
Janoski, Thomas.
Citizenship and civil society : a framework of rights and
obligations in liberal, traditional, and social democratic regimes /
Thomas Janoski.
p.   cm.
Includes bibliographical references and index.
ISBN 0-521-57198-7
1. Civil society.   2. Citizenship.   3. Civil rights.   4. Political
obligation.   5. Responsibility.   I. Title.
JC336.J35   1998
323.6 – dc21   97-8768
                                                                 CIP

A catalog record for this book is available from the British Library

ISBN 0 521 57198 7 hardback
ISBN 0 521 63581 0 paperback

Citizenship and Civil Society advances three crucial areas of citizenship theory. First, it clarifies the confusing areas of rights and obligations. Using Wesley Hohfeld's theory of law, the book shows how legal, political, social, and participation rights are systematically related to liberties, claims, and immunities. Second, the book frames the question of balance between rights and obligations in systems of restricted and generalized exchange. It makes the point that where rights and obligations do not exist in a one-for-one relationship (restricted exchange), communities and organizations will be stronger. It shows that social democratic countries have a high level of balance (i.e., high rights and high obligations) while liberal countries have a low level of balance (i.e., low rights and low obligations despite the emphasis often put on wide-ranging liberties). Third, Professor Janoski answers a number of questions about how rights developed over the past few centuries. He explains that traditional countries rely on social closure to limit rights and obligations to a rather specific population. Generalized exchange can then operate more effectively with better results than for a closed group of people. Liberal countries rely on social openness and consequently must have a lower level of rights and obligations because citizens do not want their resources given to people freely moving in and out of their boundaries. Professor Janoski then shows how power resources and state-centric theory explain the development of rights over decades and centuries. He supports T. H. Marshall's view that rights develop in particular orders, building on each other. Basic legal rights to property for men and women and freedoms of speech and religion developed first, then political rights to vote for propertied men, all men, women, and various ethnic and indigenous groups. These legal and political rights were followed by social rights. Finally, participation rights consisting of codetermination and labor market rights and protections emerged in the post–World War II period.

CITIZENSHIP AND CIVIL SOCIETY

This book is dedicated to
the citizen-advocates,
the families and children,
the volunteers,
the board members,
and the underpaid staff
of the Arc, and the
Triangle Down Syndrome Parents Group,
who together strive to bring
full citizenship to
persons of all mental abilities.

Contents

Figures and Tables

FIGURES

TABLES

Figures and Tables

Figures and Tables

Acknowledgments

This book is based on many ideas suggested to me by the late Reinhard Bendix. While I have pushed citizenship theory in many directions that Professor Bendix found untenable (e.g., participation rights), the inspiration for much of my task comes from him. I will never forget my time spent in his seminars discussing T. H. Marshall and Max Weber. In a more indirect way, but just as important, many people at the Institute for the Study of Social Change at the University of California–Berkeley provided a concrete example of a system of generalized exchange. Troy Duster should be credited for much of the organizational culture of this institute, and I specifically thank Janice Tanigawa, Robert Yamashita, Basil Browne, Joan Fujimura, Russell Ellis, and David Minkus for their diverse contributions.

This project has received support from Duke University. John Wilson, Steve Smith, Alex Keyssar, and I received a faculty thematic working group grant on "Citizenship and Civil Society" from the Center for International Studies. This group provided meetings and seminars on the topic of citizenship and brought in speakers on the topic including Andrew Arato, Craig Calhoun, Kenneth Fogelman, Volker Gransow, John Keane, and Steven Leonard. Josefina Tiryakian and Robert Sikorski were particularly helpful in facilitating the working group's activities. I am appreciative for comments made by group members: Patricia Conover, Herbert Kitschelt, Carey Pieratt, Donald Searing, Joel Smith, Steve Smith, Michael Shalev, Robert Sikorski, Edward Tiryakian, Rosemary Gartner, and John Wilson. Thanks also go to C. Robert Connor for invitations to a conference at the National Humanities Center on "The Idea of a Civil Society" and subsequent talks.

I appreciate Joel Smith's reading of the first five chapters, and John Wilson and Edward Tiryakian for reading the first three chapters. Bryan Turner and Adam Seligman also provided useful insights, especially from the viewpoint of social theory. I would also like to thank Alex Holzman

Acknowledgments

for his helpful guidance at Cambridge University Press, and the four reviewers of the prospectus and manuscript, especially Reviewer B, who provided extensive comments and timely encouragement. Thanks go to Carey Pieratt, Elizabeth Glennie, and Rahmah Abdulaleem for research assistance. Carey Pieratt's role expanded into co-authorship on a paper based on the micro-aspects of citizenship, as did Elizabeth Glennie's input in a paper related to naturalization. Their help was considerable. Finally, Amby Rice and Karen Shander did excellent work in constructing the many figures included in this book.

Lexington, May 1997

I

Introduction to Citizenship

There is no more dynamic social figure in modern history than
  The Citizen.
For centuries now, [s]he has been member and motor
  of rising social groups:
  of the urban propertied class in feudal society,
  of the new industrial class in the eighteenth and nineteenth centuries . . .
  of those who liberated themselves from dependence and deprivation –
    villeins and subjects, colonial dependents, minorities of many kinds,
    women.

Ralf Dahrendorf (1974, p. 673)

The use of rights and citizenship has exploded with groups of many
different types demanding and in some cases obtaining new rights. Many
complain of a cacophony of rights claims and the comparative silence
on obligations and duties to fulfill those rights. At the same time, immigrants in many countries clamor at the gates of industrialized nations
with claims for a new citizenship that will socially and politically integrate them into a society with opportunities to live and prosper. Rights
and duties are trumpeted and denounced with great emotion, diverse
definitions, shallow usage, and uncertain relationships between concepts.
What can citizens, politicians, and social scientists make of these claims
for inclusion, obligation, and rights of citizenship?

Although most advanced industrialized countries cover nearly all of
their inhabitants with at least some legal, political, and social rights,
citizenship rights clearly remain contentious. Citizens and subjects demand rights, but their success depends on the ebb and flow of the power
of contending political parties, interest groups, and social movements.
Many libertarian conservatives and radicals see citizenship obligations
as overly enforced, but communitarians and neo-conservatives see obligations as being in steep decline. On the one hand, Freeden sees rights
as being overwhelmingly accepted: "The concept of rights has become

one of the most reputable and positively connoted in political theory. The desirability of promoting in principle the ideas represented by the concept is far less controversial than, for example, the promotion of equality, democracy or even liberty" (1991, p. 1). On the other hand, Etzioni asks for an emphasis on obligations: "We should, for a transition period of, say, the next decade, put a tight lid on the manufacturing of new rights. The incessant issuance of new rights, like the wholesale printing of currency, causes a massive inflation of rights that devalues their moral claims" (1993, p. 5). Clearly, positions differ widely on the status of rights and obligations, which is one of a number of reasons why understanding the rights terrain is so difficult.

The claiming of rights involves many questions that would seem to be hard to deny. In terms of legal rights, one may ask today whether ethnic minorities and immigrants have freedom from attack and harassment from majorities; whether citizens can defend themselves against robbery and attack on the streets and in their own homes; whether women have the right to walk outdoors at night or to control their own bodies in clinics and hospitals; and whether developmentally delayed persons have rights to attend regular schools, to work for pay, and even to procreate. Concerning political rights, one may ask when only half the eligible citizens vote in America, are their rights really operative? When the third generation of guestworkers in Germany are denied the right to vote, how can such exclusive principles of citizenship be justified? Questions about social rights focus on whether poor or middle-income persons have rights to health care, and whether children with AIDS may attend school. We may ask whether government bureaucracies serve or simply ignore clients, and whether government workers have adequate representation on their jobs. We may ask what rights workers at private corporations have to job security, safe working conditions, and abilities to set the terms of work, rest, and production. In sum, what status do rights have in post-industrial societies, and how can they be measured and explained?

The silences about obligations appear to be irresponsible. Nearly all citizens rigorously claim the right to a trial by jury, but many avoid serving on juries for other citizens (Etzioni 1993, p. 3; Janowitz 1983). In terms of political and social obligations, many citizens demand government money from entitlement programs, yet loathe paying taxes to support entitlements for others. Some citizens feel content to watch deficits grow despite their uneasiness about the growing burdens that are being placed on future generations. Many people want protection against fraud and crime, but cannot approve measures that would prevent or inhibit lawlessness such as national identity cards, sobriety checkpoints, drug testing, and disciplinary measures in the schools. Cit-

2

izens want public defense in their communities and around the world, but are shy or afraid of serving on community watches in neighborhoods, and in the military or its more peaceful alternatives. The provision of rights to immigrants involves obligations that many native citizens easily deny. How can social scientists conceptualize, measure, and explain the creation, enforcement, or neglect of these and other obligations?

Citizenship rights were not always widespread, and at earlier points in history, citizenship rights applied to less than a tenth of the population in many nations. Rights developed through nation-building with barons gaining access to legal rights (e.g., the Magna Carta in Britain). They developed further with the bourgeoisie obtaining legal and political rights in various legal codes and constitutions during the Industrial Revolution. Many see the unique Western Enlightenment as the ideational motor of citizenship because of the rise of rational individualism, but others see it as a specific system of rights based on individualism that does not apply to other cultures (Bridges 1994, p. 6). Yet citizenship rights have widely diffused to many intellectuals and educated workers in non-Western cultures. With the world wars of the twentieth century, rights advanced for the working classes, especially after they served in the military. And rights continue to grow for gender, racial, ethnic, and ability groups. None of these processes were particularly smooth, and most were surrounded with considerable conflict, but from the twelfth to the twentieth centuries, citizenship rights have advanced in most industrialized countries. Nonetheless, the explanations for this advance are in critical need of development.

A theory of citizenship, properly conceived, should provide the tools to explain the development and balancing of public rights and obligations in advanced industrialized societies. The promise of citizenship theory is that it will also illuminate a large range of behaviors and processes concerning rights and obligations in industrialized societies.

THE MAJOR PROBLEMS FACING CITIZENSHIP THEORY

Since Marshall (1964) first crafted citizenship as an explanatory framework to explain legal, political, and social rights, a wide variety of distinguished scholars have used his theory.[1] This usage ranges from employing the concept of citizenship as part of other arguments to the more extensive explanation of citizenship, including the development of rights over decades and centuries given the inevitable conflict of capitalism and citizenship. Yet "there is still nothing which could be described as a *theory* of citizenship" (Barbalet 1988, p. 108).[2]

Marshall's tradition of theorizing about citizenship has a number of gaps that this book intends to fill. Since the mid- to late 1960s, progress toward a full theory of citizenship has been slow. In the last ten years, three important political changes have raised concerns involving citizenship: (1) the threats to social rights brought by the increasing public and even governmental attacks on the welfare state, (2) the breakdown of communist control in Eastern Europe, and (3) the increasing international claims on citizenship by immigrants and refugees. The first change concerns the internal or domestic protection of citizenship rights for poor and disadvantaged citizens, while the second change involves the re-creation of citizenship and civil society in the transition to democracy and capitalism. The third change questions the rights of nation-states to protect citizenship enclaves within country boundaries from foreigners of different racial and ethnic groups, especially when these foreigners seek relief from economic duress and political threats. Other issues are also of significance to citizenship. National identity is again prominent with new identities being molded with the unification of the European Community and the disintegration of communist regimes. And many previously subordinated citizens have increasingly moved toward new and greater rights, which has led to some backlash against those diverse citizens and particularly against foreigners. Marshall's theory of citizenship has not been adequately extended to explain many of these emerging questions of rights and obligations.

Why is there no adequate *theory* of citizenship? Citizenship can be treated simply as a concept in measuring rights and obligations. This makes citizenship part of other political theories. For instance, Bendix (1964) presents only a partial theory of the development of citizenship rights in Germany and the United Kingdom, and then drops citizenship from his analysis of Japan, India, and Russia, where he focuses more on economic development. However, the elements of a theory of citizenship exist for much wider application. Marshall provides a developmental sequence of rights for the United Kingdom, and connects this development to social forces of the bourgeoisie and then labor. Turner (1986a) provides a theory based on social movements and conflict, and Mann (1988) looks for broad causes of citizenship rights development in elite structures. Marshall, Turner, and Mann are not simply using a concept but are creating a sociological theory of the political development of rights and obligations that incorporates social movements and group conflict. Despite the presence of theories of sequencing rights, conflicts between citizenship rights and capitalism, and social movements developing identities of citizenship and rights for oppressed groups, more is needed. The requirements for an adequate theory of citizenship include clarifying the nature of citizenship rights and obligations, proposing the-

4

ories of development capable of reversals, identifying how societies and citizens balance rights and obligations, explaining domestic and external membership in the nation-state, and integrating each area into an overarching framework. Consequently, three major problems need to be addressed to advance a theory of citizenship.

First, *rights and obligations* are not adequately grounded. Not only do sociologists such as Anthony Giddens (1982) and Ramesh Mishra (1981) take citizenship rights as a hodgepodge of disparate concepts, but social advocates invoke the "currency of rights" in popular discourse for a wide range of phenomena and in return are criticized for using inflated and overblown concepts. And of course, both researchers and citizen advocates are often reminded of their frequent amnesia concerning citizen obligations. An adequate theory of citizenship must provide a much better conceptual substructure before a more dynamic theory can be developed.

Second, the *balancing of rights and obligations* has been totally ignored. At the macro-level, overall packages of rights need to be related to similar packages of obligations. Theories need be proposed as to why some nations have higher or lower levels of citizenship. At the micro-level, we need theories about how citizens balance their own rights and obligations in relation to their own identities, and what range of behaviors and attitudes citizens may assume.

Third, the *development of citizenship rights and obligations* needs to be formulated at both the macro- and micro-levels. A macro-theory needs to go beyond Marshall's linear focus on rights to include obligations. Such a theory must also address the diverse patterns that nations take from the slow and relatively steady progression of citizenship rights at low levels of obligation in the United Kingdom to a mixed and sometimes reversing sequence of legal, social, and political rights with higher levels of obligations in Germany.[3] A micro-theory needs to look at how rights and obligations are acquired over the life course, especially for children, teenagers, middle-aged adults, and senior citizens.

The theory of development requires further attention to internal and external membership. At the domestic level, this involves how dependent or disreputable groups become citizens. Who among the subjects of a nation may be accorded rights and obligations from elites to the masses and from the "normal" to the stigmatized? At the international level, this involves how nations conceptualize their own national identities, and how they frame the actualities or possibilities of integrating strangers from other countries and continents.

Finally, to be a general theory, the hypotheses of these three areas need to be put together into an overarching framework. Marshall and others have used the working classes' battle with capitalism as the motive force of citizenship. Class explains important aspects of citizenship, but this motive force is not an effective vehicle for gender, race, and ethnic groups. Turner (1990) and Janoski (1990) have proposed using both class and status as the motive force. Maslow's (1970) hierarchy of needs is sometimes seen as a motive force, and others look at rationality or social exchange. From any viewpoint, however, a theory of citizenship needs more than just class as an overarching framework.

In what Bryan Turner calls a "revival of interest" in citizenship (1990, p. 190), theorists are now responding to the challenge of extending citizenship rights into a systematic and comparative theory.[4] This book is a contribution to these efforts to build a theory of citizenship by contributing to the three areas listed above that prevent current work from becoming an adequate theory of citizenship. Illuminating citizenship requires a more penetrating and complex theoretical searchlight. In the next sections, I begin this process by framing and defining citizenship and by placing citizenship in a context of civil society. After reviewing three traditions of citizenship and choosing Marshall's approach, I present and then connect three approaches of political theory – liberalism, communitarianism, and social democratic theory – to three parallel political regimes – liberal, conservative, and social democratic regimes (Esping-Andersen 1990). These political theories and regime types will be used throughout the book. Consequently, this introduction places citizenship within a broader context in order to explain the burgeoning undergrowth of demands for rights and obligations we are now experiencing.

THE THEORETICAL TRADITIONS OF CITIZENSHIP

Three entirely different groups of theories have dealt with phenomena related to citizenship – Marshall's theory of citizenship, the Tocqueville/Durkheimian approach to civic culture, and the Gramsci/Marxist theory of civil society. In response to early studies of citizenship that focused on the concept of the citizen and political socialization, Thomas H. Marshall proposed in 1949 what most call the first sociological theory of citizenship by developing a theory of citizenship rights and obligations (Marshall 1964).[5] In a discussion of the United Kingdom, Marshall proposed a typology of citizenship rights – legal, political, and social rights – in a developmental order and balanced them with citizenship obligations – taxes, military service, and other service to the nation. Citizenship rights emerged as the result of the conflict between capitalism and equality (i.e., markets and politics). Although Marshall mainly focused on the United Kingdom, scholars subsequently applied his work to a number of other nations.

6

Introduction to Citizenship

One of the most extensive applications of Marshall's theory came at the hands of Reinhard Bendix (1964), who applied citizenship rights to the United Kingdom and Germany. Following Marshall, Bendix wrote on the transformation of these rights in the face of class inequalities caused by industrialization. His major focus was on the extension of citizenship to the working classes through rights to association, education, and the franchise. Rokkan (1966) made further contributions to studying the extension of the franchise, and both Bendix and Rokkan took what was a theory based on one nation and applied it in an explicitly comparative perspective.

Bryan Turner (1986a) pushed the developmental theory of citizenship toward conflict theory with an explicit focus on social movements as the dynamic force leading to the development of citizenship rights. Although both Marshall and Bendix included trade unions as a pressure group for extending citizenship to the masses, conflict was sometimes transparent in the development of specific rights in their theories. Turner made the role of conflict more dominant (see Mann 1986, 1988, 1994; Barbalet 1993, 1988; Kitschelt 1985; Turner 1986a, b, 1990, 1993).[6]

Second, a group of Durkheimian theories addresses the question of civic virtue. Beyond the citizenship sanctioned by law, another aspect of citizenship exists in the public sphere. It represents volunteerism in non-profit and private groups in civil society. The state does not necessarily sanction volunteering; that is, although it may be encouraged or ignored, people do not face subsequent state penalties for not volunteering. Volunteerism and civic virtues have been seen as a major component of civil society from de Tocqueville in the early 1800s to the communitarian critiques of the late 1900s (see Bellah et al. 1985, 1991; Etzioni 1993; Galston 1991; Walzer 1983, 1990; Waldron 1981; Wuthnow 1991a, b).[7]

The third group of theories related to citizenship involves Marxist theories related to reconstituting civil society, and world systems theory involving colonialism. Civil society in this tradition was introduced by Hegel and then Marx, but Gramsci significantly revised it in the 1920s (Bobbio 1988). Given the fall of communism and a distaste for state socialism, contemporary Marxian theorists are fashioning Gramsci's writings on civil society into a theory that protects against both state abuses and the greed of the market. It centers on complex democracy, social movements, and the attempts by Habermas and others to improve democratic communication (Keane 1988a, b; Cohen and Arato 1992; Hall 1995). In a sense, this approach stands between the state-centered citizenship approach of Marshall and the society-centered civic virtue approach of the Durkheimians. However, at this time, it is not entirely clear in what directions this new theory may lead (see Arato and Cohen

1984; Cohen 1982; Cohen and Arato 1992; Keane 1987a, b, 1988a, b, 1991; Seligman 1992; Sales 1991; Hall 1995).[8]

Closely related to Marxian theory is world systems theory, which links national attempts to bestow citizenship in core countries to the lack of rights in peripheral countries or with indigenous peoples. Often, the state's movement toward citizenship requires an ideology of nationalism to promote military exploitation. The obligations of citizenship may be connected to nationalism through military service to *defend* the core nation. In many ways, the state formation process is an act of closure concerning other nations and indigenous peoples (Turner 1990; Brubaker 1992, pp. 27–31; Seligman 1992). The process of achieving personhood frequently requires acts of allegiance to the nation-state, which entails the rejection or downplaying of past cultural or national memberships. Turner paraphrases Anthony Smith on this issue: "the creation of citizenship within the *gesellschaft*-like political space of the modern state may well require the subordination, or even eradication, of *gemeinschaft*-like membership within an ethnic primary group" (Turner 1990, p. 196). While citizenship subordinates ethnicity to universality within the nation-state, it may emphasize a membership in one particular state with strategies of colonialism, nationalism, and even racism. In an external manner quite distinct from civil society, these world system processes of nationalism, colonialism, and allegiance hit at the heart of citizenship development: who from inside and outside the nation may become a citizen (Janoski and Glennie 1995; Brubaker 1992; Hammar 1990; Hollifield 1992; Kritz, Lim, and Zlotnik 1992; Wallerstein 1989)?[9]

Although relying more on Marshall and Turner, I will take elements of each of these major theoretical approaches – citizenship rights and obligations from Marshall, solidarity and generalized exchange from Durkheim, civil society from Marx and Gramsci, and colonialism from Wallerstein – and put them to good work in my framework of citizenship.

DEFINITION OF CITIZENSHIP

What is citizenship? Although it is the lingua franca of socialization in civics classes, as well as the cornerstone of many social movements seeking basic rights, and a key phrase in speeches by politicians on ceremonial occasions, oddly enough, citizenship has not been a central idea in the social sciences. Six major social science surveys or dictionaries show no listing for "citizenship" or "citizen."[10] Other sources reveal definitions that reflect legal, normative, and social scientific perspectives. The social scientific definition provides the more useful conception of citizenship for my purposes of reconstructing citizenship theory.[11]

Introduction to Citizenship

Citizenship is passive and active membership of individuals in a nation-state with certain universalistic rights and obligations at a specified level of equality. Each aspect of this definition requires discussion, especially since it can be applied at both the national and individual level.

First, citizenship begins with determining *membership* in a nation-state. Internally, this means establishing "personhood" within a defined geographical territory. Out of the totality of denizens, natives, and subjects of a territory, "the citizen" is given specific rights. Personhood usually begins with a restricted group of elite citizens (e.g., the wealthy citizens of Athens, or the barons of thirteenth-century England) and then may develop to encompass a larger portion of nation state residents (e.g., the 80 to 90 percent of residents in advanced industrialized countries).[12] There are two perspectives on studying membership. The *internal approach* examines how non-citizens within a nation-state achieve membership, that is, how non citizens — stigmatized ethnic, racial, gender, class, or disabled groups – gain rights and recognition as citizens. The *external approach* analyzes how aliens from outside the nation-state obtain entrée and then become naturalized as citizens with attendant rights and obligations. Bottomore differentiates between internal and external citizenship by calling membership "substantive citizenship" and possessing rights "formal citizenship" (1992, pp. 66–73; 1993, p. 75).

Second, citizenship involves *active* and *passive* rights and obligations. Dennis Thompson (1970) sees citizenship as passive rights of existence and active rights that include present and future capacities to influence politics. Passive and active rights are very different in their theoretical implications. With passive rights alone, a beneficent dictator could rule with limited legal rights and extensive social rights in a redistributive system of income payments. Active rights bring citizens in a democracy to the foreground in politics and even economics. When citizens become directly active in citizenship rights, social scientists will be concerned with measuring the levels, causes, and consequences of participation. A good empirical example is Almond and Verba's (1965) comparative work on the various roles that citizens play one at a time or even simultaneously: the parochial or self-interested family person, the subject of the state, and the active citizen participating in the community. Thus, a stress on an active conception of citizenship may be normative, but also social scientific in that it helps construct a more complex theory of citizenship involving political and economic democracy, sometimes opposing the state (Nagel 1987, pp. 145–80). The next chapter will emphasize this distinction between active and passive rights.

Third, citizenship rights are *universalistic rights enacted into law and implemented for all citizens*, and not informal, unenacted, or particularistic.[13] Groups can advance unenacted rights as claims or proposals for citizenship rights, but since these rights often derive from norms within subcultures and are enforced by social pressures or group rules, they often conflict with norms in other subcultures. The process of enacting citizenship rights is an attempt to iron out these conflicts through universalistic rights. Further, many claims may be labeled as rights that could never be universal citizenship rights. As Giddens states, persons may have their own or group "moral imperatives" or more simply "customs" that lack universal application or state legitimation (1987, p. 320). For instance, employees working for IBM or kings of the Gypsies may enjoy specific group rights, but these rights are not citizenship rights unless they are universally applied within the country and backed by the state.[14]

Fourth, citizenship is a statement of *equality*, with rights and obligations being balanced within certain limits. The equality is not complete, but it most often entails an increase in subordinate rights vis-à-vis social elites. This equality is mainly procedural – the ability to enter the public forums of courts, legislatures, public bureaucracies, and private councils – but it may also include payments and services that have a direct impact upon substantive equality. The extent of rights actually used by citizens may also vary considerably with class and status group power (Somers 1993, pp. 602–6).

This definition differs from other conceptions of citizenship in four major respects.[15] Legal definitions of citizenship focus on simple membership which often turns on naturalization processes (Brubaker 1992; Hollifield 1992). These definitions based on the acceptance of immigrants are too narrow and will be countered by a conceptualization of internal and external membership (see Marshall 1964, p. 92; Svarlien 1964; Plano 1979). A number of other definitions focus on "being a good citizen," which consists of knowing citizenship rights but also tending to volunteer for activities (Roelofs 1957). They tend to be value-laden and are most often applied to students and newly arrived immigrants. The definition used here precludes this conception of citizenship but uses it as the separate idea of "civic virtue" in civil society.

In another direction, Turner (1990) goes too far by including "competence" in his definition of citizenship. Although "active" rights may require competence, "passive" rights (legal and social rights) do not. Consequently, competence cannot be a defining characteristic of citizenship. Mentally disabled or citizens in a coma may be incompetent for some political and participation rights, but that does not mean that they do not have legal and social rights. Deleting competence from the definition of citizenship also avoids Turner's focus on citizenship being "participation," a concept I will use in a different way in the next chapter (1990, pp. 189–90).[16]

Introduction to Citizenship

Finally, Somers and Turner emphasize citizenship as a process or practice. Somers (1993, p. 589) rejects the definition of citizenship as being a *status* of a category of persons, and instead proposes that citizenship be defined as an "instituted process," which is a "set of institutionally embedded practices" that are "contingent upon and constituted by networks of relationships and political idioms that stress membership and universal rights and duties in a national community" (p. 589). Turner (1993, p. 2) redefines citizenship as a set of political, economic, juridical, and cultural practices that "define a person as a competent member of society" and "shape the flow of resources" to them. Viewing citizenship as both a passive status and an active form of participation may solve some of their objections, but there are problems in including all processes leading to citizenship in the basic definition of the concept. These dangers include embedding too much of the explanation of citizenship in its definition and consequently confusing independent and dependent variables. The critical difference between these definitions is, I believe, that the dependent variable must be clear – citizenship rights and obligations exist when the *state* validates citizenship norms as officially legal and then takes steps to implement them. Citizenship processes as they take place within civil society between class and status groups struggling for power are not necessarily citizenship rights, but they do consist of the independent variables that constitute the explanation of citizenship. Some of the confusion here may simply be distinguishing between the concept and theory of citizenship. Processes are mostly part of the theory rather than the definition.

Citizenship rights and obligations exist at the individual, group, or societal levels. At the societal level, they refer to the development of citizenship rights and obligations in countries. At the macro-level, the focus is on the existence, breadth, and extent of universalistic rights and obligations in a society with a specified level of equality. At the group level, they concern the rights and obligations of groups to form and act, and as an explanation of citizenship, they include the ideologies and demands for rights and obligations that various class and status groups may make. At the micro-level, the individual definition of citizenship focuses on how each person sees the relationship of rights and obligations within a framework of balance or exchange. It traces the development of the "self" in relation to the state as a critical part of citizenship, especially the development of self- or community-oriented attitudes and behaviors. In the next section, I bring civil society into the discussion, which helps to maintain this distinction between state-validated citizenship rights and duties, and group-initiated claims and defenses.

CIVIL SOCIETY AND CITIZENSHIP

Citizenship concerns the relationship of the state and the citizen, especially concerning rights and obligations. A theory of civil society provides the context or "mediating institutions" between the citizen and the state (Saunders 1993, pp. 78–88). By building on Habermas's view of the public sphere (1989) and Cohen and Arato's reconstruction of civil society (1992, pp. 421–91), society can be divided into four spheres which may interact in rather distinctive ways. In avoiding the tendencies of civil society theory to be overly normative in describing the good society or excessively theoretical in delineating a history of ideas (Hall 1995; Kumar 1993), this book intends to operationalize civil society, provide the relationship between the four spheres of society – the private, market, public, and state spheres – and then connect civil society to citizenship.

Like citizenship, civil society has not been a central idea in the social sciences (Cohen and Arato 1992, pp. 29–82). As a result, the concept of civil society suffers from diverse meanings emanating from three different definitions. The early definitions of civil society by Marx and others focus on a non-state sphere of influence that emerges from capitalism and industrialization. A normative definition focuses on judging the behavior of the state in relation to its citizenry, and on whether nations develop an effective civil society that protects individuals and groups from rights abuses. The social science definition of civil society – the one used in this book – emphasizes the interaction of voluntary groups in the non-state sphere (Lipset 1981; Simmel 1956). *Civil society represents a sphere of dynamic and responsive public discourse between the state, the public sphere consisting of voluntary organizations, and the market sphere concerning private firms and unions.* This conception of civil society can be applied to all countries if they have private organizations between the state and the family.[17]

Unlike some conceptualizations of civil society and perhaps similar to Habermas's view (1989, 1996), this definition divides society into four interactive components: the state sphere, the private sphere, the market sphere, and the public sphere (see Figure 1.1).[18] However, rather than being separate as Habermas seems to think of them, there is overlap among spheres. This overlap is crucial to a theory of civil society (see also Billis 1993, pp. 156–71; Sales 1991).

The first two spheres – state and private – are not as complex as the last two – market and public. The state sphere involves legislative (law-making), executive (law-implementing), and judicial (law and constitution-evaluating) organizations. The private sphere consists of family life, networks of friends and acquaintances, and the disposition of personal

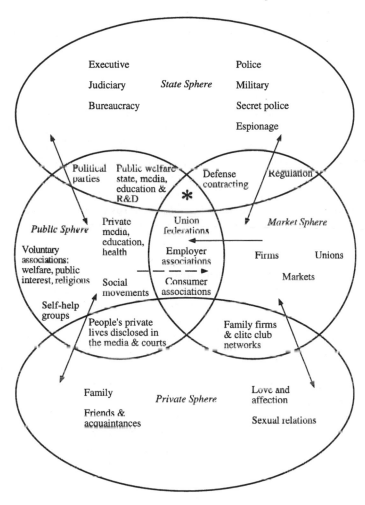

State Sphere

Executive

Judiciary

Bureaucracy

Police

Military

Secret police

Espionage

Political parties

Public welfare state, media, education & R&D

Defense contracting

Regulation

Public Sphere

Private media, education, health

Union federations

Market Sphere

Voluntary associations: welfare, public interest, religious

Employer associations

Firms   Unions

Social movements

Consumer associations

Markets

Self-help groups

People's private lives disclosed in the media & courts

Family firms & elite club networks

Family

Private Sphere

Love and affection

Friends & acquaintances

Sexual relations

* Public law corporations with tripartite control.

Figure 1.1. A conceptual diagram of the public and private spheres that locate civil society

property. The existence of the private sphere relies on a right to privacy, but in modern times, the state, market, and public spheres have invaded the private sphere (i.e., Habermas's "colonization of the life world").[19] The state now implements child abuse laws and takes children away from mothers and fathers. It also regulates divorce proceedings in the courts, often bringing private affairs into painful public scrutiny. The media may also publicize the private and intimate details of some citizens' private lives. Social movements and public debate in the public sphere directly affect families and individuals (e.g., a teenager trying to get an abortion at a family planning clinic may face tremendous pressure from demonstrators). Nonetheless, a private sphere, in which friends and family figure prominently, does exist with most citizens living large portions of their lives quietly within it.

Much private property is in the private sphere, but in a capitalist economy it is also very important in the market sphere. Theoretically within the bounds of public interest, citizens have the right to dispense their private property as they see fit. The state also gives corporations rights as a "person" to do the same; however, the position of private property vis-à-vis private organizations and businesses is more contested, especially when these organizations have a substantial impact on the public interest. Consequently, organizational property may very well be better placed in the market sphere than in the private sphere.[20]

Third, the market sphere consists of private and a few public organizations that are engaged in the instrumental creation of income and wealth through the production of goods and services. The market sphere consists of private firms and corporations engaged in business activities, and necessarily this also includes institutions that are directly involved in this process. It also includes stock markets, employer federations, professional associations, consumer groups, and trade unions. The latter two organizations are, however, generally in the overlap area of the public sphere and the market sphere since they also perform self-regulatory or negotiation functions between groups.

Finally, the public sphere is the most important but difficult item to classify because it involves a wide range of organizations. There are at least five types of voluntary associations operating in the public sphere: political parties, interest groups, welfare associations (a complex category in its own right), social movements, and religious bodies. *Political parties* are obviously related to the state, but their campaigns for state office are rooted in public discourse, and in a democracy they are rarely subsumed by the state. *Interest groups* operate in a similar way to parties, but their main function is to influence society and legislation connected to their groups' position in society. They do not as a rule present a comprehensive view of society that a party might present.

Welfare associations involve a form of "communitas." Philanthropic organizations provide funds to aid public welfare, helping organizations (Red Cross or United Way) provide direct social welfare services, and self-help groups (Alcoholics Anonymous or Downs Syndrome parents groups) counsel persons and families with similar needs. Organizations more directly involved in societal welfare are schools, hospitals, and social welfare agencies that play a large role in public discourse. *Social movements* are less organized than the other groups, and rather than using lobbying tactics like interest groups or mounting media campaigns like political parties, they use more informal techniques like demonstrations, boycotts, and protests. *Religious groups* in a theocracy would be fully integrated with the state, but religious groups in a pluralist society are generally in the private sphere except to the extent that they try to influence the welfare of the society as a whole through voluntary activities or public discourse (e.g., the abortion controversy puts many Catholic and Fundamentalist churches squarely in civil society). And federations of unions, churches, universities, sporting clubs, and so on work in the public sphere especially if they offer some service or policy recommendation to the public (rather than only to their members).

The public sphere also includes some private organizations and private governments. A corporation would fall under the market sphere in the sense of an owner utilizing private property. However, the corporation enters the public sphere voluntarily when it seeks to mold public opinion or influence legislation, especially through interest groups representing business. The corporation also enters the public sphere, perhaps involuntarily, when it threatens the welfare of communities or society. For instance, labor discord in the early part of this century pushed the human relations policies of corporations, which are most certainly internal to the corporation, squarely into the public sphere. In the second half of this century, questions of pollution and the environment brought the production and technology policies of corporations into the public sphere. Questions of racial and gender equality have done the same with formal organizations in the United States concerning harassment and discrimination claims. Of course, the boundary between the private and public spheres is always a contentious issue.

Finally, *the media* as private corporations or public agencies are inherently and overwhelmingly in the public sphere, despite their possible overlap with the market or state spheres. To a large degree, they interpret, manage, and even constitute large segments of public discourse. Inasmuch as these organizations may be state-owned (PBS to some degree, but more clearly German state-owned TV stations and the *Bundespost*), they have one foot in the state sphere and one in the public sphere. Inasmuch as media organizations are private, they, like other corporations, are based in the market sphere. But whether the media are private or public, they clearly reside in the public sphere.[21]

Thus, groups differ in their willingness to protect democracy, and this is critically related to the publicness and privacy of the various spheres. The public and private are differentially distributed among the four spheres (see Figure 1.2). The private sphere is not the only area of privacy as market organizations are largely based on private property and

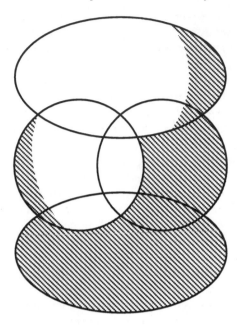

Figure 1.2. The public (unshaded) and private (shaded) in four spheres

some secrecy. Even many parts of the state are essentially private – espionage, the secret police, the military, and foreign negotiations – as are the board meetings of many voluntary associations and churches.

This approach to civil society contributes to previous theories of civil society in two interrelated ways. First, the overlaps between the public and private spheres are particularly important. Each of the three other spheres overlaps with the public sphere to produce important aspects of a developing theory of civil society. The extent of the overlaps and the size of each sphere produce a framework for comparing civil societies in pluralist, traditional, and corporatist countries (a point taken up in Chapter 5). This framework then assesses what difference these spheres make for rights and obligations, and the participation of citizens in their polity. These two aspects of civil society – overlap and size – are especially useful for comparing nations.

Second, this approach involves a theory of checks and balances of the four spheres. In other theories, the state is most often viewed in civil society theory as the danger. Civil society, especially the public sphere, provides a major check against state power along with the market sphere. Nonetheless, the market sphere may also constitute a threat to democracy and societal welfare through its creation and destruction of jobs and communities, and its powerful role in politics due to its wealth and other resources. Both the public and state spheres may attempt to check unbridled market power (e.g., in the United States, public agencies include the Justice Department and the Economic Opportunity Commission, and private groups consist of the American Civil Liberties Union and the Student Non-violent Coordinating Committee). But even the public sphere can become a danger to democracy because anti-democratic social movements also originate there (e.g., the Ku Klux Klan in the United States and the National Socialists in Germany during the 1920s were clearly not in the state or market spheres).[22]

This brings us to an important point differentiating citizenship rights and claims. While citizenship and civil society are quite different – the former refers to state-enforced rights and obligations, and the latter focuses on groups in concert or opposition – they are empirically contingent. Civil society creates the groups and pressures for political choice and state legislation, and many ideas of citizenship originate in civil society rather than in the state. Consequently, strong civil societies produce particular institutional structures that bolster citizenship, and civil society constructs much of the citizen-society discourse in terms of rights and obligations. Weak civil societies will most often be dominated by the state or market sphere. Although theories of civil society are quite similar to those of citizenship on a number of issues, civil society theory is not a theory of citizenship.[23] Civil society consists of the public sphere of associations and organizations engaged in debate and discussion. It is not the state sphere and cannot be the home of citizenship rights. Although the state may act as an advocate for some citizenship claims (e.g., the advance of disability claims), most claims for and defenses of citizenship are made in civil society through the motivating interests of class- and status-based groups. As such, civil society provides many of the independent variables that explain citizenship. However, the actual citizenship rights themselves reside in the state sphere with bureaucratic and political implementation through official protections using legal sanctions. This does not mean that this theory of citizenship is state-dominated because the debate over citizenship takes place in the public sphere, where any group or person can make citizenship claims. Different theories in themselves, citizenship and civil society combine in various ways according to three political theories.

POLITICAL THEORY AND WELFARE STATE REGIMES

Integrating political theory with macro-empirical approaches to state and society is a necessary step in bringing citizenship and civil society together in a comprehensive way. Too often these discourses have remained separated with little or no cross-fertilization. As a result, political theory lies largely untested in a comparative framework, and empirical work is devoid of the wide-ranging conceptualizations of theories of citizenship and civil society. This book intends to help close a portion of this gap, especially in matching specific political theories to particular regime types – the theory of liberalism with the liberal regimes, communitarianism theory with traditional regimes, and expansive democracy theory with social democratic regimes.[24] The fit is not deterministic, and some countries of each regime type fit the political theory better than others. Yet the parallels are striking.

Of the three major political theories, liberalism is by far the dominant theory in advanced industrialized democracies, especially Anglo-Saxon nations (Kymlika 1990; Waldron 1984, 1993). Communitarianism and expansive democratic theory have fewer partisans and tend to chip away at liberal theory from the outside (see Figure 1.3).[25] To reconstruct any of these theories would be a task far beyond the goals of this book. Instead, my task is to show how conceptions of citizenship and civil society in political theory fit the structuring of citizenship in "three worlds of welfare capitalism" (Esping-Andersen 1990).

Liberalism puts a strong emphasis on the individual, and most rights involve liberties that adhere to each and every person (i.e., negative rights or freedoms from state or social interference). There are several theories of liberalism, but my main concern here is the position of rights and obligations in this theory.[26] Although there are a few basic obligations to obey the laws (generally to pay taxes, refrain from assault and rebellion, and to serve in the nation's armed forces), liberalism places the clear weight of its ethical and moral theory behind individual and negative rights. Legal and political rights, especially civil liberties and property rights, come first and are balanced by only a few obligations. Thus, individual rights are primary and represent massive residual areas allowing the individual wide-ranging freedom of action. Social and group rights tend to violate liberal principles based on the individual, so those rights tend to be avoided. Obligations, except within their limited domain, are not at all emphasized, and social and participation rights are often difficult to incorporate in liberal theory mainly because they require more extensive obligations to work well. The relationship between rights and obligations is contractual or one of immediate reciprocity or restricted exchange; that is, for each right there is generally an equal obligation (Kymlicka 1990; Waldron 1984,1993; Putnam 1993, p. 87).[27]

Communitarianism takes a nearly opposite point of view. It puts strong emphasis on community (otherwise called society or the nation). The primary concern of the many communitarian theories is with the effective and just functioning of society. The good society is built through mutual support and group action, not atomistic choice and in-

18

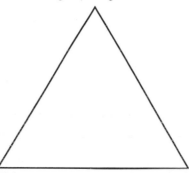

Liberalism is based on
individualism; Liberty rights
are related by contract
(restricted exchange) to only
the most essential obligations.
Rights > Obligations

**Social or Expansive
Democracy** is based on
egalitarian participation by
groups and individuals;
A full range of rights and
obligations are balanced
by both generalized
and restricted exchange.
Rights ≅ Obligations

Communitarianism is
based on strong community
hierarchy; Community
obligations are related to rights
in long term relationships
(generalized exchange) and
take priority in safeguarding
community welfare.
Rights < Obligations

Figure 1.3. Liberal, communitarian, and expansive democratic theories of rights and obligations

dividual liberty. In its extreme version, communitarianism may resemble benevolent feudal relationships where rights exist, but obligations to the whole seem to predominate so strongly as to make rights secondary. Rights that do exist pertain to protection from external enemies by the sovereign, which may entail subsidiary rights to use of the commons or provision of food in the last instance to prevent starvation. The Catholic Church's traditional conception of community often approaches this view of communitarianism. Current versions of communitarianism emphasize rights and democracy to a greater degree, but the weight of modern communitarian theory still rests on society and mutual obligations. The goal is to build a strong community based on *common* identity, mutuality, autonomy, participation, and integration (Selznick 1992, pp. 362–3). In their view, liberalism is too rights-centered (Selznick 1992, pp. 376–80), but just as liberalism does not exclude obligations, communitarianism does not jettison rights. Rights and obligations are related according to generalized exchange; that is, citizens are expected to fulfill obligations without expecting immediate returns. Rights will be fulfilled in the long run after citizens have fulfilled a large number of their obligations. Nonetheless, we can see a clear emphasis on obligations in communitarianism (Etzioni 1993; Galston 1991; MacIntyre 1981, 1983, 1990; Putnam 1993, p. 87; Sandel 1982, 1984, 1996; Sullivan 1982).

Expansive democracy theory as a social democratic approach is a lesser known and perhaps a compromise theory, but it is a third way rather than an intermediate position between liberalism and communitarianism (Singer 1993, p. xiii). It deals with an expansion of rights, especially of individual and organizational rights concerning people who have been discriminated against including most class, gender, and ethnic groups. This position can be built on Mark Warren's notion of expansive democracy in emphasizing both rights and obligations. He states that

Expansive democracy includes participatory democracy, democratic socialism, and the more radical strains of liberal democracy that stem from Rousseau, John Stuart Mill, T. H. Green, and John Dewey. These theories argue for increased participation in and control over collective decision-making, whether by means of direct democracy in small scale settings, or through stronger linkages between citizen and institutions that operate on broader scales. (1992, p. 9)

Although both communitarian and expansionary democracy theories are conceived to combat alienation and aid self-transformation, expansive democracy theory emphasizes rights to empowerment and participation, whereas communitarian theories tend to de-emphasize these rights and accentuate obligations to follow moral leadership. Expansive democracy theory rejects the emphasis on libertarian rights of individuals to pursue social mobility and build fortunes while others suffer. It also resists the communitarian obligations of citizens to promote group and community projects, while leaving rights largely behind.[28] Its emphasis is on balancing group and individual rights and obligations in both cooperative and competitive relationships. The result is a complex self-identity that fuses individual interests through participation in community activities, whether they are work, neighborhood, or welfare-related needs, but at the same time protects individual civil rights.

Each theory has its strengths and weaknesses. Liberalism rests its case on wide-ranging residual liberties that surround a small core of obligations. Social and class/status group rights are generally disallowed or integrated into liberal theory through rather painful and intermittent theoretical contortions. Yet conflicts among factions are expected and somewhat equilibrated by pluralistic political processes. Communitarianism makes obligations to a just and ethical community the core of its theory with individual rights playing a much smaller role. Consequently, it tends to ignore new claims to rights both through its theoretical scope and because of its agenda to promote neglected obligations. Expansive democratic theory is particularly suited to analyzing the empirical developments in social policy of codetermination, workers and client councils, self-administration of large state bureaucracies, and many other forms of participation.[29] This theory is useful in establishing participation rights, especially in its pursuit of the "balanced" relationship of rights and obligations.

All three political theories can be connected to their more empirically grounded welfare state regimes – liberalism with its legal and civil rights in liberal regimes, communitarianism with its tendency to emphasize obligations over rights in traditional regimes, and expansive democracy with its high levels of legal, political, social, and participation rights in social democratic regimes (Kohlberg 1992; Esping-Andersen 1990).[30] In addition to a distinctive position on rights and obligations, each regime type represents a unique configuration of civil society. Liberal nation-states have little overlap between the state, market, and public spheres. Traditional regimes often use communitarian ideas to justify a large overlap between the public and market spheres, sometimes with considerable overlap with the state sphere too. Social democratic regimes use an expansive democracy theory to justify increased participation in government and the economy at multiple levels, sometimes producing surprisingly critical rather than co-opted voluntary associations (Boli 1991).

Regime theory is based on the extension of the substance and universality of social rights, and Esping-Andersen (1990) constructs each regime from three general characteristics of the welfare state – protections against income loss (decommodification), equality in benefits, and the prevalence of public over private welfare provisions. Although regime theory is not really a typology, it can be used that way to discuss the basic features of different groups of countries. In liberal regimes the emphasis is on contingent and marginal social rights; in traditional countries the focus is on a tiered or segmented system of extensive social rights; in social democratic countries the welfare state is centered on universal and equal social rights. The indicators for the liberal regime type are means-tested welfare benefits and private pension and health spending as a percentage of all pensions. The social democratic regime type is based on the universality and equality of welfare benefit structures. And the number of occupationally distinct pension funds and the strength of civil service pensions (etatism) represent the traditional regime type.

The strength of using regime theory is that it centers itself on citizenship, but there are three weaknesses with the theory of welfare state regimes that I will deal with in this book. First, the theory does not have a clear theoretical structure. The three base variables seem to be empirical generalizations that group nicely but do not get at the theoretical core of regime types. The coupling of regime theory with political theory points to how this theory can be made more theoretically sound.

Second, the regime variables are methodologically arbitrary in a number of ways. Esping-Andersen constructed his indexes by assigning each variable a score of 0, 2, and 4, but there is no clear reason for doing this. I have recalculated these indexes using their raw scores and standardized them into indexes (Janoski 1994). Both scores can be seen in Table 1.1. Related to this reconstruction is the existence of the typology itself. Esping-Andersen avoids the presentation of a typology and relies instead on variables representing a regime type in the analysis of labor markets and stratification systems. In so doing, he has probably deflected criticism but leaves researchers guessing on which country is what regime. This is especially problematic since three countries are indeterminate on his three scales – Ireland tends toward traditionalism, New Zealand appears social democratic, and the United Kingdom resembles liberalism. However, none of these three countries are strong enough on any one variable to fall into any regime category. I will treat these countries as mixed cases rather than stretch them to fit a Procrustean regime type.[31]

Third, I will avoid the use of decommodification (removing citizens from market forces). This term is useful to Marxist theories, but less so for my purposes for two reasons. On the one hand, welfare states not only shelter citizens from markets through pensions and sickness insurance, but also reinsert citizens into work through rehabilitation and active labor market policies (recommodification, if you will). On the other hand, my approach to citizenship relies on Weber and Marshall, and decommodification does not fit their emphasis on status and other conflicts.[32]

Consequently, regime theory provides a powerful way of framing state structures and civil society for these industrialized countries. These variables will be correlated with other dependent variables such as obligations for conscription, rights measured by welfare state expenditures, and naturalization rates. Where they fit less well (e.g., with naturalization for the traditional regime type), categories will be subdivided and explained.

As a basis for social and political ideologies, these three political theories provide a way to explain the levels and balancing of citizenship rights and obligations in the three different regime structures. The following chapters will demonstrate some basic aspects of rights and obligations in three representative regime types – the United States for liberal, Germany for traditional, and Sweden for social democratic re-

Table 1.1. *Countries according to regime-type variables*
(country scores when in their own regime-type category are in bold)

Regime types:	Social democratic		Traditional		Liberal	
	(1)	(2)	(3)	(4)	(5)	(6)
Countries by regime types	Esping-Andersen[a]	Standard-ized[b]	Esping-Andersen[a]	Standard-ized[b]	Esping-Andersen[a]	Standard-ized[b]
Social democratic						
Denmark	8	+ 1.16	2	- 0.64	4	- 0.22
Finland	6	+ 0.57	6	+ 0.38	4	- 0.50
Netherlands	6	+ 0.21[c]	4	- 0.13	8	+ 0.31[c]
Norway	8	+ 0.68	4	- 0.43	6	- 0.20
Sweden	8	+ 0.85	0	- 0.70	6	- 0.41
Average	*7.2*	*+ 0.69*	*3.2*	*- 0.30*	*5.6*	*- 0.20*
Traditional						
Austria	2	- 0.29	8	+ 1.51	6	- 0.38
Belgium	4	+ 0.19	8	+ 0.79	4	- 0.64
France	2	- 0.28	8	+ 1.63	8	- 0.01
Germany	4	- 0.20	8	+ 0.54	0	- 0.95
Italy	0	- 0.63	8	+ 1.48	0	- 0.94
Average	*3.0*	*- 0.24*	*8.0*	*+ 1.19*	*3.6*	*- 0.58*
Liberal						
Australia	4	- 0.21	0	- 1.00	10	+ 0.72
Canada	2	+ 0.16	2	- 1.10	12	+ 1.56
Japan	4	- 0.98	4	+ 0.03	10	+ 0.53
Switzerland	0	+ 0.24	0	- 0.70	12	+ 0.72
United States	0	- 1.44	0	- 0.44	12	+ 1.92
Average	*2.0*	*- 0.45*	*1.2*	*- 0.64*	*11.2*	*+ 1.09*
Mixed						
Ireland	2	- 0.03	4	+ 0.24	2	- 0.51
New Zealand	4	+ 0.21	2	- 0.95	2	- 0.66
United Kingdom	4	+ 0.08	0	- 0.19	6	—[d]

[a] Columns (1), (3), and (5) refer to the Esping-Andersen scores based on assignments of 0, 2, and 4 to low, moderate and high rankings (1990, p. 74).

[b] Columns (2), (4), and (6) refer to standardized raw scores of each component variable combined into an additive index. The index ranges within +2 to -2.

[c] The Netherlands' score appears to be high on liberalism because that variable has a larger range (0-12) than the social democratic variable (0-8). The social democratic score (6 of 8 = 75%) is in fact higher than the liberal score (8 of 12 = 67%).

[d] The United Kingdom score is not reported for means tested poor relief.

gimes – and in the various civil societies of eighteen to twenty other nations.

WHY A MORE DEVELOPED THEORY OF CITIZENSHIP IS NEEDED

A revitalized understanding of citizenship is needed for four reasons. First, a comprehensive framework of citizenship provides a way to view the diverse economic and political systems of various countries in comparative research. Citizenship provides a basis of comparison between countries as different as the United States, Germany, Japan, Ireland, and Sweden. This would then help create a theory of development that covers basic and more developed rights, such as participation rights of workers councils and codetermination, which are often omitted from citizenship theories. This framework then proves vital in the analysis of citizenship development over time and the differential ordering of rights and obligations in many countries.

Second, the theory of citizenship is necessary at a more middle range to help explain several aspects of civil society and social organization. Although a theory of social movements tells us how people may organize themselves to pursue claims, it does not guide us on how and why particular citizenship rights demands are made. The left has held up the banner of workers' rights and poor peoples' welfare (and decommodification) while the right trumpets citizen obligations and alternatively abhors the active citizen but promotes the private-greedy citizen. Feminists make specific rights claims oriented toward their constituencies, as do other minority and gender groups. Corporations as legal fictions claim rights but have a limited conception of obligations. A theory of citizenship attempts to organize these claims and demands and would make predictions about resulting social movements in conflicts generated by diverse ideological bases.

Third, a theory of citizenship provides a means to understand the solidarity that holds societies together. Citizenship presumes some determinate community or civil society with some connections and networks between people and groups, and some norms and values that provide meaning to their lives. Citizenship could conceivably work in a mass society of individual choice without civil society and intermediate groups, but that society has never existed. If it did, it would be inherently unstable. Short-term exchanges with expectations of benefit for every cost tend to destroy solidarity, while long-term exchanges benefiting a large segment of the population increase it (Ekeh 1974). Consequently, the citizen approach is ultimately based on communities of responsible citizens, which are structured through civil society.

But individual citizens and their groups may be adopting post-modern and diverse values, while demanding the universalistic application of state policy toward gender, age, class, and ethnic groups (Turner 1994). Some groups may demand particularistic policies, but they will be surely opposed by other groups loathe to provide them. Bridges (1994) believes that these value changes and policy conflicts require a reconstruction of civic virtue, and he may well be correct. Nonetheless, while most theories of citizenship require the universality of rights and obligations, each universalistic right benefits certain groups more than others (workers councils benefit male workers more than female workers, while social rights to day care often directly concern women more than men). Thus, the participation of a diversity of citizens expresses specific claims for citizenship, but these "post-modern groups" can make their claims for new rights (and obligations) in ways that will benefit them specifically *and* others. Done in this way, these rights still fall within the bounds of universal citizenship.[33]

THE OBJECTIVES OF THIS BOOK

This book does not attempt to cover all aspects of citizenship, but rather to explicitly advance three areas of citizenship theory – clarifying rights and obligations, balancing rights and obligations, and delineating the development of rights over time. The book does not attempt to test various theories, but only to provide enough evidence to show how variables could be operationalized and hypotheses tested. Consequently, it is divided into three parts: Chapters 2, 3, and 4 focus on the basic framework of citizenship rights and obligations; Chapters 4 and 5 examine the balance of citizenship rights and obligations at the theoretical, macro-, and micro-levels; and Chapters 6 and 7 delineate the short- and long-term development of citizenship rights.

Chapter 2 establishes the framework of rights. It examines the logic of Marshall's legal, political, and social rights, and the addition of participation rights. Although rights lie in an area of deep philosophical controversy, Hohfeld's categories of rights – liberties, claims, powers, and immunities – illuminate the meaning and structure of rights for social science purposes. The result is a foundation that provides enough theoretical scope to cover major innovations in citizenship rights from bodily control to workers councils.

Chapter 3 addresses the puzzle of why obligations are generally ignored in social science research and much of our public discourse on rights. This chapter divides obligations into what can legitimately be called citizenship obligations, and what falls into the category of civic virtue, which is not directly part of citizenship. People fulfill obligations more often than they are given credit for doing; for instance, many of us respect others' civil liberties and pay taxes nearly every day. However, social researchers must more directly address obligations, and this can be done by a more comprehensive use of lower level positive and negative sanctions. Finally, I develop the concept of "responsible patriotism" that embodies overall conceptions of citizen obligations.

Chapter 4 presents the basic features of restricted and generalized exchange as a way to approach the variable aspects of organizing rights and obligations. Generalized exchange promotes solidarity and long-term focus on societal benefits, while restricted exchange operates in the short term with a focus on individual social mobility. Some people see rights and obligations in a balance with both being relatively low, other people see rights and obligations in a balance with citizenship saturating their environment, and still others explore various imbalances of rights over obligations. The restricted exchange approach (for every right there is an immediate and expected obligation) tends to result in immediate and sometimes greedy responses. Where generalized exchange exists (rights and obligations are more loosely but still ultimately coupled), rights and obligations filter through society in diverse ways in a system that requires high amounts of trust. Nonetheless, variation is present, and this can be analyzed by a typology of citizens – incorporated, active, deferential, privatized, and marginal – that encompasses varying degrees of these two types of exchange.

Chapter 5 examines how generalized or restricted exchange operates in the web of voluntary associations that makes up civil society. The organization and operation of this web, which takes different forms in liberal, traditional, and social democratic regimes, mediates between the citizen and the state under various combinations of generalized or restricted exchange. The exchange implied in each regime is crucial for each citizen's quality of life. My argument is that liberal regimes will be low in rights and obligations, while the other two regime types will be high in both. Further, liberal regimes are not the unanimous leaders in voluntary association membership. Social democratic countries are also very high in voluntary association membership, especially when church voluntary activities as a substitute for the welfare state are controlled. This chapter ends with the synthesizing of citizenship, civil society, and social exchange theories.

In the next two chapters, the focus changes to the development of citizenship rights and obligations, first with an internal or domestic approach and then with an external world systems perspective. In discrimination, sacrifice, and bureaucratic approaches, states and civil societies extend citizenship within a larger concept of state mobilization. Chapter 6 searches for explanations of long-term patterns of citizenship rights development over decades. What forces bring about cooperative versus competitive citizenship patterns, and what forces bring about greater or lesser bundles of rights? The answers come from a model of the social policy process that stresses demands from status and class groups, and the structure of state processes. Citizenship rights and obligations are an outcome, but also an input through citizenship ideologies. This model of internal development is synthesized with overlapping and mutually exclusive structures of civil society, which then distinguish rights and obligations according to liberal, communitarian, and expansive democracy ideologies in their respective liberal, traditional, and social democratic regimes.

Chapter 7 takes the viewpoint of citizenship rights development over centuries and looks at the development first of legal and political rights, and then of social and participation rights. It presents a model of medieval constitutionalism and increasing war preparations that may be mediated to develop democracy, and then focuses on a Boolean approach to the development of legal, political, social, and participation rights. The approaches of both decades and centuries stress the complementarity of power resources or social movements approaches (Korpi and Turner) and state-centric or elite approaches (Skocpol and Mann). Chapter 7 shifts focus to the sequencing of four exemplars of each of the four citizenship rights, and then the sequencing of sixteen different rights. The results show distinct sequencing patterns for each regime type. The concluding chapter examines the importance of citizenship rights and obligations, how nations move to different solutions to solve basic human needs, and how future research analysts may incorporate this theory for citizenship rights and regime theory.

2

The Framing of Citizenship Rights:
Expansion, Clarification, and Meaning

What are we like?
We are rights-conscious and individualistic, at least as compared to people in the past. There is a central concern with the development of the self and the molding of unique individuals. The core mechanism for constituting the self, according to the prevailing point of view, is through free and unrestrained choice, exercised with regard to many and competitive options.

Lawrence Friedman (1990, p. 5)

Strong democracy . . . rests on the idea of a self-governing community of citizens who are united less by homogenous interests than by civic education and who are made capable of common purpose and mutual action by virtue of their civic attitudes and participatory institutions rather than their altruism or their good nature.

Benjamin Barber (1984, p. 117)

Citizenship rights are at the same time indisputable and subject to extension, and controversial and an object of curtailment. Some see freedom as maximized through market choices made by individuals (Friedman 1990), while others see freedom requiring the community to combine peoples' efforts through discourse in common purpose (Barber 1984). To understand citizenship rights within this broad range of opinion, this chapter surveys, analyzes, and frames rights under citizenship as universalistic rights enacted into law, and not informal, unenacted, or particularistic rights.[1]

This chapter will establish the logic of citizenship rights through five points. First, it establishes the range of rights in T. H. Marshall's theory. Second, Marshall and Bendix use citizenship rights in an implied cross-classification of action (active and passive) and arenas (political and economic), which undergirds their theory. But they leave the active and economic cell empty. This chapter extends citizenship rights to include this cell under a fourth right of participation and then reviews classifications of the four rights of citizenship and some data on their levels in three regimes. Third, after reviewing criticisms of Marshall's citizenship rights typology, the theoretical integrity of legal, political, social, and participation rights are clarified using Wesley Hohfeld's categories of rights – liberties, claims, powers, and immunities. Finally, the question of personhood – how subjects come to be recognized as citizens within their own societies – is examined.

EXPANDING CITIZENSHIP RIGHTS THEORY

Marshall, Bendix, and Turner accept the tripartite citizenship rights schema and lump disparate rights together; consequently, citizenship rights theory experiences difficulty when confronted with rights such as collective bargaining, workers councils, codetermination, workplace protest, and client rights to control bureaucracies and organizations. Marshall used residual categories, which he called a "secondary system of industrial citizenship," to describe the bargaining and negotiation over rights and duties between private parties. This parallel and supplementary welfare system has been highly criticized. Giddens claims that Marshall's industrial citizenship simply extends civil rights (1981, p. 229; 1982, p. 172), but Marshall clearly saw industrial citizenship as separate from citizenship rights. Giddens conceives of "industrial citizenship" as "economic civil rights" – union organization, bargaining, and striking – that are different from civil and political rights, but this too is problematic. Giddens sees "something awry in lumping together such phenomena with civil rights in general" (1989, p. 172). Consequently, Bendix (1964, p. 80), Turner (1986a, pp. 46 and 85), and Giddens (1982, 1989) do not reach a satisfactory solution to Marshall's secondary system of rights.[2]

In referring to civil rights as "the legal state of being" and political rights as "the legal power of doing", however, Bendix provides the basis for a fourth right that clarifies some of these problems (1964, pp. 78–9). *Being* means that one has rights, which is a passive position, much akin to "liberties" and "claims." *Doing* means that one has the meta-right to create rights, which is an active process described by "powers."[3] Rights can also be classified according to public and private spheres. Public rights include civil and political rights – the rights to be protected in public courts and to help develop public laws. Private rights involve interventions into individual economic well-being at home or at work, or the creation of rights in largely private areas such as organizations and markets (seeTable 2.1). Bendix implicitly cross-classifies types of social action (passive/active) and arenas of state-backed citizenship rights

Table 2.1. *Citizenship rights as a dichotomy of action and institution*

		Civil society	
		Public sphere: (Politics)	*Private sphere*: (Markets)
	Passive: Being, status, or having rights	(1) Legal rights	(2) Social rights
Type of rights	*Active*: Doing, capacity, or creating rights	(3) Political rights	(4) Participation rights

(public/private) without recognizing that participation rights fill the last cell.

The result of this recasting of citizenship is four rights, which are detailed in Table 2.2. Legal rights for individuals are mostly liberties.[4] First of all, they include procedural rights to access the court system and receive fair treatment therein. There are three different kinds of substantive rights. Expressive rights refer to the freedoms of speech, religion, and privacy. Bodily control rights refer to a person's inherent right to bodily integrity and include freedoms of sexual practices and control over medical interventions into internal bodily processes. The professed right to have an abortion would come under this category. Bodily control rights also include protections from physical assaults from other persons (muggers and murderers), and assaults from the environment (pollution and environmental accidents). Property and service control rights include rights to property and choices about residential location, occupation, and social mobility. Finally, legal rights also refer to the expressive rights to choose friends, spouses, and companions, and the organizational rights to form unions, businesses, and political parties.[5]

Political rights include citizens' rights to vote and participate in the

Table 2.2. *Four types of citizenship rights*

Legal rights	Political rights	Social rights	Participation rights
A. Procedural rights 1. Access to courts and counsel 2. Right to contract	*A. Personal rights* 1. Enfranchisement of the poor, gender groups, ethnic/racial groups, age categories and immigrants 2. Rights to run and hold office 3. Rights to form and join a political party	*A. Enabling and Preventive rights* 1. Health services 2. Family allowances 3. Personal and family counselling 4. Physical rehabilitation	*A. Labor Market Intervention rights* 1. Labor market information programs 2. Job placement programs 3. Job creation services
3. Equal treatment under the law 4. Right of aliens to immigrate and citizens to emmigrate		*B. Opportunity rights* 1. Pre-primary education 2. Primary and secondary education	*B. Firm and Bureaucracy rights* 1. Job security rights 2. Workers councils or grievance procedure rights
B. Expressive rights 1. Freedom of speech 2. Freedom of religion 3. Choice of friends, companions and associates 4. Right to privacy	*B. Organizational rights* 1. Political lobbying 2. Political fund raising 3. Legislative and administrative consultation 4. Political bargaining	3. Higher education 4. Vocational education 5. Educational assistance for special groups	3. Client participation in bureaucracy or self-administration 4. Affirmative action and comparable worth 5. Collective bargaining rights
C. Bodily Control rights 1. Freedom from assault and unsafe environment 2. Medical and sexual control over body	*C. Naturalization rights* 1. Right to naturalize upon residency 2. Right to information on naturalization process 3. Refugee rights	*C. Distributive rights* 1. Old age pensions 2. Public assistance 3. Unemployment compensation	*C. Capital Control rights* 1. Codetermination rights 2. Wage earner and union investment funds 3. Capital escape laws 4. Anti-trust laws 5. Regional investment and equalization programs
D. Property and Service rights 1. Hold and dispose of property and services 2. Choice of residence 3. Choice of occupation	*D. Oppositional rights* 1. Minority rights to equal and fair treatment 2. Political information and inquiry rights 3. Social movement and protest rights	*D. Compensatory rights* 1. Work injury insurance 2. War injury pension 3. War equalization 4. Rights infringement compensation	
E. Organizational rights 1. Employee organizing 2. Corporate organizing 3. Political party organizing			

political process. They also involve the procedures for electing political representatives, creating new laws, and running for and holding political office. Political rights for organizations may include raising campaign funds, consulting with legislators on proposals, nominating political candidates, and lobbying for particular policies. Political rights include protections for aliens and refugees including access to a reasonable naturalization process. Finally, political rights include oppositional rights to protect minorities, to protest, and to demonstrate, and enabling rights of citizens to obtain government information and conduct political inquiries (e.g., the Freedom of Information Act).

Social rights are public interventions into private spheres to support citizens' claims to economic subsistence and social existence. They alter the private market's distribution of resources. Social rights are largely individual and consist of four parts. Enabling rights concern health and family services to assure the basic functioning of citizens in society. Opportunity rights allow citizens to get the necessary skills for work and cultural participation through elementary, secondary, and higher education assistance. Distributive rights provide transfer payments to assure that workers, retirees, the disabled, children, single parents, and all other citizens receive economic subsistence. Finally, compensatory rights provide compensation payments to disabled veterans, injured workers, and citizens whose rights have been abridged in some way (e.g., payments to Japanese Americans who were interned during World War II and to German Jews who were put in concentration camps). Thus, social rights range from distributive rights with money payments to enabling and opportunity rights with many personal services.

Participation rights involve the state's creation of rights in private arenas, whether in market or public organizations. Just as political rights are public powers of action, participation rights are state-assured private powers of action. They refer to the individual and group rights to participate in private decision making through some measure of control over markets, organizations, and capital. Labor market intervention rights involve public participation in assuring employment for citizens in job placement, retraining, and job creation programs. Organizational participation rights can range from individual rights to participate in decisions at work in codetermination and workers councils, to community rights to participate in health care and environmental impact decisions. They can even include interventions into private political, religious, or ethnic organizations.[6] For instance, legislatures that have passed laws to ensure union democracy (e.g., the Landrum-Griffin Act in the United States) could also require political parties to have democratically based conventions every year. Participation rights could even mandate religious councils that would assure female political and participation rights to be priests in the Catholic Church. Capital participation rights involve worker and public participation in decisions about investment in firms and capital flows within and outside the country (e.g., wage earner funds in Sweden).[7]

Participation rights can also be viewed on three levels concerning actors and the directness of participation. Under indirect participation, the government is given the power to intervene in labor markets, organizations, and capital markets to promote the citizen's interests (e.g., the National Labor Relations Board, European social or labor courts, and the Department of Justice's Anti-Trust Division). This is participation in the weakest sense – indirect participation through representatives voted into political office. Under direct participation rights, workers, clients, or customers would have rights to help make personnel decisions in organizations or markets and involve members in workers councils or other self governing bodies. With group participation rights, labor and management representation on self-administered organizations, much like the German Federal Institute of Labor, would be midway between intervention rights and direct participation rights.[8] These quasi-governmental agencies (QUANGOs) mix state intervention with union and employer representation.

In sum, this discussion leads to the conclusion that the essence of public or political democracy resides in civil and political rights, and the heart of private but largely economic democracy exists in social and participation rights.

THE PRACTICE OF CITIZENSHIP RIGHTS

Advanced industrialized countries clearly differ according to the amount of rights they accord their citizens. Table 2.3 shows that violations of legal rights (columns 1 and 2) appear to be higher in liberal countries than in the other two regimes. Political and social rights are much higher in traditional and social democratic regimes (columns 3 and 4). And participation rights are high in traditional regimes, moderate in social democratic regimes, and nonexistent in liberal regimes (column 5). These totals are summarized in Table 2.4. While many measures of these four citizenship rights could be included in the tables, the measures presented in Tables 2.3 and 2.4 suggest that rights are more dense and protected in social democratic regimes. On the other hand, as rights continue to grow they may reach a point of saturation where greater obligations to enforce those rights yield a heavily regulated society that drains legal and political liberties.[9]

In Table 2.5 we see a different ranking of countries on the basis of legal and political rights listed in Humana (1993). Humana selected

Table 2.3. *Citizenship rights in three regimes*

Regime and country	(1) Homicide	(2) Prisoners	(3) Voting	(4) Social spending	(5) Works councils
Social democratic					
Denmark	5.7	47	83%	13.8%	0
Finland	2.4	75	64	9.1	0
Netherlands	—	27	87	22.6	2
Norway	0.9	47	82	13.6	0
Sweden	1.5	55	91	15.5	1
Average	*2.63*	*50.2*	*81.4*	*14.92*	*0.6*
Traditional					
Austria	2.3	87	92	18.5	2
Belgium	—	27	95	18.8	2
France	4.6	40	86	19.2	1
Germany	3.8	77	87	15.5	2
Italy	4.3	60	90	15.1	1
Average	*3.30*	*58.2*	*90.0*	*17.42*	*1.6*
Liberal					
Australia	2.0	60	94	7.7	0
Canada	—	94	69	9.7	0
Japan	1.5	45.5	74	8.2	0
Switzerland	2.0	54	89	11.4	0
United States	8.0	426	53	9.1	0
Average	*3.38*	*135.9*	*76.8*	*9.22*	*0.0*
Mixed					
Ireland	—	60	62	11.5	0
New Zealand	2.5	60	89	—	0
United Kingdom	1.6	77	76	11.3	0

DEFINITIONS AND SOURCES (by column number):
(1) The homicide rate per 100,000 persons is from 1987-89 and comes from the U.N. (1993).
(2) The incarceration rate is the prisoners per 100,000 persons from 1980 to 1986 and comes from national yearbooks, except for countries that come from the U.N. (1993) and Mauer (1994).
(3) The percentage of the electorate voting in major elections in the 1980s (Lane and Errson 1991 and national sources).
(4) The percentage of GNP spent on social security programs in 1965, 1975, and 1985 (OECD 1991).
(5) The presence of workers councils and codetermination in 1990 (0 for none, 1 for one form, and 2 for both forms) (see Janoski, McGill, and Tinsley 1997).

thirty-five different types of legal and political rights for his scale, and for the most part the advanced industrialized countries are all quite high on the total scale (only Japan is below 90). Table 2.5 lists the total score in the column 7 with a selection of the rights exhibiting the most variance in the first six columns. These rights show results similar to those in Table 2.4: social democratic countries have the highest rights scores, the traditional regimes are in the middle, and liberal regimes have the lowest scores.[10]

The United States in particular has a low total score of 90, which is

Table 2.4. *Summary of citizenship rights in three regime types*
(group ranking in parentheses)

Regime and country	(1) Legal rights: homicide	(2) Legal rights: prisoners	(3) Political rights: voting	(4) Social rights: spending	(5) Partici- pation rights
Social democratic	2.63 (1)	50.2 (1)	81.4 (2)	14.9 (2)	0.60 (2)
Traditional	3.30 (3)	58.2 (2)	90.0 (1)	17.4 (1)	1.60 (1)
Liberal	3.38 (2)	136.3 (3)	76.8 (3)	9.2 (3)	0.00 (3)

SOURCES: All numbers are averages from Table 2.3.

based on having cruel and unusual sanctions (capital punishment), other rights problems with interrogations of lower-class and ethnic groups, invasions of privacy through wiretapping, and weak forms of legal aid. Some may protest that Humana's list ignores some important rights, for instance, the right to be free from government interference in business and the right to bear arms. However, questions of business interference are rather mixed, with the United States having a considerable degree of government intervention in regulation and anti-trust law. The right to bear arms is a more serious question. Although citizens can obtain gun permits in many European countries for various reasons, this application procedure certainly does not exist as a right in most countries (liberal Switzerland would be an exception with militia weapons in the majority of households). This may prevent citizens from quickly mounting a rebellion against an oppressive government, but it does not entirely preclude people from eventually gaining arms. On the other hand, the right to bear arms most certainly contributes to the astoundingly high homicide rates, high incarceration rates, and right-wing militia activities in the United States. Clearly, the right to bear arms also cuts against other legal rights and results in the violation of many citizens' rights to bodily integrity and property. Although the legal rights listed in Table 2.3 – homicide and incarceration rates – may be problematic as evidence of the lack of rights because they are outcomes, they reflect actual failures to implement rights to bodily integrity.[11]

As another but indirect measure of the level of rights in different regimes, the willingness of states to sign and ratify international human rights agreements indicates the acceptance of more universal human

Table 2.5. *Legal rights expressed as protections against violations of rights in eighteen countries*

Countries and regimes	Against illegal disappearances	Against torture or intense interrogations	No capital punishment (year stopped)	Against political censorship	Against invasion of personal privacy	For free legal aid for the poor	Total human rights score
Social democratic							
Denmark	Y	Y	Y (1978)	Y	Y	y	98
Finland	Y	Y	Y (1972)	Y	Y	Y	99
Netherlands	Y	Y	Y	Y	Y	Y	97
Norway	Y	Y	Y	Y	Y	Y	98
Sweden	Y	Y	Y (1972)	Y	Y	y	98
Average	3.00	3.00	3.00	3.00	3.00	2.60	98.0
Traditional							
Austria	Y	y	Y	Y	Y	y	95
Belgium	Y	Y	y	y	Y	y	96
France	Y	y	Y (1981)	Y	y	Y	94
Germany	Y	Y	Y (1949)	Y	Y	y	98
Italy	Y	y	Y (1944)	y	Y	y	90
Average	3.00	2.40	2.80	2.60	2.80	2.00	94.6

Liberal							
Australia	y	y	Y (1985)	y	y	y	91
Canada	Y	y	Y (1976)	Y	Y	y	94
Japan	Y	y	N	Y	y	n	82
Switzerland	Y	Y	Y	Y	Y	Y	96
United States	Y	y	n	y	y	n	90
Average	*2.80*	*2.20*	*2.00*	*2.60*	*2.40*	*1.80*	*90.6*
Mixed							
Ireland	Y	Y	Y (1990)	Y	Y	y	94
New Zealand	Y	Y	Y	Y	Y	Y	98
United Kingdom	y	y	Y (1964)	Y	Y	Y	93

NOTE: Y=strong yes for protections, y=maybe yes, n=maybe no, N=strong no for protection

The scoring is done as follows: Y=3, y=2, n=1, N=0

SOURCES: All scores come from the Humana (1993) and refer to the country's position on human rights as of November 1991. The total score is a combination of 35 different categories of rights, and range from 64 in Mexico to 99 in Finland.

rights in the international civil society. Although there are some inherent differences in the ability to sign and ratify these documents in federalist countries, which tend to be liberal regimes, signing agreements does rest on many significant civil rights positions (e.g., the United States will not ratify a treaty against capital punishment because it allows executions). As with the other tables listed above, social democratic regimes score high on signing covenants, traditional regimes are moderate, and liberal regimes are the lowest (see Table 2.6).

From this presentation of rights, we can see that countries have some interesting differences in levels of citizenship rights. These results are by no means conclusive, and they will be pursued further in Chapter 5.

THE NATURE OF CITIZENSHIP RIGHTS

Political rights refer to the right to participate in the public arena and are largely procedural, but the content of legislation is not usually part of political rights themselves. Thus, legislation is not synonymous with the substance of any kind of right. Legislation may also deal with many laws that have no affect on citizenship rights. In the same way, the legal system itself is not synonymous in substance with any particular right but underlies all rights since state laws create citizenship rights. All rights make use of legislation and law, but citizenship rights are distinct universalistic entities. Thus, legal rights allow one to protect various freedoms and liberties, political rights allow a procedure to extend those freedoms, social rights provide services or payments to insure economic and political survival, and participation rights refer to procedural forums within firms, bureaucracies, and other private institutions. These rights are usually but not exclusively plied in particular institutional forums: civil rights are mainly exercised in the courts; political rights are primarily used in voting, legislating, and protesting; social rights are often activated by government bureaucracies; and participation rights are involved in councils and participatory commissions.

Table 2.2 presents the range of rights to measure where countries may stand on each citizenship right, but these citizenship rights are neither necessary nor inalienable rights. These statements on rights refer to the range of rights that various groups have asserted, and not an argument for the "human rights" that nations should offer. As Turner states, "the notion of abstract Human Rights (possibly in association with some commitment to natural law) no longer commands widespread intellectual support" (1990, p. 190; Martin 1993, pp. 72–97). Human rights are often used as an appeal to ethical conscience or sympathy, but they do not have legal standing, and consequently the state does not maintain and promote them. Citizenship rights exist to the extent that a claim is advanced by a particular group, and they are confirmed when the state enacts and enforces the rights to some degree. Innate or natural rights usually refer to preexisting claims that may exist as informal legal norms, rather than enacted rights (Martin 1982). As such, they do not enter the realm of citizenship rights until they are at least politically asserted as a universal right in the public domain. Thus, citizenship rights theory, as presented here, is not a normative theory because it avoids human and natural rights as its main focus of study. And in doing so, it does not say that society should have particular rights or that various rights are inherently human. It is instead a theory enabling researchers to measure the success or failure of groups claiming rights of many different kinds in many different countries.[12]

CITIZENSHIP RIGHTS AND PRIOR THEORETICAL DIFFICULTIES

The extension of the citizenship rights framework solves many theoretical difficulties. First, Marxists and others claim that Marshall's theory forces us to think of trade unions and workers making economistic demands (Turner 1986a, pp. 50–1). But the concept of participation rights covers more than wage and consumption issues. It includes the rights to participation in production on the shop floor and even refers to controlling labor and capital markets. The expanded version of citizenship rights theory can examine the contradictions between labor and capital as they are played out under state social policies in countries that have enacted participation rights, rather than leave them as residuals beyond the pale of citizenship.

Second, Mishra charges that citizenship rights, as conventionally defined, exclude occupational benefits and voluntary ways of meeting needs. He is right by definition. Particularistic benefits accruing from a private firm or charity cannot be universalistic citizenship rights (Turner 1986a, p. 92). If legislated, participation rights to collective bargaining may in practice deal with occupational benefits, but these benefits are the results of the rights, not the actual procedural participation rights themselves. Thus, citizenship rights do not apply to private benefit programs or to voluntary benefits such as charity because these actions are not part of a universalistic state policy. Further, private benefits are narrow in scope and application and are created in wholly different arenas – philanthropic grant-making and private bargaining rather than democratic politics (Mishra 1981, pp. 30–8). In this area, Mishra confuses citizenship rights programs with the many private aspects of social welfare in civil society.

Table 2.6. *The ratification and signing of human rights accords as of January 1994 in three regimes*

Country by regime type	Conventions, covenants and protocols neither signed nor ratified (signed but not ratified in parentheses)	Number signed and ratified	Number signed but not ratified	Total Score[a]
Social democratic				
Denmark	(EXP) AHR AFR	10	1	10.5
Finland	AHR AFR	11	0	11.0
Netherlands	(RC) EXP AHR AFR	9	1	9.5
Norway	AHR AFR	11	0	11.0
Sweden	EXP AHR AFR	10	0	10.0
Average		10.2	0.4	10.40
Traditional				
Austria	EXP AHR AFR	10	0	10.0
Belgium	OCP (NW) MM (TP) AHR AFR	7	2	8.0
France	NW (MM) AHR AFR	9	1	9.5
Germany	OCP AHR AFR	10	0	9.5
Italy	MM (NW) AHR AFR	9	1	9.5
Average:		9.0	0.8	9.40

Liberal				
Australia	MM EXP FF AHR AFR	8	0	8.0
Canada	MM EXP FF (AHR) AFR	8	1	8.5
Japan	OCP (RC) NW MM TP FF AHR AFR	5	1	5.5
Switzerland	OCP (RC) (WD) PRW NW MM EXP AHR AFR	4	2	5.0
United States	(ESC) OCP RC (WD) (NW) (MM) EXP FF (AHR) AFR	2	5	4.5
	Average	*5.4*	*1.8*	*6.30*
Mixed				
Ireland	MM (TP) EXP AHR AFR	8	1	8.5
United Kingdom	OCP NW EXP AHR AFR	8	0	8.0
New Zealand	EXP FF AHR AFR	8	0	9.0

[a] The total score adds 1 point for a ratification and signing, and 0.5 points for a signing each of the thirteen different conventions. Ratifications cannot occur without signings, and the range is 0 to 13.
DEFINITIONS: *ESC*: International Covenant on Economic, Social and Cultural Rights. *CP*: International Covenant on Civil and Political Rights. *OCP*: Optional Protocol to the International Covenant on Civil and Political Rights. *RC*: Convention on the Right of the Child. *WD*: Convention or the Elimination of All Forms of Discrimination Against Women. *PRW*: Convention on the Political Rights of Women. *NW*: Convention on the Nationality of Married Women. *MM*: Convention on Consent to Marriage, Minimum Age for Marriage and Registration of Marriages. *TP*: Convention against Torture and other Cruel, Inhuman or Degrading Treatments or Punishment. *EXP*: Convention for the Suppression of the Traffic in Persons and the Exploitation of the Prostitution of Others. *FF*: European convention for the Protection of Human Rights and Fundamental Freedoms. *AHR*: American Convention on Human Rights. *AFR*: African Charter on Human and Peoples' Rights.
SOURCES: Cook (1994) and Lawson (1592).

Third, participation rights clear up the problems having to do with "industrial citizenship" because these formerly residual rights are distributed among three formal citizenship rights. Organizational civil rights are no different under the law whether they concern unions or businesses.[13] Organizational political rights include trade union rights to action and protest in the formal political system. With questions of collective bargaining, strikes and shop floor participation come under participation rights. They are government interventions into firms and markets to back workers and employers in mutual negotiations, not the legal and political rights to organize trade unions (Bendix 1964). Consequently, what Giddens vaguely refers to as "economic civil rights" breaks down into portions of legal, political, and participation rights with the particularistic elements excluded (1982, p. 172).[14]

Fourth, the recognition of participation rights counters criticisms that the welfare state creates a dependent society (Andrain 1985, pp. 21–30; Leonard 1983, p. 80; Mead 1986). Participation rights not only assure worker participation in private firms but also apply to clients and community participation in welfare bureaucracies. Thus, participation rights can cover many previously ignored rights within welfare states including citizen initiatives, workers and clients councils, state laws to prevent mergers or acquisitions (e.g., Minnesota laws to protect major corporations from hostile takeovers), and newly emerging forms of women's participation (Hernes 1987, pp. 135–63; Galie 1988; Foster 1980). Participation rights provide an alternative, somewhat complementing but also competing, justification for citizen welfare with the voluntary sector and privatization approaches (Culpitt 1992, pp. 81–182).

CLARIFYING CITIZENSHIP RIGHTS AS RIGHTS

Citizenship rights are not unidimensional, which Hohfeld's (1978) well-known typology of rights demonstrates.[15] Hohfeld differentiates rights into liberties, claims, powers, and immunities. One exercises a liberty without others being obliged to help. A claim imposes a correlative duty on others to help respect and protect the right. Thus, a claim requires cooperation and is bounded, whereas liberties are relatively open.[16] Powers are cooperative controls that may be imposed on others. The opposite of powers are immunities that allow escape from controls and deliver us back to a particularistic version of personal liberties (Hohfeld 1978; Weale 1983, p. 125). My extension of Marshall's conception of citizenship rights meshes with Hohfeld's typology of rights (see Table 2.7).

Civil or legal rights are *liberties* and are more open-ended. A citizen

Table 2.7. *The relationship of citizenship rights to Hohfeld's categories of rights*

Hohfeld's categories	Citizenship rights
1. *Liberties*: The right to unilateral protections or actions. Liberties refer to each individual's ability to act or not act in any way that they please so long as others are not directly hurt.	1. *Legal rights:* Legal rights generally refer to freedoms of religion, speech, due process, and general rights to use the legal system to protect other rights.
2. *Claims*: The right to goods or services that require correlative duties from others. Unlike liberties, claims require the positive and supportive action of other persons.	2. *Social rights:* Social rights include educational and medical services, and tax support for cash payments for welfare and social security. Those who use their social rights depend upon others to pay taxes for those services and transfer payments.
3. *Powers*: Powers include the right to cooperatively control other persons or properties.	3.a. *Political rights*: By voting, citizens cooperatively control the agenda for political action in the future. By holding office, citizens control other citizens and society in a more direct way.
	and
	3.b. *Participation rights*. By participating in workers councils, members of organizations help set the course and policy for their firms. By participating in self-administration, involved interest groups set policy directly related to their constituents.
4. *Immunities:* Immunities include the right to escape powers or claims.	4. *Legal rights:* As an exception to universalistic principles because of a deprivation of rights in the past, legal rights can refer to compensation for aggrieved groups. Affirmative action and veterans compensation are examples.

has the liberty to choose his or her religion and express his or her opinion on an issue. Yet liberties require tolerance of each other's choices and state protections of those choices. Political and participation rights are *powers* that represent cooperative rights where persons and groups must work together to activate these rights. They are mainly procedural. Social rights are *claims* that depend directly on others to pay unemployment and public assistance benefits so that another citizen may receive subsistence. Thus, liberties are more unilateral, and powers and claims, multilateral.

But *immunities* are particularistic. For instance, special income tax exemptions written into law for oil investors would be an immunity from civil obligations to pay taxes; and affirmative action and veterans employment benefits that apply to only a segment of the citizenry would be an immunity from labor laws and personnel rules applying to employment. However, immunities violate the universalistic requirement of citizenship rights, and they can only be considered citizenship rights when they are used as a tool to achieve larger universalistic goals. Although both affirmative action and oil depletion allowances are immunities, only affirmative action is a citizenship right because it attempts to achieve equality of opportunity put into deficit by systematic violations of civil, political, and social rights. Oil depletion allowances refer to no such denial of citizenship in the past.[17]

Hohfeld's classification shows that citizenship rights are varied. Critics such as Nozick (1974) more often than not refer to individual liberties as the only kind of right, whereas rights, especially powers and claims, encompass a variety of social actions.[18] Conservative critics even exaggerate the unilateral nature of liberties and overlook the individual tolerance and complex institutions that are necessary to define and protect these rights. For instance, not only the courts and police, but also the institutions of civil society – bar associations, civil liberties unions, ethnic associations, religious organizations, electronic media, and the publishing industry – protect civil rights.

Critiques by Mishra and Giddens also confuse the varied nature of rights. Mishra says that social rights are concerned with the "distribution of the social product," whereas civil and political rights "set the rules of the game."[19] He concludes that "logically social rights do not belong to the same category of norms as civil and political rights" (1981, pp. 32–3). Indeed, social and participation rights are different from civil and political rights. Not only are social rights in the private (economic) rather than the public (political) realm, but social rights are "claims," rather than "liberties" like civil rights, or "powers" like political rights. Thus, citizenship rights differ qua rights (Hohfeld 1978; Weale 1983).

The Framing of Citizenship Rights

Giddens and Mishra fail to see this complex differentiation of rights. Giddens demonstrates this confusion when he complains about the "lumpiness" and diversity of citizenship rights (1982, p. 172). He also modifies social rights as "economic civil rights" (1987, p. 200–9), but later seems to call for a new class of rights called "economic civil rights" (1982, p. 172; 1989, pp. 268–9; see also Held's extensive critique, 1989, pp. 162–84).[20] Further, critics cannot have it both ways. Mishra criticizes Marshall for not including every conceivable right under citizenship rights in his discussion of private benefits and philanthropic giving, but he reverses himself to say that his citizenship rights do not logically belong to the same category and that including social rights goes too far.

From another direction, some exchange theorists attempt to make rights the basis for nearly all social action. Although Coleman (1990, pp. 49–54) invokes half of Hohfeld's theory of rights, he expands rights to the realm of all social action. According to Coleman, a person "has a right to carry out an action or to have an action carried out when all who are affected by exercise of that right accept the action without dispute" (1990, p. 50). This enlarges the concept of rights to include all activities where action is simply conceded. However, this expansion violates most conceptions of rights. In Coleman's rights perspective, rights are based on a direct "power-weighted consensus" (1990, p. 53), but in most other views, rights are once removed from power and the consensus has been predetermined. Market relations are rights in the sense that one has the right to private property including the ability to sell and buy such property. Market outcomes are not rights but rather the results of bargaining. Bargaining outcomes are simply not rights activities.[21] Interest groups and the state may bargain in the creation of rights, but once rights are established, their bargaining over the existence of the right more or less ends. In Dworkin's terms (1977), rights are trumps, and those trumps were established before the game begins; their value may even fluctuate, but their operational effects are "dedicated," "hardwired," or predetermined. Coleman's usage of rights is to build a more general exchange theory about social behavior, and not to understand the state's provision of citizenship rights.[22] But this approach is far too broad for a theory of citizenship.

Thus, this extended approach to citizenship rights is composed of four different kinds of rights. As a result, sociologists using citizenship rights theory can avoid the criticisms of both the right (Nozick 1974; Dworkin 1977, 1981; Mead 1986) and the left (Giddens 1982, 1989; Mishra 1981) and avoid the over-extension of the rights formula to overall social interaction (Coleman 1990).

PERSONHOOD AND THE RIGHT TO BE RECOGNIZED AS A CITIZEN

Persons knocking at the door of citizenship organize into social movements and interest groups because they are often excluded from formal participation in civil and political activities. Turner emphasizes that citizenship rights are "the outcome of social movements that either aim to expand or defend the definition of social membership" (1986a, p. 92). He finds that the long-term consequences of these social movements have been to push and universalize citizenship rights for an ever widening array of "persons." Yet at the same time, citizenship is an act of closure about a group of people it calls citizens, and consequently states and societies are very particular about whom they call citizens.

Hoffman (1986, p. 83) presents a useful typology of persons who claim citizenship, to which I add a category. There are four categories of claimants not already citizens: stigmatized humans, impaired humans, potential humans, and human-like non-humans.[23] *Stigmatized humans*, first of all, are the most common category of candidates for citizenship, whether class-denigrated poor, gender-disqualified women, status-degraded racial or ethnic groups, or gender-despised homosexual groups. Each group tends to be thought unable to perform the duties and accept the rights of citizenship because of short-sighted interests that will not benefit the community, such as selling their votes, being swayed by their husbands or caretakers, or not having enough education or mental capacity to make a decision. Minority religious and gay groups are perhaps the exception to this generalization in that objections to their having rights are clearly based on cultural or value dissensus. Although established citizens may object to the preferences of any group, these other two groups are not stigmatized by incompetence but rather by opponents' claims that foreign religions, domestic cults, or gays destroy the basic values of society and hence the survival of the dominant group. For instance, Muslims may destroy Christian culture (or vice versa), and gays may threaten the survival of straight culture. Their primary offense is to alter the basic value systems of the nation. But any of these groups may and do form social movements to promote their acceptance and access to rights and obligations.

Second, the group of *impaired humans* may come from established citizen groups, but their competence to fulfill rights and obligations is questioned because of physical or mental disabilities that preclude action or good judgment and establish dependence. Physically disabled groups have mounted a strong campaign for rights, especially through the Center for Independent Living at the University of California at Berkeley (Shapiro 1993). With relatively small and usually material adjustments

46

(e.g., wheelchair access or orally operated typing mechanisms), people with physical disabilities can operate in society with little difficulty as full citizens. Mentally disabled groups have had more problems because self-advocacy has proved to be more difficult. Nonetheless, the inclusion movement in schools, employment, and leisure has brought about changes in many American schools in order to integrate these students. Employment is following close behind with the support of a number of important employers (Sailor et al. 1989).[24]

Third, *potential humans* include the fetus in the womb, accident victims in a permanent coma, unconscious patients, or aged citizens who have lost all thought and activity processes other than involuntary life sustenance. The rights and status of the fetus have been and will likely be debated for some time. The fetus cannot effectively communicate, but the permanently impaired and non-communicative citizen is also in a difficult position. While many speak of the rights of these citizens, few speak of their obligations. Some might argue that they have rights to a fixed amount of care, at which point they may have an obligation to allow resources to be used to save others. This, however, would be an extremely controversial point, as it involves euthanasia and denial of services.

Finally, there exists a category of *human-like non-humans* or *quasi humans*, such as corporations, nations (ethnic groups, races, and even religions), and offices. Corporations have been accorded rights; however, these rights really represent groups of people (e.g., shareholders and to a lesser extent employees). The groups and the corporation are different in some ways, including separability, but corporate rights are a form of group rights. In fact, the connection of the group to the corporation for collecting profits is through dividends, but separation of the corporation from the group for the purposes of limited liability is the major advantage of corporate existence with rights (i.e., when the corporation loses money the stockholders cannot be sued for debts). Group rights can lead to difficulties, whether they are corporate, ethnic, or other groups. Although group rights can legitimately exist, it makes sense to accord them a status that is much less forceful than individual rights whenever individual and group rights are in conflict because organizational rights are derivative from individual rights (Dan-Cohen 1986, pp. 102–13).[25]

Corporate rights lead to a systematic class and size bias. First, corporate stockholding requires financial resources beyond survival needs. Those close to survival minimums will not invest in stock. Although stockholding may be a universal right connected to property rights, it will not be an exercised right for a large portion of the population. This leads to a clear class bias. Second, corporations can acquire large resources and considerable power. Individuals and communities often face this power with comparatively minuscule resources. Consequently, countervailing power resources are necessary to balance their bargaining. Labor organizing, codetermination, workers councils, and environmental monitoring laws have been some of the many ways to do so.

Another important difficulty in dealing with group rights concerns the loss of universality when cultural rights are accorded to racial and ethnic status groups – African Americans, American Indians, New Zealand Maori, Canadian Inuit, French Canadians, Australian Aborigines, Belgian Flemish and Walloons, and many others. These groups may demand rights to protect the integrity of their culture through particularistic rights that may be based on past deprivations of rights (i.e., the issue here is not affirmative action justified as compensation but group solidarity based on culture). The problem is that social resources will be guaranteed to promote a culture in which everyone cannot participate. Formal statements on group rights are rewritten into the Spanish constitution that grants autonomy to the many language-based regions of the country, and the former Soviet Union's approach to autonomous language-based (but not religious) republics (Rothschild 1981). One position is extremely critical of viewing citizens as deculturized, non-ethnic persons, and often status groups strongly support this position (Gray 1989). Another position sees the granting of cultural or group rights as being dangerous because it violates the primacy of individual rights (Howard 1992, pp. 97–9; Dan-Cohen 1986; Van der Wal 1990). A more positive approach attempts to justify group rights (Kymlicka 1995a, b). Clearly, these debates can be differentially justified in communitarian and liberal political theories.

But there are three major problems with group rights. First, group rights are inherently particularistic and may become discriminatory. They are usually advocated by minority groups who want full expression of their culture through rituals and social structures. When other groups live among these minority groups, the others become strangers with no cultural rights themselves.[26] A state based on citizenship embraces universalistic citizenship rights and must avoid advocating religion or ethnic cultures based on particularistic values. The complete achievement of group rights for ethnic and other groups would lead to a feudal system of particularistic communities with entirely different legal and social systems (see Dahrendorf's criticism of sectoral citizenship for a similar but non-ethnic example; 1974, p. 693). Rights to free movement and employment would become strained because a system of group rights encourages separatism. Ethnic groups may argue that the nation-state already advocates a dominant ethnic culture, and this is most certainly true. But that cultural component needs diversity through multiculturalism rather than being counterbalanced by another set of particularistic rights. Consequently, countries based on citizenship can increase their public rituals based on minority cultures, but they should not balkanize their societies with particularistic rights with private rituals.

Second, group rights require representation of the group, and group leaders, rather than the citizens themselves, become invested with the rights. These results may lead to charismatic leaders fanning ethnic hatreds when citizens themselves may not be so concerned about the group (indeed, this lack of ethnic support may even be given as evidence for the necessity of group rights). Reactions against such group-led ethnic rights can be seen in demonstrations in Belgium in 1996 and the non-separatist vote in Quebec in the 1990s. Third, eventually some ethnic groups may seek self-determination and liberation through secession. This is often not a problem for the ethnic leaders who desire independence; however, it is a clear threat to the state and larger society advocating universal citizenship, and it can result in painful civil wars and other conflicts.[27] In the end, many ethnic and racial group problems can be better solved through participatory structures that allow greater democratic control over local and regional resource distributions.[28]

For a society that prefers equal treatment and social mobility through universalistic rights, group rights based on ascriptive criteria cannot be given primacy. Group rights will lessen occupational and geographical mobility and, if pursued in full, will lead to segregated ethnic communities that are sub-states and societies in and of themselves. These sub-societies will then develop tensions between themselves and increase ethnic conflict. Inequalities and injustices can be handled without group rights through compensatory immunities, general social programs, multicultural policies, and participation rights. In a society based on citizenship, individual core rights must be protected on a universalistic basis, and group rights can be based on achieved but not ascriptive statuses. Some ascriptive group rights can be established for holidays and symbolic purposes, which all citizens may be allowed to participate in, but these rights come at a third level of importance behind basic citizenship rights in a society based on equal treatment. Of course, societies can be based on principles other than citizenship, and they can establish group rights as primary. The consequences may be seen in the Serb, Croat, and Muslim conflict in the former Yugoslavia.

Any group in a democratic system, however, may have the political right to obtain citizenship rights that will apply to all but at the same time uniquely improve their own group's position (e.g., a univeralistic poverty program could disproportionately help a poor minority group, or a universalistic rape prevention program could primarily protect women against rape). Minority protections may help this process, but proportional election rules will be most effective in allowing minority groups to form parties and to elect representatives to national legislatures. Countries without proportional procedures may ignore minority concerns, pay attention to such concerns through indirect representation (e.g., white senators representing African American interests in the United States), or attempt the invention of convoluted gerrymandering or double voting schemes (Guinier 1991a, b).

CONCLUSION ON RIGHTS

Social scientists have used citizenship rights theory as a conceptual ruler for measuring democracy and the welfare state, but that approach has become somewhat limited because it did not look into the principles behind Marshall's categories. In Western societies, rights in a logical system of law have grown to protect various groups in vulnerable positions. That system is supported by principles of political and economic democracy. One of Marshall's basic principles shows the movement toward economic democracy through social rights, and this extension of passive citizenship rights to more active rights paves the way for participation rights, a category that is implicit in Bendix and Marshall's conceptual base.

The approach to citizenship rights theory outlined here differs in a number of other ways from present citizenship theories. First, citizenship rights theory provides a clear framework of theoretically grounded rights and obligations. The use of Hohfeld's categories clarifies many previous confusions about the lumpiness of rights categories. Second, the addition of participation rights pushes citizenship rights into the center of more recent welfare state controversies and democratic struggles. Third, the emphasis on stigmatized, impaired, potential, and quasi-humans in pursuing personhood helps predict the difficulties that each category will probably encounter in achieving rights. Finally, the discussion of the prioritization of individual, achieved-group, and ascriptive-group rights avoids troublesome conflicts that groups rights can often lead to.

Many current studies most often use citizenship rights theory only when democracy or the welfare state is threatened, for example, the rollback of legal or social rights in the United States and United Kingdom (King and Waldron 1988). They need to understand the many conceptual underpinnings of citizenship rights. The addition of participation rights offers the further ability to analyze worker participation in the firm (codetermination and works councils), the local citizen involvement in initiating and implementing policy (community action programs and *Burgerinitiativen*), citizen participation in investment (socially conscious investment funds and wage earner funds), and client participation in social policy and media regulation.[29] Previous approaches to citizenship rights have failed to keep up with these new developments in industrialized countries since World War II.

Thus, the expansion of Marshall's theory points citizenship rights analysis into many areas previously unexplored by systematic rights analyses and will allow a more detailed analysis of rights in three regime types. Chapters 5, 6, and 7 will present hypotheses and some data to pursue the apparent differences between rights and obligations in social democratic, traditional, and liberal nations.

3

Reconstructing Obligations and Patriotism: Limitations, Sanctions, and Exchange in a System of Rights

All authority comes from the People.
But the People can only maintain this authority through its obedience.
For if it allows itself to disobey the Citizens to whom it has given power,
then everything is lost, there can no longer be Laws, or peace, or public
safety.
The citizen who disobeys public authority disobeys himself.

Jacques-Pierre Brissot (1789)

A veteran returning from Korea went to college on the GI Bill; bought his
house with an FHA loan; saw his kids born in a VA hospital; started a
business with an SBA loan; got electricity from the TVA and, then,
water from a project funded by the EPA. . . .
His kids participated in the school-lunch program. . . . [They] made it
through college courtesy of government-guaranteed student loans.
His parents retired to a farm on their social security, getting electricity
from the REA and the soil tested by the USDA. When the father became
ill, his life was saved with a drug developed through the NIH; the family
was saved from financial ruin by Medicare.
Our veteran drove to work on the interstate; moored his boat in a channel
dredged by Army engineers; and when floods hit, took Amtrak to Washington to apply for disaster relief. . . .
Then one day he wrote his congressman an angry letter complaining about
paying taxes for all those programs created for ungrateful people.[1]

Jonathan Yates (1988, p. 12)

To many, obligations invoke the specter of coercion and totalitarianism,
yet recent social commentary has lamented the lack of obligations in
society and social theory. Some have mounted an attack on "the greedy
citizen" who focuses only on entitlements, denies responsibility, attacks
the state when obligations are mentioned, and commits some minor
crimes with impunity.[2] Others seek to reconstruct a social society, but
are puzzled that "citizen duties and state rights" get little "more than a
token mention, more often, not a whisper" (Selbourne 1991, p. 96). Like
the everyday lawbreakers described below, many citizens believe that

they are entitled to government-backed rights but recognize few if any obligations to society through the state:

We [Americans] are a nation of law breakers. We exaggerate tax-deductible expenses, lie to customs officials, bet on card games and sports events, disregard jury notices, drive while intoxicated . . . and hire illegal child care workers. . . . Nearly all people violate some laws, and many people run afoul of dozens without ever being considered or considering themselves criminals. (Adler and Lambert 1993, p. 1)

This chronic avoidance of obligations is puzzling because not only do rights require obligations for their fulfillment, since no right may exist without an obligation to help make the right exist, but obligations must also constrain each person's bundle of citizenship rights to make any system of rights workable. T. H. Marshall clearly supports this position: "If citizenship is invoked in the defense of rights, the corresponding duties of citizenship cannot be ignored" (1964, p. 123). Rex Martin states that a right always implies or has attached some closely related duty on others in a democratic system of rights, and that rights must be promoted and maintained by use of obligations with the backing of the state (1993, pp. 29, 82–4; Singer 1993, p. 5). Janowitz agrees with Marshall on citizens' obligations to pay taxes, pursue an education, and serve in the military and that a "balance of citizenship rights and citizen obligations" is necessary (1980, pp. 1, 3–10).

Nevertheless, citizenship theories, liberal political theories, and many citizens themselves have tended to ignore duties and obligations (Carens 1986, p. 31). Janowitz is on the mark when he says that "the long-term trend has been to emphasize and elaborate citizen rights without simultaneously clarifying the issues of citizen obligation" (1980, p. 1).[3] But what students of citizenship must realize is that obligations enforce rights, and without enforcement, rights will not exist (Lockwood 1996; Martin 1993).[4] How can researchers theoretically conceptualize rights for citizens as individuals and in groups without an adequate understanding of obligations?

Intense interest in citizenship obligations has come from two entirely different directions in the last fifteen years. First, the neo-conservatives attacked the lack of responsibility in the welfare state, especially in their claim that welfare recipients do not fulfill their obligations to look for and find work (Mead 1986). Second, with the advent of communitarian influences in public policy, Etzioni (1991, 1993), Galston (1991), and others, while not being so one-sided as neo-conservatives, nevertheless criticize a society where citizens demand rights but abhor obligations. For instance, over 90 percent of the citizenry demand the right to a trial by their peers, but only 14 percent are willing to serve on a jury to fulfill that right (Janowitz 1983, p. 8; Etzioni 1993, p. 3). While obligations have received more and more attention, little is known about what citizens in advanced-industrialized countries believe their obligations to be, and what factors lead to those beliefs. But before empirical work can progress, sociology needs to clarify citizenship theory concerning the actual role played by obligations, and how obligations and rights work together.

This chapter will approach obligations from what could be called a "mediated social control" perspective on obligations. Although obligations need to be strengthened and enforced, citizenship theorists need not fall prey to the reactionary emphasis on punishment. Instead, obligations need to be controlled in a more functional, flexible, targeted, and delimited way. In reasserting but limiting obligations, this chapter takes five steps to (1) identify citizenship obligations and show why they are necessary, (2) place obligations in a system of rights and obligations with restricted and generalized exchange, (3) show how rights can be delimited and safeguarded with notching mechanisms, (4) offer positive and lower-level negative sanctions to enforce obligations, and then (5) view each citizen's obligations vis-à-vis a "new" reconstruction of patriotism based on allegiance rather than obedience.

WHAT ARE CITIZEN OBLIGATIONS?

Citizenship obligations may range from the sometimes vague but other times enforceable requirement to respect another person's opinion and position in life (i.e., general tolerance) to state-enforced civil obligations including conscription and taxation under the penalty of imprisonment (Heath 1976, pp. 50–60; Hohfeld 1978; Phillips 1986). Table 3.1 details the obligations of citizenship that correspond to the rights outlined in Table 2.2. This table of obligations provides much more detail than Janowitz's mention of taxes, education, and military service (1980, pp. 8–16). These obligations can also be viewed as general types. *Support obligations* consist of paying taxes, contributing to insurance-based funds, and working productively. *Caring obligations* to others and to oneself require a person to respect others' rights, care for children and a loving family, and respect oneself by pursuing an education, a career, and adequate medical care. *Service obligations* include efficiently using services, and actually contributing services – be it voter registration, health care for the elderly, "pro bono" work in public defense for lawyers, volunteer fire fighting, or youth service.[5] *Protection obligations* involve military service, police protection, and conscription to protect the nation by bearing arms or caring for the wounded, and social action to

54

Table 3.1. *Four types of citizenship obligations*

Legal obligations	Political obligations	Social obligations	Participation obligations
A. Interpersonal obligations 1. Respect other's rights to liberty, free speech, religion and property 2. Respect laws of contract, association, and equal treatment	*A. Interpersonal obligations* 1. Vote and participate in politics 2. Be informed and exercise the franchise wisely 3. Respect democracy and not make unreasonable demands	*A. Enabling and preventive duties* 1. Pursue prudent health care 2. Raise a loving family 3. Maintain a safe and clean environment	*A. Labor market obligations* 1. Duty of those receiving services to actively pursue work 2. Duty of employers to cooperate with government and unions to provide programs
B. Organizational duties 1. Organizational duty to promote the general welfare 2. Respect individual rights 3. Respect laws duly made by government	*B. Organizational duties* 1. Cooperate with other groups in the operation of politics 2. Follow political laws and regulations	*B. Opportunity obligations* 1. Pursue education to best of one's ability 2. Pursue career to the benefit to society 3. Tolerate social diversity	*B. Firm/bureaucracy obligations* 1. Ensure equity and productivity in the organization 2. Safeguard firm competitive information 3. Respect all groups in participatory process
C. Enforcement and implementation obligations 1. Provide resources for the legal system 2. Assist in assuring the domestic tranquility (militas) 3. Respect and cooperate with police in assuring legal rights	*C. Enforcement and implementation obligations* 1. Provide resources to protect and operate democratic system 2. Protect nation from threats by active service in the military (draft) 3. Protest and overthrow governments that violate rights	*C. Sustenance/economic obligations* 1. Recipients of unemployment or public assistance should look for work 2. Respect other's social rights and the need for transfer payments	*C. Capital participation obligations* 1. Protect and promote the economy 2. Provide for capital funds through savings
		D. Enforcement and implementation 1. Provide resources for social rights 2. Help less fortunate by voluntary government and association service	*D. Enforcement and Implementation* 1. Provide resources for programs 2. Invest in national industries

internally protect the integrity of a democratic system through social service, protests, or demonstrations.

As with rights, obligations have been implemented differentially in three different regimes, and in Tables 3.2 and 3.3 one can see the different levels of obligations that three regimes place on their citizens. Social democratic countries have the highest level of tax obligations with more than ten percentage points over liberal regimes and about three over traditional regimes. Social democratic regimes also have considerable conscription obligations (highest with 59.5 percent of soldiers being conscripts, but much lower than traditional countries on penalties). Liberal countries have the lowest conscription obligations with only the United States having considerable conscription in the last forty years (column 4). Recalling similar results with rights, one can posit a hypothesis of balance between rights and obligations, and this hypothesis will be discussed further in Chapter 5.

However, as with rights, obligations may conflict with other obligations and with other noncorresponding rights. For instance, the obligations to respect liberties (i.e., freedom of person) may contradict political obligations to protect the society from foreign threats (i.e., military conscription); or respect for laws and other persons' liberties (i.e., tolerance) may conflict with obligations to overthrow governments that systematically violate democratic principles (i.e., obligations to protect democracy). Societies may clearly negotiate many different compromises between rights and obligations in an overall system of citizenship.[6]

THEORIES OF POLITICAL OBLIGATIONS

Sociological theories of obligations are not very well developed. This can be said despite the large amount of work done in the area of political theory concerning obligations. Political theorizing often exists as a deductive exercise of rational individuals – an exercise that does not always mesh well with a sociological theory of citizenship that takes group negotiations and institutional socialization much more into account. Philosophers seek absolutes that clearly justify a position, while social scientists look for variation to explain outcomes. Nonetheless, political theory provides many useful insights that are helpful in delineating a theory of citizenship obligations.

Political theory has generated three basic approaches to the problem of obligations focusing on frameworks of consent,[7] alternative foundations,[8] and alternative frameworks[9] (Hirschman 1992). I will take from each basic approach to obligations in political theory to begin constructing a theory of citizenship obligations in three parts: (1) incurring consent with recipience and acceptance in restricted exchange, (2) accepting

Table 3.2. *Taxes as percentage of GNP in three regimes (average of 1965, 1975, and 1985 figures)*

Social democratic regimes		Traditional regimes		Liberal regimes		Mixed regimes	
Denmark	40.0	Austria	38.7	Australia	28.0	Ireland	32.0
Finland	34.0	Belgium	39.7	Canada	31.0	New Zealand	28.7
Netherlands	41.0	France	39.3	Japan	22.0	United Kingdom	35.3
Norway	42.0	Germany	35.3	Switzerland	27.7		
Sweden	43.7	Italy	32.3	United States	28.3		
Average	*40.1*	*Average*	*37.0*	*Average*	*27.3*	*Average*	*32.0*

SOURCE: OECD (1991, 1987a, b).

Table 3.3. *Conscription and National Service in Three Regimes*

Countries: by regime types	(1) Conscripts as a % of the armed forces in 1982	(2) Length of basic service in months in 1982	(3) Penalties after rulings in months in 1982	(4) Number of years of draft from 1951-90
Social Democratic				
Denmark	30.4	9	15	40
Finland	73.7	8	12	40
Sweden	73.0	10	4	40
Norway	72.3	12	12	40
Netherlands	48.3	15	24	40
Average	*59.5*	*10.8*	*13.4*	*40.0*
Traditional				
Austria	68.9	6	4.5	40
Belgium	33.8	10	36	40
Germany	46.3	15	60	38
France	51.9	12	24	40
Italy	65.4	12	48	40
Average	*53.3*	*11.0*	*34.5*	*39.6*
Liberal				
Australia	0	0	0	—
Canada	0	0	0	0
Japan	0	0	0	0
Switzerland	0 [a]	1 [a]	—	0
United States	0	0	0	22
Average	*0.0*	*0.2*	*0.0*	*5.4*
Mixed				
Ireland	0	—	—	0
New Zealand	0	—	—	0
United Kingdom	0	0	0	0

[a] Swiss reserves are conscripted for an initial four week training period and a two week training obligation in subsequent years. This four week training period is taken as one month of service. The first variable is zero because there are no conscripted regular armed forces. If conscripted reserves were taken to be regular armed forces, this variable would be a misleading 92.5%.

SOURCES: Mellors and McKean (1984, pp. 33-38), the International Institute for Strategic Studies (1966/67 and 1992/93), and national sources.

state legitimacy with generalized exchange, and (3) limiting obligations
with supererogatory acts and notching mechanisms.

Obligations after the Recipience and Acceptance of Rights

Citizenship theory needs to carefully recognize the context from which
obligations emerge. From context, the degree to which an obligation
applies depends upon "accepting" versus "receiving" rights (Simmons
1979).[10] Acceptance implies that a citizen tried to obtain the right, suc-
ceeded, and willingly or knowingly benefited from it. Citizens who "accept" rights formally incur obligations. However, citizens may "receive"
benefits from rights but not recognize that they benefit (i.e., unknowingly
take advantage of a public good) or not willingly accept the benefit (i.e.,
be under direct coercion or duress). According to some versions of political theory, citizens who merely "receive" benefits do not formally
incur obligations. For example, a disoriented veteran may be placed into
an inappropriate rehabilitation program that he or she has not re-
quested, or a welfare client may be forced under pain of losing benefits
into a training program that may be useless. Many citizens may also
simply not receive a benefit and thus do not incur the associated obligation. For instance, the uninsured unemployed do not incur obligations
to look for work deriving from the social right to unemployment insurance.

One should be careful about accepting these consent or contract theories, and it is helpful to take a sociological or socialization approach
to incurring obligations. Children grow up receiving many benefits without acceptance, that is, they do not consent to the receipt of rights. A
baby benefits from rights to medical care but cannot fulfill any obligations. A child who gets a dollar for a weekly allowance is not aware
that the state regulates and monitors the monetary supply, prosecutes
forgers, and regulates foreign exchange. A teenager who is provided
schooling may not consent to that schooling and might rather watch
movies or hang out all day. Nonetheless, the state in most industrialized
nations obligates that child to attend school. Some of the obligations
may be the result of acceptance, but many are not even known and some
may even be resisted. Nonetheless, societies obligate minors to perform
many actions, allow them to escape many others, and provide them with
a restricted bundle of rights. Consequently, young citizens may feel the
force of obligations without giving consent, and we all gradually accu-
mulate obligations and rights in our years before adulthood (Tussman
1960; Jones and Wallace 1992).

Although not uniformly, adult citizens are subsequently given some
choice as to whether certain rights and obligations should be incurred.

59

By that time, new citizens having reached the age of consent have accumulated a history of benefit and obligation performances. One could declare that upon reaching the age of twenty-one, they no longer consent to the draft, taxes, schooling, obeying traffic signals, police powers, and so on; however, their past history and societal adherence to laws interfere with this withdrawal from obligations. For instance, the middle-class citizen having benefited from schooling, police powers, zoning, and any number of benefits declares on his or her twenty-first birthday that he or she no longer consents to any of these actions and is therefore not obligated to provide taxes for them. The new citizen must explain away past benefits, and this may be difficult. The state may require that the citizen reimburse the state (and society) for prior benefits before being released from obligations. For instance, the Soviet state required Jewish emigrants to reimburse the state for education received in secondary and tertiary schools. While these Soviet actions were punitive because of other acts of discrimination and repression against Jews in the Soviet Union, the action had a certain logic based on obligations. One cannot suddenly declare oneself to be a libertarian after benefiting from state and social services in the past.

The distinction between accepting, receiving, and not receiving a benefit is particularly important for minority groups and dissenters. Minority groups who are discriminated against often do not receive benefits. Although they may be expected to conform to obligations, in reality they may have few such obligations. For instance, educational rights for many American blacks prior to 1954 were often prone to systematic denigration, and arguments can be made now that they are still insufficient (Anderson 1982). It is questionable whether many African Americans actually received these benefits, and as such, they would be under different obligations than others who clearly benefited from high-quality education. To expect minority groups to respect the civil and political rights of others when minority rights are violated is a problem.[11]

Systematically dissenting groups may have little discretion in dealing with rights lest they lose rights that protect their dissent by ignoring obligations. If a dissenting group continually benefits from rights, they are in a weak position to deny obligations (e.g., protesters during the 1960s being on food stamps). If dissenting groups rebuff such rights, they can more easily ignore obligations. If they totally repay the costs of receiving past rights and benefits, they are on strong grounds to ignore obligations. While few groups have attempted to repay the costs of past benefits, others have chosen to wean themselves off benefits to successfully claim their release from obligations. Groups, such as the Amish and Hutterites, who have rejected many benefits have a clean slate on many obligations despite having benefited from the liberties such as the freedom of religion. Nonetheless, friction persists on issues of conscription, soil banks, social security, and education (Thomson 1992, p. 440).

One major disadvantage of the consent approach to incurring obligations in the discussion of socialization and dissenting groups is that it heavily relies on restricted exchange between rights and obligations. A sociological approach, while benefiting from the accounting for recipience and acceptance, must consider a system of rights held together by rights and obligations in a more complex relationship. Although restricted exchanges of rights and obligations do occur within the recipience theory, much citizenship behavior involves the more loosely coupled relationship using generalized exchange.

Accepting Obligations with Legitimacy

Part of the communitarian thesis states that "some responsibilities do not entail rights" or that the connection employs long-term circular exchange rather than short-term reciprocal exchange. Consequently, the more restricted exchange relationship implied by Simmons in the previous paragraphs is inappropriate, and generalized exchange with "people helping people who help other people" needs to be added to the analysis (Ekeh 1974; Etzioni 1993, p. 4). This is not a simple theoretical addition to make the ties between rights and obligations more palatable. Generalized exchange actually operates in a very different way from restricted exchange. It is true that some responsibilities may not necessarily directly entail rights; nonetheless, there is a tie or connection for many rights and obligations. Further, one may mistake nonreciprocal ties (A gives to B, B gives to C, and C gives to A) as not directly tying rights and obligations together, but they do so in an indirect way. This is exactly what generalized exchange adds to the analysis.[12]

Walzer (1970, 1983) and Etzioni (1993) appear to be avoiding a contractual and narrowly instrumental view of the connection of rights and obligations, and embracing a more community-oriented view of generalized exchange (Ekeh 1974). Most citizens do not calculate their everyday balances of rights and obligations like they might balance their checkbook. For example, today I have volunteered here and received rights there, and thus being in balance, I need not help the elderly blind woman having difficulty crossing the street. This position is defensible in avoiding the constantly calculating citizen, and its claim that people do establish a view of overall balance (or legitimacy) is built into the generalized exchange position. People do not expect immediate and reciprocal returns from the people they help, but they do expect to see their returns materialize over time in building a decent life in a more or less just society.

61

Consequently, rights and obligations may be more loosely coupled in longer-term relationships, but nonetheless, they are coupled because of prior motivations toward and receipts of benefits. This loosely coupled relationship is covered by the concept of legitimacy, but its weakness in social science lies in that it is often vague and difficult to measure. The generalized exchange concept, which will be developed in the next chapter, attempts to trace peoples' conceptions of rights and obligations over time and to correct for that vagueness.

Limiting Obligations

In establishing limitations on obligations, Fishkin (1982) presents three zones of action – indifference, moral requirement, and supererogation. Actions are then differentiated into categories of amorality (no issue of morality involved), morality (clearly right or wrong), and heroism (supererogatory acts of exceptional morality). In the end, we are obligated to save someone's life at only small costs to ourselves (e.g., open the refrigerator door for a small child trapped inside). Obligations clearly do not apply in supererogatory situations where heroic actions are necessary at great cost of life and limb to the volunteer (e.g., jumping into a torrential river to rescue an unconscious child when it is highly probable that both the child and rescuer will die). The importance of this position is that there are moral positions where people are obliged to act, non-moral positions where they can be indifferent, and moral positions where they may avoid exceptional heroism. This is a useful viewpoint toward everyday life during calm periods of history.

However, at other points in time, the state asks for heroism from its citizens, and the sanctions of treason and cowardliness are not far removed. For instance, on D day when young soldiers were put on Omaha Beach, the state made rather incredible demands on these citizens for heroism. But for those who refused to board the launch vehicles, severe punishments were waiting in the wings. On one end of the scale of intensity of obligation, serving in the military during wartime would require a great deal of heroic behavior. Consequently, these actions are often backed by strong sanctions (e.g., death by firing squad for abandoning a position at the front). At the other end of the scale, voting for taxes to support the poor and homeless provides a clear position of morality that relieves the everyday citizen from supererogatory acts (e.g., using up all their savings and selling all their assets to run a mission for the poor). While citizenship obligations cannot totally rule out supererogatory actions, they do provide a mechanism for delimiting extraordinary charity and supporting state-run programs based on a clear morality of helping large numbers of needy people in great difficulties.

Reconstructing Obligations and Patriotism

Three instances of scale – obligation, recipience, and action – help the citizen and state differentiate between these positions on obligation. The *scale of obligation* refers to the number of situations falling under an obligation; the *scale of recipience* refers to the number of persons who would be affected by the obligation; and the *scale of action* is the number of citizens who could perform the actions connected to an obligation (Fishkin 1982, pp. 46–7). Because each scale presents dangers of free riding, the state must further obligate and sanction the citizen to perform these actions. The larger the number of situations, needy persons, and citizens who can potentially help, the more citizens will be overwhelmed by need while having much less personal connection to the problem. These positions of scale lend themselves to empirical operationalization.[13] Zones of indifference can be constructed differently for many citizens (what may be the philosopher's nightmare of no objective position may be the sociologist's delight in finding adequate variation). Hence, individual obligations are indirect through taxes and are handled by state programs when they apply to large numbers of citizens helping a large number of needy persons in many different types of situations (i.e., the scales of obligation, recipience, and action are high). Individual obligations are direct when the needy are few in a unique situation and only one person can respond (i.e., the scales of obligation, recipience, and action are low). These principles of limitation clearly differentiate individual and state-enforced obligations and reinforce paying taxes for social welfare as a moral act, and not paying taxes, no matter what the efficiency complaints might be, as an immoral act.

Limitations on obligations can also be pursued from the conflict of rights perspective. Etzioni and Galston present a position on obligations that emphasizes the enforcement of sanctions (e.g., obligation to stay sober while piloting an airplane, and obligation to care for one's own children). This enforcement, however, involves conflicts between the rights of passengers and pilots, and children and parents. Although Etzioni does not use this terminology, he basically regards these situations as ties between competing civil rights and gives the tie-breaking role to overall societal welfare.[14] Yet the lack of a right to privacy in avoiding drug testing may lead to a serious consequence for the pilot (i.e., a long prison term for endangering the lives of many people). Before the fact, rights to avoid testing and rights to fly safely are simply probabilities that may be small (probability of crashing or being caught with residual drugs in one's system). After an accident, the results would be known, and their impact could be highly detrimental. But this leads back to ties between two different individual rights. Giving society the ability to break the tie between intensely felt rights of equal intensity does not solve the problem of one or the other person's rights being violated, but it does produce a society that is workable and beneficial for large numbers of people (Etzioni 1993; Waldron 1993; Nozick 1974).[15]

Nonetheless, benefit for the majority may be misery and torture for the minority, and this is why basic and somewhat unconditional civil rights are necessary. Etzioni's position here is to safeguard the erosion of rights by having the state act only under four conditions: (1) there is a clear danger, (2) no reasonable alternatives exist, (3) the decisions in favor of society are least intrusive, and (4) efforts are made to minimize damage or treat the effects of constraining a right (1993, pp. 177–90). These "notching mechanisms" strive to prevent the gradual and sometimes unobserved erosion of individual rights. These mechanisms will not satisfy the elegance demanded by liberal-individualist theory, which may accept inaction as the result of theoretical indeterminacy. But this liberal-individualistic inaction causes people to suffer a real loss of rights (e.g., men and women die on a train driven by a drug-taking conductor). Etzioni and other communitarians argue that these are definitely unbalanced outcomes that require the sanctioning of obligations rather than the privileging of inactivity through rights. When Waldron discusses whether citizens have a "right to be wrong," the answer becomes contingent on likely consequences. The notching principles seem to be enough to distinguish between sanctioning someone "yelling 'fire' in a crowded theater" when there is none, and tolerating a partisan "yelling scurrilous attacks" in the heat of a political debate.

Rex Martin, based to a certain extent on John Rawls, comes to a similar position on the conflict of rights from the entirely different approach of safeguarding civil rights, especially those of prisoners who explicitly have violated the basic rights of other citizens. He establishes the following general principles to decide on basic conflicts of rights:

1. With the scope and possession of rights, determine whether the persons involved are citizens and whether and in what way the rights apply to the situation at hand;
2. Identify and locate rights in conflict due to overlapping areas between rights;
3. Establish competitive weights for each right in their zone of overlap based on each right's distance from its core principles;
4. Establish tests that will apply the weighing system (e.g., the clear and present danger rule, but many other rules exist);[16] and
5. Restrict the scope of competing rights by partitioning rights from each other and eliminating the zone of overlap (Martin 1993, pp. 110–26; Rawls 1982, pp. 9–12, 26, 56–74; Waldron 1993, pp. 203–24; Gostin 1995; Wellman 1995, pp. 200–41).[17]

Operating on the principle that citizenship rights are universal rights supported by "mutually perceived benefits" among the citizenry, Martin restricts these conflict reduction principles, which constrain some rights to favor others, by three considerations: (1) no reasonable alternatives exist, (2) the rights constriction is a temporary or interim procedure (not a lifelong restriction), and (3) the intent is to improve the overall system of equal rights for the mutual benefit of all (Martin 1993, pp. 109–18).[18] The wide application of this conflict reduction procedure by constitutional delegates, political legislators, legal practitioners, and concerned citizens establishes a system of rights that harmonizes its demands on society and individuals (p. 115). The result is somewhat similar, though much more complex, than Etzioni's notching principles.[19] However, it is a common practice that takes place in most courts on a daily basis.

Martin then moves from the conflict of rights to the actual violation of rights by lawbreakers. After an extended discussion of punishment, he concludes that governments should tailor the question of punishment to specific characteristics of the crime. The total forfeiture of rights for prisoners is not sound (1993 p. 281). Principles of penalties, compensation, and rehabilitation may all play a role in punishment, but rights to have medical attention, to work productively, and to avoid torture are still unquestionably present (pp. 284–97). As with the conflict of rights, the violation of rights entails punishment applied according to the violation, but it does not remove all rights. Thus, Martin takes a careful approach to constraining rights where rights conflict, even in the case of imprisonment for serious crimes. The end results are notching mechanisms even more far-reaching than those of Etzioni. Yet at the same time, it is an approach that explicitly sanctions lawbreaking.

There is great value in all three of these approaches. The first group of theories of political obligation tried to tie specific obligations to specific rights (e.g., Simmons). While exclusive reliance on restricted exchange was a problem, Simmons's concepts of recipience and acceptance represent important contingencies for the application of citizenship obligations. The second approach tries to put obligations and rights into a system of generalized exchange, whether we call that system a community (e.g., Walzer) or a democratic system of rights (e.g., Martin). Walzer's position goes even further in this legitimacy position by finding obligation to be based in the community which is not obviously and directly connected to the state. While a direct connection to the state is preferable for citizenship theory, this position is helpful in establishing a system of rights with principles of socialization based on generalized exchange (Tussman 1960). Thus, the restricted exchange position of Simmons in the first group and the more generalized exchange of Walzer in the second group are both possible as contingent hypotheses. The third group of theories help establish limitations on heroic obligations and justify taxes for social rights, and the "notching principles" carefully control the enforcement of obligations from the common problem of rights conflicts (indeed, nearly all obligations involve conflicts of and subsequent constraints on rights).

THE APPLICATION OF SANCTIONS

As citizenship rights in general are clearly different from civic virtue, citizen obligations and sanctioning are also not the same as social concern or vengeance. Obligations require rational sanctions by the state, just as rights must have enforcement or maintenance by the state. Rights and obligations are laws, not vague feelings of responsibility or influence between the state and citizens, or citizens and their peers. As Michael Ignatieff states:

> The language of citizenship is not properly about compassion at all, since compassion is a private virtue, which cannot be legislated or enforced. The practice of citizenship is about ensuring everyone has the entitlements necessary to the exercise of their liberty. As a political question, welfare is about rights, not caring, and the history of citizenship has been the struggle to make freedom real, not to tie us all in the leading strings of therapeutic good intentions. (1989, p. 72)

Citizenship obligations, duties, or responsibilities require sanctions with some connection to the state, or they are not part of citizenship theory. But these sanctions need not be severe and negative. The following approach to sanctions attempts to enforce but not overly coerce citizens.

Emphasizing Positive and Lesser Sanctions

Sanctions can be positive or negative, and they begin early. Attending school is an obligation to children until their sixteenth birthday in the United States. Positive sanctions include gold stars for good attendance in grade school, National Honor Society pins for academic performance in high school, and rights to use the items or facilities made or improved by sweat equity projects (Brown 1995, pp. 146–7). Negative sanctions include after-school detention, expulsions from school, truant officers apprehending children who skip, and even courts punishing parents who fail to send their children to school. The weight of sanctions in schooling seems to be heavily on punitive sanctions. However, positive sanctions can be further developed. Educators have proposed additional positive sanctions such as longer vacations or trips on holidays for children who attend every day or do well at school in a modified and lengthened school year.[20]

Sanctions for adults may also be positive or negative. Negative sanctions may be severe, such as the death penalty or denying freedom of movement to incarcerated citizens convicted of felony crimes. But the results of these negative sanctions acknowledge failure concerning the prisoner, and a society that excessively relies on imprisonment will find this route to be costly and tremendously coercive.[21] Instead, emphasis could be on positive and lesser sanctions. Positive sanctions include status rewards publicly recognizing those who fulfill duties (e.g., patches, medals, or certificates), recognition in the media, and other symbolic rewards. Negative sanctions may include small specific punishments such as fines, publicizing those who have not carried out obligations, and actually removing the rights of citizens by denying the use of public facilities (such as denying the use of a park for a month to persons who litter). Publishing in the newspapers the pictures of children truant from school, students expelled from class, fathers delinquent in child support, and persons who commit crimes can be important. Schools with disciplinary problems have changed dramatically when video cameras in the hallways can replay offensive student behavior in disciplinary hearings. Some neighborhoods in the United States with high crime rates have used video patrols to "widen the observability" of illegal cruising, johns soliciting prostitutes, gang intimidation, and graffiti painting (Brown 1995, pp. 132–5).[22] For convicted lawbreakers, developing community service sanctions not only sanction behavior but also involve complex emotions of empathy that may be beneficial.

There are a number of approaches to "lesser sanctions" that can be implemented. Lesser sanctions can be put in place by communicating the failure to fulfill responsibilities to the community. This can be done by increasing observability, experiencing the emotions of sanctions more deeply, and citizens' participating in sanctioning.

Increasing Observability

Many societies, however, have become unable to enforce lesser sanctions as they have moved from closely knit neighborhoods with strong social pressure to more anonymous suburban and urban settings with little social closure. Nonetheless, a range of positive and negative sanctions is necessary for adequate social control in any society. If previous mechanisms of social control have broken down due to the disappearance of most communities in small towns or ethnic neighborhoods in large cities, other mechanisms can be found. There are dangers of overly coercive societies with unbearable social pressures using excessive applications of negative sanctions, but there are also the equally important dangers of anarchy and a shredded social fabric that come with the avoidance of sanctions. In a positive vein through voluntary but extensive participation, the "co-housing movement" builds communities that maximize observability through architecture and community meals.

For effective sanctions to exist in the first place, citizens in the community and the police must have knowledge of and access to citizens and other residents. The Japanese police conduct two surveys each year to find out who lives in the neighborhoods located in their district or *Koban* (Bayley 1976, pp. 17, 84–6). Germany and Sweden also have address registries and national identity cards that facilitate community knowledge. Police also cooperate with social service professionals in successfully tracking fathers who fail to pay child support (Glendon 1989, pp. 217–27).[23]

Second, sanctions need to be enforced in a positive way. The way to enforcement is not enhanced by police as strangers arriving to arrest offenders but rather is enhanced by local police who know people in the community and can counsel potential conflicts and help mobilize community groups to provide observation and social pressure. Indeed, police should move from enforcement by arrest or citation after the commission of a crime, to enforcement through mediation and conciliation before the crime. In effect, police need to engage in public discourse within the civil society to do their jobs effectively. In Japan, the police and neighborhoods interact to produce crime prevention associations composed of resident volunteers working closely with police in every neighborhood in the whole country (Bayley 1976, p. 91). Other organizations such as Friends of the Police and the Women's Apartment House Lock Troop exist for other cooperative endeavors. These activities make police an active, observed, controllable, and consultative aspect of every community. Although Japan is somewhat unusual because its neighborhoods are organized into *han* or *cho-kai* governance on a wider number of social welfare issues, negotiation and observability are being embraced by police with community mediation centers in the United States and Europe.

As a third general principle, much of these positive and negative sanctions in Japan rest on observability. As Hechter and Kanazawa (1993) show in their inventory of Japanese life, from their thin house and room walls to their methods of small group social pressure, Japanese citizens are as a matter of daily life closely observed at home, in the neighborhood, and at work. The United States has the least observability, with more suburban single-family dwellings, and teenagers living most of their day away from parents, teachers, and other adults in age-segregated settings. Europe is in between the United States and Japan with more group activities and closer neighborhood living than the United States, but to a lesser extreme than Japan. Much of this is not a new principle, as Jacobs (1960) has written some time ago about observability on city streets leading to safe neighborhoods and liveable cities. While societies do not need Orwellian monitoring by "big brother," community observation is necessary for socialization and both positive and negative social control. And socially monitored and controlled observability naturally leads to soft sanctions, rather than harsh sentences in prison.

Experiencing Sanctions through Shame and Empathy.

Beyond information, shaming and empathy can be effectively used if certain conditions are met. Stigmatizing shaming must be avoided where shame becomes a badge of honor or causes subjects to internalize deviant labels (Braithwaite 1989, pp. 66-7). "Reintegrative shaming," on the other hand, employs communication between community members (i.e., even community social pressure and gossip) and then provides supports to help the offender. Direct confrontation is avoided, but the subject knows that talk about him/her has occurred; labeling is avoided because the citizen who avoids responsibility is led in concrete steps toward fulfilling obligations in the future (Bergmann 1991, pp. 144-6; Braithwaite 1989, pp. 75-7; Hamilton and Sanders 1992, pp. 136-7; Byrne, Lurigio, and Petersilia 1992; Grasmick, Bursik, and Arneklev 1993).

"Restorative justice" involves establishing empathy through the direct interaction between the victim and the offender. The offender is held accountable through fines or services to be provided to the victim, but more importantly the offender has to deal with the victim's emotions (Wright 1991, pp. 112-31). The Japanese tend to accept more restorative sanctioning than Americans, and the Japanese tend to employ it more often (Hamilton and Sanders 1992, pp. 75-88, 135-56; Hechter and Kanazawa 1993; Braithwaite 1989, pp. 74-5). There are, of course, situations where this should not be applied as with the cases of obsessive stalkers or rapists who would be rewarded by the additional contact. However, these rights violators can be put in programs where they must be responsive to other victims (e.g., discussing their misdeeds before women's protection groups).

Citizen Participation in Sanctioning

Sanctions raise legitimate concerns about coercion – a point of continual concern throughout this chapter. But sanctions can be monitored in formal channels through community participation in various community advisory boards (Pateman 1979). Many European nations exercise greater sanctions through advisory boards (e.g., the *Weise Ring* protecting victims' rights and giving advice on sentencing in Germany), and the principles of active participation in policing are clear and sometimes applied in American Neighborhood Watch Programs (Bayley 1976; Ames 1981).[24] Brown mentions a number of additional cooperative developments in neighborhoods: search parties for children, informally enforced community curfews, neighborhood mentoring programs, and group parenting by single mothers and elder neighbors (1995, pp. 129–59).

While Germany requires that residents file their new addresses after they move with the police, the authorities protect the privacy of information so much that the decennial census was held up for a number of years due to questions about the constitutionality of privacy provisions in the questionnaire.[25] Information in residential registries is protected by a board of governors that observe and protect confidentiality. In Japan, police knowledge of each person's location remains at the local *Koban* office and cannot be sent to national computer databanks or higher levels of the state. The Swedes protect privacy so much that the identities of suspects cannot be revealed during trials in case they are innocent – not even the identity of the suspected assassin of the late Prime Minister Olof Palme. Swedish police also work with citizen advisory groups (1950s–1960s) and Crime Prevention Councils (1970s–1980s) (Archer 1985, p. 265; Becker 1973, p. 109; Alpsten 1974, pp. 32–3; Brewer et al. 1988).

Finally, citizens in both Germany and Sweden fulfill obligations and provide for the treatments called for in the notching mechanisms by paying for welfare state and social services, which creates a tax burden nearly twice that of the United States.[26] These and other lesser sanctions could be closely monitored and applied in any society. Thus, establishing observability, restoring lesser sanctions, using restorative justice and reintegrative shaming, and limiting obligations through consultative policing and notching principles are mechanisms that can make the society's positive and negative sanctioning of obligations more effective and legitimate. In the end, observability, sanctioning, and community control can lead to more effective enforcement of many citizens' rights without meaningful loss of others' rights.

THE RECONSTRUCTION OF PATRIOTISM

In this section, nationalism and national identity will be examined with a reconstruction of patriotism through responsible patriotism. Many scholars have a difficult time dealing with a citizen's obligations to the nation-state.[27] Should citizens be nationalists, patriots, revolutionaries, agnostics, cynics, or simply subjects? Smith views nationalism as "an ideological movement for attaining and maintaining autonomy, unity and identity on behalf of a population deemed by some of its members to constitute an actual or potential 'nation' " (1991, p. 73) that "shares a historic territory, common myths and historical memories, a mass, public culture, a common economy and common legal rights and duties for all members" (1991, p. 14). Unfortunately, the ways that many nationalist movements have maintained unity and identity have led to assertions of superiority and aggressive actions, and this has led to grouping nationalism with other "-isms" like sexism and racism.

A less benign characterization of nationalism than Smith provides recognizes nationalism as a possible social problem. It would be like the following:

I am an Xian. Nation-state X is a superior nation. I see goodness in Nation X and support it through good and bad times. I am inexorably proud of being an Xian.

This approach to nationalism shades into imperialism and leads to aggressive behavior on the part of states to take or retake territory that "justly" belongs to such a superior state. A major problem is that elite and mass belief systems will devolve from the culturally centered approach defined by Smith to the more aggressive definition that has produced war and great suffering.

Many sociologists and political scientists implicitly prefer "national identity" to nationalism. National identity involves political community that implies "at least some common institutions and a single code of rights and duties for all the members of the community" in a "well demarcated and bounded territory" within which members identify and belong (Smith 1991, p. 9). This more neutral stance leaves out the territorial component since many nations, especially those in diasporas, lack a specific territory:

I am an Xian. Being Xian entails having $X_1, X_2, \ldots, X_n$ beliefs, values, rituals, myths, emotions, rationalities, language, and other characteristics. I am proud of these characteristics and intend to maintain them.

This definition is largely cultural, and while it would be appropriate for many purposes in social science, it is a problem for citizenship theory because national identity is entirely passive toward the state. Having a national identity or selecting some features of it entails no commitment to fulfill obligations, and requires no necessary position toward citizenship at all. As a result, this approach comes perilously close to denying citizenship because if you deny obligations you ultimately deny other citizens' rights.

By following at least partially in Janowitz's footsteps in his book *The Reconstruction of Patriotism*, consider the following position of "responsible patriotism":

I am a citizen of X. I support X's policies when I think that they are mostly just. I do not support and try to change X's policies when I think they are wrong. I see virtues and flaws in X, and I take responsibility for them.

This position of patriotism allows both assent and dissent.[28] It drops the totalizing social movement aspect of negative nationalism that seems to require true believers but retains the possibility of social movements for or against current policies. It retains the citizens' relationship to the state, which is not necessarily present in national identity and which can be overwhelming in extreme patriotism. Martin also makes a critical distinction between assent and dissent (1993, pp. 188–206) by rejecting "obedience to the state" under political obligation, but accepting the more critical yet positive term of "allegiance," which allows for patriotism with dissent and periodic civil disobedience (Pateman 1979, p. 165).

The position of responsible patriotism also requires that the citizen take an active position toward the state.[29] It does not allow the easy position of the passive cynic who criticizes the state but makes little or no investment in his or her own society (Janowitz 1983). Responsible patriotism is also preferable to positions of world citizenship, which many citizenship scholars regard as an impossibility since citizenship requires some form of closure (Brubaker 1992; Aron 1974).[30] It is preferable to the agnostic position of support and change without emotional involvement because the agnostic position could hardly motivate one to sacrifice anything to support other peoples' rights. Responsible patriotism unifies the nation-state, rather than dividing it, which national identity might do if it evolved into ethnic competition between groups.[31]

Although Selznick has a similar view toward patriotism, his position draws attention to another element missing from or perhaps redefined in the responsible patriotism concept: "In pledging allegiance to the nation 'as a project' we identify ourselves with an idealized past, accept responsibility for failures as well as successes, and promise to care for the community's well-being" (1992, p. 390). Selznick's definition accords with responsible patriotism, but his reference to "nation" reminds one of how easily "nation" implies an ethnically based group (*ethnie*). A definition that allows multiculturalism would have to be more careful about sharing common myths and historical memories in a mass and public culture. A common economy and common legal rights and duties for all cultural groups would imply more of a "constitutional patriotism" used by Habermas (1994, p. 27), and the mass and public culture would be a civic culture that allows for a diversity of religions and ethnic customs. Habermas indicates that constitutional patriotism would be based on rights and obligations of many groups, and that many multicultural societies show that a particular "political culture" as "the seedbed of . . . constitutional principles" does not require that all citizens share the same language, culture, or ethnic origins. Instead, the political culture serves as "the common denominator for a constitutional patriotism" that sharpens citizens' awareness and respect for multiple cultures (1994, p. 27). The result is a concept that allows for freedom of movement for migrants and minorities with assurances of full rights, duties, and belonging. But it also requires that the myths and historical memories of the state and society be in the public sphere and shareable by all ethnic, racial, gender, class, and ability groups.

CONCLUSION

Obligations have been ignored because they had become a taboo topic after the totalitarian regimes of the first half of the century. Yet after lying fallow in the post World War II period, obligations are receiving renewed attention. Much more is being written and spoken about obligations to care for one's self and family, to develop one's education including self-discipline, and to protect the nation peacefully or even militarily. These obligations must be closely watched and prevented from going too far in a coercive direction, for while rights cannot exist without obligations, obligations can exist without rights. That many citizens do not realize this is reflected in a rather sad quote from David W. Brown (1995, pp. 2–3):

It seems that the more you and I do as we like, the less you and I get what we want. We are avid consumers and . . . don't know what to do with the waste stream that our consumption produces. We go where we please and find our highways congested and our favorite recreational areas crowded with strangers. We seek professional attention for our manifold physical complaints and then complain when health costs make professional attention almost prohibitive. We celebrate sexual freedom and mourn the loss of friends to AIDS or deplore the costs of supporting unwed teenage mothers. We walk out on marriages that aren't working and are confronted by a generation of sullen and angry children.

From this chapter's review of obligations in a system of rights, six conclusions are clear. First, rights and obligations are intimately related. The existence of rights is predicated on the simultaneous presence of obligations. If societies ignore obligations, they will never enforce many of their rights. Second, obligations are not always related to rights in a one-to-one contractual manner as in restricted exchange. Instead, they are often related together in a larger system of rights and obligations that entails some restricted exchange but also large amounts of loosely coupled generalized exchange. Third, personal obligations are limited by the persons affected, the number of situations occurring, and the enormity of the action needed. Where problems are large and numerous, responsibilities tend to be widely distributed and ultimately carried out by the state. Hence we help the poor through taxes and collective efforts, rather than facing heroic responsibilities by ourselves. Fourth, obligations need to be carefully watched to avoid going too far in a coercive direction. Democratic societies develop "notching mechanisms" to scrutinize problem situations to allow rights to be delimited and modified where conflicts exist between them. These notching mechanisms also require that the least intrusive methods be implemented, that sanctions be monitored by public bodies, and that damage created by the constraints on rights should be treated or minimized. Fifth, with these limitations and safeguards, positive and negative sanctions need to be enforced to make rights meaningful. Areas in which this can be done include positive rights, reintegrative shaming, restorative justice, increased social observability, and community social pressure. And sixth, these citizenship processes within a system of rights lead to a position of "responsible patriotism" that rejects "obedience to the state" to embrace "allegiance to a state with constitutional procedures of citizen participation, political dissent, and multiculturalism."

4

Citizen-Selves in Restricted and Generalized Exchange

What citizens do politically is not just a matter of their social and economic circumstance, it is also a matter of the particular outlooks they have about politics and the specific values they may seek to express.
Geraint Parry, George Moyer, and Neil Day (1992, p. 172)

A continuing source of resistance to the use of exchange models in sociological theory is that they seem to reduce all forms of social relationship to market models of contract, when clearly the specific and calculated character of market exchanges marks them out as rather distinctive.

At the same time exchange in a more general sense is a very useful tool in social analysis: in any relationship (from love to hate) something is given and something is taken. We can make progress by defining the field of exchange generally and by then locating different types of exchanges more precisely within that field.
Colin Crouch (1990, p. 69)

Having discussed rights and obligations, it is clear that they are related to each other in some way. Often these and other social relationships are seen in terms of pure self-interest and individualism (e.g., rational choice and social exchange theories). At other times, rights and especially obligations may be cast in terms of altruism and caring (e.g., normative, communitarian, and many feminist theories). The use of multifaceted exchange models combined with Weber's theory of social action can help us move away from viewing these relationships as being one or the other (i.e., constant and dichotomous) and conceptualize rights and obligations in terms of a more complex relationship (i.e., variable and continuous). In his work and the quote above, Colin Crouch makes just such a recommendation by going beyond the market principles to more generalized forms of exchange, and consequently this chapter will introduce restricted and generalized exchange as different alternatives that can motivate the same person. This will allow the analysis of relationships where "individualism and altruism appear to be combined in complex ways" (Wuthnow 1991a, p. 21). Thus, rights and obligations become embedded in two theories of exchange – restricted and generalized exchange – and these systems are maintained by trust and the enforcement of sanctions. From different combinations of these two diverse processes of interaction, totally different views about the social may develop.

Although rights clearly relate to obligations, few social scientists have attempted to define that relationship in any way.[1] Lyons indicates that "it is commonly held that rights 'correlate' with duties" (1970, p. 45) and goes on to say that rights may or may not correlate with duties or obligations (pp. 54–5). Marshall showed that there has been a "changing balance between rights and duties" (1964, p. 129). In one of the few attempts to balance citizenship rights and duties, Andersen (1987) sees the ties between rights and duties eroding because Scandinavian citizens want it all – "The Christmas Eve Theorem."[2] However, aside from calling for a restoration of "a clear psychological connection between rights and duties" to prevent a welfare state breakdown, Anderson has no overall theory of this important relationship. I will approach this implied balance of rights and obligations through exchange.

TWO IDEAL TYPES OF CITIZENSHIP EXCHANGE

Debates between rational choice and more norm-oriented perspectives on behavior have suffered from a dichotomous idea of behavior and attitudes. If behaviors or attitudes contain one iota of self-interested behavior, then they are motivated by self-interest and *not* by altruism. However, if every behavior and attitude is motivated by self-interest, self-interest itself becomes an uninteresting topic. It becomes useless to pursue because there is no variation to be explained – every behavior and attitude is simply self-interested. Many social scientists believe this is not so. This chapter will try to differentiate between self-interested and other-interested behavior by dropping the self-interest and altruistic dichotomy in favor of restricted and generalized types of exchange (Ekeh 1974; Damon 1980; Leach 1983; Lévi-Strauss 1969).

Self-interested behavior takes place in the short term, focuses on material well-being, targets the individual's own person, and consists of mutual reciprocity.[3] Self-interested behavior occurs within the realm of restricted exchange. In short, self-interested behavior involves a mutual exchange of material goods or services between two persons within a short period of time (i.e., A gives to B and B gives to A).

On the contrary, *other-interested behavior* takes place in the medium to long term, focuses on material or spiritual well-being, targets group or societal interests, and consists of generalized exchange involving univocal or one-way reciprocity. Other-interested behavior is the exchange of material or spiritual goods and services from one person to others without direct reciprocity. These exchanges form a chain so that eventually some specific or general benefit may accrue to the initiating parties. Since these exchanges take a long time to complete and no benefit is forthcoming, they tend to be closer to other-interested than to self-interested behavior. If what one presumes to be self-interested behavior takes the interests of all of society into account over decades or longer, how does it differ from "community, societal, or world interest"? It doesn't. If acting to preserve the rain forests is "enlightened self-interest" that benefits many others, then it is "other-interested behavior." Also, other-interested behavior often includes exchanges that involve large elements of spiritual contentment, self-esteem, social adjustment, social prestige, or feelings of moral righteousness.[4] Finally, other-interested behavior is more oriented toward groups, generations, and society, while self-interested behavior is inherently oriented toward the individual or one's own group. This division of behavior into self- and other interests helps to avoid the "pure altruistic" trap often laid by "interest determinists," whether they be rational choice theorists, Freudians, or Marxists (Sears and Funk 1991; Putnam 1993, pp. 88–9).[5]

Self- and other-directed behaviors can be effectively examined by focusing on the balance of rights and obligations in two different types of exchange. The two main ideal types of citizenship interaction over rights and obligations in any society bear similarities to communal and market types of action. Each has its own type of exchange.

Restricted Exchange

Restricted exchange exists most often in markets. This is exchange by which a person gives something to another and immediately receives something in return. You may give one dollar to a baker and immediately expect a loaf of pumpernickel bread in return. This type of exchange applies to buying and selling, various types of barter, and even exchange between co-workers (i.e., a trade of clients, cases, or working hours) (see the top half of Table 4.1). The proscribed time limits – most often the immediacy of a few seconds, days, or monthly payments with credit – are important and closely watched. The longer the period for return payment, the more likely that the late reciprocators must pay monetary interest or suffer a diminution in social power. This exchange involves "mutual reciprocity" where A and B both give and receive, rather than "univocal reciprocity" where A may give to B but receive from a third party, and B may receive from A but give to another party (Ekeh 1974, pp. 46–52).[6]

Table 4.1. *Types of restricted and generalized exchange*

	Individual to individual	Individual to group	Group to group
Restricted Exchange:	(1) *Singular:*	(3) *Group*:	(5) *Over-lapping*:
	A $\leftrightarrows$ B	A $\leftrightarrows$ CDEFG	ABCDEF $\leftrightarrows$ CDEFGH
	(2) *Multiple:*	(4) *Societal:*	(6) *Mutually exclusive:*
	A $\leftrightarrows$ B $_{time\,1}$ A $\leftrightarrows$ B $_{time\,2}$ A $\leftrightarrows$ B $_{time\,3}$	A $\leftrightarrows$ BCDEFGHIJK	ABCDEF $\leftrightarrows$ GHIJKL
Generalized Exchange:	(7) *Chain:*	(8) *Closed:*	(10) *Over-lapping:*
	A → B → C → D → E → A	A → BCDE, B → ACDE, C → ABDE, D → ABCE, E → ABCD	ABCD → BCDE → ... WXYZ → XYZA
		(9) *Open:*	(11) *Mutually exclusive:*
		A → BCDE, B → CDEF, C → DEFG, D → EFGH, ... Z → ABCD	ABCD → EFGH → IJKL → ... WXYZ → ABCD

Citizen-Selves in Restricted and Generalized Exchange

By looking at items 1 through 6 in Table 4.1, we can see the variation in types of restricted exchange. First, *singular exchanges* occur only once. For instance, singular exchange between transporters and illegal aliens may occur only once and is not made based on state-enforced rights to property, but rather how much both parties might benefit from the exchange. The illegal alien does not have recourse to future exchanges or the legal system to back up the claim; nevertheless, the market bargains continue to be made. Similarly, a "fence" who sells stolen property does not operate from rights, but rather on a negotiated and bargained relationship that results in varying degrees of mutual satisfaction (Steffensmeier 1986). Power and possession in a market transaction are strong descriptions of the social process being undertaken.

In singular exchange, isolated and unique dyadic exchanges exist (Ekeh 1974, p. 51).[7] For instance, one-time market relations could resemble drug transactions with little trust where parties to the conflict take extreme precautions. For example, two parties, relieved of weapons, exchange goods by being at opposite sides of a fifty meter circle. Each places its goods down at one point and slowly moves around the circle to pick up their goods at the other point. If anyone defects, he or she cannot take both the drugs and the money. However, even here there is a small amount of trust that each will follow the minimal rules and others will simply not attack the bargaining site to steal the goods. As the examples of the illegal alien and the fence show, rights are not necessarily involved in these examples.

Second, *multiple exchange* requires repeated exchange and trust by both parties that the other person will supply a quality product because at the time of a trade one cannot fully know its quality. For instance, a car or computer may break down after a few weeks, which is usually not known by the buyer at the time of the exchange. Exchanges where there is no intention of further exchange (anonymous spot markets) are then the most risky, because one party may get away with selling bad goods. In these kinds of multiple exchanges, business lunches and gifts are used by salespersons to build trusting and committed relationships onto a market relationship. Gifts and even community volunteering establish their reputations and, even more importantly, create strong bonds that reach beyond transitory market relationships (Smith-Lovin 1993, p. 285). Salespersons work very hard at this. Thus, business professionals try to get away from restricted exchange and atomistic market relationships as much as possible, but consumers may find it difficult to do so.

Community observation of exchange reinforces pre-, present-, and even post-contractual solidarity. Community observation comes horizontally (other persons making similar and visible exchanges) and chronologically (the same persons making repeated and remembered exchanges). One result might be a service culture with considerable trust being established with people of quality reputations. Community observation may even be institutionalized with new organizations intended to monitor goods and promote trust, such as the Chamber of Commerce, the Better Business Bureau, and Consumers Union.

Some philosophers try to apply this simple restricted exchange format to the language of rights and obligations. For the purposes of citizenship rights, this approach covering all rights and duties is misleading (e.g., Lyons 1970; Sumner 1987, pp. 129–62; White 1984, pp. 56–73). Although exchanges of property and services can be justified and perhaps enforced under rights to property or even under various liberties, the nature of other rights and duty relationships are not well captured by use of restricted exchange concepts. To characterize market relationships in rights terms is an abuse of terminology. Buying bread or batteries, illegally transporting aliens, or fencing stolen property bear little on the language of rights and responsibilities. In legal market transactions, one has the right to bargain, but the results and outcomes of all bargained relationships are not rights. Thus, restricted exchange, especially as it relates to bargaining relationships, supplies a poor casement for rights and obligations.

In the second category of individual to group exchange, things get more complicated. In *individual to group exchange*, one person exchanges goods and services with the sum total of individuals in a group or society (i.e., items 3 and 4 in Table 4.1). Group-restricted exchange takes place with slightly longer-term relationships than individual exchange.[8] For example, a person (i.e., A) pays dues to a neighborhood association or taxes that go into the state's general fund that benefits many people (i.e., BCDEFGHIJK). The neighborhood association or state representing those people gives back services of equal value to that person. This exchange can still be relatively short-term (i.e., in the same or next year).

Problems with individual to group exchange develop when more long-term or indirect returns are involved. On the one hand, two persons – say, Ms. Young and Mr. Old – pay state income tax in Kentucky, and the state constructs and maintains highways that both persons use every day. When improvements are made in the roads, Ms. Young and Mr. Old notice the improvements, and the exchange is reciprocated in their minds. On the other hand, Ms. Young and Mr. Old also pay property taxes to the county for the school system. While Ms. Young's children are in the county, Mr. Old's children are grown, were educated in California, and now live in Michigan paying taxes for Mr. Old's grandchildren in a district thousands of miles away. Mr. Old asks why he should pay for schools in Kentucky that are of no direct benefit to him or his family. Leaders more interested in generalized exchange argue that schools benefit society as a whole, and that Mr. Old benefits through greater productivity and less social pathology, but this argument does not work under restricted exchange. The social psychology of the immediate bargain in restricted exchange often causes Mr. Old to severely discount generalized exchange arguments operating over the long term. What is important are the more "immediate" benefits received for the taxes. This expectation of relatively immediate exchange between the two parties is a core idea in restricted exchange. If pushed to the extreme in citizen to state relations, this idea leads to "the supermarket state," where the state sells all the goods necessary to customers who want them. However, this "supermarket state" can no longer be the collective actor that does what individuals and groups need and cannot do themselves – that is, provide public goods for those in need (Bulkeley 1991).[9]

Third, *group to group exchange* operates on similar principles (see items 5 and 6 in Table 4.1). Groups expect equal and immediate payback in all restricted exchanges. Thus, in our example of the roads and schools, we could be talking about a trade association of traveling salespersons favoring expenditures on roads versus an environmental group of hikers who want park expansion, or a group of parents who want better schools versus retirees with no offspring who want lower taxes to suit their reduced incomes. The same principles of restricted exchange can easily apply to interactions between mutually exclusive interest groups. Groups with overlapping memberships will be more inclined to compromise and understand the others' positions; however, this will weaken internal solidarity as members who expect restricted exchange will be disappointed and may quit the group.

Restricted exchange, however, does not lay the base for interaction through strong interpersonal contact between parties. Restricted exchange tends to rely on a larger and impersonal exchange system rather than create intensive interaction. Trust is a factor to some degree only in multiple exchanges, and following Durkheim, many sociologists recognize that an underlying "pre-contractual solidarity" is necessary for any market relation to work (Durkheim 1933, pp. 215–19). However, restricted exchange, whether singular or multiple, builds fewer bonds between parties than the more general type of exchange because it is predicated on minimal trust. The one-time drug deal is perhaps the extreme, but even in most business dealings each party "restricts" his or her interests to the things being exchanged and avoids most other aspects of each bargainer's welfare. Business contacts, for instance, despite a history of long-term gift exchange – trading gifts with company emblems, exchanging beers after work, or giving presents at the weddings of each others' grown children – often disappear when a salesperson encounters serious illness or is fired. If groups are overlapping (i.e., salespersons belong to the Lutheran church and the American Legion Post), ties will last longer. Nonetheless, instrumental ties remain instrumental. A democratic government with rights and obligations with a civil society based on trust requires more. The instrumental nature of restricted exchange may be fine for market transactions in the economy, which have an intended self-limiting quality, but it does not well serve political rights and obligations in a political community.

Generalized Exchange

Generalized exchange relies on "univocal reciprocity," where goods or services flow in one direction – A gives to B, but B does not give back to A. There are three different types of generalized exchange. First, individual to individual *chain* exchange according to Peter Ekeh (1974, p. 50) consists of the following (see item 7 in Table 4.1):

In generalized exchange no party gives to the party from whom he (she) receives. Thus, given five persons, generalized exchange operates as a unitary system as follows:

A→B→C→D→E→A, where "→" signifies "gives to."

A simple example comes from families where parents overwhelmingly help their younger generation of children, and those children when they grow up do the same to another generation. Teaching and mentoring could be viewed in the same way.[10]

Second, individual to group exchange constitutes another set of generalized exchange principles. *Closed generalized exchange* involves exchanges within a fixed group of people. For example, person A hosts a dinner party for friends BCDE, with each person in that group reciprocating in kind at a later date (see item 8 in Table 4.1). In the opposite direction, the group gives a birthday party for one individual among a stable group of friends. The dinners and birthday parties among families or closely knit groups of friends are examples that require trust to last at least a year for the exchange circle to be completed. The main point is that the group has clear and definite closure.

Open generalized exchanges involve a changing group, and this makes generalized exchange more complicated and difficult. Open exchange relationships have less social closure and require more time, people, and trust. In an open system, the original group in the exchange (i.e., ABCDE) has disappeared by the sixth exchange, unlike the previous examples where all people remain part of every exchange (see item 9 in

Table 4.1). One simple example would be birthday and dinner parties among people in neighborhoods where there is a great deal of geographical mobility (e.g., highly mobile academic, military, diplomatic, and corporate families). Often these groups require active organizers and socializers to reinforce trust, and these organizers are often provided by the organization or institution (military commanders or corporate executives create social committees). Some of these kinds of generalized exchanges could take a lifetime to complete, and they may even run for two or three generations. On the whole, they may involve rewarding people known to be givers even though these people may not have given much to participants in the present group. Whether they last long periods of time depends upon social stability and effective institutions with reinforcing norms.

Third, generalized exchange may involve overlapping or mutually exclusive groups. In *overlapping generalized group exchange*, a group exchanges unilaterally with another group that has substantially similar membership to the first group (see item 10 in Table 4.1). Although no direct return is received, this exchange is easy to accept because in each exchange the first group helps its members who also belong to the second group. Liberal theory based on overlapping memberships and cross-pressures basically works according to this principle (Pestoff 1977, pp. 4–5; Lipset 1981, p. 77). And *mutually exclusive generalized exchange* involves univocal exchanges between groups with no membership overlap (see item 11 in Table 4.1). The incentives for this exchange are concerned with societal functioning rather than group rewards. Through interests in society as a whole, each group knows that the survival of society depends on cooperative relations between groups, just as the mobile families often need to protect their kind but not necessarily their own kin in exchange. These relationships tend to exist between internally competing and mutually exclusive groups such as labor and management or Protestant and Catholic groups in corporatist and consociational bargaining systems.

Closed generalized exchange may be the intermediate point between individual to group restricted exchange and open generalized exchange. Under restricted exchange, taxpayer C expects in-kind repayment, but under closed generalized exchange, if he or she learns to wait their turn as neighbor A gets something this year and neighbor B the next year, then they will get something in the third year. Under open generalized exchange, each person's receipt of goods becomes more insecure and uncertain. The taxpayer looks to more general repayments for the overall welfare of the group. A larger group with some generalized exchange is needed to catalyze this relationship since it will not generally build itself up from individual interests. Whether groups in exchange are overlapping or mutually exclusive has tremendous implications for civil society, and this makes generalized group exchange more complex than restricted group exchange. In the next chapter, liberal polities are characterized as being composed of overlapping groups (i.e., many people belonging to different groups), and corporatist systems composed of closed or mutually exclusive groups (i.e., workers stay in working-class groups, and university graduates stay in their own groups).

In generalized exchange, however, problems with defection and/or "free ridership" create a need for more widespread forms of social action (Yamagishi and Cook 1993, p. 245). Social control measures are necessary for sanctioning. First, social norms can be internalized through primary and secondary socialization (Axelrod 1986). For instance, states, religions, and families socialize their members to share and help their fellows in need, and some internalize these values. The Boy Scouts perform service projects as an expected part of their advancement processes. Second, social pressure can be applied through informal norms, much like those constructed by the informal work groups in the relay switch assembly rooms at the Hawthorne Western Electric plant (Homans 1950). Third, subgroups may exert power over other subgroups within a setting, resulting in the first group's dominance as with whites and blacks in the southern United States in the first half of this century. Fourth, norms incorporating generalized exchange can be modeled after significant others who show the positive and proven results of their actions. This status signaling takes place through reputation whereby people may also model high-status behavior. Fifth, people belong to groups such as voluntary associations and religions that practice generalized exchange and exert pressure on members to do the same. Families and groups may engage in the planned promotion of generalized exchange in the future, although present behaviors may mask such plans. Finally, formal laws enacted by the state may encourage generalized exchange by providing incentives or penalties (Axelrod 1986, pp. 1102–8).[11]

As indicated at the beginning of this chapter, the use of exchange terminology does not imply an economic exchange or even a sociological exchange theory approach. As Bernd Marin states, this concept of "generalized political exchange" is intended to "criticize and even break with traditional exchange theories" and "to link policy studies and theorizing on governance and interest intermediation to network thinking and network analysis" (1990, p. 13). Further, these approaches to exchange do not require conscious calculation. Initially, people may formulate strategies and plans that subsequently become so repetitive that they are hardly thought about. These modes of interaction become traditions and even norms. Parents, teachers, and pastors socialize children and students into these modes of interaction by explaining that "sharing, caring, and helping without direct payment" is the way we do good. Consequently, these one-time conscious methods of interaction then become accepted and more opaque to rational explanation.

In the opposite direction, the cause of exchanges may be accidental or non-rational, but subsequent explanations invent a rationality (see Durkheim's distinction between historical and functional causes). Thus, the concepts of restricted and generalized exchange provide a theoretical and empirical tool to analyze group to group phenomena in a rigorous rather than either an impressionistic or polarized fashion.

SOCIAL ACTION AND FORMS OF EXCHANGE

An understanding of Max Weber's forms of action can be most helpful with traditional and emotional action as well as differentiating different types of rationality (see Table 4.2). Item 1 in Table 4.2 indicates that traditional action is composed of conventions, local norms, and informal sanctions that may be negotiated locally or embedded in organizational cultures. These items refer to norms, rituals, and institutional assumptions that tend to continue to exist because they were once useful and may continue to be useful in different ways. They may be efficient, or if not, they continue to exist because we do not have the time and energy to rationally contest our everyday culture and methods of living, or because they now benefit various groups in society. Sometimes they can be rather cumbersome; other times they are highly efficient. Item 2 refers to emotional or affectual action. These are emotional interactions with others that are preset culturally or socialized within particular families, classes, or status groups. They can be destructive or constructive in terms of love, caring, or violence. Emotional action can be viscerally reactive, motivationally cultivated, or strategically manipulated. Both traditional and emotional action tend to be ignored by rational strategists, but they are important especially in propelling action by means of motivation and mood.

Social movements thrive on emotional energy (Collins 1993; Barbalet 1993, pp. 49–55). It is not individually rational to absorb clubbings, threats, insults, and bullets at the beginnings of a social movement. It is rational to overtake and jump on a bandwagon. Emotional energy derived from observed suffering and injustice, and the counterfactual imagining of a new order, push people and groups to take actions that appear to be fundamentally against their health and material well-being. These emotional resources are especially necessary for persons involved in demonstrations, protests, and riots. The result of these shared deprivations in the line of fire will be a greater group solidarity and emphasis on generalized exchange.[12]

Table 4.2. *Social action through behavior and sanctions:*
Tradition, practical rationality, and formal rationality action

Forms of action	Behavior	Sanctions
1. *Traditional action:* Applied within communities, families, or relationships	*Conventions, local norms, and habits:*	*Informal sanctions:*
Cultural and institutional assumptions	Caring for yourself and others in daily life (e.g., eating, cooking, cleaning, grooming and driving).	Interpersonal hints and messages about proper behavior (e.g., subtle suggestions and general popularity).
2. *Emotional or affectual action:* Applied in personal and wider social venues *Cultural and institutional assumptions*	Emotional interactions with others from love (e.g., child care, dating, sex, and marriage) to hate (e.g., swearing, arguing, and fighting).	Stronger interpersonal feedback on personal behavior (e.g., social pressure from family, peer groups, and others).
3. *Everyday rationality:* Applied within groups.	*Broader norms and social pressure:*	*Social sanctions and pressures:*
Substantive rationality: "Value Systems Deductions"	General rules about fitting into groups (e.g., rules about conversations at work or in the neighborhood about noise, politics, religion, and entertainment, etc.).	Social pressures from work and neighborhood groups (e.g., supervisor sanctioning work behavior, co-workers or neighbors making complaints to others).
Practical rationality: "Rule of Thumb Calculations"	Rules about getting specific things done (e.g., rules about job payment, operating machines, buying and selling goods, keeping children healthy).	Sanctions and social pressure about calculative procedures (e.g., workers and managers evaluating work, significant others evaluating parents).
4. *Strict rationality:* Applied to society as a whole	*Secular law, religious law, and professional codes:*	*Coercive sanctions: exile, incarceration, and fines:*
Theoretical rationality: "Theoretical systems"	Idealistic and social mores, laws, and taboos congealed into a regulated way of life (e.g., religious codes for congregational behavior, world views of philosophers).	Formal ideologies or religious theology may exile, shun, fine, request penance, or otherwise formally punish deviant behavior.
Formal rationality: "Formal calculation or procedures"	Formal laws and procedures (e.g., the formal legal system backed by the state, professional procedures in law, business or medicine; and financial calculations for long-term rationality).	Formal punishments for specific violations certified by courts, professional or scientific boards (e.g., execution, incarceration, fines, censure, loss of license to practice).

NOTE: This table builds on Max Weber's theory of social action (Weber 1978; Kalberg 1980).

Citizen-Selves in Restricted and Generalized Exchange

Rationality is the most misunderstood aspect of social action because its processes depend on the multiple ways a goal can be set (see items 3 and 4 in Table 4.2). Rational choice theorists prefer to see practical rationality as the logical processes of getting things done in everyday life, and formal rationality as the more institutionalized formal calculations and procedures embodied into bureaucratic law, idealized science, and procedural politics. The difference between these two forms of procedural rationality is mainly the level at which it takes place: an individual in everyday situations or groups in institutionalized settings. Much of rational choice theory is based on this inductive procedure at an everyday or societal level (see cells 1 and 3 in Table 4.3).

However, value-based rationality using deductive reasoning is often ignored as a basis for human action, which is a problem because values are important in determining goals (see cells 2 and 4 in Table 4.3). At the same level as practical rationality, substantive rationality is based on value system deductions from congregations, neighborhoods, local politics, or a myriad of traditions about what should be done in everyday situations. At the higher level of abstraction, theoretical rationality is deduced from an action or idea's fit within a systematic group of ideas or theories such as Catholic dogma, Roman law, or Tory political theory. These are larger forms of rationality often connected to the workings of a group as a whole in an institutional context and deductively arrived at from value systems. Table 4.2 relates these forms of social action to behavior and sanctions and gives some examples of traditional, emotional, and rational behaviors and sanctions.

In large measure, restricted exchange applies to procedurally based rationality with practical rationality based on rules of thumb and formal rationality based on calculation and procedures. Generalized exchange matches with the value-based forms of substantive rationality and the more ideological or theory-based theoretical rationality. Traditional, emotional, and rational forms of social action are not mutually exclusive, and consequently any action is a combination of emotion, tradition, and rational action.

TRUST AND EXCHANGE

Trust is an important aspect of any exchange, but more so for generalized exchange. Trust can be defined from a number of directions, but two aspects of trust – predictability and social concern – are important (Barber 1983; Gambetta 1988a; Lorenz 1992).[13] Predictability involves having an expectation that stability or manageable change exists in society and our interpersonal relationships. In Bernard Barber's terms, this

Table 4.3. *The basis and level of four types of rationality*

		Basis:	
		Procedural or inductive	*Value-based or deductive*
Level:	*Everyday*	(1) Practical rationality	(2) Substantive rationality
	Institutional	(3) Formal rationality	(4) Theoretical rationality

means that citizens expect that the "natural order – both physical and biological – and the moral social order will persist and be more or less realized" (1983, p. 9). This is a very broad definition, but it does focus on social stability, and for all intents and purposes it encompasses Barber's second definition that sees trust as involving peoples' expectations that others will perform their role expectations in a technically competent manner: mothers will adequately feed their babies, managers and owners will make products and profits, and doctors will treat their patients (1983, p. 15). These expectations of stability and competence can be broken down into many distinctions (e.g., institutional or interpersonal, family or professional, and weak or powerful), but they do not necessarily imply any empathy or feelings for the people involved.

The second form of trust involves positive concern, which is similar to Barber's conception of trust as fiduciary obligation and responsibility. It refers to our expectations that the person in whom we trust will have our best interests at heart. This positive concern may involve as much as the love of a parent or spouse, or as little as the fiduciary responsibility of a stranger acting as a guardian or trustee. In either case, the issue is not a predictable outcome, but rather the person's motive. The trusted person takes action because they actually care or must legally be concerned about you.

These two forms of trust are entirely different in analytical form. As a result they may overlap, occur alone, or not occur (see Table 4.4). In cell 1, another may be trusted for both predictability and positive concern. Many children strongly trust their mothers to competently prepare

88

Table 4.4. *Trust as predictability and
positive concern*

		Personal Concern:	
		Positive	*Negative*
	Yes	(1) Strong trust (Close friend, relative, or parent)	(3) Wary trust (Predictable acquaintance or enemy)
Predict-ability:	*No*	(2) Faithful trust (Children, or God who acts in mysterious ways)	(4) No trust (Unpredictable acquaintance or enemy, or uncontrol- lable natural force)

(e.g., destroying bacteria by cooking) and lovingly present (e.g., giving favorite foods) a meal for them. On the other hand, a sister may trust in the positive concern of her little brother, but hardly believe that her little brother's actions are competent or predictable (see cell 2). In the diagonally opposite cell, an enemy may be totally predictable but have malevolent intentions toward us. Nevertheless, this predictability forms at least some sort of trust through stability. And in the last cell, we may have an enemy who, lacking all positive concern for us, is entirely unpredictable.

Each type of exchange is based on and reinforces some sort of trust or solidarity, but restricted and singular exchange provides less trust, and group-focused generalized exchange produces more trust. This is because restricted exchange only involves predictability, whereas generalized exchange adds a considerable amount of positive concern to predictability. In fact, positive concern is a major motive in producing generalized exchange. Positive concern can be so strong that a parent may expect no return at all from a child.

Time and community are important for developing trust. Although restricted exchanges are inherently short-term, generalized group exchanges or even individual exchanges are usually long-term exchanges that may take years to cycle. Restricted exchange can operate with great mobility and little community but requires state institutions to enforce the exchange paradigm with property rights (i.e., that one may exchange what he or she owns) and a legal system that backs enforceable contracts. Generalized exchange operates better with strong community and worse with extensive social mobility (Walzer 1990). When someone within the circle of exchange leaves (social or geographical mobility) before paybacks are completed, group members feel cheated and abandoned. Investments made in friendship and "particular capital" (Collins 1987, 1988) are lost as is a part of each person's self.[14]

Restricted exchange produces little trust for many reasons. Individual cost-benefit calculations to gain as much as possible drive the market bargainer. While procedural fairness may be present, the parties engaged in bargaining are not concerned with any particular outcome of fairness (not to mention positive concern) concerning the other and certainly not with the larger commonweal. After the transaction, the market bargainer is under little obligation. If the bargainer can gain more, he or she will not incur any particular obligations beyond the bargained exchange. These kinds of outcomes typically occur in market transactions, and they are often lauded as a benefit of a market system.

If, however, citizens approach rights and obligations intending to maximize personal benefits, then citizenship becomes commercialized, and citizenship can no longer protect against the market. This makes citizenship writhe in self-contradiction. The purpose of citizenship rights and obligations in the first place was *not* to be the first and most basic provider of market goods (Warren 1992, pp. 17–21; Marshall 1964). Instead, citizenship was intended to improve long-term development through direct and indirect institutionalization and redistribution. Citizenship is neither intended to function like a market, nor can it replace the market. Citizenship is intended to correct the market. If people become what Mouritzen calls "demanding citizens," they pursue their self-interest without regard to obligation or repaying society for rights, and in turn without providing for generalized exchange that lays the basis for the development of trust and societal development (Mouritzen 1987; Leca 1990, p. 187). Demanding citizens, who are the source of many criticisms of rights, destroy the realm of political rights and obligations, which are supposed to be above bargaining (Dahrendorf 1974, 1986, 1987; Glendon 1991; Mead 1986). Rights are pushed back into the market relationship.

Rights-based theories rely on a basic principle of equality, which must maintain rights and obligations to counterbalance market outcomes. The capitalist or market-based state allows firms and individuals to amass fortunes or go bankrupt. But a bankrupt citizen stripped of civil rights and obligations as a natural outcome of market processes (i.e., not because of a heinous crime) is a contradiction in terms of citizenship. At the point of bankruptcy in rights, the conflict between citizenship and capitalism may even disappear because the market has overwhelmed citizenship. The realm of rights and obligations, which is to apply equally to all citizens, then becomes mired in the realm of unequal bargaining power, which finds many of its roots back in the arena of capitalist market relationships.

Social interaction exists on many interaction levels, especially in exchanging emotions, feelings, and conceptions of the world. Much of interaction is involved in establishing oneself as a secure individual largely based on warmth and attention received from and given to other persons. Rational exchange itself cannot go on without values, and individuals need to construct their own sense of values even before exchange goes very far. When restricted exchange permeates social interaction, trust evaporates into bargaining power. In generalized exchange, people are more likely to construct a reflective "self," while in restricted exchange, people are less likely to do so. When A engages in a restricted exchange where B expects a generalized exchange, there is a sense of an emptiness on B's part. The result is that exchanges become narrower and less room is made for the self and community discourse. Thus, restricted exchange without trust impoverishes the subjective construction of realities and values from generalized exchange relationships. The same principles apply to interest groups and societies that develop collective identities about their own values and purposes. This is not an attack on restricted exchange, which has its place in the impersonal market, but it shows the weakness of pushing restricted exchange into citizenship rights and obligations in the public sphere.

Generalized exchange preserves this realm of political and economic equality. It requires patience, an ability to look for the larger group or societal results, and the general building of social trust. Rights are no longer tightly connected to obligations, and people give away time and concern for others, invest in socially aware projects and voluntary activities, and even pay taxes for widespread social results rather than their own immediate returns. This does not mean that citizens should not expect efficient results, but it does mean that they do not demand an immediate and totally "personal" good or service for themselves. Being overly concerned with "What's in it for me" is not part of citizenship. Paying for employment programs provides the right to work for large numbers of potentially unemployed persons, and in the generalized cycle of exchanges this results in reduced poverty, pathology, and crime. Employers paying for employment training in Germany may not provide their firm's employees for the next year, but employers provide for highly skilled employees for the whole nation. All employers benefit. Movement from restricted to closed generalized and/or open generalized exchange is a difficult process based on trust. It often needs social intervention by the state, voluntary associations, or private governance mechanisms for catalytic support.

THE DEVELOPMENT OF THE CITIZEN-SELF

The process of gaining citizenship rights and assuming citizenship obligations and then losing them is a gradual one that is curvilinear over the life course. First, gaining rights and obligations generally takes place within a family and becomes more conscious during adolescence (Demo 1992, pp. 310–16; Jones and Wallace 1992, pp. 18–23, 146–51; Morgan 1984). During adolescence teenagers learn many citizenship processes through civic education in the schools and participation in the neighborhood and community. Children and adolescents to some degree are provided with rights they have not earned and in a sense are born with an obligational deficit. For adolescents or children to take a heavily "restricted exchange" view toward rights and obligations requires that they ignore or denigrate the embeddedness of their position in family and society.

Consequently, citizens emerge out of this dependent position to engage in various types of exchange being already indebted with emotional and sometimes rational obligations toward family and community. The rational being, making calculations independent of all persons and institutions, is perhaps the furthest from the actual development of citizenship that one might imagine. And to a large degree, adolescents and young adults are doing their utmost to construct a viable self at this time that will take rights and obligations into account. This self ultimately intervenes between rational calculations and actions. They realize that they must develop some independence from parents and the state (as experienced in the school) before they can fulfill obligations. Adolescents seek independence but usually realize that many of their obligations can only be fulfilled in a long-term process of generalized exchange. In the family, it becomes an obvious form of generalized exchange – my parents gave to me, and I will give to my children. This exchange rarely reaches closure (i.e., giving parents can never be totally recompensed by the children). Thus, much of one's self-construction arises around various sorts of generalized exchange bounded by family, networks, and community.

Second, independence and hence citizenship diminishes during old age (Demo 1992, pp. 317–38). Participation in work tends to cease with retirement, while political and other forms of participation, especially voluntarism, frequently increase for a number of years (Chambré 1987). Nonetheless, with failing health and deteriorating mental condition, many older citizens often give up their freedom to guardianship while being under care of relatives or nursing homes. When older citizens are hospitalized and unconscious, many major decisions are made by doctors and immediate family with informed consent (Barber 1983, pp. 141–9). Family and medical personnel may even decide to avoid extraordinary measures to save the older citizen's life. Thus, the extent of citizenship rights and obligations is directly connected to independence, and when a person is at the beginning and end of life, his or her condition of dependence lessens their ability to take advantage of rights and to fulfill obligations.

Citizens form a self-concept in relation to the state with its rights and obligations, which they express to others (Portis 1985, pp. 461–72; Roche 1987, pp. 375–81). Modern theories describe the self as not only dynamic but also multifaceted. Markus and Wurf even refer to the self as a confederation of actual-, ideal-, ought-, and even counter-selves (1987, pp. 301–3; Demo 1992). This helps explain why attitudes are not consistent and may not predict behavior. People interpret and reinterpret their reasons for engaging in citizenship behavior. Markus and Wurf indicate that "individuals often rewrite their personal histories to support a current self-view" (1987, p. 316). On the other hand, the self is not solely a reflection of what significant others see in one. After the self develops in childhood and adolescence, it becomes a complex coherent structure in its own account and is not a simple reflective mechanism.

The important role of the "self" is perhaps why pure exchange theory is not useful, although this approach has provided many insights into bargaining and power relationships (Bacharach and Lawler 1981; Cook 1987). Social exchange theory and rational choice theory have a limited view of the "self."[15] In a sense, the self does not exist as a research problem, probably because both theories tend strongly toward behavioral outcomes, and subjective states such as the self are denigrated. Nonetheless, exchange theories note a weakness in their approach because they have trouble locating what different people value. Fromkin and Snyder (1980, p. 75) say that "the study of social behavior as a single act of exchange has bred a benign neglect of a host of important variables and related processes," and they go on to list these as "uniqueness," "self-identity," "self-image," among others (pp. 59–75). References to the "self" in social exchange theory are rare, unless of course we include the subjectively barren concept of "self-interest."[16]

In exchange theory, the implicit encounter with the "self" comes in constructing a theory of value (Emerson 1987; Friedman 1987).[17] Emerson states that sociology has "a strong incentive to rethink the question of a cardinal concept of utility" and "what social exchange theory now needs is a theory of value based upon empirical psychology" (1987, pp. 12–13). Without an apparent conception of the self, exchange theory ends with a static and simplistic view of values. Ethics and religion are banished to pure metaphysics. After all, what is the self but a mechanism of self-reflection of others' values and a person's own values?

As an exception, James Coleman (1990) has produced a theory of purposive social action that assumes utility maximization by the "rational actor in economic theory" (p. 14) and has a conception of the self. But the self is not adequately treated in this theory either. Coleman's theory of the self uses labels that parallel symbolic interactionism; (that is, the "object self" is the "me," the "acting self" is the "I," and the "judge" is the "significant other" (p. 507).[18] One might wonder how a theory that firmly places itself in an objective interest category (i.e., rational choice) can find itself so compatible with a subjectivist theory (symbolic interactionism). In some parts of his explanation, he makes analogies between the "I and me" with the "agent and principal" (p. 504), which is hardly appropriate since the micro-agent can hardly take the money and run to another personality. Although Coleman discusses objective and subjective interests, he does not really resolve this basic contradiction.

Coleman shows how rational actors may adopt the interests of others by developing an expanded self through internalization of others' interests – mothers' internalizing their childrens' interests, fans identifying with favorite movie stars, fellow soldiers who have shared extreme deprivation helping each other, hostages dependent on captors moving toward identification, and lovers internalizing their loved one's interests. These identification processes can take place through empathy, complementarity, claims, authority, or cathexis (Coleman 1990, pp. 157–62, 519–20, 948–9).

Coleman's discussion of the self and internalization appears to be a promising start toward a synthesis of rational and interactionist theories; however, he abandons this path. When Coleman refers to the "looking glass self" (p. 525), he indicates that "this conception of an actor is . . . an extreme," and he tries to disqualify it by saying that rationality might enter in at an earlier point (1990, p. 526). In the end, Coleman recognizes the "self" as an effective controller of rationality, but then effectively bans it from his theory. Coleman does intimate that multiple selves exist, but he fails to follow up on what could be a coalition theory of multiple selves within the individual, and his odd example of Ford Motor Company as a corporate self does not help the argument.[19] Coleman could push coalition theory further into the self and come up with a rational choice theory of goal formation and decision making, which would be a profitable synthesis, but he chooses a simpler path back to rationality.[20] Consequently, even this exceptional development of exchange theory cannot maintain the self as an important concept.

The weakness of social exchange and rational choice theories is their failure to conceptualize meaning or value. Elster comments that rational choice theory "is first and foremost normative, . . . it tells us what we ought to do in order to achieve our aims as well as possible," but "it does not, in the standard version, tell us what our aims ought to be" (1989, p. 3). This is where the self comes into play because it is constructed and then functions to select values and set goals.

CITIZEN-SELVES WITH RESTRICTED AND GENERALIZED EXCHANGE

The construction of the citizen self is largely symbolic and often indirect. Many of the interaction ritual chains of rights and obligations involve few goods being directly exchanged with the state. Sales taxes may be overlooked in their daily toll, but yearly income taxes are not. Some people receive monthly checks from the government, but many others do not. Some people are conscious of the state when they drive on the interstate freeways and local roads, but most are not. Although a few people may seek out class action suits over prayers at graduation ceremonies, most do not. Even groups that face discrimination and are denied rights do not directly interact with the state (although the police would be one such direct interaction). Instead, they read about the state in the newspapers, watch the TV news, and then engage in discussions with other citizens (through equity or social comparison theory). Thus, the state is brought down to social interaction level with friends and acquaintances involved in interaction rituals.

A typology of six different types of citizen-selves motivated by value involvement and behavioral activity can be constructed from working-class images of society (Bulmer 1975; Lockwood 1975; Goldthorpe et al. 1969) combined with Almond and Verba's (1965) classification of citizens. This typology – incorporated, active, deferential, cynical, opportunistic, marginal, and fatalistic citizen-selves – incorporates conceptions of restricted and generalized exchange within a context of active or passive social motivation and allegiant or oppositional positions (see Table 4.5).[21] The incorporated citizen is generally part of the elite, or feels that he or she is. They identify with party and governmental interests, and actively participate and support party goals. Self-interest may be involved as far as they have a political job or appointed position, but

Table 4.5. *The citizen typology by action position and value involvement*

Action position – Behavior	*Value involvement* – Belief		
	Allegiance (Value rationality)	Apathy/Self-interest (Instrumental rationality)	Alienation (Value rationality)
Active (Citizen participant)	1 Incorporated citizen	2a Opportunistic citizen ↑ ↓	3 Active citizen
Passive (Citizen subject)	4 Deferential citizen	2b Opportunistic citizen 6a Marginal citizen ↑ ↓	5 Cynical citizen
Inactive (Neglected citizens and aliens)	7a Fatalistic loyalist	6b Marginal citizen	7b Fatalistic opposition

it is usually not dominant because most will never be compensated for the large amounts of time and money they volunteer for their beliefs. The incorporated citizen is part of the regime, not the grassroots opposition, and is in the middle spectrum of pragmatic politics. The incorporated citizen tends toward generalized exchange; however, in dealing with specific politicians, especially from the opposition, exchange will be highly restricted.

The active citizen participates in the activities of the polity, has concern for the people in the group, and exhibits a large degree of generalized exchange behavior. However, the active citizen is often engaged in conflict with established elites and most often approaches problems from the grassroots level. The active citizen often belongs to a political party, social movement, or some other active association to be active in proselytizing an ideology of change. The active citizen is not necessarily left or right, but tends to be in the opposition and the more radical of each political persuasion. This citizen can include social reformers of an established party, grassroots organizers of any political position, or radical revolutionaries with an activist orientation. The active citizen tends toward generalized exchange because this person believes that much can be done altruistically (i.e., for "the people" or "the country"). However, in dealing with specific politicians, especially from the opposition, exchange may also be highly restricted.

The deferential citizen accepts authority and the leadership of elites but does not strongly internalize the goals of the party or state. The deferential citizen follows tradition and socialization from family experience, but avoids most political activities. Deferential citizens tend to be neither conservative nor radical, although the leadership of elites may come from either direction. The deferential citizen tends toward generalized exchange because this person believes that much is being done for him or her by elites, and sometimes exchange will be tradition-oriented, that is, highly ritualized. The deferential citizen will not be oriented toward political participation and will tend to leave that to elites; however, he or she will vote and contact politicians for help when in trouble.

The cynical citizen is similar to the active citizen but does not carry out his or her means of political participation because it is impossible to really do anything about political situations. The cynical citizen may talk about the necessity of generalized exchange, but since implementing it is not possible, he or she generally ends up acting out of restricted exchange. As a result, this citizen ends up being passive and often bitter critics of politics and the state.

Opportunistic citizens are highly motivated to make rational decisions about material interests that affect their short-term and immediate interests.[22] The opportunistic citizen does not participate in political activities unless these activities directly affect his or her interests, involve substantial income or major services, *and* can actually achieve the desired outcomes. Otherwise the opportunistic citizen lapses into his or her own private world of interests. In general, politics and ideology are uninteresting to the opportunistic citizen. This citizen represents the self-interest concept with a free ridership approach and tends toward restricted exchange because this citizen believes that nothing is being done for free or altruistically. The opportunistic citizen is guided by restricted exchange with time horizons focusing on short-term paybacks. With the rise of individualism in the United States and Europe, this type of citizen-self has been identified as the "demanding citizen" responsible for the breakdown of community and other social institutions.[23]

The marginal citizen is extremely detached and alienated from the system. He or she has low resources and little power to act politically. Persons in poverty and under extreme emotional distress fit into this category. Most of the time these sorts of citizens will not have the time or resources to vote or volunteer opinions. They are often targets of policymakers since they may participate in deviance, riots, or crime. Outside forces or fate control much of the behavior of marginal citizens, which causes their behavior to appear irrational (extremely short-term) or survival-oriented. However, highly restricted exchange with others may often occur through "street sense." Immigrants as marginal citizens simply owe allegiance to another community or country, and they pursue extremely restricted exchange in one setting but may react in a generalized way to family and friends in another society.

Fatalistic citizens were not included in the Almond-Verba schema; however, one can also use Thompson et al. (1990) to delineate fatalistic loyalists and fatalistic opposition positions, which take no action at all but have distinctive value positions.

This typology of citizen-selves can be seen as a cross-classification of value involvement and action position (Almond and Verba 1965, p. 21; Thompson, Ellis, and Wildavsky 1990, pp. 219, 247–8).[24] First, value involvement concerns accepting the value position of the dominant political regime, which ranges from allegiance to apathy and alienation. The citizen's affectual relationship to the regime is consequently an important and defining dimension of the typology. Incorporated and deferential citizens identify with the regime, whereas activist and cynical citizens oppose it. The regime may benefit or repress the marginal and opportunistic citizens, but they have little value involvement and more apathy toward the regime. Second, action position refers to behavior including active participation, deferential subjection, and inactive domination or disability. Citizenship activity ranges from little to extensive participation. In the area of political rights, this includes doing nothing, voting, contacting a representative, campaigning, or running for office (Verba, Schlozman, and Brady 1996; Verba and Nie 1972).

Many of the cells in Table 4.5 are clear: the incorporated citizen with active allegiance, the active citizen with active alienation, the deferential citizen with passive allegiance, and the cynical citizen with passive alienation. The opportunistic, marginal, and fatalistic citizens are more complex. The opportunistic citizen lies in the apathetic value column because action depends critically upon self-interest rather than a political value position. Consequently, the opportunistic citizen will range between action and passivity but not be particularly allegiant or alienated since his or her values lie within. The marginal citizen also lies between passivity and inaction due to an often temporary or powerless position in society.

Of course, this typology could not possibly cover all reactions, and it is limited to the citizen-self and not the many other aspects of self processes. Nonetheless, the typology provides a starting point for examining the construction of the citizen-self and the place that restricted and generalized exchange play in this state-citizen interaction.[25]

Citizens interact with others on issues of rights and obligations through a network of close friends and outward toward a larger group of weak ties. The result is that opinions toward, for instance, the welfare state are formed through discussion in primary groups and the larger groups that they touch: work groups, voluntary associations, churches, ethnic groups, and so on. Citizens form a self-concept in relation to rights and obligations, which they express to others (Portis 1985, pp. 461–72; Roche 1987, pp. 375–81). This citizen self-concept may range from a complex interactive self based on generalized exchange and extensive trust, or a self-interested self based on restricted exchange and suspicion. Hypotheses 4.1 through 4.6 attempt to explain citizenship behavior using this citizenship typology.

> *Hypothesis 4.1: The active and incorporated citizens: Activism for or against a regime will be correlated with higher education, income, occupation, social class, and cultural capital, and citizens will actively balance the exercise of rights with a performance of obligations.*

Although Parry, Moyser, and Day (1992, pp. 9–16, 225–37) see the impulse to participate coming from instrumental, communitarian, educative, and expressive models, these impulses can be divided into two – self-oriented and community-oriented participation. Occupation and education will fit a self-oriented model in predicting professional and interest group (e.g., veterans and trade union) participation. Socialization variables linked to cultural capital and social trust will fit a community-oriented model in predicting community service participation such as working in soup kitchens and voluntary associations to help the needy (Janoski and Wilson 1995).

> *Hypothesis 4.2: Status transmission from parents to children – occupation, education, and income – helps most to explain self-oriented participation. Parental socialization by modeling after parental participation (i.e., cultural capital in action throughout the community) creates social trust that explains community-oriented participation.*

Considerable debate surrounds the causal direction of both parts of this hypothesis. The behaviorists contend that high personal efficacy causes participation (i.e., persons with high cultural capital and economic resources choose to participate because they can get things done). The developmentalists contend that participation causes increased personal efficacy and self-esteem. Evidence seems to support both theories, but they can also be complementary due to time order differences (Berry, Portney, and Thomson 1993, pp. 260–80; Finkel 1985, 1987; Janoski and Wilson 1995; Janoski, Wilson, and Musick in press).[26]

> *Hypothesis 4.3: The opportunistic citizen's self-concept will be based on opportunism dominated by restricted exchange. Their active interest in social mobility explains their preference for rights and distaste for obligations.*

The opportunistic citizen is a product of upward or threatened downward social mobility. Although the opportunistic citizen is the perfect human identity for rational choice theory, this opportunistic citizen is socially constructed and not representative of the human condition. As Portis comments, "the very pursuit of personal interest presumes a self-concept which entails normative social commitment" (1985, p. 471). The process of social mobility usually involves and may indeed require the repudiation of obligations to prior communities and families of origin (e.g., the upwardly mobile "Ear'oles" repudiate the "Lads" who are destined for the factory gates; Willis 1977). Their movement to new and higher social class or status groups is most often incomplete; consequently, they may often maximize their rights and minimize their obligations in new and old groups.

> *Hypothesis 4.4: Deferential citizens tend to participate little and are the product of lower social class, less education, limitations on cultural capital, and lower but still somewhat steady occupations. They balance rights and obligations at a lower level than their more active citizens, yet are conscious of maintaining this balance.*

> *Hypothesis 4.5: The cynical citizen believes that nothing can be done despite all efforts to improve things. Cynical citizens will take advantage of rights but not see the value of fulfilling obligations.*

> *Hypothesis 4.6: The self of the marginal citizen is based on a value system from another subculture or counterculture. Their lack of interest in balancing rights and obligations is due to their temporary immigration or permanent entrapment. At the same time, they often have serious rights deficits. Fatalistic citizens are similar, but they have no base in an alternative culture or country.*

The incorporated, active, and deferential citizens will tend to balance rights and obligations. The opportunistic citizen will push for greater rights than obligations, and the marginal and fatalistic citizens will generally suffer greater obligations than rights. Cynical citizens are difficult to predict. In their hearts they are active citizens pursuing balance, but in their minds they know things will not work out, and consequently they may be closer to the opportunistic citizens in obtaining what they can. The social class position of the cynical citizens may make a big difference on this point with some higher social class persons pursuing balance, and the many lower social class persons needily grasping rights. Both the cynics and the marginal citizens are to a large degree strangers within their nation, and consequently more subjects than citizens.

THE STATE, TRUST, AND CITIZENSHIP

The state, of course, does not have a neutral position concerning the citizen-self because it wants to include incorporated and deferential citizens as a rule, and the opposition wants to recruit active and even cynical citizens. Consequently, the state acting for the benefit of society seeks to create ritual and socialization processes that will fashion citizen-selves conducive to state interests. To do this, two things are necessary: (1) actual social mechanisms to induce citizenship, and (2) trust in the state.

First, the social mechanisms to create citizenship involve the important socialization functions of the educational process. Socialization in the schools includes civic education expressly oriented toward rights and obligations. The critical part from the state's perspective is socialization toward obligations, and so students recite pledges, sing anthems, and hear stories of citizens fulfilling state obligations (e.g., stories of heroes and heroines fighting wars or creating needed institutions). They are also activated in some school systems toward doing voluntary activities, which for many has a lasting effect (Janoski, Wilson, and Musick in press).

Through socialization for citizenship in the schools, the state lays a base of values that it hopes are sufficiently internalized by students so that they will withstand subsequent criticism and frustration (Fogelman 1990, 1991; Ichilov 1990). Especially problematic is the transition to adulthood when adolescents typically rebel against parents. This same rebellion can be focused against the state but not as much unless reinforced by unpopular laws or wars. Two entirely different class processes tend to develop with citizenship socialization. For some lower-class men and a few women, the state offers "full maturity" through military service (e.g., "join the Army and become a man" or the Marines want "a few good men"). For students in the higher social classes who go to college, much of the education process will consist of debunking the simplistic citizenship messages usually presented in earlier citizenship training. Many of these students will be heavily socialized toward participation in voluntary associations and actual participation as state representatives. As potential elites, they will carefully weigh or bracket these debunking messages with attitudes of noblesse oblige.

Second, in traditional and social democratic regimes, citizens must grant a higher level of trust. Their view of the state is that higher levels of rights and obligations can be provided for the overall purpose of benefiting the citizens of the nation-state. These citizen's conceptions involve a higher level of participation (e.g., worker councils and yearly political party conventions) and operate on some form of generalized exchange, although the extent of generalized exchange may vary. In traditional regimes, the deferential citizen fits more of a communitarian model with more trust, while marginalized and fatalistic citizens see themselves as simply being subject to state actions that may be arbitrary. In the social democratic regimes, there is a strong emphasis on the active and incorporated citizen.

Hypothesis 4.7: Trust in the state will be high in social democratic countries with less in traditional countries and the least in liberal countries.

Because of these two social mechanisms, the typical citizens of liberal, social democratic, and traditional polities differ. The ideal pluralist citizen seems to be the opportunistic citizen who makes relatively few demands on the state and fulfills relatively few obligations. The opportunistic citizen is not particularly curious about and may not believe in the positive concern of the state, but instead wants to know what opportunities might exist for exerting his or her self-interest vis-à-vis the state. Restricted exchange will be the modus operandi. The market is particularly attractive to this citizen, and rights and obligations controlled by the state will be kept more or less at a minimum. Although opportunistic citizens will attempt to increase whatever rights and shed whatever responsibilities that they might have toward the state, they tend to learn that in a society of equals, everyone cannot have privileged access to the state. Hence, their opportunism is somewhat tempered.

Hypothesis 4.8: Social democratic regimes will have more active and incorporated citizens, while liberal regimes will have more opportunistic, cynical, and marginal citizens.

The social democratic and traditional regimes are more threatened by modern social changes than the liberal form of active citizenship. Opportunistic citizenship relying on markets and often based on social and geographical mobility reduces generalized exchange. The active citizen requires more stable network connections of community often based on union, party, occupation, gender, or extended family. This form of citizenship requires the trust of predictable compatriots and of positive concern. The active citizen is threatened by social and geographical mobilities that disrupt communities and families (Walzer 1990, pp. 11–5; Dagger 1981, pp. 726–9). He or she will also be threatened by the increasing size of place brought by urbanization and the increasing division of labor (Dagger 1981, pp. 721–6).

CONCLUSION

This chapter has provided the theoretical skeleton of exchange, social action, trust, and citizen-selves. Its main intent is not to proselytize for either type of exchange, but rather to treat these processes as variables in society and interpersonal relations that will help explain citizenship outcomes (England and Kilbourne 1990, p. 168). Consequently, both restricted and generalized exchange exist at varying levels of trust and efficiency in public and market spheres with emotion, tradition, and four different types of rationality being necessary to explain citizenship behavior. Although exchange provides a mechanism for conceptualizing why and how people take the actions they do in the realm of citizenship, it does not mean that all actions are calculated. Each of the types of exchange listed above can occur through socialization with traditional or emotional action, and there may not be calculation or ranking of alternatives. For instance, many forms of restricted or generalized exchange may simply be internalized from primary socialization so that consciousness of them may be slight indeed. And the typology of citizen-selves operationalizes these concepts of exchange at the individual level.

This chapter also does not attempt to dictate the types of citizen-selves that are generated in advanced industrialized countries. Surely there is great variation among and within societies. However, the typology is presented to guide research in this direction rather than assume rational action or ignore this area altogether.

5

The Balance of Rights and Obligations through Nesting, Civil Society, and Social Closure

> If citizenship means anything, it means a package of benefits and burdens shared, and accepted, by all.
>
> William Galston (1991, p. 250)

> There are various ways in which it is possible for a closed social relationship to guarantee its monopolized advantages to the parties. (a) Such advantages may be left free to competitive struggle within the group; (b) they may be regulated or rationed in amount and kind; or (c) they may be appropriated by individuals or sub-groups on a permanent basis and become more or less inalienable. The last is a case of closure within, as well as against outsiders. Appropriated advantages will be called "rights."
>
> Max Weber (1978, p. 43)

Given that varying levels of citizenship exist, how do societies and their constituent groups and categories organize rights and obligations in their relationships to the state? The explanations proposed here will differentiate between liberal, traditional, and social democratic regimes in how they operationalize restricted and generalized exchange. This is in part because much of the citizenship literature seems to pinpoint self-oriented versus other- or community-oriented behavior in the construction of civil society and effective state mechanisms (Dahrendorf 1974; Janoski and Wilson 1995). This chapter will first explore the macro-relationship of rights and obligations in a double-relationship of capitalism and state redistribution. It then discusses liberalism, traditionalism, and social democracy as defining basic regimes of generalized and restricted exchange that demonstrate the principles involved with voluntary associations in civil societies. Third, a number of macro-hypotheses are presented about the relationship of citizenship rights and obligations in three regimes.

The Balance of Rights and Obligations

NESTING CITIZENSHIP RIGHTS AND OBLIGATIONS WITHIN CAPITALISM

The question of balancing rights and duties is not a simple question because it is composed of both interpersonal and group process – citizen-state, citizen-group, and group-state – embedded within the institutions of markets and politics. Historically, the old feudal order of particularistic rights and duties was upset first by the reformation and the birth of individualism (Wuthnow 1989), and second by a massive increase in wars and markets, which created new inequalities (Downing 1992; Tilly 1991; Mann 1986, 1994). During industrialization in the developing democracies, new duties were discounted since obeying the market overwhelmed the old political rights and duties, but over time some political groups sought to control the market through political and then social rights.[1]

But the question of balance is extremely complex because this question exists on two levels. The first level asks What is the relationship of citizenship to market inequalities emanating from the mode of production, or more generally "politics versus markets"? (Esping-Andersen 1990, 1985). Lenski saw this as citizenship reestablishing "the importance of need" (1966, p. 83–4). Within the realm of political membership, the second level asks more specifically What is the relationship of citizenship rights and obligations? In this two-stage consideration of balance, the second stage of citizenship is nested as a corrective to the imbalances created by the market and war in the first stage.[2] Consequently, rights and duties in the second stage may be very much out of balance but nevertheless in a disequilibrium or sub-state equilibrium that makes up for market imbalances.

As Marshall indicated in his essay on the rise of citizenship in the United Kingdom, the coming of industrialization and a market economy brought a great deal of instability for the masses, and large fortunes for many of the bourgeoisie. Some of the former rulers and aristocrats survived the market revolution to some extent, but they made concessions and adjustments through legal and some political rights to the bourgeoisie. Any system of rights and duties in the political realm requires a certain amount of stability, but the rise of markets was creating considerable turbulence in the relationship of rights and duties. Dagger (1981, pp. 724–9) argues that residential mobility destroys a sense of community, and hence, the rights and duties of community citizenship.[3] Walzer elaborates that geographical, social, and marital mobilities destroy feelings of citizenship (1990, pp. 11–15). These forces for mobility disengaged many gears of social control, the casement for rights and obligations, and produced a society where market inequality could have full sway.

In the 17–1800s, with massive change and unstable rights, the bourgeoisie, aided by market forces and the state, shed duties to the poor and overwhelmed most mass political protest. Rights and duties were clearly out of balance, and due to massive mobilities involved in the enclosure acts and the industrial revolution, citizenship participation and rights were severely reduced. The market, supported by basic liberal rights, dominated the political and citizenship rights of the masses previously embedded in medieval constitutionalism (Downing 1992). While citizenship rights were growing first with the nobles and then with the bourgeoisie, this growth was still beyond the reach of peasants and workers. Thus, although the major categories of markets and political action were out of balance, it would be ludicrous to expect rights and obligations of individual citizens (i.e., peasants and workers) and groups (i.e., trade unions and churches) to be very much in balance. Legal, political, and social rights were overwhelmed by obligations to work enforced by the workhouse and debtor's prisons, and secondarily by military obligations. The church provided some solace, but it had begun a retreat from its strong position in politics during feudalism to a more modest place in the public and private spheres under capitalism.

The subsequent rise of citizenship and its concomitant rights and duties in the nineteenth and twentieth centuries need to be seen against this background of market forces nearly overwhelming prior feudal and agrarian rights and obligations, which were largely communitarian. Although the power of the bourgeoisie and the state and the extent of mobility and social control varied from country to country, the basic principle of nesting rights and obligations within markets and politics remains the same.

Marshall states that we must examine "the conflict between egalitarian measures and the free market" (1964, p. 131) and asks "Is it still true that the basic equality can be created and preserved without invading the freedom of the competitive market?" (p. 77). His answer is "no." In the post–World War II period, Marshall asks What is the "changing balance between rights and duties?" (p. 129). His answer is that "Rights have multiplied, and they are precise." However, only a few duties exist that are compulsory, while most citizenship obligations have faded into vague or informal duties and responsibilities (p. 129). Oddly enough, Marshall's statements in 1949 have a strangely modern tone in being similar to present-day neo-conservative and communitarian complaints that rights have overwhelmed duties (Mead 1986; Glendon 1991; Etzioni 1991). But exactly the opposite had prevailed in the eighteenth and nineteenth centuries.

Given this brief historical background, one might ask why should politics and markets or rights and obligations ever be in balance? Societies rarely reach a complete equilibrium because inequalities are constantly reproduced by markets and other social mechanisms (e.g., class conflict, patriarchal families, or ethnic discrimination). Nevertheless, given these social forces that discount rights and accentuate obligations of lower social classes and status groups, societies do maintain and develop material and symbolic conceptions of balance. When imbalance is perceived, the affected groups will push to correct these deficits between rights or obligations, and they will only go so far as their relative differences in social power will allow. Whatever social balance that might exist depends on prevailing ideologies and levels of various groups' political power, and how much social movements representing subordinated groups and categories of people can mobilize in pursuit of their interests. While not pretending to solve these problems of balance, the nesting framework just outlined puts them in a more solvable context.

INSTITUTIONS AND EXCHANGE

Whether rights and obligations are related through restricted or generalized exchange, both social processes occur within the context of and sometimes motivated by institutions. Social institutions are not social structures of class, race, gender, or other social categories; rather, they are patterned interactions set up and controlled by formal and informal norms (Steimo, Thelen, and Longstreth 1992, p. 11). Simplifying a complex terrain, institutional theory can be seen as composed of three basic approaches. First, institutionalization refers to the formation of informal groups within organizations or networks. These groups develop their own conceptions of what rights and obligations should be, just as the Hawthorne workers created their own norms for output restriction, sociability, and simple cooperation.[4] Second, institutionalization refers to the structuring of organizational forms creating norms of group behavior and organizational identity. They refer to political structures, democratic norms, and participation in voluntary associations.[5] And third, institutions refer to the macro-structuring of large domains of society including the family, education, media, medicine, legal system, economy, and polity. This larger view of institutions refers to how organizations, groups, and the public are tied together in functioning networks in a segment of society that has a particular and persisting coherence.[6] Within these three types of institutions – informal groups, organizational forms, and broad segments of society – a complex web of norms and positions are constructed for a wide variety of reasons from highly instrumental purposes of making money or controlling people, which may be highly restricted exchanges that are project-oriented, to sector-organizing fields of socialization and education with more generalized forms of exchange.

These institutions at the macro-level are primarily in the areas of state and public organizations and societal institutions. They are constructed in a long-term evolutionary process, although some major changes may be evident in revolutions or military occupations. These institutions become a complex combination of incentives, rules and norms, sanctions, and organizational forms. These institutions and especially political institutions (being careful not to equate complex interactions with the simple presence of political structure) construct particular types of macro-exchange leading to different balances of rights and obligations.[7]

To use an ideal type, societies can build institutions that promote diverse aims of quality of life, or institutions that primarily benefit some people more than others (Weaver and Rockman 1993a, b; Bellah et al. 1991, pp. 3–18; March and Olsen 1989, pp. 53–67). For instance, societies may structure families that have happy or liveable couples, loving and socializing children, industrial relations institutions that create satisfied employees and lead to few strikes, and educational institutions that lead to effective and enthusiastic learning environments, or just the opposite. These institutions are built through interpersonal and group norms. They play a major role in how societies construct individual relationships to the state vis-à-vis rights and obligations, and how groups do the same.

POLITICAL SOCIOLOGICAL MODELS AND REGIME THEORY

Three welfare state regimes were put together with three models of political theory in Chapter 2, but these same regimes with their theoretical base can be matched with four models of political sociology – pluralist, elite, corporatist, and mass society (Held 1987; Esping-Andersen 1990, pp. 24–9). In the pluralist model, interest groups are kept at arm's length for fear of corruption and/or bias (Held 1987, pp. 186–220). This does not mean that interest groups have no effect, but rather that interest groups can influence any policy by campaign contributions to representatives, expertise and proposals for legislation, and public statements about their support or opposition of particular proposals in the media (see part 1 of Figure 5.1).

Often these groups have great staying power and influence, even after scandals involving their constituents, since the public easily moves on from one issue to the next with little media memory. The result is that interests must be continually aggregated in the legislative process, which not only makes the process slow and cumbersome, but limits potential consensus since each interest group is implicitly encouraged to push its one or two issues (sometimes through veto processes). The pluralist approach, as a whole, depends on liberal interpretations of rights and obligations that are diverse and clearly focused on the individual. In the welfare state, benefits are frequently modest and means-tested. The state encourages market solutions to many social problems, and the public sees the state as the solution of last resort. As for political theory, pluralist states emphasize liberalism, which gives rights precedence over obligations. The United States is a good example of a pluralist regime along with Canada and Australia.

An elitist model of governing corrects for the optimism and blind spots of the pluralist model (Held 1987, pp. 143–85; Dahl and Lindblom 1976). Peak institutions and their experts are highly influential in the governance of citizenship policies, and little direct democratic participation is present. The form of government in traditional regimes may vary from being a somewhat elite-controlled or benevolent pluralism, to a business dominated system where peak corporations control outcomes with little input from labor, grassroots, or other organizations. The main point is that business generally has as much or even more power than the state (see part 2 in Figure 5.1). Traditional welfare states emphasize principles of subsidarity by elite organizations from the church to the trade unions and base their benefits on social insurance principles rather than general revenues or means tests (Shelton 1992). The state encourages regulative solutions, and the market can often be extensively organized into somewhat noncompeting firms. In terms of political theory, traditional regimes are based on elite-guided communitarianism that emphasizes obligations as opposed to rights in society. France is a good example of a traditional regime based on elite principles.[8]

The neo-corporatist model aggregates interest groups into peak federations, which are then formally or informally involved in the policy process (Held 1987, pp. 214–20; Lehmbruch and Schmitter 1982). The result is, at minimum, the direct consultation of interest groups, and at most, the self-administration of many aspects of government by peak federations at local, regional, and national levels (see part 3 in Figure 5.1). However, this participation is not as confusing as pluralism because interests are aggregated and the consensus-building process is embedded in institutions. Consociationalism is similar to neo-corporatism, but instead of the class-based groups of labor and employer federations, status groups are based on either religion or ethnic preferences. In terms of political theory, neo-corporatism corresponds to expansive democracy theory, where rights and obligations are more in balance. The social democratic countries – Sweden, Norway, and Denmark – are good examples of corporatist regimes with the Netherlands being consociationalist.[9]

To some degree, neo-corporatism is like an eighteenth century mar-

1. Pluralist Model

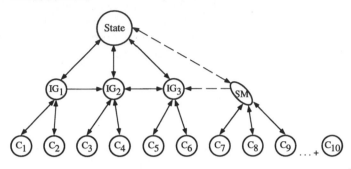

3. Neo-Corporatist Model

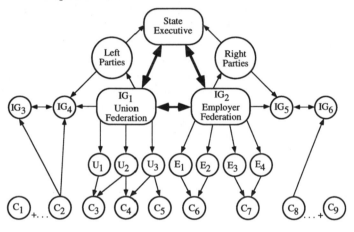

NOTE: IG_n = Interest group; C_n = Category of persons;
SM = Social movement; U_n = Trade union; E_n = Employers.

Figure 5.1. Four models of political sociology – pluralist, elite, corporatist, and mass society

riage because the social partners are linked (apparently) for life. To alter the situation produces a major restructuring of politics. Constitutions protect rights, but interest group involvement is an even more effective protection against rights violations. Once federated interest groups are heavily invested in a particular policy process, it is difficult to dislodge them (Regini 1995). Groups not represented may have difficulties because their interests must be indirectly represented by the three major powers.[10] The labor movement may have a universalistic ideology that will protect many subordinate groups, but this ideology may not go far

The Balance of Rights and Obligations

2. Elitist Model

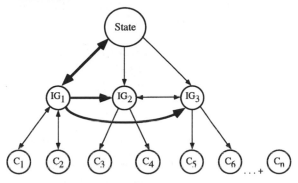

4. Mass Society Model

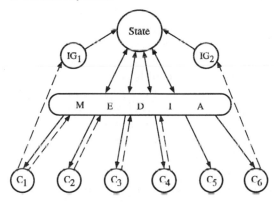

enough to protect gender or ethnic interests. The SPD in Germany protects guestworkers, but it does not go as far as an interest group of guestworkers would for the naturalization of Turkish workers and their German-born sons and daughters. Though nominally represented by labor unions, women's groups may also fall through the cracks for the same reason.

All three of these models are somewhat threatened or altered by the mass society approach to politics where the media have increasing influence in the political process. While other models place the media as one of many interest groups and civil society theory reserves the public sphere for the media, mass society theories make the media dominant (Neuman 1986; Iyengar 1991; Kornhauser 1959) (see part 4 in Figure 5.1). The United States is the best example of this model because of the deterioration of parties and the influence of political advertising and network news sound bites; however, the mass society model operates much less clearly in most European countries. At this point in time, the mass society approach is more of a tendency than a current and concrete reality.[11]

Thus, important theories of political sociology can be combined with three regime types and three political theories. Interest groups function in a different way in each system; as a result, civil society in each regime type is somewhat different.

REGIME DIFFERENCES IN CIVIL SOCIETY

Each of these approaches to political governance develops a different map of civil society. The various groups in civil society – religions, political parties, media, social movements, interest groups, watchdog groups, welfare organizations, and leisure groups – are structured according to the extent of overlap between the public, and other spheres. The liberal regime using pluralist principles nearly avoids overlap between state, public, and market spheres. Traditional regimes are a mixed type of corporatist and elitist elements with the state sphere strongly overlapping with the market and public spheres, which themselves overlap much less. The democratic-corporatist arrangement has the largest numbers of overlapping spheres at each intersection, especially the tripartite intersection of state, public, and market spheres (see Figures 5.2 and 1.1 for the basic structure of civil society). While these three systems hardly exhaust the number of different political systems (see Held [1987] for more democratic models), they do provide us with an adequate starting point to theorize about civil society in advanced industrialized countries.[12]

First, the nature of the overlap between spheres differs between regimes. The liberal regime concentrates its voluntary and welfare state organizations in the public sphere and much less in overlapping areas with the market or state spheres (see the United States in Figure 5.2). Political parties will always overlap with the state, and labor unions and employer federations will generally overlap with the market sector. But parties, unions, and employers overlap little with the state in providing social and government services. In pluralist societies, religious groups and voluntary associations of the welfare state will be entirely in the public sphere with little or no direct state control or support.[13] Although making some contributions, profit-oriented firms and the state will keep their distance from permanently supporting organizations in the public sphere.

By contrast, the social democratic regimes maximize the number of overlapping areas (see Sweden in Figure 5.2). Religion has an important

The Balance of Rights and Obligations

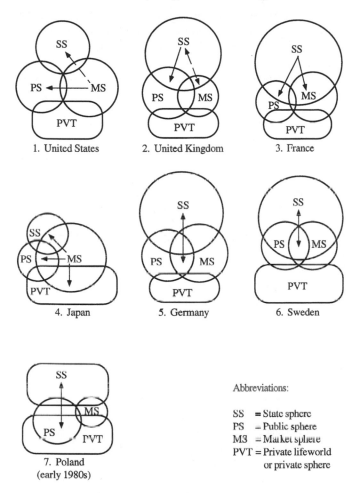

Figure 5.2. The public and private sphere in eight countries

connection to the state and often receives public subsidies through taxes. Labor and capital organizations overlap with the state government administration of welfare services and in peak political bargaining. Self-administration of government functions with employers and unions is a particularly important overlapping area of social spheres in neo-corporatist nations with social democratic regimes. Part of the media may also be subsidized by the state and public sector, whereas most liberal regimes will leave the media mostly to the market sphere. And finally, voluntary associations will often exist on full or at least partial state subsidies.

Traditional regimes share some characteristics of social overlap with social democratic regimes; however, they often have much less overlap between unions, employers, religion, or voluntary associations (see France in Figure 5.2). Either the state or business will have more overall influence on society. These traditional countries are quite mixed in their patterns; nonetheless, elites tend to play a more dominant role, and mass participation is rather secondary.[14]

Second, the size of the public sphere varies in different countries. Pluralist and social democratic countries will have a much larger public sphere than traditional regimes. The United States and Sweden have large public spheres, as measured by voluntary participation, media discussion, voluntary study groups, and participatory structures, while Germany and France have smaller public spheres. The communist countries, of course, had very small and carefully controlled public spheres, but the solidarity movement created an unusually large public sphere in Poland (see Poland in Figure 5.2). The communist successor states are just now developing civil society anew.

Third, there are important differences in the basic assumptions of these three forms of political organization. *Assimilation* or guiding all citizens toward a relatively uniform culture underlies most liberal-pluralist countries. This belies an optimistic belief that class and ethnic differences can be overcome relatively easily. Consequently, society need not be arranged around these differences. The end result is that institutions such as schools and media may emphasize common citizen backgrounds and heritages (often stressing myths of unity), but very little will be done in an organized way to intervene in society to organize or promote relations between various groups. Policy actions to alleviate group conflict will tend to be of a relatively temporary nature of a few years and will arrive in a more ad hoc fashion.[15]

Under neo-corporatism or consociationalism in social democratic regimes, a deep diversity in social cleavages is recognized as a permanent problem that cannot be overcome by pluralist politics. In corporatism, there is the basic assumption that class differences are so great that labor and management must have their own representatives in integrative institutions. This representation must be led by the state and civil society itself. For religiously or ethnically diverse countries like the Netherlands or Belgium, consociationalism as a "status-group" as opposed to "class-based" corporatism leads to major divisions that create separate institutions with group participation at every level. Most policy decisions will be of a longer-term nature and will be systematically applied within each sphere (labor, media, welfare, etc.). In class-based regimes, formal systems of social courts, workers councils, self-administration, and the like will be legislated and implemented. Political myths recognize the different cultural or class interests but tend to emphasize their commonality (i.e., the "social partners," labor and capital, work together to ensure the commonweal of the society).

Traditional regimes may also assume corporatist or consociationalist structures, but these regimes are much more based on an elitist model. Expenditures on an elite civil service are more than double those in the social democratic countries, and the number of public pension schemes is from two to six times more. Meanwhile the equality of pensions and other benefits is twenty to thirty percentage points below that in social democratic countries (Esping-Andersen 1990). As a result, these traditional regimes may be corporatist but of an elitist variety.

Traditional regimes that are less directly corporatist (e.g., France and Italy) establish elite controls and assume assimilation with a dominant culture. Elites also dominate politics but without labor or ethnic group participation. However, bargaining in France tends to occur at the peak level after mass mobilizations and general strikes. In either case, the elites seem to be able to enforce a peak bargain periodically. French elites allow considerable immigration but give French culture and language hegemonic support. Directly consociational and ethnically diverse countries like Belgium have developed similar processes based on two languages (Lijphart 1968, 1984).

GROUP EXCHANGE IN LIBERALISM, TRADITIONALISM, AND SOCIAL DEMOCRACY

Liberalism, traditionalism, and social democracy produce their own characteristic forms of social exchange. Liberal democracies tend to rely more on restricted exchange, and indeed many social forces of modernization focusing on rational and individualistic social choices seem to come from this polity. It is relatively unique in its problems of veto group politics. Traditional regimes tend to rely on more generalized exchange than pluralist regimes but less than social democratic countries. Traditional regimes stress obligations rather than rights, and the political system is elite rather than pluralist. At the same time, traditional regimes also have a type of restricted exchange that is based on insurance payments, individual payment responsibility, and elite competence (i.e., you pay health premiums, you get well-administered insurance benefits). Social democratic regimes stress generalized exchange utilizing general revenues rather than targeted insurance. Its approach is backed by universalistic and egalitarian ideologies (Schmid, Reissert, and Bruche 1992; Crouch 1990; Therborn 1992b).

The balance of rights and obligations between groups may exist in four different forms: individualism/traditionalism, civic virtue, pluralism,

Table 5.1. *The organization of civil society by exchange and openness*

	Degree of openness:	
	Closed (mutually exclusive groups)	*Open* (overlapping groups)
Restricted	(1) Individualistic behavior with outsiders, competing familism between groups, or insurance-based traditionalism	(2) Pluralism (overlapping interest groups with complex lobbying)
Generalized	(3) Neo-corporatism (interest intermediation and tripartite bargaining)	(4) Civic virtue (voluntary associations, public interest groups, rotating credit associations, public cooperatives)

Type of exchange:

and corporatism. In Table 5.1, these four different forms are presented as the result of a cross-classification of types of exchange and the nature of the groups involved. (These exchange processes are diagrammed in the "group to group" column of Table 4.1.) Individualistic behavior represents a liberal society where citizens interact in competitive market relationships (cell 1 in Table 5.1). Groups tend to act in a similar way, often forming alliances but usually well below the federation level required for corporatism. As a result, groups in pluralist societies tend to play a necessary but smaller role than in other regimes. Familism represents restricted exchange between groups which have closed themselves off from one another. Each clan or gang competes in a zero-sum battle for societal resources, and often the results are negative-sum. Traditionalism develops from these closed groups where cooperation and trust are difficult, but they are developed through insurance payments based on restricted exchange and elite controls and coordination. Sicily is the negative-sum case of closed and restricted exchange with the Mafia, while Germany is a positive-sum case where elites establish insurance-based trust funds (Gambetta 1988b; Pagen 1988; Banfield 1958).

In the opposite case, civic virtue represents generalized exchange with open or overlapping groups (cell 4 in Table 5.1). In this situation, groups cooperate with considerable trust to produce positive-sum outcomes. This form of civic virtue is unstable and hard to maintain, yet it does exist in many voluntary organizations such as the United Way, Alcoholics Anonymous, and rotating credit associations. However, the first and fourth cells in the table are more like ideal types than the other two mixed cells.

The restricted exchange and open groups (cell 2 in Table 5.1) represent pluralism with strong norms of liberal competition and distrust of government. The openness of groups keeps the restricted exchange from becoming coercive as people move freely from group to group. Nonetheless, without extensive cooperation, the pluralist model lacks effective policy as the state continually defends against factionalism.

Neo-corporatism represents a closed group situation (cell 3 in Table 5.1) where the various groups recognize that they can fall into amoral familism or destructive war if they simply fight against each other. Consequently, they agree to cooperate at a higher level, and this produces overlapping spheres in civil society. The result is greater cooperation but little mobility between groups. Since cells 2 and 3 are mixed models that are closer to political reality for most countries discussed in this study, they are discussed next.

The liberal regime is based on political pluralism that illustrates a form of restricted exchange where interest groups interact with the state and each other in a one-to-one bargaining arrangement. However, each group's membership overlaps to some degree with many other groups, and consequently there is some basis for agreement between groups (Lipset 1981, pp. 211–26; Rawls 1993, pp. 133–72). Individuals may be cross-pressured into more tolerance. Thus, a modified and constantly changing consensus can be reached periodically. This membership or micro-overlap is different from the overlapping spheres of civil society because it focuses on the common memberships of individuals in different groups, not the sharing of duties between public, state, and market organizations. For example, since Mr. Smith belongs to the American Legion, the United Auto Workers Union, and the Parent-Teacher Association, he can talk to Ms. Jones who belongs to the National Organization of Women, the American Nursing Association, and the Parent-Teacher Association because they have common interests from their membership in the parent-teacher group. Other times, however, pluralism demonstrates a great deal of confusion and jockeying for position. The end result is somewhat similar to the much maligned pluralist concept of "equilibrium," which can sometimes fall into "business as usual gridlock" or "ungovernability." This situation represents a network of groups that in many ways counteract each other's power and only rarely gain enough consensus to make major changes through government (Neuman 1986, pp. 35–6; Pestoff 1977; Lipset 1981, pp. 211–26, 267–73).

Neo-corporatist groups are composed of more mutually exclusive membership; that is, blue-collar workers belong to unions while white-collar managers belong to the employer federations, or there were few mixed marriages of Flemish and Walloons in Belgium or Catholics and Protestants in the Netherlands. The end result is a form of mutually exclusive group to group exchange that operates on the assumption that membership does not seriously overlap. Since group differences are so great, these groups could be locked in long-term and potentially disastrous struggles (i.e., zero- or negative-sum games). To reduce the potential for self-destructive conflict between groups, more formal and sometimes informal corporatist arrangements are put into place with the state operating as a mediator. The result is a system of regulated exchange that does not result from individual or cross-pressured consensus, but from the agreement of coalitions within a three-party system – labor, management, and the state, or two or more status groups and the state (Pekkakarinen, Pohjohla, and Rowthorn 1992; Boswell 1991; Crouch 1990, 1992b; Traxler 1990). This nonoverlap in group membership ultimately leads to a formal and cooperative overlap between groups represented in councils or on boards, which causes an overlap between spheres of civil society. When overlapping membership begins to occur with greater social mobility in class-based corporatism or intermarriage in status-based consociationalism, then corporatism will tend to break down, just as when social mobility declines and major class/caste cleavages eliminate cross-memberships, pluralism loses its raison d'être.

Again, traditional regimes are in the middle, but with less overall participation and membership. The missing elements are powerful groups that will represent the mass of workers, religious, or ethnic groups at a peak level.

SANCTIONING GENERALIZED AND RESTRICTED EXCHANGE IN A DEMOCRACY

While some group leaders may participate in voluntary altruism, many are socialized into cooperative behavior by informal social pressures of fellow groups, constituents, and customers and by formal state laws. In considering the eight sanctioning mechanisms mentioned in the previous chapter – reputation, modeling, membership, planning, social pressure, dominance, and formal law – this section presents examples of sanctioning mechanisms that reinforce generalized or restricted exchange in pluralist and corporatist societies (Axelrod 1986, pp. 1102–8).

In nations where citizens are members of groups and those groups are members of large federations, a greater capacity for generalized exchange exists simply through the mechanism of membership. German or Swedish workers who are members of unions are secondarily socialized into a trade union ideology that supports solidarity and collective action. Demonstrations and/or strikes periodically give these workers a chance to act on the basis of that ideology. And while acting, workers who defect are under extensive observation so that punishment through social pressure or membership sanctions are highly likely. Consequently, corporatist societies with high unionization will demonstrate support for generalized exchange within the trade union through membership, social pressure, and internal bylaws. Many of these trade union members, however, will not need extensive monitoring because they have internalized trade union norms through trade union social functions while they are growing up in working-class families. Thus, primary socialization exerts an important effect.[16] Employer federations will often demonstrate the same results in response to defections in lockouts or centralized agreements. These groups need closure for effective socialization processes to work.

In pluralist nations with little unionization and ineffective federations (i.e., unable to actually bargain centralized labor agreements), internalization and social pressure have much less effect. Social mobility may critically weaken the internalization of generalized exchange in trade unions as the sons and daughters of worker families achieve education and assume work in middle-class institutions and organizations. Instead, restricted exchange in less dense networks tends to dominate in middle-class culture. Unions tend to bargain in a more individualistic way leapfrogging each others' gains or losses. Yet at the same time, these same persons who may reject ideologies of group membership accept ideologies of openness and mobility that allow foreigners to naturalize and lower-class/status individuals to work their way up through educational and occupational merit.

As an example of the state playing a catalytic role in encouraging generalized exchange through formal law, consider why the German employer associations and the vast majority of firms as their members provide vocational training for businesses throughout society rather than only for the sole needs of any one firm. In this example, free ridership is handled in two ways. First, formal law in Germany requires that employers above a minimum size belong and pay dues to a chamber of commerce, which regulates apprenticeship programs. While a firm may

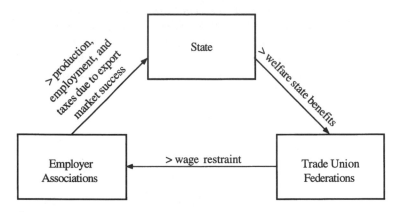

Figure 5.3. Neo-corporatism as a system of generalized exchange

choose not to involve itself in apprenticeship training, it must still pay dues to the chamber to maintain training. The result is adequate financing; however, the government has little or nothing to say about how the chamber or its firms actually produce most of the training. Social pressure by other firms through membership in associations then provides additional force on individual firms to go along with the apprenticeship program. A few firms may still refuse to cooperate, but norms and state sanctions are arrayed to back up the generalized exchange program for the vast majority of employers. The system engenders cooperation, which is based on large-scale but not perfect trust (Franz and Soskice 1994; Janoski 1990).[17]

The basic logic of neo-corporatism also exhibits generalized exchange. The state and secondarily employers meet to plan economic growth and influence the trade union federations to accept wage restraint. This enables the employers to increase production and employment with the side effects of increased export market success for them and higher revenues through taxes raised for the state. The state then legislates the welfare state benefits (i.e., the social wage) for the trade unions. This process is diagrammed in Figure 5.3. Although this system of exchange has reached its limits under neo-Keynesian economics, it worked well for a number of years in the neo-corporatist countries, and new forms of generalized exchange will undoubtedly emerge.

In a pluralist system, the state may enact formal laws to reinforce the restricted nature of exchange. In the United States, anti-trust laws were passed to increase competition in the free market, and as such, they reinforce the restricted nature of exchange in American business. At the same time, these laws discourage the establishment of cooperative business chambers, federations, or networks that are so successful with employers in Germany and Japan and also tend to mitigate against state industrial policy (Campbell, Hollingsworth, and Lindberg 1991). Antitrust meshes with meritocratic ideologies that allow everyone an opportunity to advance in a competitive world of restricted exchange.

REDISTRIBUTIVE EXCHANGE, EMOTION, AND SOCIAL MOVEMENTS

While rights and obligations may be balanced at a high or low level of benefits, social movements may also play a role in redistributing rights and obligations by increasing rights for their own members and obligations for other groups. In a sense, social movements thrive on disrupting the current balance (whether an equilibrium or a stable disequilibrium) by pressuring for the increased recognition of their members as citizens, and then increasing their rights and sometimes their obligations.

Social movements will have a highly emotional component for two reasons. First, social movements make major efforts to change the identity of their membership. Whether workers, women, minority ethnic or racial groups, or disabled persons, each member's identity will be under reconstruction. This process of consciousness raising will be a highly emotional process, and people may be activated to participate at new and more intense levels. Second, since members are often being asked to perform activities that they consider to be out of the ordinary – demonstrations and protests – and that others see as disruptive, high amounts of emotional energy will be necessary for countering dominant social viewpoints. Social movement leaders may even make what appear to be irrational decisions in terms of forestalling movement goals in order to intensify the consciousness and hence the solidarity of the members in the social movement itself. Restricted exchange tends to be denigrated in these highly charged group settings.[18] Instead, social movements will emphasize processes of generalized exchange as members drop their direct self-interest and make occasional and sometimes repeated sacrifices for the group as a whole.

These processes within social movements will tend to emphasize group membership obligations over individual rights, and also over the rights and obligations of the general citizenry. For example, demonstrators have obligations to their movement to show up at the target site and protest; however, in the process they may be violating what much of society sees as an obligation to respect property and the general public order. These citizens must choose between the social movement's new values and the society's established values. This battle over the loyalty of these citizens creates an instability within citizenship with confusion over competing claims of rights and obligations. If the social movement is strong enough, it eventually changes the programs and eligibility rules of citizenship.

EXPLAINING RESTRICTED AND GENERALIZED EXCHANGE AT THE MACRO-LEVEL

Four sets of hypotheses are particularly important in looking at citizenship and exchange at the macro-level: (1) social structure and closure, (2) political-economic institutions and civil society, (3) state policies and balancing citizenship rights and obligations, and (4) voluntary associations and the state. The first set of hypotheses concerns social structure and generalized exchange. The homogeneity of a nation creates a general sense of closure that promotes generalized exchange. Mourtizen proposes that "The more homogeneous the population in a country, the more important will ideology tend to be in the formation of citizens' spending preferences; and the more heterogeneous the population in a country, the more important will private benefit indicators or self-interest measures be" (1987, p. 432). Thus, we should expect the "opportunistic" or "demanding" citizen under restricted exchange to be driven by individual cost-benefit calculations in the heterogeneous United States where class and status crosscut and where groups overlap. The "active" or ideological citizen under generalized exchange will be motivated by party and interest groups' ideologies where either class or status groups are dominant (i.e., where groups are mutually exclusive). For instance, in more homogenous Sweden, the Social Democratic Party and LO ideologies will tend to keep their members focused on generalized exchange in a large group, rather than on individual or subgroup outcomes. Similar ideological processes operate within the confessional pillars in the Netherlands where status groups are dominant. These ideologies are part of the ways that individuals and groups establish their identities. Consequently, where class or status dominate the formation of groups in civil society, individuals can more easily clarify their position vis-à-vis the community; where class and status crosscut, individuals will have trouble maintaining a group identity and be more likely to choose self-oriented positions.

Hypothesis 5.1: Generalized exchange will develop in societies that have either class or status (but not both) group divisions, and these exchange processes will be promoted by group ideologies that will provide the basis for generalized exchange within the individual self processes of citizens and group members. Restricted exchange will develop where class and status distinctions crosscut and group ideologies tend to be ineffectual.

The Balance of Rights and Obligations

Hypothesis 5.2: Liberal societies should rely more on restricted exchange in the construction of political and economic institutions, while social democratic and traditional societies will rely more on generalized exchange.

Social democratic countries will be closer to the traditional corporatist regimes on this issue than pluralist regimes because social democratic regimes have considerable overlap between diverse groups through cooperative institutions.

Hypothesis 5.3: Liberal societies will develop greater overlapping membership in groups within civil society, especially in the realm of voluntary associations. The more overlapping memberships, the more generalized exchange in rights and obligations in voluntary associations and institutions in the public sphere. Traditional corporatist societies will not develop generalized exchange through overlapping voluntary associations or organizations. Instead they overlap through more formal mechanisms of overlapping institutions in civil society. Social democracies will incorporate both forms of overlap but tend more toward neo-corporatism.

The structure of the school systems in these three regime types is a good example. In Germany, working-class, middle-class, and university-bound students attend entirely different schools with little in the way of integrative mechanisms, while in the United States students tend go to the comprehensive high school where everyone attends sports and social activities together whether they are going to the university or on unemployment.[19] Social democratic regimes like Sweden tend to put students in the same schools but with very different curricula. In these three approaches, overlapping memberships are created, molded, or totally avoided. In the end, the generalized exchange of rights and obligations in institutional overlap with mutually exclusive groups in corporatist systems will be stronger than cross-pressured membership in voluntary associations in liberal societies since the former are more formally structured and involve greater resources. The public sphere of voluntary associations in liberal regimes, however, will have greater potential to oppose the state (Putnam 1993; Boli 1991).

Hypothesis 5.4: Social inequality – measured by income inequality and social mobility coupled with social closure – has a complex relationship to generalized exchange of rights and obligations: (a) social democratic countries generate high equality, moderate social mobility, and moderate social openness and will exhibit "open" and "overlapping" generalized exchange; (b) traditional regimes with high inequality, low social mobility, and extreme social closure will have "closed" and "mutually exclusive" generalized exchange; and (c) liberal regimes with moderate inequality, high social mobility, and very open societies will have "overlapping" and "mutually exclusive" restricted exchange.

123

Table 5.2 shows some evidence for this complex social inequality hypothesis in eighteen countries. Social democratic countries have the most income equality as demonstrated by their low post-tax and standardized Gini coefficients (.321 and .279 compared to .398 and .411 for traditional and .341 and .352 for liberal regimes). Class crystallization is highest in the traditional regimes with high social immobility (.273 compared to .247 for social democratic and .228 for liberal regimes), or conversely, low total social mobility (63.5 compared to 73.0 for social democratic and 72.0 for liberal regimes). Social closure as measured by standardized naturalization rates shows that traditional regimes are the most closed (1,662 naturalized per 100,000 aliens), while liberal regimes are very open (4,803) and social democratic regimes not far behind (4,027). In traditional societies, high levels of both internal closure in the stratification system and external closure in refusing to integrate immigrants leads to a hierarchical type of society where generalized exchange can be maintained. In liberal societies, low levels of these three types of closure lead to highly restricted exchange that makes boundaries hard to maintain. Social democratic regimes achieve the difficult task of maintaining some sort of closure with moderate mobility and naturalization while maintaining open generalized exchange. By their very nature, openness and generalized exchange processes are somewhat contradictory and hard to maintain in the same system. What is interesting about social democratic regimes is that they can combine social mobility and openness. Walzer (1990) and Portis (1985) make a more general prediction about mobility by adding geographical, marital, and other movements to social mobility that destroy community and a sense of generalized exchange.

The second set of hypotheses involve political institutions, civil society, and generalized exchange. Because the structures of social mobility, civil society, and politics differ, exchange relations between groups about rights and obligations vary in each regime type.

> *Hypothesis 5.5: Generalized exchange will develop in societies where the state formally encourages participation in cooperative and corporatist organizations.*

The state acting as a catalyst may take place through regulatory sanctions (e.g., laws that state that all employers must contribute but need not participate in corporatist arrangements) or participation in community organizations for political and social concerns (e.g., self-administration mechanisms to promote solidarities and prevent conflict development). However, the state does not dictate the actions of groups, and generalized exchange depends on both types of overlap to some degree.

The Balance of Rights and Obligations

Quantitative tests of these hypotheses may be rather difficult, and case studies should be more useful in ferreting out generalized exchange. Nonetheless, comparative and historical analyses have shown that traditional corporatist and social democratic societies are well known for structuring economic competition into cooperative mechanisms (Katzenstein 1984, 1985). Recall the two examples of cooperative apprenticeship systems and wage restraint just discussed. Also, corporatist countries seem to establish cooperative trade and educational associations that work with industry within the country and then compete quite heavily with foreign firms for international trade (Pekkarinen, Pohjola, and Rowthorn 1992). These more cooperative mechanisms also extend to industrial relations (Crouch 1992b; Marin 1990) and the development of trade (Johnson 1982).

Third, the balance of rights and obligations differs according to regime type. Obligations have a direct connection to rights in generalized exchange. Where obligations are low, more restricted exchange prevails. Little or no attention has been given to the macro-balance of rights and obligations; nonetheless, the following hypothesis has some support.

> *Hypothesis 5.6: The greater the willingness to fulfill obligations through paying taxes and serving in the military, the greater the development of legal, political, social, and participation rights. From a higher level of balanced rights and obligations comes greater generalized exchange. From a lower level of balance comes more restricted exchange.*

Traditional and social democratic regimes will exhibit this greater willingness to fulfill obligations, while liberal regimes will not. Social democratic regimes will pay the most taxes and receive the higher level of rights; liberal regimes pay low taxes and receive fewer rights. When looking at Humana's human rights scores for industrialized countries, which are composed of 100 items, social democratic regimes have the highest correlation with legal and political rights ($r = +.74$, $p = .0005$), while the liberal regime variable has a strong negative correlation ($r = -0.53$, $p = .04$). Traditional countries are clearly in the middle ($r = -.10$, $p = .68$) but not significantly correlated (see Esping-Andersen 1990, pp. 69–78; Janoski 1994, pp. 55–6, 86 for regime scoring; see Humana 1993 for the rights measures). In a simple regression equation, the social democratic regime variable explains over 43 percent of the variation in the human rights variable. These results based on Humana's measures show that social democratic countries have the highest legal and political rights, and liberal countries the lowest (see Table 2.6 for the total country scores). Other results are possible with different measures like Freedom House; however, the Humana variables are much

Table 5.2. *Internal and external measures of class and social closure*

	Gini index of income inequality, 1970 [a]			Social mobility, circa 1970		Natural- ization rate
	Pre-tax Gini	Post-tax Gini	Standard- ized house- hold Gini	Social [b] immobility	Total [c] social mobility/ fluidity	
Social democratic						
Denmark	—	—	—	.283	—/—	3,133
Finland	—	—	—	.231	—/—	3,504
Netherlands	.385	.354	.264	—	—/.16	2,854
Norway	.354	.307	.301	.196	—/—	5,810
Sweden	.346	.302	.271	.279[b]	73/-.17	4,836
Average	*.362*	*.321*	*.279*	*.247*	*73.0/.005*	*4,027.4*
Traditional						
Austria	—	—	—	—	—/—	2,960
Belgium	—	—	—	.297	—/—	848
France	.416	.414	.417	.278	65/.16	2,002
Germany	.396	.383	.386	.218	62/.13	838
Italy	—	.398	—	.299	—/.12	—
Average	*.406*	*.398*	*.411*	*.273*	*63.5/.137*	*1,662.0*

Liberal					
Australia	.313	.312	.354	.215	70/-.23	7,223
Canada	.382	.354	.348	—	-/-	9,879
Japan	.335	.316	.336	.229	73/-.20	1,242
Switzerland	—	—	—	—	-/-	1,426
United States	.404	.381	.369	.238	73/-.20	4,246
Average	*.359*	*.341*	*.352*	*.228*	*72.0/-.210*	*4,803.2*
Mixed					
Ireland	—	—	—	—	53/.16	269
New Zealand	—	—	—	—	-/-	2,544
United Kingdom	.344	.318	.327	—	—/-.09	*18,004*

[a] The Gini indexes come from Sawyer (1976). A higher score means more social inequality.

[b] The social immobility score from Xie (1992) is φ - Q_x and a higher score means less social mobility. However, the social immobility score for Sweden is probably too high.

[c] The total mobility rate (TMR) and fluidity scores (β) are from Erikson and Goldthorpe (1992, pp. 195 and 381). A higher score means more social mobility.

richer in detail and do not automatically support the case that everything is fine in liberal countries.

But these correlations reveal little about balance, whose evidence can be seen in Table 5.3. In column 1, the average taxation level is highest for the social democratic countries (40.1%) followed by the traditional (37.1%) and then the liberal countries (27.4%). Column 2 shows a standardized variable representing conscripts as a percentage of the armed forces and length of basic service (see Table 3.3). The average standardized score for social democratic countries (+0.76) is slightly higher than traditional countries (+0.71), which is much greater than liberal countries (−1.60). Social democratic and traditionalist countries strong in corporatism or consociationalism (Austria, Belgium, Denmark, Finland, the Netherlands, Norway, and Sweden) all have considerable conscription programs, and many of these programs also allow for hazardous nonmilitary tasks and service-related programs for the benefit of society. The corporatist conscription programs with their more continuous fulfilling of obligations and extensive volunteering in alternative community service have a strong generalized exchange component. Pluralist or liberal countries (Australia, Canada, New Zealand, and the United States) did not have conscription programs in the 1980s or 1990s, tend to avoid conscription in peacetime, but may reinstate conscription in time of war (Stern 1957; Moskos and Chambers 1993). After wartime, the liberal regimes emphasize restricted exchange with specific benefit programs for veterans and many means-tested programs for others.[20] Thus, on the whole, the social democratic and traditional regimes are much higher on obligations than the liberal regimes.

The four rights on specific measures I have selected are much higher in social democratic and traditional countries than in liberal regimes. On legal rights in column 3, social democratic regimes have the least incarcerated prisoners per 100,000 persons, the traditional regimes next, and liberal regimes nearly double (averages: 50.2 < 58.2 < 136.3 and still higher at 63.4 excluding the United States). The averages of the total Humana human rights scores (see Table 2.5) represent a positive rather than negative measure of rights, and they also reflect this trend (98.0 > 94.6 > 90.6). Political rights were measured by the percentage of the population voting in column 4.[21] Traditional regimes were the highest (90.0%) with social democratic regimes not far behind (81.4%), while liberal regimes were clearly the lowest (67.7%).[22] Social transfers as a percentage of GDP were highest for traditional regimes (17.4%), with social democratic (14.9%) and liberal regimes (9.2%) lower. And participation rights showed the traditional regimes highest on codetermination and workers councils (1.6), while social democratic nations had some participation rights (0.6) but liberal nations had none (0.0). All

The Balance of Rights and Obligations

four measures of rights flow in the same direction with liberal regimes being on the bottom for each of the four variables.

Rights and obligations are strongly and positively correlated, which indicates that a balance of rights and obligations forms at different levels – low rights beget low obligations in liberal regimes, moderately high rights match moderately high obligations in social democratic regimes, and high rights beget high obligations in traditional regimes.[23] The tax and conscription measures in advanced industrialized societies are strongly correlated with political, social, and participation rights. Although this selection of measures of rights and obligations can be disputed and should be supplemented with more extensive measures, these results demonstrate the plausibility of the argument that rights and obligations are in some sort of balance.

> *Hypothesis 5.7: Regimes with the most and least support for the welfare state tend to generate the use of general revenue funds. In social democratic regimes, the greater the use of general revenues, the greater the generalized exchange. In traditional regimes, heavy reliance on insurance based benefits results in restricted exchange. And although the use of general revenues in liberal regimes is a form of generalized exchange, they are used at a low level while the welfare state is heavily guarded by means tests, which reverts back to restricted exchange.*

The use of general revenues allows citizens to support a wide range of social benefits as they are needed. Insurance-based revenues target benefits for those who made the insurance payments. If you don't pay the premium, you don't get the benefit. Even more of a restricted exchange are the means-tested benefits provided to poor people. They must demonstrate through a disclosure of poverty or other measure of inadequacy that they qualify for a benefit. Social democratic regimes rely more on general revenues and avoid means tests, and consequently they provide greater universal coverage and overall generalized exchange. Traditional-corporatist regimes are more bound to insurance-based benefits, and liberal regimes are well known for their extensive use of means-tested benefits. Schmid, Reissert, and Bruche (1992) have shown how these different financing schemes result in large differences in active labor market policy in six European countries.

Fourth, the structure of civil society as measured by voluntary associations and their relations to the state differ according to regime type. Following in the tradition of Tocqueville, many claims have been made that the United States has the highest percentage of its population involved in voluntary association activity in the world. This is an oft repeated claim that is applied to liberal societies in general. This claim, however, is misleading because liberal regimes substitute voluntary as-

Table 5.3. The levels of rights and obligations in three regimes

	Citizenship obligations		Citizenship rights			
	(1)	(2)	(3)	(4)	(5)	(6)
	Support: Taxes as % of GNP	*Service:* National Service Index	*Legal:* Prisoners per 100,000	*Political:* Voters as percent of citizens	*Social:* Social transfers over GDP	*Participation:* Work councils and codetermination
Countries/ Regimes						
Social Democratic						
Denmark	40.0%	-0.22	47	83%	13.8%	0
Finland	34.0	0.94	75	64	9.1	0
Netherlands	41.0	1.05	27	87	22.6	2
Norway	42.0	1.40	47	82	13.6	0
Sweden	43.7	1.18	55	91	15.5	1
Average	*40.1*	*0.76*	*50.2*	*81.4*	*14.9*	*0.6*
Traditional						
Austria	38.7%	0.56	87	92%	18.5%	2
Belgium	39.7	0.002	27	95	18.8	2
France	39.3	0.79	40	86	19.2	1
Germany	35.3	0.99	77	87	15.5	2
Italy	32.3	1.19	60	90	15.1	1
Average	*37.1*	*0.71*	*58.2*	*90.0*	*17.4*	*1.6*

Liberal						
Australia	28.0 %	-2.25	60	94 %	7.7 %	0
Switzerland	27.7	1.01	54	48	11.4	0
Canada	31.0	-2.25	94	69	9.7	0
Japan	22.0	-2.25	45.5	74	8.2	0
United States	28.3	-2.25	426	53	9.1	0
Average	*27.4*	*-1.60*	*136.3* [a]	*67.7*	*9.2*	*0.0*
Mixed						
Ireland	32.0%	-2.25	60	62%	11.5%	0
New Zealand	28.7	-2.25	60	89	—	0
United Kingdom	35.3	-2.25	77	76	11.3	0

[a] Without the United States, the average is 63.4, which is still higher than the social democratic and traditional regime types.

SOURCES/CONCEPTS: Sources are listed by column number:

(1) Taxes as a percentage of GDP are an average of 1965, 1975 and 1985 (OECD 1991).

(2) The national service variable is a standardized index of the basic length of compulsory service in months and conscripts as a percentage of the Armed Forces. The -2.25 scores represent zeros on both measures. Both figures are for 1982 and they come from columns (1) and (2) in table 3.3.

(3) The incarcerated population per 100,000 persons from 1980 to 1986 comes from the UN (1993), Mauer (1994), and national sources.

(4) The percentage of the population voting in national elections are for 1982 and come from Piven and Cloward (1988, p. 5).

(5) Social security transfer expenditures include sickness, old age, family allowance, public assistance, and other transfers. They average 1968, 1979 and 1985 and come from OECD (1991);

(6) The participation variable adds the presence of legislated works councils and codetermination on corporate boards. It comes from Stephens-Huber and Stephens (1982) and national sources.

sociation activities for a strong welfare state, which makes voluntary association activities in social democratic regimes appear lower. But voluntary associations in social democratic regimes are actually quite strong, and often state organizations in Scandinavia perform welfare functions just as well or much better than underfunded voluntary associations and piecemeal church-based efforts in the United States. Statistics showing the levels of voluntary association membership and participation in three regime types are shown in Table 5.4 (Curtis, Grabb, and Baer 1992, p. 143). Once churches are taken out of United States figures, these numbers drop from being the overall leader on membership (47.1%) and participation (18.9%) in voluntary associations to fifth and sixth respectively (see columns 2 and 6). Sweden is second overall on membership (68.1%) and fourth on participation (26.1%), but it rises to first without church membership (64.9%). When union participation is subtracted, Sweden still remains strong. German membership and participation are high for the traditional category; but it does not approach the levels of either the liberal or social democratic categories. On the whole, traditional regimes are much lower on voluntary association membership and participation. When churches are taken out to get a more comparable figure for liberal societies and when unions are taken out to eliminate the bias of corporatist societies, the end result for each category is that social democratic countries have greater passive membership (41.1%) compared to the traditional (21.1%) and liberal (34.9%) regime types, and social democratic (18.4%) and liberal (18.0%) regimes are both higher on active participation than traditional regimes (13.8%). When these figures are translated into union and church memberships in Table 5.5, liberal societies are much more active in churches, while social democratic regimes are high on union participation. On overall membership and participation – excluding unions, churches, and Japan because it is an outlier – the social democratic (41.1% for membership and 18.4% for participation) and liberal regimes (39.2% and 21.0%) are about equal (Hardacre 1991).[24]

Hypothesis 5.8: For very different reasons, voluntary association activity will be greater in social democratic and liberal societies than in traditional corporatist societies.

Liberal societies are not the unmitigated leaders in voluntary association activities. Instead, liberal societies tend to stress church activities, usually as a partial substitute for the welfare state, and social democratic regimes tend more toward union and political participation. Traditional regimes, while being stronger than liberal societies on union participation, tend toward low participation as one would expect in an elite system.

On the issue of the quality of discourse in civil society, social democratic regimes have an advantage because many of the liberal regime's voluntary associations are engaged in tedious welfare state functions. As a result, voluntary associations in liberal regimes are often buried in the details of fund-raising and distributing goods and services to the needy. These activities are particularly prone to co-optation by elites and the state due to their control of private and public funding, and voluntary associations tend to avoid controversy for fear of alienating donors. Voluntary associations in social democratic regimes have the ability to be much more independent and engaged in critical discourse. Although the state may provide much of the social democratic regime funds for voluntary associations, they are not reduced to fund-raising efforts and are surprisingly critical of state policies (Boli 1991, pp. 118–20; Pestoff 1977).[25]

> *Hypothesis 5.9: Discourse over politics will be more political and policy-oriented in social democratic societies because fewer voluntary associations are tied up in private church activities and fund-raising for welfare programs.*

Voluntary associations, especially those operating in the welfare sector, that are dependent on uncertain and discretionary funding from a wide range of donors will not want to alienate potential supporters by critical or political positions. On the other hand, right- or left-wing sects may be highly political and controversial, but they are often closed in their membership and tend to generate their funds from their own members. They can afford to alienate nonmembers, but this does little to improve the quality of discourse in civil society. The combination of the neutrality of the majority of voluntary associations and extremely polarized position of a small but important number of closed groups often results in an impoverished public discourse.

SYNTHESIZING CITIZENSHIP, CIVIL SOCIETY, AND SOCIAL EXCHANGE

Legitimacy may come in many forms: a widespread belief in "the people's home" and welfare state in Sweden, a sense of "social contract" in the United Kingdom, or even the often positive attitudes toward the indirect generalized exchange of "trickle down economics" operating through restricted exchange in the market in the United States. When beliefs in legitimacy are not widely shared, benefits through generalized exchange weaken, and regimes lose stability or break down. Since the turn of the century and especially after the Keynesian revolution in policymaking, the state is seen by the public as ultimately responsible for social exchange. Legitimacy rests on a widespread belief that some aspect

Table 5.4. *Voluntary association membership and participation in three regimes*

Regimes and countries	VA membership only				VA membership and active participation			
	(1) Total VA	(2) VA minus church	(3) VA minus union	(4) VA minus church and union	(5) Total VA	(6) VA minus church	(7) VA minus union	(8) VA minus church and union
Social Democratic								
Sweden	68.1 %	64.9 %	43.5 %	39.4 %	26.1 %	19.8 %	24.3 %	18.0 %
Norway	61.9	59.5	43.1	40.2	23.3	21.0	19.9	17.6
Netherlands	62.8	48.8	59.1	43.6	24.7	20.2	24.2	19.6
Average	*64.2*	*57.7*	*48.6*	*41.1*	*24.7*	*20.3*	*22.8*	*18.4*
Traditional								
Belgium	42.6	37.0	30.2	25.3	20.7	17.9	19.9	17.1
France	27.2	25.1	21.9	19.7	15.3	13.6	14.1	12.4
Germany	48.6	42.7	38.3	32.0	21.2	16.8	19.8	15.4
Italy	25.9	22.9	21.3	18.2	17.6	15.0	15.7	12.8
Average	*34.2*	*28.8*	*26.7*	*21.2*	*18.4*	*15.2*	*17.1*	*13.8*

Liberal								
Australia	61.0	50.3	52.3	39.7	26.7	20.4	26.0	19.6
Canada	58.2	44.3	53.2	36.9	32.9	25.5	32.1	24.6
Japan	30.0	23.8	20.8	14.3	13.4	10.5	12.1	9.0
United States	72.7	47.1	69.5	41.2	31.8	18.9	31.7	18.8
Average	*55.5/*	*41.4/*	*49.0/*	*33.0/*	*26.2/*	*18.8/*	*25.5/*	*18.0/*
	63.9[a]	*47.2*[a]	*58.3*[a]	*39.2*[a]	*30.5*[a]	*21.6*[a]	*29.9*[a]	*21.0*[a]
Mixed								
Ireland	51.5	34.3	45.6	25.5	21.0	16.6	20.4	15.8
United Kingdom	51.3	44.1	42.5	31.0	19.6	16.3	19.0	15.5

[a] The second figure for the liberal countries is calculated without Japan, which is an outlier. However, the arguments do not really change whether Japan is in or out.

SOURCE: The proportion of respondents reporting voluntary association memberships comes from Curtis, Grabb, and Baer (1992, p. 143).

Table 5.5. *Active and passive membership in church, union and other*
voluntary associations

Regime types	Church associations		Trade unions		All other associations (excludes church and union)	
	(1) Passive	(2) Active	(3) Passive	(4) Active	(5) Passive	(6) Active
Social democratic	6.5%	4.4%	15.6%	1.9%	41.1%	18.4%
Traditional	5.4	3.2	7.5	1.3	21.2	13.8
Liberal	14.1/16.7[a]	7.4 /8.7[a]	6.5/5.6[a]	0.7/0.5[a]	33.0/39.2[a]	18.0/21.0[a]
Mixed	12.2	3.8	7.3	0.6	28.3	15.7

NOTE:
Passive (columns 1 and 3) refers to membership only, while active (columns 2 and 4) refers to
membership and active participation in voluntary associations.
[a] The second figure for liberal countries (i.e., after the slash) excludes Japan, which is an outlier on
voluntary association membership among liberal countries.
SOURCE: Figures are calculated from previous table. Church figures are "total VA memberships" minus
the "VA memberships minus the church" (Column 1 - column 2 for passive and column 5 - column 6 for
active). Union figures are "total VA membership" minus "Voluntary associations minus union
membership." All other associations are "total VA membership" minus church and union memberships.

of a generalized exchange system is working (whether direct generalized
exchange or the trickle down results of restricted exchange), while ille-
gitimacy consists of rampant beliefs that only self-interest through restricted exchange works without wider benefits.

In Table 5.6 the different aspects of citizenship, civil society, and
exchange are put together to portray the type of political system that
evolves in each regime type. Using state citizenship, five measures of
rights and two measures of obligations are ranked according to regime
type (H for the highest, M for the moderate or middle regime, and L
for the lowest average of regime types, and summarized in the bold face
capital letter). The picture that emerges of each regime type synthesizes
the previous discussion of political theory and its evidence in numerous
tables (see Figure 5.4).

Social democratic regimes have a high level of rights and obligations,
with high voluntary association membership and participation. Their
societies are tied together through open and overlapping forms of generalized exchange with a strong welfare state that does not overwhelm
but complements a strong civil society. They are relatively open to immigrants from other countries. Social democratic countries tend to be
corporatist political systems with strong generalized exchange in a system that has increasingly moved toward civic virtue and openness. They
follow an expansive democracy theory, but openness and generalized
exchange are brought together in sometimes a difficult combination.

Table 5.6. *Synthesizing citizenship, civil society and social exchange*

	Balance of rights and obligations in state citizenship:		Nature of civil society:		Types of societal exchange (table 4.1)	Political system and movement (table 5.1)
	Rights[a]	Obligations[b]	VA membership[c]	Social closure[d]		
1. *Social democratic regime*	HMMMH **M** Moderately high level of rights with a high level of obligations.	HH, **H**	H_tMHH, **H_t** High voluntary association membership in a moderately open society.	LMM **M**	Generalized: a. overlap b. open. Extensive use of general revenue in welfare state.	Expansive democracy that is open but unstable. Corporatist system moving toward civic virtue with moderate individualism.
2. *Traditional regime*	MHHHM **H** Moderate level of rights and obligations.	MH, **M**	LLLL **L** Low voluntary association membership in a closed society.	HHHH **H**	Generalized: a. mutually exclusive b. closed. Extensive use of insurance-based funds.	Communitarian theory; corporatist system with little movement toward civic virtue or individualism.
3. *Liberal regime*	LLLLL **L** Low level of rights and obligations.	LL **L**	H_tHMH, **H_t** Moderately high voluntary association membership in an open society.	MLL **L**	Restricted: a. overlap b. mutually exclusive. Both general revenue and insurance finance, but expenditures are low.	Liberal theory moving toward both civic virtue and individualism; Pluralist system moving toward civic virtue with strong individualism.

NOTES:
Letter scores below are averages of regime scores on variables indicated below and listed in previous tables. The averages are indicated by: L=low, M= moderate, H=high, H_t=tie with other regime; the summary of these averages is in bold.
[a] Rights (from table 5.3 except where indicated): Legal rights – Prisoners per 100,000 persons, high rights equals a low incarceration rate; Political rights – Voters as a percent of eligible citizens; Social rights – social transfers over GDP; Participation rights – works councils and codetermination; Human rights index from Humana (from table 2.5).
[b] Obligations (from table 2.5): Taxes as a percent of GNP; National service index.
[c] Civic participation (from table 5.5): Overall VA membership, Overall VA participation, VA membership without churches and unions; VA participation without churches and unions.
[d] Social closure (from table 5.2): Income inequality as measured by Gini index, social immobility, and naturalization rates in 1980-89.

Liberal regimes have a low level of rights and obligations, which are made up for by a high level of voluntary association activities, mainly by churches and non-profit social welfare agencies. Civil society is very active but not very critical in these countries, which are the most open in the world to immigrating strangers. Exchange processes in society are restricted to a large degree with both overlap and mutually exclusive

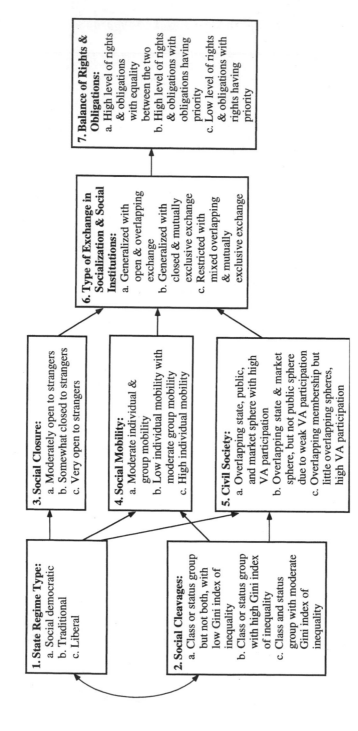

Figure 5.4. A model explaining the balance of rights and obligations in three regimes (a = social democratic; b = traditional; c = liberal)

exchanges occurring. Thus, these countries are based on liberal theory with pluralism enveloping the somewhat contradictory elements of civic virtue of voluntary groups and extreme individualism.

Traditional regimes probably have the highest level of rights and obligations, which may contribute to voluntary association activities in civil society being the weakest of the three different regime types. Social closure is strong with naturalization policies that allow only a small number of immigrants to become citizens, but this is consonant with high rights and obligations. After all it is easier for liberal regimes to offer citizenship to the world if they give few rights and ask for minimal obligations. Like the social democratic countries, traditional regimes rely on generalized exchange, but types of generalized exchange that are nearly opposite. Their generalized exchange is closed and done through groups that are largely mutually exclusive. The social welfare system operates in a similar way of relying on insurance-based funds that make membership and its boundaries patently clear. Traditional regimes are clearly based on communitarian theory with a corporatist system that encompasses much less civic virtue of voluntary groups in civil society than other regimes.

What may be surprising in the comparison of these three regimes is that social democratic regimes seem to violate some aspects of common trade-off theories. Liberal and traditional regimes tend to form a continuum whereby a country can be open and have low rights and requirements, or it can be closed and protect high rights and requirements. The social democratic countries are both quite open with very active voluntary sectors, but at the same time exhibit generalized exchange and high levels of rights and obligations. While this may be due to social democratic countries' small size and fear of external economic threats, or lower defense expenditures, social democratic countries demonstrate that openness and cooperation through generalized exchange is possible in a number of countries.

CONCLUSION

This chapter reconceptualizes and specifies the relationship between rights and obligations according to two different levels of balance. First, rights and obligations are nested within the political sphere that is intended to countervail the power of markets. This relationship may be more or less in balance depending on the efforts made by a country and society to equalize these two social institutions. As a result, no simple balancing relationship will exist between rights and obligations without consideration of what political compensation is being made to counter the effects of the market. Second, rights and obligations form a rough balance in different regime types. Liberal countries have low rights and low obligations, traditional countries have high rights and high obligations, and social democratic countries are in between. This was shown in a correlation of legal, political, social, and participation rights in eighteen countries. While further explanations are needed with other measures of rights and obligations, this analysis has shown the plausibility of a "relative" balance theory based on differing amounts of political power.

Another aspect of balance concerns the process through which it occurs. Rights and obligations fit into an ideal-type continuum between restricted and generalized exchange. Some societies may exhibit either extreme depending upon their history and structure of social relations, and any society exhibits a mix of restricted and generalized exchange at any one time. Social democratic societies and those traditional societies based on full corporatism exhibit trust based on generalized exchange with relatively closed class and status groups. Liberal societies generate trust through more restricted exchange with overlapping memberships in relatively open groups, but suffer the danger of atomistic selfishness with groups pursuing veto politics and narrow self-interest. But balance is complicated by exchange in that fulfilling obligations or rights may come immediately from the involved person or group, or it may come with considerable delay from a far distant and even unknown person or group. This makes conceptions of balance much more complicated than previous theories have indicated.

The approach outlined in this chapter bears on a number of citizenship controversies. First, the universalistic push for individual citizenship rights and obligations, while coming from solidaristic class and status group movements, has the ironic effect of reducing social solidarity and trust. The universalization of trust vitiates the mutuality of small group interaction upon which trust ultimately depends (Seligman 1992). The promotion of social mobility destroys solidarity in a similar way. Participation rights demonstrate a way to mitigate the universalizing tendencies of large bureaucracies and make small group participation or representation the foundation of political and economic institutions. This partially avoids the problems of alienation that have been assumed to be genetic to the welfare state, but not the effects of social mobility.

Second, the increasing demand that citizen obligations should be matched by clear and necessary rights plays directly into the very market-oriented, restricted exchange system that citizenship rights were designed to correct. Generalized exchange not only provides the trust for a mature view of citizenship that promotes equality, but it also promotes the social values of citizenship or civic virtue that the "demanding citizen" seems to lack. The consequences of state institutions and policies that avoid real participation (i.e., not a weak form of advising) and promote the "your tax buys this benefit" market approach (i.e., a check-off on tax forms designating where tax monies shall go) should be clear – a short-term contractual relationship of citizens to the state and little concern for other citizens' needs or interests. While free ridership by opportunistic citizens is an active concern of responsible citizens, states may enlarge this group of selfish citizens by promoting an explicit "buy and sell exchange system" between rights and obligations.

Third, the closure of nations by restricting immigration or of organizations by restricting employment or education leads to greater possibilities of generalized exchange and consensus. As Brubaker reminds us, citizenship is "not only an instrument of closure," but it is also "an object of closure" (1992, p. 31). Neo-corporatism in traditional and to some extent social democratic systems is more apt to provide this closure, while pluralist liberal regimes will not. Neo corporatism also leads to higher rights and obligations, on which immigrants tend to rely, but then adds moderate social closure toward political rights. Nonetheless, states can consider policies that will maximize closure and at the same time promote tolerance. This can especially be done by promoting neighborhoods and communities by making complementary rather than overlapping borders even if this is not optimal in other ways (i.e., efficiency). For instance, employment service, pension office, welfare office, health clinic, political jurisdictions (from city, to county, to federal), court boundaries, phone area codes, and many more boundaries can be made coterminous. This reinforces community and a sense of closure (i.e., an idea of who belongs) rather than dispersing citizens to offices throughout a larger region. Tolerance can be maintained by programs that promote the understanding of foreign cultures, and the active assimilation of aliens through naturalization and exchange programs. But they need to avoid massive immigration programs with little or no control, or suffer the diminution of generalized exchange.

6

Incremental Change in Citizenship over Decades: Power Resources, State Structures, Ideology, and External Forces

The power resources approach expects class to be one of the major determinants of conflicts of interest in Western societies, holds that inequality in the distribution of power resources is of central interest but assumes that the degree of inequality can vary over time and between countries, and accords political democracy an important role in the processing of conflicts of interest.

Walter Korpi (1989, pp. 309–10)

A "structured polity" approach to explaining the origins and transformation of national systems of social provisions . . . draws our attention to four kinds of processes: (1) the establishment and transformation of state and party organizations through which politicians pursue policy initiatives; (2) the effects of political institutions and procedures on the identities, goals, and capacities of social groups that become involved in the politics of social policy-making; (3) the fit . . . between the goals and capacities of various politically active groups, and the historically changing points of access and leverage allowed by a nation's political institutions; and (4) the ways in which previously established social policies affect subsequent politics.

Theda Skocpol (1992, p. 41)

Citizenship is the outcome of class struggles, war, migration and egalitarian ideologies.

Bryan Turner (1986a, p. 67)

Four approaches to the development of rights and obligations in advanced industrialized countries are brought together to form one model in this chapter. When dealing with "subjects" (i.e., internal non-citizens), one approach focuses on the strength of class and status groups in social movements, and another stresses the comparative capacities of state bureaucracies and institutions in creating, administering, and enforcing rights. Another approach considers univeralistic ideas of citizenship and party coalitions. In viewing non-citizens, a fourth approach focuses on state mobilization or reaction to external political and economic forces

– wars, depressions, or colonization – to affect the inclusion of foreigners into the realm of the nation.

The first approach – power resources theory – focuses on the dynamic engine of citizenship rights, which comes from those groups that lack rights.[1] Emerging citizens prepare the way for change in citizenship rights in two ways. First of all, new citizens enlarge the definition of personhood. This has come in incremental advances as the result of major waves of political action: eliminating property as a criterion of citizenship, then gender, ethnicity, race, disability, sexual preference, and even other issues. Second, each group of emerging citizens has different problems, and as a result each group demands different citizenship rights solutions. Social movements and interest groups representing these emerging citizens may be empowered or reduced by economic, demographic, ideological, or international developments.

The second approach – state-centric theory – focuses on constraints and opportunities afforded by state structures. States structures and institutions are crucibles in which citizenship rights are formed, and states are among the agents that protect and maintain citizenship rights. The different structures of executives, parliaments, bureaucracies, and courts have a tremendous impact on the structure and survival of citizenship rights. Although state structures are created at a specific time and may change, these structures often appear as constants or constraints on citizenship development. In comparative research, state structures lay bare the constraints or opportunity structures with changing points of access and leverage allowed by a nation's political institutions within which social movements, interest groups, and parties operate. State-centric theory also allows differential modes of state mobilization for leaders' and bureaucrats' interests with the effects of political institutions on their identities, goals, and power.

Third, ideologies and political parties are closely connected to interest group proposals, but they take on a cultural life of their own in comparisons between countries and regimes. Universalistic policies are much more oriented toward citizenship than more particularistic ideologies or those with little thematic unity. Ideologies must also be meshed with diverse ideas in coalition governments where compromises must be made. However, my approach still gives primacy to political economy forces with cultural elements taking a subordinate but important role.

The fourth approach of external effects involves war, colonization, and migration to colonizing and settler countries. Direct colonization creates contact with diverse cultures and nations with at least some intermarriage and cultural diffusion. Although colonization involves oppression, many natives will eventually be co-opted and become eligible for immigration and naturalization. In settler nations indigenous populations are stripped of their rights, especially land rights, and the state invites immigrants from cultures similar to that of the former colonizer to come and live. Finally, universalistic ideology plays an important role in social democratic states where colonization and settling have played little or no role. Social democracy opens itself to asylum seekers and guest workers who then can obtain naturalization at a much higher rate than in traditional regimes. This external approach to citizenship is by far the least developed though Turner (1986a, pp. 71–3, 1993a, pp. 14–15), Janoski and Glennie (1995a, b), and Soysal (1994, pp. 36–44, 136–62) stress its importance.

These approaches focus on decades mainly in the post–World War II period rather than on centuries, which makes them more useful and specific in formulating hypotheses about the recent growth or decline of citizenship rights. Ten to fifty years allows enough time for development to take place (e.g., pension policies change over the post–World War II period) but avoids the multiple stages of development that make political economy entirely different and difficult (e.g., one can hardly speak of left party power causing pensions in the 1700s). The first two theories are sometimes thought to be mutually exclusive explanations of policy, but although they overlap to some degree, they primarily provide complementary explanations. One covers *pressures* that enact policy, and the other constrains the *forms* that policy will take. The third approach covers how much social closure a particular society might have due to war and migration and covers both pressures and forms from an entirely different perspective of "looking inward."

MEANS OF THE EXTENSION OF CITIZENSHIP

Citizenship rights may be advanced in four ways: discrimination extensions of citizenship by social movements from below; public goods and elite extensions of citizenship through bureaucracies and policy experts from above; sacrifice extensions of citizenship from below caused by state mobilization for war dictated from above, and naturalization extensions of citizenship to foreigners (see Figure 6.1).

First, *discrimination extension* concerns the development of social demands by groups that have been excluded from citizenship rights and obligations. In social research, this view often focuses on why diverse discrimination patterns develop in different countries. In some sense, this question goes back to the initial formation of the nation-state and the state's relationships to ethnic, racial, and other nations. In settler countries, immigrating colonials deal with indigenous natives and the motherland, but the colonizers often encourage slavery and large waves of immigration. In some European nations and Japan, populations are

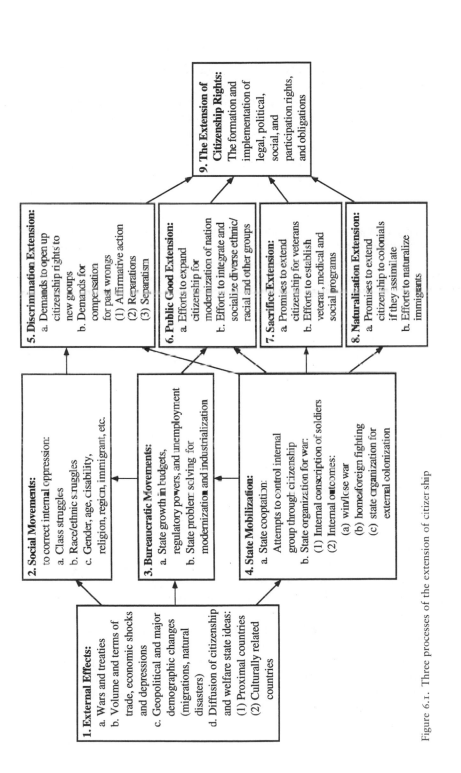

Figure 6.1. Three processes of the extension of citizenship

9. The Extension of Citizenship Rights: The formation and implementation of legal, political, social, and participation rights, and obligations

5. Discrimination Extension:
a. Demands to open up citizenship rights to new groups
b. Demands for compensation for past wrongs
 (1) Affirmative action
 (2) Reparations
 (3) Separatism

6. Public Good Extension:
a. Efforts to expand citizenship for modernization of nation
b. Efforts to integrate and socialize diverse ethnic/racial and other groups

7. Sacrifice Extension:
a. Promises to extend citizenship for veterans
b. Efforts to establish veteran, medical and social programs

8. Naturalization Extension:
a. Promises to extend citizenship to colonials if they assimilate
b. Efforts to naturalize immigrants

2. Social Movements: to correct internal oppression:
a. Class struggles
b. Race/ethnic struggles
c. Gender, age, disability, religion, region, immigrant, etc.

3. Bureaucratic Movements:
a. State growth in budgets, regulatory powers, and unemployment
b. State problem solving for modernization and industrialization

4. State Mobilization:
a. State cooptation: Attempts to control internal group through citizenship
b. State organization for war:
 (1) Internal conscription of soldiers
 (2) Internal outcomes:
  (a) win/lose war
  (b) home/foreign fighting
  (c) state organization for external colonization

1. External Effects:
a. Wars and treaties
b. Volume and terms of trade, economic shocks and depressions
c. Geopolitical and major demographic changes (migrations, natural disasters)
d. Diffusion of citizenship and welfare state ideas:
 (1) Proximal countries
 (2) Culturally related countries

more settled, and conflicts tend to be based more on class (or caste for the Gypsies and Burakumin).

Second, *public goods extension* takes place by technocratic bureaucrats and social policy experts from the academy who propose solutions to social problems in the interests of the public. Professionals offer reasons for different social policies that will improve sanitation, diet, income maintenance, employment, and political participation. These programs may also benefit the careers of professionals and organizational growth of various agencies, but whatever latent benefits, the policies must be justified in terms of some public goods. For the most part, these forces stem from within the state and policy-making communities (Burstein 1991; Knoke et al. 1996). Some effects may come from the diffusion of policy innovations; however, these international effects are always mediated through internal policy domains that may resist many influences from abroad.

Third, the *sacrifice extension* of citizenship results from the external mobilization for war and is pressed by veterans and civilians who have risked life and limb for the country. After the country's soldiers suffer death and injury in order to promote national interests, war service clearly establishes their personal or family needs for social and other rights. Because veterans' difficulties often stem from completing onerous obligations to the state, veterans have a very strong claim to citizenship rights. However, due to differing national circumstances of war and internal politics, states can respond to these needs with particularistic veterans' or universalistic citizens' rights.

Fourth, the *naturalization extension* of citizenship brings groups from outside the country into citizenship status. This occurs as the result of state mobilization for war and control of weaker countries, or it may result from state efforts to populate a country taken from an indigenous population. This extension of citizenship takes place through relatively short processes of marriage, war service, or other qualifications such as being from a specifically recognized country (e.g., Ireland to the United Kingdom, or Finland to Sweden), and a longer process of naturalization by learning the language, customs, and politics of a new country or nation.

These four methods of extending citizenship fit into the power resources, state-centric, and naturalization theories. The first extension of discrimination with social movements fighting for personhood and interest groups obtaining specific policies corresponds with power resources theory. The second extension concerning public goods reflects the constraining bureaucracies and state structures of state-centric theory. The third extension involving sacrifice ties both theories together with state mobilization. It has one set of effects through pro- or anti-war movements and veterans programs, as male veterans from dominant groups form status groups to pursue their own rights agenda, and subordinated minorities press for equal rights after completing their war service obligations. It has another set of effects through changing state structures in the military and central state, which are often institutionalized through historical conflicts. The naturalization extension results from state mobilization, which clearly involves state-centric theories delineating the state structures and institutions that constrain naturalization processes. But it also involves power resources theory in describing the social movements that eventually develop among the foreign-born population and the naturalized population that eventually represents their ethnic groups.

CONFLICT AND THE MOBILIZATION OF RESOURCES

Each approach to citizenship involves considerable conflict. Although citizenship theory has been criticized for playing down conflict, it is clearly a central part of citizenship theory. Conflict enters into citizenship rights theory at three entirely different levels. First, newly emerging and established interest groups battle over the extension of "personhood" to new citizens and the advancement of citizenship rights. Conflicts take place between both class- and status-based groups. Class groups include trade unions and employers, left and right parties, and the intelligentsia. Status groups cover ethnic, racial, women, religious, and veterans groups (Turner 1988, pp. 42–64) and may crosscut class groups rather than only dwelling within class groups (Parkin 1982, pp. 98–9). Usually status groups are based on largely ascriptive characteristics (race, ethnicity, tribe, or gender), but they can be somewhat volitional or achieved (veteran and gay).[2] Status groups are clearly "not the creations of the division of labor or the productive system" (Parkin 1982, p. 98), but the main point is not so much the generation of the group, but its composition: how much does the group crosscut class lines and pursue goals at least somewhat different from class groups? The politics of citizenship will be simpler when either class or status dominate; politics will be more complicated and often fragmented when powerful class and status groups are mixed. Thus, conflict between these two generic groups produces diverse social policy struggles.

Second, inherent theoretical conflicts can occur between rights. Rights in the abstract can contradict, especially in how they are bundled into ideologies for established and emerging interest groups. For instance, taxation violates property rights, health care may violate freedom of religion for Christian Scientists, and affirmative action may violate universalistic citizenship concerns about equal treatment before the law. Or on a deeper level, the liberal reliance on individual rights has serious consequences for ethnic groups that would pursue group rights through more communitarian assumptions. Following Marshall's insights, Fraser and Gordon (1993) explain the more general conflict between civil (legal and political) rights and social (social and by implication participation) rights. These theoretical conflicts are sometimes useful in analyzing specific social policy outcomes, but they must be grounded in group action or run the danger of reification.

Finally, many argue that citizenship and capitalism are inherently in conflict (Pinker 1981; Barbalet 1988, p. 77; Quadagno 1987, pp. 114–15). According to Lipset, Marshall conceptualizes conflict between citizenship and class (1981, p. x) and even sees a "war" between citizenship and capitalism (1981, pp. xxii, 16). Esping-Andersen (1985) sees this conflict as occurring between politics and markets. Citizenship rights themselves can be perceived as being divided between capital and labor: legal and political rights largely result from bourgeois power in the rise of capitalism, while social and participation rights often come from worker power in the welfare state. However, using this more abstract line of argument alone can also lead to the reification of rights (i.e., rights develop according to their own internal logic) and gloss over actual developments. Focusing only on capitalism and citizenship also tends to downplay the role of status groups, which often do not fit the capitalist-citizenship dimension. For instance, we can hardly characterize women's or veterans' battles for social programs as primarily a conflict between citizenship and class.

Thus, citizenship theory involves conflicts between interest groups, between theoretical outlooks toward rights and obligations, and between capitalism and citizenship itself. More powerful analyses in the future will be sensitive to each of these multiple conflicts between rights.

A MODEL OF CITIZENSHIP RIGHTS DEVELOPMENT

The model of the internal development of citizenship presented here is based on social demands and state structures with the subordinated influences of ideology and external events. The development of citizenship rights can be generally explained by broad avenues of political economy with complex interactions of status and class group demands. State structures emanate from the coercion path of state growth through state institutions structured through policy domains and streams. In discussing the role of political regime types in developing policy, I will offer a number of hypotheses regarding the twenty-to-thirty-year development of citizenship rights. The two main factors – social demands and state formation – and the subordinate influence of citizenship rights ideology under parties and coalitions explain citizenship rights development.[3]

Incremental Change in Citizenship over Decades

These factors cause citizenship rights to develop in diverse ways, and reverses as well as extensions are possible.[4] An outline of the theory can be seen in Figure 6.2 (Janoski 1990). American, German, and Swedish examples are used to illustrate each regime type in this approach to the explanation of citizenship rights development.

Social Demands by Social Movements and Interest Groups

Socially rooted demands emanating from class and status group struggles are most frequently used by sociologists to explain social policy (Korpi 1989; Esping-Andersen 1990; Shalev 1983).[5] As social demands came from class and status group pressures, labor unions pushed for recognition and extension of the welfare state, and senior citizens represented by their votes and/or those of their sons and daughters created pressure for pensions. In Germany and Sweden, class demands came through labor unions demanding citizenship rights. For instance, the "worker question," which dominated social policy discussion in Sweden and Germany during industrialization, led to class demands for social policy advances. The major difference between the two countries, however, was that the Swedish Social Democrats were able to forge an alliance with the farmers and the agrarian party in less industrialized Sweden, while the German Social Democrats were unable to do so in heavily industrialized Germany.[6]

Status groups in the United States demanded increases in citizenship rights with less success. Status had a double emphasis due to the massive immigration of European peasants and the enslavement of African Americans centuries well before the welfare state. The result before World War II was a "socialization emphasis" in the American welfare state that pushed social unity through homogenizing high schools and social work programs, from which African Americans were most often excluded (Janoski 1990). After World War II, social rights programs emphasized transfer payments and some employment programs for blacks, while many ethnic immigrants had largely made it into the working or middle classes. The native American workers, including the second generation of earlier immigrants, pursued defensive actions through craft unions, veterans movements, and upward mobility before World War II. Although trade unions pursued a more unified approach after the war, social demands remained split by the crosscutting demands of status (especially race, ethnicity, and gender) and class.

These differences can be seen more generally for the countries in each of the three regime types in Table 6.1. The social democratic countries have the highest trade union strength (62.8% in column 1) and high extension of collective bargaining agreements (81.0%), and traditional regimes are not far behind in union strength (46.4%) with even larger

149

Table 6.1. *Power resources, social movements and state structures in three regimes*

Regimes and countries (ranked by column 1)	Power resources variables					State-centric variables		
	(1) Union strength/ CB range	(2) Left party power	(3) Demonstrations	(4) Riots	(5) Franchise as organizing issue[a]	(6) Self-administration	(7) Strong ministries-labor[a]	(8) Proportional rep.[a]
Social democratic								
Sweden	82/83%	45%	2.4	0.9	Y	2	Y	Y
Denmark	71/–	45	5.8	1.2	Y	1	Y	Y
Norway	62/75	49	4.2	0.3	Y	2	Y	Y
Finland	65/95	27	0.9	0.9	Y	2	y	Y
Netherlands	34/71	31	1.3	0.6	Y	2	Y	Y
Average	*62.8/81.0*	*39.4*	*2.92*	*0.78*	*3.0*	*1.88*	*2.8*	*3.0*
Traditional								
Austria	59/98	51	2.1	2.6	Y	2	Y	Y
Belgium	73/90	30	5.7	4.5	Y	0	Y	Y
Italy	40/–	42	3.0	5.4	Y	0	y	Y
Germany	38/90	44	3.7	1.7	Y	2	Y	Y
France	22/92	28	7.1	3.2	Y	1	y	Y
Average	*46.4/92.5*	*34.6*	*3.90*	*3.10*	*3.0*	*0.86*	*2.6*	*3.0*

Liberal								
Australia	52/80	43	4.8	0.7	N	0	n	N
Canada	33/38	9	1.4	1.4	N	0	n	N
Japan	32/23	33	1.8	1.2	Y	0	n	Y
Switzerland	32/53	25	6.5	2.4	Y	0.5	N	N
United States	23/18	0	10.8	4.1	N	0	N	N
Average	*34.4/42.4*	*22.0*	*5.06*	*1.96*	*1.2*	*0.10*	*0.6*	*0.6*
Mixed								
Ireland	53/–	14	31.3	4.0	Y	1	N	Y
United Kingdom	50/47	44	12.3	6.5	N	0	y	N
New Zealand	43/67	50	6.7	0.4	N	0	y	N

NOTES:

[a] Y=yes, y=maybe yes, n=maybe no, N = strong no. The letters are averaged by assigning scores: Y=3, y=2, n=1, N=0. CONCEPTS AND SOURCES (by column number):

(1) Trade union strength is the percentage unionized 1970-85 with the following exceptions: Austria 1985, Finland 1983-5, Denmark 1984-5, France 1983-5, Norway 1974 and 1985, and United States 1985 (Bean 1989), the extension of collective bargaining circa 1990 (OECD 1994, p. 173).

(2) The percentage of left party power is for 1970-85 and comes from Cook and Paxton (1992) and national sources. The communist party is counted only in Italy and France and the United States excludes the Democratic party.

(3) Demonstrations per 1,000,000 citizens is the average number of demonstrations from 1953-77 divided by the average population (Taylor and Jodice 1983, Taylor and Hudson 1972).

(4) Riots per 1,000,000 citizens is the average number of riots from 1948-77 divided by the average population multiplied by 1,000,000 (Taylor and Jodice 1983, Taylor and Hudson 1972).

(5) The franchise as a labor organizing issue in the early 1900s.

(6) Self-administration in the welfare state scored a maximum of 2 for welfare and labor market policy.

(7) Strong ministry or department of labor and weak veterans affairs department.

(8) Proportional representation that allows small parties to form and be represented in the legislature.

extensions of bargaining agreements (92.5%). Liberal regimes are much lower in trade union organization (34.4%) and bargaining extensions (42.4%). In terms of left party power, social democratic (39.4% in column 2) and traditional regimes (34.6%) are both much higher than liberal regimes (22.0%). While liberal countries lack trade union or left party power, they tend to be higher with demonstrations and riots (5.06 in column 3) than social democratic (2.92) and traditional (3.90) regimes, but most of this effect comes from the United States with its more crosscutting status groups. Thus, the effects of class power can be seen in trade union power and more ordered industrial relations, while the crosscutting effects of group power based on class or status lead to greater reliance on demonstrations and social movements.

Korpi has stressed the impact of the labor movement on the development of state policies, and this has been shown to be the case in much of Europe. He has been criticized for not including social movements other than the labor movement, but gender, ethnic, and racial movements can easily be brought into the theory as competing and/or cooperating social movements. Turner has backed this approach toward social movements and citizenship in theoretical developments.

Integrating social movements into a model with state structures in a theory of citizenship brings civil society into play since social movements emanate from the public sphere of individuals and groups who coalesce around a group goal in order to oppose recognized interest groups and different state structures. Thus, the structure of civil society has a tremendous impact on the role that social movements may play. In liberal societies, social movements play an important role in breaking into the business-as-usual lobbying of established interest groups. In the United States, the winner-take-all political system makes third and subsequent parties extremely difficult and frustrating to establish. Consequently, social movements become an frequent outlet for frustration and the development of new rights. If successful, social movements become absorbed by a dominant political party, and their lobbyists are listened to in day-to-day affairs in the capital. Unsuccessful movements may continue without impact if their social base is strong, but others may simply die. Emphasis on social movements is due to a fertile mix of classes and status groups because of an openness to industrialization, tolerance of social mobility through frequent occupational changes, and an openness to immigration and new status groups. Thus, social movements play a stronger role in liberal countries than in the other two regimes.

Social democratic systems operate in an entirely different way. New ideas and concerns become represented comparatively easily due to proportional elections and the formation of minor parties in their system. Social movement involvement can take place in three ways. First, social movements lead to new political parties, but for the most part these parties remain small and marginal. Only in a few cases do these parties grow and develop – labor or social democratic parties are the primary example as yet to be followed by another mass party. A successful social movement and political party can bring about the corporatist system and place their interest groups in major policy roles. Other parties including the greens (environmental parties) have not yet achieved such a role. While multiple parties absorbing social movements is a source of stability, it is also a source of rigidity in that other and often smaller social movements find it hard to break into the corporatist system. Centralized corporatism may also become so separated from its grassroots members that wildcat strike waves within the labor movement may also result (Wilson 1990, p. 70; Otter 1983; Bergmann and Müller-Jentsch 1983; Jacobi, Keller, and Müller-Jentsch 1992; Kjellberg 1992; Rucht 1991; Eyerman and Jamison 1991).

Second, social movements in corporatist systems can lead to political parties that form coalitions with established parties. These parties gain some access to direct corporate bargaining, but their role may be strategically large or kept quite small. If the small parties are critical to coalition success, they have an influence on at least one of the corporatist partners. And third, corporatist systems channel social movement issues and energies into the corporatist mechanisms for conflict resolution (Wilson 1990). This may be a less preferred outcome to non-labor activists due to the denigration of movement militancy and energy, and because the corporatist social partners control the process. This is another corporatist equivalent to issue absorption in a pluralist system. Thus, representation through political and social democracy will be greater in social democratic and traditional regimes than liberal regimes because of these economic and political institutions that channel conflict.

Hypothesis 6.1: Social Movements under Stability: Liberal regimes will demonstrate high social movement activity with protest demonstrations and riots, and these activities will tend toward particularistic rights and immunities (e.g., affirmative action rights for blacks, special education for the disabled, etc.). Social democratic and traditional regimes will channel social conflict through class- or status-based institutions that bargain over wages and benefits, and other conflict will be represented through additional political parties participating in coalition bargaining.

Hypothesis 6.2: Political and Social Democracy under Stability: Social democratic arrangements in the postwar period are established by slightly more politically democratic institutions and stronger attempts to institutionalize economic democracy at many different levels, especially social and participation rights. Liberal countries are characterized by much less economic democracy.[7]

Citizenship and Civil Society

During periods of crisis when new conflicts arise, especially from status groups and new class groups, institutions must change quickly. Traditional regimes are more elitist and have great difficulties with changing their institutions. The more fragmentary nature of liberal regimes allows them to make these adjustments under uncertainty more easily. Social democratic regimes appear to be more flexible with their institutions; however, in many ways they have not been as severely tested as traditional regimes due to their largely semiperipheral status in the world system. As a result of these previously effective institutions, especially those solely oriented toward class that are somewhat brittle during periods of momentous change, the hypotheses reverse their positions for each regime under crisis.

> *Hypothesis 6.3: Social Movements in Conflict: Despite increasing violence and social movement activities during a major sociopolitical crisis, social movements under liberal regimes will be less violent than traditional regimes.*[8]

> *Hypothesis 6.4: Political and Social Democracy during Periods of Crisis: Liberalism will be more effective in implementing new democratic institutions under crisis and more democracy will be preserved. Traditional regimes will lose major citizenship rights. Social democratic regimes will be in between.*

State Structures and Institutional Cultures

Second, the formation of the state, which consists of administrative, judicial, educational, military, and representative institutions, also explains major comparative differences between nations (Skocpol and Orloff 1986, p. 241; Alber 1987, pp. 200–7). State formation for the purposes of social policy consists of the bureaucratic structures of the welfare state, the form of political parties, and the power of labor-oriented offices in the cabinet.[9] Where the bureaucracy precedes the franchise, a powerful organizational precedent is set that becomes amenable to self-administration and a strong ministry of labor. Where the franchise precedes the bureaucracy, third-party bureaucracies are implemented to overcome patronage, and labor has a much weaker position in the government. Because of divergent state structures, countries vary on "state capacities" to rigorously pursue social policies (Skocpol and Orloff 1986; Quadagno 1987, p. 119; Ruggie 1984).

Self-administration in the welfare state has major implications for citizenship rights. In Weimar Germany, the unions and employer associations self-administered social policy from pensions to health insurance in a neo-corporatist structure of social welfare with participation rights.

Incremental Change in Citizenship over Decades

The formation of self-administration in Germany was aided by the early creation of an elite bureaucracy, which was penetrated by trade union and employer representatives in self-administration, partly because the franchise was an organizing issue (Janoski 1990).[10] Union representatives gradually replaced the employers or foremen as chairmen of the funds, and these institutions – covering pensions, industrial injury benefits, health insurance, and other programs – became known as the "third pillar" of the German labor movement. These state structures left an indelible imprint on the German welfare state.[11]

The development of welfare state structures in the United States went instead from patronage structures to third-party bureaucracies. Because an elaborate bureaucracy did not form until after the franchise was achieved, patronage jobs in the bureaucracy were an expected benefit from government. But the Progressive Movement lashed back against widespread patronage and corruption with a reform program: social work and the high school to socialize the "immigrants," and a civil service to promote employment by merit in the government (Skocpol 1992; Janoski 1990; Schefter 1977).

Self-administration did not develop in the United States. The civil service guarded against corruption and patronage but also latently prevented labor/management participation. For instance, the 1933 Wagner-Peyser Act mandated federal and state advisory councils on a tripartite basis; however, Secretary of Labor Frances Perkins and others ignored the councils and pushed the civil service into the agency. Thus, employer and union input was blocked by appointed bureaucrats (Skocpol and Orloff 1986, pp. 241–3; Schefter 1977, pp. 423–9; Robertson 1981, pp. 121, 150–5). The results in these two countries were weak welfare state bureaucracies administered by middle-class bureaucrats in the United States, and strong self-administered bureaucracies administered by labor and employer representatives in Germany.

The development of the state was quite different in Sweden. Although some early laws were passed on factory inspection (1889), state subsidies for sickness funds (1891), and old-age pensions (1913), the state superstructure of participatory bureaucracies did not really develop (Olson 1988, pp. 4–5). Although a strong and centralized state had emerged out of Sweden's imperial past, the most significant development was when the trade unions obtained complete control over most of the unemployment funds and, as a result, were seen as the authority in charge of unemployment compensation. This is domination rather than self-administration, and it allowed the labor movement to grow in strength and penetrate the bureaucracy (Rothstein 1991, 1995). Self-administration eventually developed in the Labor Market Administration (AMS) with the tripartite participation of labor, management, and the state (Rothstein 1995, pp. 74–100). However, much of the rest of the welfare state remained under the control of the state and the dominant party coalition controlled by the Social Democrats.[12]

The bureaucracy's control over most of the welfare state was, however, strongly constrained by powerful neo-corporatist bargaining. In its historical development, much of the past bureaucracy was seen as biased, and new organizations and personnel were created (Stråth and Torstendahl 1992, pp. 28–30). For instance, the AMS has a reputation for hiring union representatives, much like the Veterans Administration in the United States has a reputation for hiring veterans. Thus, Sweden does not have the powerful continuity of participation in welfare bureaucracies that Germany exhibits. Further, trade unions as an essential part of neo-corporatist bargaining have a strong impact on the implementation of policy in many other welfare agencies because the Social Democrats have been in power for such a long time. Rather than internal participation through self-administration or works councils, Sweden exhibited strong external participation. As Stråth and Torstendahl put it: "The basic network of the state of participatory capitalism consisted of a strong government, preferably with a stable majority in parliament, a rapidly expanding administration with strong vertical integration, and a consensus among capital and labour that an increase in the purchasing power of the working class was needed" (1992, p. 30). Thus, state formation in Sweden is superficially similar to state development in Germany but very much unlike state processes in the United States.

At a higher level, the German Ministry of Labor was powerful, the United States Department of Labor was weak, while the Swedish Ministry of Labor was again in between. During the Weimar Republic, the Ministry of Labor administered a wide array of policies: pensions, labor law, child welfare law, job creation policies, unemployment compensation and relief, veterans' benefits, war widow benefits, public housing, some job training programs, and medical programs. This vast range of policies completely outstripped the scope of other labor ministries in most other countries (Barclay 1974, p. 248). The ministry's power also included final say over arbitration in industrial disputes and strong leverage in the labor market with monopoly power over job placements.

In the United States, the Department of Labor has always been weak. A cabinet-level Department of Labor was not established until 1913, and its mission was diffuse (Robertson 1981, p. 80). During the New Deal and later, the department lost regulatory functions over railway labor, union organizing, coal mining, industrial mediation, immigration, children, and job creation (Lowi 1979, p. 82; Grossman 1967; Lombardi 1942). Although it gained occupational safety and some mining duties in the 1970s, the Department of Labor still remains weak.

In Sweden, the Ministry of Labor was much stronger than in the United States, but weaker than in Germany. The Swedish ministry controlled some important policies, but not family allowances and educational programs for immigrants. However, with very strong labor and social democratic party power, the Swedish labor movement was able to penetrate many different ministries rather than just one. As a result, Prime Minister Olof Palme could claim that all government ministries are ministries of labor. Many other aspects of state formation also affect citizenship rights, but these examples are enough to illustrate the point.

The state-centric variables can be seen for the other countries in Table 6.1. Both social democratic and traditional countries had the franchise as a union organizing demand, while liberal countries already had the franchise, so this did not help blend trade union and democratic causes (see column 5). Consequently, the early adoption of mass voting proved to be a detriment to social policy development for the working classes in liberal countries. Self-administration with tripartite control by labor, management, and the state is strongly present in social democratic countries (1.88 in column 6), less so in traditional (0.86) countries, and hardly at all in liberal regimes (0.10). The ministries of labor are strong while the ministries of veterans affairs are weak in the traditional and social democratic countries, but the reverse holds in most of the liberal countries (see column 7). State structures of proportional representation were widely available in social democratic and traditional countries, but much less so in liberal nations (see column 8). Thus, state-centric variables help explain social policy developments in these three regimes even though they are frequently difficult to quantify.

Three basic factors address the variations of policy formation factors within state-centric theories – policy domains, issue trade-offs and political thresholds, and policy streams. First, within each country different *policy domains* may produce entirely different policy results (Burstein 1991; Knoke and Laumann 1982).[13] A policy domain is a substantive area of the policy formation, implementation, and evaluation process that attains some closure with regard to other policy domains, (e.g., much of the discussion in the previous section has delineated a labor policy domain) (Knoke et al. 1996). Within a policy domain, experts and politicians, who have differential occupational socialization, interpret policy goals, theories, and methods in similar ways.

Each policy domain develops around a substantive set of issues, encourages the establishment of organizations from interest groups to government bureaucracies, and develops a specific kind of institutional culture. For instance, the American health policy domain includes the American Medical Association, medical schools, the National Institutes of Health, and other organizations specific to their area. The labor market policy domain includes the American Vocational Association, state employment offices, the Employment and Training Section of the Department of Labor, the AFL-CIO, and so on. Each domain tends to have a dominant professional orientation: medical researchers and doctors dominate the health domain, and program administrators and labor economists dominate the labor market domain. As one might expect, medical doctors as a group have different worldviews and much greater resources than labor economists, and consequently their incentives and motivations differ substantially. The power and culture of each one of these occupational groups may vary considerably from country to country. For instance, the presence of self-administration brings unions and labor researchers into many decision-making arenas that they might not otherwise see. As a result, the political economy and institutionalization of each sector will differ by country.

Because domain cultures may vary greatly based on differential occupational socialization and the influence of diverse groups, issue creation and recognition will be structured in entirely different ways. Political culture arguments as they are often made at a national and policy-wide level are not so applicable. Instead of a cultural code that is embedded in the political identity of a nation and applies to the centuries of history, the production of culture approach is much more useful, especially in occupational socialization and the construction of issue networks (Petersen 1979; Dimaggio 1994; Knoke et al. 1996). Although we find general variations between nations in political culture, more finely tuned studies of policy domains will find domain cultural factors being more important in many comparisons. This approach is consonant with state-centric theory in many ways and is an extension of their work concerning domain culture.

The second approach to diversities in policy comes from *trade-off theories*. Nations have only so much in the way of resources, and when they are generous on one type of policy, they must be stingy with others. Some of these trade-offs will be consistent like the war and welfare trade-off, but variations will occur because countries make compromises among policies at different levels. Other trade-offs may be unique, such as the active labor market policy and public assistance trade-off in Sweden, or the failed social welfare and labor reform trade-off in American politics. Trade-off theory has close ties to power resources theory since it involves strategies of interest groups and political parties. But trade-off variations are between domain relations, while most of the policy domain explanation is due to within domain processes. These trade-offs are connected to political thresholds. The typical model of citizenship policy assumes that social demands, bureaucratic pressures, and state structures exert a continuous and effective pressure on the political mechanisms in various countries so that policy will be produced. To some degree this becomes a bit of a transmission belt theory that does not recognize the overall organization of policy actors and institutions. Trade-off agreements must take these issues past a critical threshold before policies will actually be passed.

A third factor, which also causes the direct input-output model to derail, is the contingent position of policy streams.[14] Developed by Kingdon who drew on the garbage can model of organizations, the policy streams approach indicates that policy will be enacted (or implemented or put on the agenda) when three unrelated policy streams converge (Kingdon 1984; Sabatier 1991; Cohen and March 1974). The *problem stream* consists of social science and journalistic identification of real world problems and actual efforts made to solve them. The *policy stream* concerns bureaucrats, advocates, researchers, and practicing professionals in a specific policy domain proposing possible policy solutions. And the *political stream* consists of elected and interest group representatives who present policy positions and eventually enact legislation, and politically active bureaucrats and professionals in the field who implement and evaluate policies. The political stream is consistent with the coalition issue discussed above, but the two other streams are additions to most explanations of policy, although case studies often refer to them.[15]

Real political action comes with the convergence of these three policy streams. What Kingdon's approach suggests is that an interaction effect variable is necessary in addition to problem recognition and political power. Consequently, the confluence of these three policy streams makes the analysis of policy considerably more contingent and removes the deterministic element of the building forces of any one element.[16] In liberal countries, the streams tend to converge much less often, and when they do, little time is available for action. Constant mobilization of policy and polities is necessary in the face of major problems. For instance, Knoke et al. (1996, p. 26) found that German labor policy domains with self-administration and codetermination had more integrated labor-management communication than United States and Japanese policy domains. Disciplined parties, incorporated interest groups, and interpenetrating bureaucrats who can maintain a foothold in politics and the civil service also give many European countries an ability to draw the policy and political streams together.

Hypothesis 6.5: In social democracy and traditional regimes: (1) policy domains are tighter with more communication, (2) political thresholds are lower with more trade-offs possible, and (3) the problem, expert, and political streams are much more closely linked than in liberal regimes.

Citizenship and Civil Society

Synthesizing both the power resources and state-centric theories from the perspective of citizenship theory brings social movements and their constraints to the forefront. Although Marshall spoke of conflict and the labor movement, he seemed to do so at a distance and with little or no generality to include social movements based on race, religion, gender, or disability. Turner not only brought social movements to the forefront of citizenship theory, but also made them the major carrier of social change through "a process of social conflict and negotiation" (1986a, p. 85). Thus, bringing power resources theory together with state-centric theory puts social movements in the driver's seat of innovation in citizenship rights and obligations. Marshall said little of state structures directly; however, he had much to say about the king and the state. The reason he could not come up with an explicit state-centric theory was probably because he was only studying one country – the United Kingdom. For state-centric theory, comparisons with other states are not only helpful but are the strongest application of this theory.

Although some may protest that this synthesis is contradictory, others would maintain that it can be complementary (Hicks and Misra 1993; Huber, Ragin, and Stephens 1993; Janoski 1990). Both social demand and state processes operate at the same time but in different ways. Social movements based on power resources provide the *pressure for change* in citizenship rights. State structures form constraints and bureaucracies often constitute the *form of change* in citizenship. These two processes can be totally compatible (Janoski 1990).[17] The trade unions, women suffragettes, or civil rights protestors demand change, but the bureaucratic experts in particular state structures constrain opportunities and provide the vehicle for that change. There are arguments that the bureaucracy co-opts change, and this may constitute a conflict between pressure and form. The co-optation approach is characteristic of elite theory (Domhoff 1986/87, 1987; Piven and Cloward 1979), and it is in opposition to both the state-centric and power resources theories. However, in many cases there is little conflict between form and pressure.[18] For instance, old-age pensions could have been implemented in many different ways depending on state structures and bureaucracies in different countries, but whatever the country, social movement pressure led to the change, which created a policy that social movements demanded. This does not resolve all conflicts between these sometime competing theories, but it does show that for the most part they are compatible.

Ideologies, Parties, and Coalitions

A third group of factors wedged between power resources and state-centric theories – citizenship ideologies and structure of parties – make a major difference in the development of citizenship rights ([4] in Figure 6.2). Germany and the United States are at opposite ends of the spectrum on this issue, and while Sweden is more similar to Germany, some critical differences make coalition outcomes totally different. The social democratic parties in Germany (SPD) and Sweden (SAP) were not hard to form under a proportional system of government, and both parties gained strength in the early 1900s. The German SPD took power in 1918–19, but the Swedish SAP had to wait much longer (Lewin 1988). A major factor in the social democratic parties' drive to power was their ability to combine the demand for working-class franchise with union organizing. With proportional representation as a precondition that enabled a labor party to solidify with a small percentage of the vote, union organizing and political demands marched shoulder to shoulder in formulating a relatively consistent ideology. The system also led to party discipline and an ideological approach to politics in both countries.

American democracy, however, was well established before industrialization. The unions and radical parties could not make the franchise a working-class issue and thus lost a major opportunity for ideological convergence. Because of winner-take-all elections and the separation of powers, new parties were very difficult to start because losers lose everything, rather than being represented on the basis of the proportion of votes they garner. Because small parties could only be symbolic in the United States, third parties were brief episodes in this American system. National interests converge as consensus parties are subject to multiple class- and status-based interest groups rather than developing specific ideologies and party discipline of their own. Craft, industrial, and socialist ideologies clashed among themselves and further battled with gender, ethnic, and racial ideologies. Market ideologies stressing restricted exchange are especially strong in comparison to Europe (see the strong success of Milton Friedman's *Free to Choose* in the United States versus the lesser popularity of Rüdiger Soldwedel's *More Market in the Labor Market* in Germany). Thus, the American party system encouraged a fragmentary rather than comprehensive approach to ideology (Lowi 1984; Brody 1983; Lipset 1977).

In Germany and Sweden, the social democratic parties and the unions developed a coherent ideology of class-based social policy with a foundation in participation rights. In Germany, Fritz Napthali (1929) provided the structure and goals of self-administration and Eduard Heinemann (1929) the social theory of capitalism. Napthali saw self-administration pervading many areas of social policy and thought that the 1927 employment service law would lead to the spread of self-administration and participation throughout society. Swedish ideology was not as well developed at this time, and Swedish labor, as well as

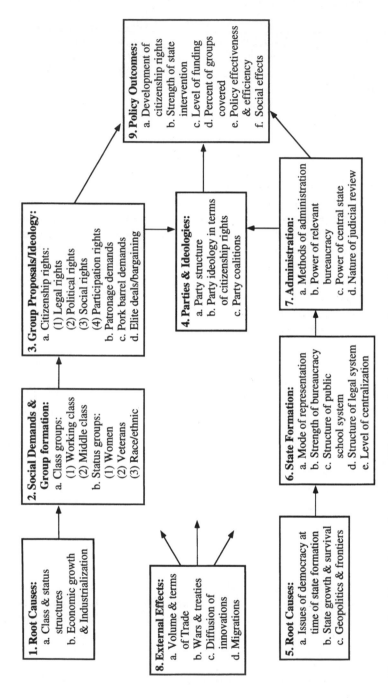

Figure 6.2. Social demands, state formation, and ideology in the development of citizenship

much of European labor, often looked to the Germans for inspiration. Similar developments with an emphasis on political, social, and then economic democracy came later in Sweden during the 1930s and 1940s with Per Albin Hansson and in the postwar period with Rudolph Meidner (Olson 1988, p. 7). Unions in both countries developed special schools, libraries, and cultural institutions to spread this ideology in the worker subculture, which was particularly strong compared to that in other countries (Lidtke 1985). By the 1960s-1970s, international social policy experts switched their searchlight for new ideas toward Sweden.

The critical difference in the development of German and Swedish labor concerned their relative abilities to form coalitions. The Swedish labor movement, though loathe to do so at first, established effective ties with the farmers and their agrarian parties (Baldwin 1990; Esping-Andersen 1990; Lewin 1988). On the negative side, this may have been due to the relative weakness of industrialization in Sweden, but on the positive side it points to the possibilities of coalition with a farming class that was relatively independent of dominant and repressive landlords. Thus, Swedish farmers, having a tradition of democracy and independence, could combine with the labor movement and make a coalition that would press effectively for citizenship rights for both workers and farmers – the overwhelming majority of the country's citizens (Baldwin 1990; Esping-Andersen 1990). The German labor movement could not make this coalition during its rise to power in the Weimar Republic (Abraham 1986). The consequences are well known. This difference manifests itself in the political parties and their ideologies, but much goes back to state structures in the development of the Swedish state (Downing 1992, pp. 187–93, 206–11). In other countries, left coalitions of reds and old greens (farmers), reds and liberals, and reds and new greens (environmental parties) are important.

In the United States, left parties withered under adverse political structure and direct coercion, while labor-leaning parties developed a socialization ideology around civil and political rights with a delayed push toward social rights. The native working class did not develop a unified subculture since it was busy with defensive social mobility against immigrants and blacks. The AFL pursued its own narrow course, while ethnic and racial groups established cultural and self-help organizations. Even the blue-collar communities that formed around factories were often status- (i.e., ethnic) rather than class-based (Kornblum 1978). Ethnic groups frequently exerted their social policy influence through political machines in the cities with little influence in Washington. Consequently, ethnic and racial subcultures supplanted a working-class subculture. Although the southern democrats representing a control-oriented conservatism based on race combined with the Democratic party of the North and West over the last century to produce a democratic coalition (Shelley 1983), this de facto coalition was based on trade-offs rather than a labor-based ideology of social policy. Instead, under the banners of opportunity and individualism, the ideologies of "interventionist and self-help" social work and "economistic and job control" unionism developed together, while the South constituted a backwater of racial control (Perlman 1928; Janoski 1990, chs. 2 and 3).

Positioning parties and ideology in a central place does not mean that either one is the dominant factor in the generation of citizenship and social policies. However, ideology develops along with state structures and class and status group interests. Ideas may have an independent effect when interests are clouded. Thus, group interests and state institutions are the "tracklaying vehicles" in the development of citizenship rights with ideologies operating at times to switch the tracks of history, but group interests have the ultimate power to override ideology and lay new track (Mann 1986, p. 28; Sewell 1985; Skocpol 1985).[19]

External or World System Effects

What has been presented so far is primarily an internal model of development, but external effects as a fourth group of effects in this model can also have an important impact on citizenship rights (see [8] in Figure 6.2) (Dryzek and Goodin 1985). War may produce an egalitarian or divisive effect: wars that are lost and fought on home soil promote a general welfare effort, while wars fought on foreign soil promote the interests of a particular status group of veterans returning from overseas. Winning World War I allowed veteran status groups in the United States to press for and eventually obtain a special welfare system in the Veterans Administration in 1930 – mainly for native-born workers – while diluting demands for universalistic welfare and labor market programs. And from an earlier war largely fought on southern soil, Civil War veterans in the North had gained pension benefits that were effectively denied to the massive wave of central and southern European immigrants who came to America around the turn of the century (Skocpol 1992; Sanders 1980; Orloff 1988, pp. 45–52).

German veterans were submerged in the general social policy thrust, especially after World War II, and this led to a stronger labor movement. Losing World Wars I and II strengthened universalistic welfare policies in Germany, while winning them weakened overall support for a universalistic welfare state in the United States. Veterans groups exist in Germany, but they are not the mainstays of social policy development.

The impact of the World Wars on Sweden is more difficult to measure because it was neutral; consequently, veterans did not return to Sweden demanding their own welfare state, nor did the country have the solidarity and leveling brought about by a war occupation or loss. In effect, the war itself had an indirect effect on Sweden because neutrality left the Swedish economy largely intact, which allowed the labor movement to continue to promote the welfare state after the war. Although the worldwide depression from 1928 to 1935 also created government interventions into labor markets by Germany and the United States, only the Swedish government was able to follow up on its Keynesian programs during the depression with continued growth in the welfare state and labor market policy after the war (Gourevitch 1986). The Weimar government never really got started with Keynesian demand management because of the constraints of war reparations but Nazi demand-stimulation programs were implemented. The depression era experiments in the United States were drowned out by veterans benefits, the Marshall Plan, and other postwar programs (Janoski 1990).

External effects also come from the differential integration of foreign immigrants into the polity, but the extension of citizenship to strangers comes with strings attached. The Roman Republic blatantly used citizenship as a form of social control in conquered lands. Mann (1986, p. 254) even speaks of the "invention of extensive territorial citizenship" as the "decisive edge" that gave Rome its political advantage over Carthage and other competitors (Sherwin-White 1939; Nicolet 1988; Riesenberg 1992, pp. 56–84). This principle has similar effects in the colonial and settler countries concerning their relations toward immigrants and indigenous populations.

Work in this area has not been extensive, but Brubaker (1992) tries to explain why France is more open than Germany in allowing immigrants to become citizens by using "cultural idioms," or ways of thinking and talking about nationhood. He shows that cultural idioms were either forged in the French Revolution or evolved over time in Germany. However, the key may lie in the fact that regime structures and colonization processes create three different positions toward naturalization and social closure: liberal countries have the highest naturalization, social democratic regimes have moderate naturalization, and traditional regimes are split into colonizing countries with moderately high naturalization and non-colonizers with very little integration of foreign immigrants (Freeman 1979).

In Table 6.2, these naturalization figures are divided by the size of the foreign community in various countries from 1980 to 1989. From this table it can be seen that regime structures and organization for colonization have a major impact on naturalization rates, which demonstrate a country's willingness to integrate strangers. Among social democratic and liberal regimes, state mobilization and attendant ideologies strongly

Table 6.2. *Explaining social closure measured by naturalizations per 100,000 aliens in 1980-1989*

Regime type and country	Imperial colonization[a]	Settler coloniza-tion with indigenous decline[b]	Standardized naturalization[c] rate 1980-89
Social democratic countries			
Denmark	0.4	-15.9	3,133
Netherlands	5.7	0.0	3,504
Norway	0.0	-8.5	2,854
Finland	0.0	-3.5	5,810
Sweden	0.1	-3.3	4,836
Average	*2.07*	*-6.24*	*4,027.4*
Non-colonizing and mostly traditional countries			
Belgium	0.0	0.0	848
Japan[d]	0.0	0.0	1,242
Germany	0.0	0.0	838
Ireland[d]	0.0	0.0	269
Average	*0.00*	*0.00*	*799.3*
Colonizing and mostly traditional countries			
Austria	0.3	0.0	2,960
France	0.9	0.0	2,002
United Kingdom[b]	16.1	0.0	18,004
Average	*5.77*	*0.00*	*7,655.4*

impact on naturalization. Among traditional countries, colonization or its absence makes a critical difference. Colonization expands the military and consequently citizenship since pressures for citizenship will increase where volunteers and especially conscripts serve in the military. These regimes send soldiers all over the globe and respond to native colonial claims for citizenship by offering immigration and citizenship. Non-colonizers are more complex. Some stay focused on internal social control through the military and expanding their boundaries via their neighbors. After defeat, they form closure around their countries and allow little naturalization. Other non-colonizers such as Ireland are not involved with expansion, but they too form closure around their nation and culture for more defensive purposes.

Regime type and country	Imperial colonization[a]	Settler coloniza- tion with indigenous decline[b]	Standardized naturalization[c] rate 1980-89
Settler and/or liberal countries			
Australia	0.0	-76.5	7,223
Canada	0.0	-95.6	9,879
New Zealand[d]	0.0	-28.9	2,544
Switzerland	0.0	0.0	1,426
United States	0.0	-93.2	4,246
Average	*0.00*	*-58.84*	*5,067.6*

[a] Colonization is the ratio of the population in all colonies divided by the population of the colonizing country measured every ten years between 1855 and 1955. All colonization under 50 years is deducted as occupational control (Janoski and Glennie 1995a).
[b] Indigenous decline is the percentage decline in indigenous population from 1800 to 1920 (Janoski and Glennie 1995a).
[c] Naturalization rates are naturalizations per 100,000 resident aliens (Janoski and Glennie 1995a,b).
[d] The following countries are reclassified according to the most appropriate regime type: colonization and traditional regime for the United Kingdom, non colonization and traditional regime for Ireland, and settler country under liberal regime for New Zealand. Japan was considered a traditional regime prior to WWII.
SOURCES: These data were taken from national statistical yearbooks, ministry reports, and ministry communications with the author. For details on sources see Janoski and Glennie (1995a,b).

Liberal countries that were once colonized countries develop an inclusive conception of citizenship rights.[20] But the process of developing "the breadth of citizenship" in the former colonies is connected to settler interests in territorial expansion and labor shortage, combined with a campaign against the rights of indigenous peoples. Thus, the development of open immigration is a process that involves some "safe haven" for immigrants but also some persecution of indigenous populations – American Indians, Maori, Aboriginals, Saami, Tasmanians, and other native groups. The denial of property rights to indigenous peoples for their land creates a labor shortage that draws large amounts of immigration from the colonizing nation, its continental neighbors, and later the rest of the world (Connor 1972; Sheehan 1973; Wilmer 1993; Burger 1987; Thornton 1986).

> *Hypothesis 6.6: The New World Anglo-Saxon settler colonies eradicated large segments of the indigenous population and in so doing created a labor shortage. In liberal countries where settlement occurred, the rate of decline in indigenous peoples from 1840 to 1950 will correlate with the naturalization rates of these countries. The end result is the creation of an ideology of openness and practice of large-scale naturalization.*

Once immigration and naturalization policies are backed by social institutions and political ideologies, citizenship processes become difficult to stop. When natives protest immigration because of its economic and social competition, "the nation of immigrants" and "huddled masses" ideologies will protect assaults against immigration.

Immigration creates competing status groups, disrupts the social demands of native groups, and depresses wages for native groups in labor markets (Briggs 1992; Hollifield 1992; Layton-Henry 1985; Freeman 1994; OECD 1987c).[21] Native workers may have some opportunity for social mobility since immigrants will usually take low-paying jobs, but they must be ready and willing to pursue this mobility. For those who do not, their wages will tend to drop to immigrant levels. Native citizens will pursue social policies that will benefit them more than immigrants and oppose the extension of universalistic policies. These political and social divisions resulting from a lack of closure on citizenship will lead to a pattern emphasizing legal and political rights, which the natives will have an advantage in pursuing, and restricting social and participation rights. Indeed, the offering of full social and participation rights to foreigners during mass immigration would create a massive burden on citizen obligations of taxation and state institutions. Consequently, social rights will be slow to develop, and they will tend to be guarded by means tests when they finally appear. This liberal model is based on permanent settler countries, which are often very liberal regimes and societies (e.g., Australia, the United States, and Canada).

Social democratic countries have quite high naturalization rates. In Table 6.2, naturalization rates for Nordic countries are over 2,000 while all other non-colonizers are much below that figure. Further, the naturalization rates for Sweden and Finland are above that of three of five liberal countries including the United States. There appear to be four reasons for Nordic countries to be so high. First, three of these countries were colonizers in a previous period of history. Sweden's connection to colonization reaches back to the occupation of Gdansk, the burning of southern German towns, and the voyages through the Volga to Russia.

Denmark was involved in Africa, Iceland, Norway, and a number of other areas. Norway can even claim a colony in Vinland, in what eventually became America. Although this was too long ago to exert the political economic effect of empire, it may have had a cultural effect, and Swedes in particular sometimes make reference to their occupation or colonization of Finland, Poland, Germany, and Russia. Second, all four countries have a state church and strong if not hegemonic left party power in the post–World War II period, which combines two forms of universalistic ideologies. Third, these countries have had some indigenous decline (see column 2 in Table 6.2), which clearly did not cause a labor shortage but may point to the effects of cultural contact and the eventual acceptance of an indigenous population. And to soften the high Nordic rates just a bit, the Nordic countries have more lenient naturalization procedures between themselves, which is reflected in their special naturalization regulations for their fellow Nordic countries. These first three factors point to how Nordic naturalization may be connected to a number of historical factors related to the social democratic regime type.[22]

> Hypothesis 6.7: A universalistic ideology in the social democratic regimes backed by a state church, distant colonization, and indigenous population causes naturalization rates with full political and legal rights to be high, and this same ideology will support strong social and participation rights.

The traditional countries are split by colonization. Traditional countries with high rates of colonization will have moderately high naturalization because the longer the colonization effort lasts, the more the colonizer has problems with social control. The colonizer will gradually offer citizenship to the native population in order to control the colony. This effect will be greatly enhanced by the colonials serving in wars to support the parent country (Headrick 1978). This is graphically depicted in Figure 6.3.

Under colonization, the development of citizenship takes place in four relatively long-term stages: repression, colonial control, military service, and subsequent immigration. In the repression stage, the military of the colonial power uses force to colonize the country, sometimes with a divide and rule strategy and other times not. This stage contributes to the internal development of citizenship within the colonizing country, which is mentioned above, but it does not contribute to tolerance and openness to other national and ethnic groups. These four stages take at least fifty years of colonization. Being neither liberal nor social democratic countries, Britain and France are good examples of colonizers.

For naturalization to occur in large numbers, colonial natives must first assimilate into the colonizer's culture and support colonizer values

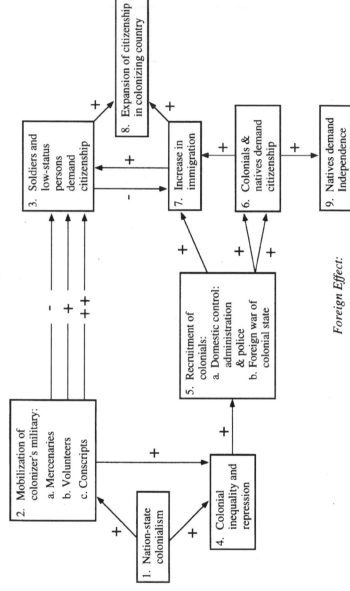

Domestic Effect:

Foreign Effect:

Figure 6.3. The effects of colonization on citizenship

(e.g., the Portuguese in Angola issued *assimilado* identity cards) (Albertini 1971, pp. 517–23). The eventual result will be greater racial and ethnic diversity in the colonizer's country, and even more demands for the extension of citizenship by the colonizer's natives. This process will not be without considerable conflict and discrimination, but the eventual result will be an extension of citizenship.

> *Hypothesis 6.8: When countries go beyond occupation and colonize for more than fifty years, they become more open to colonial natives naturalizing as citizens of the metropole. This openness will be greatest when colonizers: (1) express universalistic values, (2) conscript foreigners into their armed services, (3) have national security reasons to integrate foreigners, and (4) stress cultural pluralism.*

Traditional countries without this much colonial experience maintain parochial and intolerant attitudes toward immigrants that seek to become citizens of their lands. Because colonization needs a strong state, these non-colonizing countries are either weak states or recently strengthened states (i.e., within the last 100 years). Without colonization reaching the social control stage, the state has no incentive to offer naturalization. Immigration from and emigration to the colonies does not occur, and consequently naturalization is low. Each of the non-colonizing countries experienced emigration not to a colony but to a foreign country.[23]

> *Hypothesis 6.9: Non-colonizing countries will avoid naturalization because they (1) express their political and cultural values in a particularistic way, (2) restrict their armed services to favored ethnic groups, (3) have strong national security reasons not to integrate foreigners, and (4) stress cultural and ethnic purity in the face of large-scale emigration.*

The non-colonizer scenario of closure applies most clearly to Germany and Japan.

CONCLUSION

Citizenship rights and social policies in the short and medium run (ten to fifty years) are explained by four factors: (1) social demands based on class and/or status groups engaging in social movements, (2) state structures that aided or restricted citizenship rights formation and implementation, sometimes with direct elite involvement by maintaining structures from previous periods or critical compromises, (3) the internally contingent factor of citizenship rights ideology and political parties, and (4) the externally contingent factors of world events and population movements. Citizenship rights themselves can be developed through discrimination, public goods, sacrifice, and naturalization extensions of the policies of advanced industrialized countries. This chapter has presented a comprehensive explanatory model using power resources and state-centric theories – including the innovations of coalition formation and policy streams research – along with ideology and external forces for citizenship.

The overall attempt of this chapter has been to fuse these different approaches to citizenship over decades to half centuries. Turner questions whether there is "a single version of citizenship" or whether there are "many diverse and different formulations of citizenship principle in different social and cultural traditions" (1993a, p. 9). On the one hand, this chapter has shown that the regime-type approach is capable of providing three different formulations of citizenship for advanced industrialized countries. On the other hand, it tries to fuse power resources, state-centric, and external naturalization theories to provide one explanatory framework. Turner says that a "unitary theory of citizenship is inappropriate" (1993a, p. 11), and it is certainly true that all countries should not be put on the Procrustean bed of Marshall's developmental model of the United Kingdom. Nonetheless, a theoretical framework at a general level of abstraction can prove useful in delineating the major differences between advanced industrialized countries. The model presented here is not offered as a complete synthesis, but rather as pointing the way toward the necessary integration of internal and external factors that will help to explain citizenship rights. The next chapter will show that these external factors of war and migration become even more important over the centuries.

7

Momentous Change in Citizenship over Centuries: From Wasps to Locomotives in the Development and Sequencing of Rights

The critical factor in the emergence of citizenship is violence – that is, the overt and conscious struggle of social groups to achieve social participation. The primary instance of this violence is class conflict and we can define the main issue in class relationships about an issue about genuine participation and control. . . . These social movements have historically had their most significant impact under conditions of war, and warfare thus represents the second illustration of violence as the basis of citizenship.

Bryan Turner (1986a p. 26)

Over the last thousand years, European states have undergone a peculiar evolution: from wasps to locomotives. . . . Tribute-taking states remained fierce but light in weight by comparison with their bulky successors; they stung, but they didn't suck dry. As time went on, states – even capital-intensive varieties took on activities, powers and commitments whose very support constrained them. These locomotives ran on the rails of sustenance from civilian population and by a civilian staff. Off the rails, the warlike engines could not run at all.

Charles Tilly (1991, p. 96)

The long-term development of citizenship over many centuries involves war and international conflict. This chapter formulates two comparative approaches that explain the long-term development and the ordering of citizenship rights in liberal, traditional, and social democratic regimes. The first approach attempts to explain the initial formation of each type of citizenship right. The two similar historical models – one from 1200 to 1815 and the other from 1789 to 1945 – deal with the changing nature of the state exerting coercion and capital-structuring demands. This approach brings three works together: the long-term historical discussion of the military revolution with its burdens and then total war (Tilly 1990; Downing 1991), which connect most clearly to state mobilization as elite strategies; the extension of social demands through social movements in cities and then factories (Korpi 1989; Tilly 1990);

and state structures in the development of the modern state (Skocpol 1992). Throughout there is the explanatory tension of social movements (bottom-up from Turner) and elite strategies (top-down from Mann) in explaining citizenship rights.

The second approach builds on Marshall's developmental theory, which has received surprisingly little attention except for social rights (see Abbott and Deviney 1992; Hicks, Misra, and Ng 1995), by ordering four to five rights within each category of citizenship rights (e.g., political rights include the rights to vote for propertied men, then working-class men, women, and minorities). It then compares the sequencing and overlap of legal, political, social, and participation rights over time as an initial test of Marshall's theory of citizenship rights progression.

The macro-historical approach to citizenship rights development examines the transformation of rights within European countries over seven centuries. Most existing theories in this literature touch on many citizenship issues; however, they do not always explain citizenship rights development per se. Dictatorship and democracy, or the welfare state are the most frequent foci. The formation, sequence, breadth, and extent of citizenship rights themselves have been ignored. Nonetheless, each of the following initial approaches to rights provides an excellent theoretical and empirical starting point that guides analysis of the development of citizenship rights in different countries. It is particularly important to differentiate between the more or less gradual development of rights in the United Kingdom and the leap to social and participation rights with legal and political rights reversals in Germany.

THEORIES OF THE DEVELOPMENT OF CITIZENSHIP OVER THE CENTURIES

In explaining the diverse ordering of rights over centuries, six theories of the long-term development of citizenship are especially useful: (1) Turner's use of Barrington Moore's trajectories of dictatorship and democracy, (2) Mann's elite approach, (3) Korpi and Esping-Andersen's use of power resources theory, (4) Flora and Alber's developmental perspective, (5) Therborn's inside-outside approach, and (6) Tilly and Downing's focus on war and citizenship.[1]

First, Turner (1986a, pp. 62–3) follows Moore's four paths of development: the capitalist/parliamentary revolutionary approach of France, England, and the United States; the capitalist/fascist reactionary development of Germany and Japan; the communist revolutionary development of Russia and China; and the mixed pattern of India (1966, pp. 413–38). In more recent work, Turner (1990, pp. 200–9) elaborates on Moore's categories: revolution in the public context (France), passive democracy with gradualism (England), liberal pluralism in the private sphere (United States), and plebiscitary authoritarianism in the private sphere (Germany). These four categories emerge from a cross-classification of (1) the direction of demands for citizenship – from elites or from subordinates – and (2) contested arenas – public or private spheres of action. Moore's thesis develops from peasant organization, but to a large degree it seems to be undergirded by a mode of production argument, which is developed in the subsequent work of Skocpol (1979), Paige (1975), and Stinchcombe (1983). Turner concludes that "radical citizenship is the outcome of class struggles, war, migration, and egalitarian ideologies" (1986a, pp. 67–75). Turner's mechanism focuses on social movements based on class or status, but beyond a critique of Marshall he does not elaborate on the sequencing of rights.

Second, Mann emphasizes class in his typology of the development of citizenship, but he focuses almost entirely on elite strategies – liberal, reformist, fascist, authoritarian monarchist, and authoritarian socialist regimes (1988, p. 190). As a result, his approach tends to subordinate social movements and social demands or views them as being co-opted. Mann also adds a twist to his theory by distinguishing between countries that switch strategies over time, which is a potentially important addition to developmental explanations. In the early twentieth century, for example, the United Kingdom switched from a "reformist" pattern to a "liberal pattern," and Germany from an "authoritarian monarchist" to a "fascist pattern." Mann also identifies fascism as a viable alternative path of rights development that has never seen full fruition. When coupled with Turner's theory, Mann's top-down approach is quite useful. The driving force from his more general work consists of organized power in an IEMP model of ideology, economy, military, and state politics. While Mann's approach is quite Weberian and makes extensive use of T. H. Marshall, it also does not explicitly theorize the development of citizenship rights.

Third, Korpi (1989) and Esping-Andersen (1985, 1990) focus much more on the Scandinavian countries as welfare state leaders, which the other typologies tend to ignore. Esping-Anderson uses "welfare state regimes," which are being used throughout this book. While a complete and comparative theory of sequential rights is still nascent, the regime approach provides a power resources theory with an emphasis on the relative strength of working classes in coalition with other classes. However, power resources do not predict status-based movements (i.e., women and ethnic/racial groups) very well. Recently, both scholars have done much more to include women's groups (Korpi 1994; Esping-Andersen 1990). This strain of theory, however, has a great deal to say about social rights, but little to contribute about the other three citizenship rights.

Fourth, Flora and Alber (Flora and Alber 1981; Flora 1988) provide for three categories of citizenship development – liberal/reformist, monarchist/ reformist, and communist paths to differentiated citizenship. The liberal/reformist countries (the United Kingdom, United States, Canada, Australia, and Switzerland) more or less followed Marshall's progression of civil, political, and social rights. The monarchist/reformist nations of the late 1800s and early 1900s passed more social rights than other Western countries, while political rights were often restricted. Sweden, Norway, and Denmark developed extensive social and participation rights, but Germany, Austria, and Italy were slow in developing civil and political rights and under fascism endured systematic political and civil rights tragedies. After World War II, West Germany, Italy, and Austria reemerged with comprehensive civil, political, social, and even participation rights. After peasant revolutions, communist countries gave immediate precedence to social rights and social equality, especially through the "right to a job," but they lagged in civil and political rights. The strength of Flora's theory is its explicit focus on the ordering of social rights. For my purposes, they suggest external hypotheses based on elites and a fascist route to citizenship, as does Mann. But their theory remains somewhat functionalist, and it is difficult to isolate specific causes other than growth and differentiation.[2] Sweden and Germany are especially troublesome because they are in the same category but demonstrate entirely different trajectories of rights.

Fifth, Therborn has done extensive studies of the rise of political democracy and universal suffrage (1977, 1992a, b). He builds an inside-outside theory from a two-by-two classification of elite opposition (whether policy comes from the top-down within the country or from international pressures or diffusion) and pressures for democracy (whether they come from the bottom-up inside the country or from cross-national acceptance). For him, democracy develops in the "pioneering European route" from a battle of internal forces of modernization against an internal "old order" in the United Kingdom and France (internal, internal), while it develops in the "externally induced modernization" route from external "forces of modernization" against an external colonialist threat in Japan and China (external, external) (1992a, pp. 64–5). The mixed cases are (1) the "Anglo-New World" route with internal forces of modernization battling an external old order of the British Empire (external, internal) in the United States, New Zealand, and Australia; and (2) the "Southern-New World" route where external elites try to influence national politics (i.e., former Anglo-Saxon colonizers who have been transformed over the centuries into liberal democratic advisors and bankers) and push democracy against an anti-democratic military order consisting of internal elites in South America and Africa (internal, external). While Therborn's work resembles Turner and Mann's classifications to some degree, its dual focus on inside and outside forces is different, and he focuses on a wider array of countries. Nonetheless, in explaining "pioneering" Europe, both of Therborn's causal explanations are internal and cannot explain major variations within the European continent (e.g., Sweden and Germany) with a mechanism that appears to be similar to power-resources theory.[3]

Sixth, Tilly and Downing focus on the critical role that war-making plays in the development of citizenship. Tilly (1991) focuses on two paths of state formation. In the coercion path, the concentration and accumulation of the means of coercion (soldiers, technology, and strategy) lead to the growth of states. In the capital path, the accumulation and concentration of the means of production lead to the growth of economies and cities, which influence the overall form of the state. In the last one hundred years, the two paths combine into a coercive/capitalized state, which is necessary because economic production and scientific research now underlie military power. More coercion than capital leads to authoritarian states with few rights (e.g., Germany developing out of the underindustrialized Prussian state), while more capital than coercion leads to an elite democracy that is either neutral or allied in a confederation (e.g., cantonal Switzerland and the Netherlands). Different combinations of both lead to more or less democratic regimes under a coercive/capitalized state, and as history has entered the second half of the twentieth century, both types have moved toward more mass-based democracies.

Downing (1992) makes a similar argument but with more focus on citizenship rights. Late medieval Europe had representative assemblies that predisposed Europe toward political democracy. But the military revolution consisting of mobilization and then modernization required states to control societies for more and more resource extraction. This revolution diminished democratic forces. Some countries avoided military revolution and preserved democratic-constitutional government by finding alternative methods of financing war beyond domestic sources. Both Downing and Tilly argue that under certain conditions the avoidance of heavy burdens on local communities in giving either taxes or conscripts for the military contributed to greater legal and political rights.[4]

Even though each theory is not always directly concerned with rights and obligations, does not target the precise mechanisms causing citizenship, and often has little to say about the ordering of legal, political, and social rights, parts of these six approaches can be synthesized into a developmental theory of citizenship rights. Obviously, more specific theories focusing on citizenship development are needed. A developmental theory of citizenship rights should simultaneously address the causes of the initial and complete formation of rights programs and the differential ordering of all four rights. Only after these specific questions are framed can hypotheses about an explanatory developmental theory of citizenship rights be proven.

A FRAMEWORK FOR THE DEVELOPMENT OF RIGHTS FOR CITIZENS

The variables of state coercion and capital control lead to citizenship regimes and their corresponding rights and obligations. Each variable fulfills a different role at different times, and hence I will present two versions of the model – one from 1200 to 1815, and the other from 1789 to 1990. There is some overlap in time periods because some processes operate at different times in a number of countries during periods of transition.

Consider Tilly's wasp metaphor at the beginning of the chapter in which state coercion and capital control are interwoven (1991, p. 96). Adding a little to his metaphors, the quote can be modified to describe the movement of capital from bees (the early cities) to locomotives (the advanced industrialized economies), and the state from wasps (the kings and nobles' sporadic war-making) to juggernauts (the mass mobilizing and technologically advanced war machines). This chapter, then, is about how states moved from being hard-working agricultural bees and contentious but intermittent military wasps to becoming locomotives continuously generating economic goods and military juggernauts bringing military destruction, and what effects this had on citizenship.

The first model is operationalized with four sets of variables from Tilly (1991) and Downing (1992) – medieval constitutionalism, war pressures, financial escapes, and the legal and political outcome (see Figure 7.1). According to Downing, nobles with the kings and peasants with their landlords established "medieval constitutionalism," which was a proto-democratic system of rights and obligations (Downing 1992; Sandoz 1993; Holt 1993). The cities extended and accelerated this phenomenon, and the result was the capital route to citizenship operating through the class-based groups created by cities. This path operated from 1200s to 1700s, and even to 1815, depending on the time and place. But over time, city elites and artisans tended to give way to workers and industrialized elites in the next model. The crucial variable is how the state responded to the pressures of war. The path between

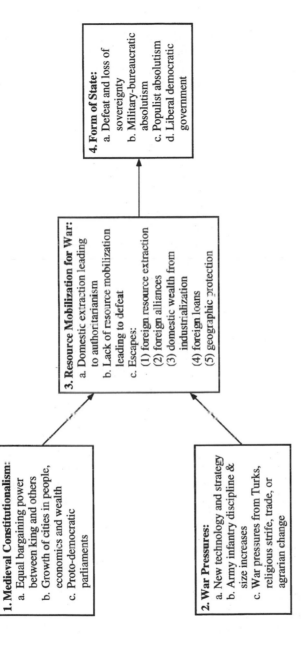

1. Medieval Constitutionalism:
a. Equal bargaining power between king and others
b. Growth of cities in people, economics and wealth
c. Proto-democratic parliaments

2. War Pressures:
a. New technology and strategy
b. Army infantry discipline & size increases
c. War pressures from Turks, religious strife, trade, or agrarian change

3. Resource Mobilization for War:
a. Domestic extraction leading to authoritarianism
b. Lack of resource mobilization leading to defeat
c. Escapes:
  (1) foreign resource extraction
  (2) foreign alliances
  (3) domestic wealth from industrialization
  (4) foreign loans
  (5) geographic protection

4. Form of State:
a. Defeat and loss of sovereignty
b. Military-bureaucratic absolutism
c. Populist absolutism
d. Liberal democratic government

Figure 7.1. The development of citizenship 1200–1815

"medieval constitutionalism" and liberal democracy is mediated by solving financial and resource problems related to the pressures of ever increasing wars. Those states that had to rely on domestic resources established military-bureaucratic absolutism, while those that could avoid overtaxing their subjects (i.e., by forming alliances or financing wars with loans, foreign pillaging, or commercial success) developed some form of liberal democracy (Downing 1992, pp. 18–55).

Following Tilly (1991), coercion and capital lead to different emphases. The coercion route was generally followed by the princes in the countryside. The capital route leads to the accumulation of economic resources and its concentration in extractive, commercial, and manufacturing ventures. This leads to the development of a market system and the continued development of cities. Cities before the Industrial Revolution amount to a social movement based on capital, led by entrepreneurs and skilled craftsmen in a hive of economic activity. They created production and trade, which increasingly included foreign states, but they also demanded independence from the patrimonial state of the kings and for themselves within the city. The city air makes you free and relatively equal, and bourgeois groups in the cities formed constitutional forms of self-government that led to legal and political rights (Downing 1992, pp. 26–31).

This model operated until the Industrial Revolution was unleashed, when another variable superseded the cities as a growth mechanism – industrialization with an ever growing and more complex economy that combined with mechanized war. The newer model still has the same paths of capital and coercion, but their components are reordered. The capital path generates classes, gender groups, and ethnic groups concentrated in occupations or unemployment, rather than petite bourgeois owners and skilled craftsmen. Like commercial and craft capital leading to mass mobilization in the cities, industrial capitalism led to social movements based on trade unions. In the 1870 to 1945 period, labor was the strongest social movement in pushing social welfare in most European countries, with gender and ethnic groups being either subordinated within or excluded from the citizenship rights agenda.[5] Labor has pursued political, social, and participation rights with greater success in the social democratic and traditional regimes, and less success in the liberal regimes.

In the later model from 1789 to 1990, the coercion route comes from the accumulation of political power through means of physical control (e.g., expropriation, torture, incarceration, and threats) and the increasing labor control through technology, organization, and strategy (see items 5 and 6 in Figure 7.2). These military processes begin with land-

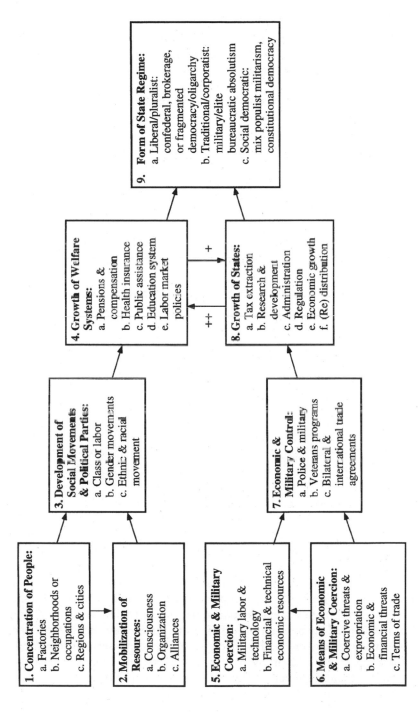

Figure 7.2. The development of citizenship, 1789–1945

9. Form of State Regime:
a. Liberal/pluralist: confederal, brokerage, or fragmented democracy/oligarchy
b. Traditional/corporatist: military/elite bureaucratic absolutism
c. Social democratic: mix populist militarism, constitutional democracy

4. Growth of Welfare Systems:
a. Pensions & compensation
b. Health insurance
c. Public assistance
d. Education system
e. Labor market policies

8. Growth of States:
a. Tax extraction
b. Research & development
c. Administration
d. Regulation
e. Economic growth
f. (Re) distribution

3. Development of Social Movements & Political Parties:
a. Class or labor
b. Gender movements
c. Ethnic & racial movement

7. Economic & Military Control:
a. Police & military
b. Veterans programs
c. Bilateral & international trade agreements

1. Concentration of People:
a. Factories
b. Neighborhoods or occupations
c. Regions & cities

2. Mobilization of Resources:
a. Consciousness
b. Organization
c. Alliances

5. Economic & Military Coercion:
a. Military labor & technology
b. Financial & technical economic resources

6. Means of Economic & Military Coercion:
a. Coercive threats & expropriation
b. Economic & financial threats
c. Terms of trade

lords and nobles and then spread to the nation-state. This leads to the state extracting resources from society to provide labor and money for military exploits. As time goes on, the state adds more and more duties, moving from the earliest to the later stages of Titmus's theory of the state's "progression of biological interests" in war (1963, pp. 79–82).[6] In his theory, the state's concern about coercion comes in four stages: (1) the quantity of soldiers and their pay, (2) both the quantity and quality of soldiers, (3) the quality and quantity of the population as a whole, and (4) the social production of high-quality countries through regulation and mobilization of the population, industry, research, and other aspects of society. When the fourth stage is reached, the industrial economy becomes a locomotive, and its war machine a juggernaut.

By the twentieth century, the coercion path tends to combine economic and the military processes. Military coercion through threats and expropriation takes on a new dimension with economic growth providing greater carrying capacity for more soldiers, and then greater military technology to emphasize the education of soldiers to perform technological tasks – operating and maintaining artillery, tanks, aircraft, and missiles. Human resources are especially important since the state needs soldiers to fight with complex strategies and new weapons, and skilled researchers to develop new military technologies. The result fuses military coercion and economic power with both being dependent upon each other. The state now reaches Titmus's last stage of total mobilization for war.

The military becomes an important means for the advance of citizenship, especially when there is conscription for total war as in the French revolutionary wars, the American Civil War, and the two world wars (see the "sacrifice extension" of citizenship in the previous chapter). Immigrants and subordinated ethnic and racial groups can greatly improve their chances for citizenship by serving in the military. The state gives rights and benefits to those who fulfill its most demanding obligation. Because total war makes such strong demands on labor power, new skills and opportunities in the war economy were opened up for previously excluded groups such as women and ethnic minorities. Their integration into equal citizenship is intensified where civilians suffer war injuries through bombing or occupation (e.g., French women won the vote only after their extensive participation in the Resistance during World War II). This internal process is not entirely new since states had to bargain with citizens and subjects to get them to serve in the monarch's armies, but with mass mobilization, interest groups and social movements organize much of the mass response to bargaining, and solutions become more formal and universalistic.[7]

The result of class and status mobilization in social movements leads to a new emphasis on citizenship rights, with the extension of political and legal rights to the masses, and the initial creation of social and participation rights. The coercive path through the state has also reached the centers of production, research, and education. The eventual result was a tremendous growth in the welfare state.

Liberal, corporatist, and social democratic regimes have approached these events over the last 400 years in different ways. In traditional countries, emphasis on landholding estates exercising coercion without extensive capital development in cities, as in Prussia, has led to institutions emphasizing coercion and control (Downing 1992, pp. 84–112; Tilly 1991). In more liberal regimes with cities and free markets, as in the United Kingdom and United States, extensive economic development led to less coercion and social control. In what later became a social democratic regime, Sweden developed a strong but not coercive state. With little capital development, Sweden during its imperial period (1620 to 1719) extracted resources from outside the nation through tribute, pillage, and loans, allowing lower taxes and limited conscription in the villages (Downing 1992, pp. 187–211; Sawyer 1982). These differential processes have left residual institutions and mass attitudes that strongly affect the state and the development and ordering of citizenship rights.

From these liberal, traditional, and social democratic approaches to politics and social movements, a number of hypotheses can be proposed involving (1) the mechanisms of development, (2) the overall development of rights over the centuries, (3) the ordering of rights between regime types, and (4) the trade-off between political and economic democracy. The first two items refer more to the causal explanation of development, which is taken first, while the latter two items refer to testing Marshall's theory of development, which is pursued in the second half of this chapter.

EXPLAINING DIFFERENT DEVELOPMENTS OF CITIZENSHIP RIGHTS

The overall development of citizenship over the centuries divides into three periods: 1200 to 1815 for legal and political rights, 1789 to 1980 for legal and political rights, and 1883 to 1990 for social and participation rights. This does not mean that each right did not develop in other periods, but that much of the most important developments of each right occurred within each of the specified time frames.

In Table 7.1, the variables for Tilly and Downing's analyses are presented for seventeen countries. The first seven variables represent medieval constitutionalism (independent variables IV1, IV2, and IV3) and war pressures (IV4, IV5, IV6, and IV7), which are more or less the same for the first nine countries. Most of Europe had a proto-democratic base and at the same time tended to face increased war pressures in the 1600s and beyond. Japan, Russia, and China had no such proto-democratic heritage, and their progress toward military-bureaucratic absolutism was more or less assured. The remaining nine countries with a proto-democratic base and war pressures mobilize either internal or external resources (IV8, IV9, IV10, and IV11). Countries that avoid domestic resource mobilization and its attendant repression tend toward liberal democratic governments. For example, the British case is able to mobilize foreign wealth through success in colonial wars and semi-sanctioned piracy, establish alliances at critical points in time, rely on resources from loans and then a strong economy during the Industrial Revolution, and, finally, be in a safe geopolitical position vis-à-vis other warring countries. A country only really needs one of these variables, so the United Kingdom is rather overdetermined. Sweden, for instance, is not particularly isolated and had only moderate economic growth. However, it was able to rely on somewhat rationalized logistics and foreign pillaging (IV8) to supply its troops on foreign soil during the Thirty Years War, and when the Northern War left Sweden relatively defenseless, alliances (IV9) prevented the Russians from taking the country (Downing 1992). The Netherlands relied on their economic strength (IV10) and even on their unique geography by flooding their dike system at opportune times (IV11) (see Mann 1993, pp. 19–20 on geopolitical position).

On the other hand, Prussia, Austria, and Spain had fewer protections and for very different reasons had to intensively mobilize their domestic economy and polity. Prussia did this most efficiently with the least amount of resources (e.g., poor land and weak economy), while Spain did so primarily in one province (Castile). These countries where war pressures forced the intensive mobilization of domestic resources eventually developed oppressive and rationalized absolutism. France is a special case with absolutism developing out of the Thirty Years War, and then various forms of democracy after the French Revolution. Downing treats the Napoleonic interlude as an instance of populist absolutism, a brand of absolutism that is weaker and more temporary than military-bureaucratic absolutism, which is more strongly internalized into war machine institutions. A controlled form of democracy followed with many ups and downs. Thus, France exhibits three possible outcomes at different times, but I will treat it as mostly a liberal democracy.

The last three columns in Table 7.1 refer to proto-states that were not independent during the period under question but were influenced by the conditions of this era. Belgium ends up developing much like the Netherlands, and Finland and Norway are quite similar to Sweden. Although these three countries are subordinate at this time, they have the basis for development into a liberal or social democracy. However, Italy is a very mixed case with some democracy in its city states before unification.[8] Although Italy has many of the preconditions for liberal democracy, it lacks an effective escape from military-bureaucratic absolutism. Only a weak case can be made for alliances (not protectors), some economic development in the cities, and a small measure of geographic protection in the Alps to the north and sea to the south. Yet Italy did not have clear military-absolutist institutions. Italy will continue to be a major contradiction in the next period.

The results in Table 7.1 fully support the Tilly/Downing explanatory approach with no contradictions in explaining the six liberal democracies (the positive cases) and the three military-bureaucratic regimes (the negative cases).[9] The eastern states of Russia, Japan, and China lack the preconditions for democracy because they have extremely unequal bargaining power, weak cities, and no independent parliaments. On the whole, the summary explanation of Downing and Tilly's theory is quite good.

From Downing and Tilly on the earlier centuries, the explanation moves to legal and political rights in the seventeenth through twentieth centuries. Table 7.2 outlines the variables and countries in a Millsean chart using data from Downing (1992), Stephens (1989), Lipset (1981), Luebbert (1992), and Baldwin (1990).[10] Emerging from the previous period, military-bureaucratic authoritarianism (independent variable IV1) does well in explaining the rise of fascism.[11] The exception is Italy, which could be considered a populist absolutist government since it was not run by regimenting institutions.

The variables inspired by Barrington Moore – economically and politically strong landed upper class (IV2, IV3), economically moderate but politically weak bourgeoisie (IV4), and a strong state (IV5) – line up fairly well for fascist coalitions and governments. The landed upper class has a high amount of economic and political power in absolutist countries. The United Kingdom is an exception on the political power of the landed class, but this was overcome by bourgeois elites benefiting from an early Industrial Revolution (Rueschemeyer et al. 1992, pp. 95–8). Australia had both economic and political power invested in the landed class because it began as an authoritarian colony of convicts, but this was overcome by immigration from the democratic United Kingdom. Consequently, these contradictions are minor.

Two countries could be considered mixed cases on the power of the landed gentry. Italy is not only a mixed case, but the bourgeoisie plays an entirely different role because they unite with the landed upper classes, but not as a weak and dominated partner (Rueschemeyer et al. 1992, pp. 103–6). The country is not dominated by a landed aristocracy, but

Table 7.1. *The development of legal and political rights, 1200 to 1815*

Country[a]	UK	FRA	SWZ	NET	DEN	SWE	PRU	AUS	RUS	JPN	CHI	BEL	FIN/NOR	ITA	POL
Variables															
A. Medieval constitutionalism from 1200 to 1500 establishes proto-democratic procedures:															
IV1	Y	Y	Y	Y	Y	Y	Y	Y	N	N	N	Y	Y	Y	n
IV2	Y	Y	Y	Y	Y	Y	Y	Y	N	N	N	Y	Y	Y	n
IV3	Y	Y	Y	Y	Y	Y	Y	Y	N	N	N	Y	Y	Y	N
B. War pressures increase tremendously pressing the state to find more resources in men and money:															
IV4	Y	Y	Y	Y	Y	Y	Y	Y	Y	Y	Y	Y	Y	Y	Y
IV5	Y	Y	Y	Y	Y	Y	Y	Y	Y	Y	Y	Y	Y	Y	Y
IV6	y	Y	y	Y	Y	Y	Y	Y	Y	Y	Y	Y	Y	Y	Y
IV7	y	y	y	y	y	Y	Y	Y	Y	Y	Y	y	y	y	y
C. Ways that nation-states could escape the pressures of military bureaucratic absolutism:															
IV8	Y	y	Y	Y	Y	Y	N	N	N	N	N	Y	y	n	N
IV9	Y	Y	N	N	Y	Y	N	N	N	N	N	Y	N	y	N
IV10	Y	y	N	N	Y	y	N	N	N	N	N	Y	N	y	N
IV11	y	n	n	Y	N	n	N	n	Y	n	n	N	N/n	N	n

186

D. Dependent variables: Political outcomes affecting legal and political rights:

DV1	N	N	N	N	N	N	N	N	Y	Y	Y	Y
DV2	N	y	N	N	Y	N	N	N	N	N	N	N
DV3	N	N	N	N	N	N	N	N	N	N	n/y	N
DV4	Y	y	Y	Y	N	N	N	N	y	y	N	N

NOTE:

Variables in first column, countries in first row. Y=Yes, N=no, n=maybe no, y=maybe yes

ᵃ Countries in order of presentation: United Kingdom, France, Switzerland, Netherlands, Denmark, Sweden, Prussia, Austria, Spain, Russia, Japan, China, Belgium, Finland and Norway combined, Italy, and Poland.

INDEPENDENT VARIABLES:

IV1=Relatively equal bargaining power between kings and nobles, and between nobles and peasants; IV2=Strength of towns and cities as capital accumulation and commercial trading centers; IV3=Existence of relatively independent parliaments, assemblies, and/or peasant communes; IV4=Innovations toward expensive technologies such as rifles, cannons, and large armies; IV5=Disciplined infantry with increased army size and an increasingly complex organization; IV6=War pressures with Turks in the East in Europe and from the West in Asia, increasingly violent religious strife between Christians, hostilities caused by international imperialism and agrarian transformations; IV7=Increasing extraction of resources from inside or outside the country for survival purposes; IV8=Foreign resource mobilization through sacking, imperialism, or other means; IV9=Alliances with other countries reducing war resource needs; IV10=Advanced economic development with large monetary reserves enabling independent resources or public debt; IV11=Geo-political isolation that allows protection from enemies;

DEPENDENT VARIABLES: DV1=Defeat and prolonged subordination or colonisation by another nation; DV2=Military and bureaucratic absolutism; DV3=Populist absolutism reverting back to democratic government; DV4=Liberal Democratic government for some (i.e., not the masses).

the Po Valley and the south are in coalition enough to cause similar effects. The American South could be considered similar to Prussia due to its landed upper classes and weak bourgeoisie. However, the South did not dominate the United States, and the Civil War proved just the opposite.[12] If slavery had extended to Pennsylvania and Ohio, the Confederacy might have behaved like Prussia and thus have led the United States to an authoritarian outcome. Consequently, the United States works well, but Italy remains a messy ad hoc explanation.

The economic and even political power of the bourgeoisie are in dispute in Germany (IV4). Unlike the rural domination in other authoritarian regimes, Germany experienced a strong industrial revolution in the latter part of the nineteenth century. This makes an assessment of bourgeois political and economic power somewhat problematic. Stephens cannot place Germany into definite yes or no categories since the relative powers of the landed bureaucracy and the bourgeoisie were in a rather mixed and regionalized situation (Rueschemeyer et al. 1992). Nevertheless, Prussia clearly fits the hypothesis, and Bavaria is not far behind. Many other regions of Germany, especially the heavily industrialized Ruhr area, do not clearly fit Moore's hypotheses. However, Prussia and Bavaria are politically dominant in the united German state and rule the overall classification of the country.[13]

Other variables from Moore's and Stephen's hypotheses are a bit mixed. The revolutionary break with the past has contradictions (IV6). Switzerland, Australia, Canada, and New Zealand have not had what would be considered a revolution. Further, the Glorious Revolution in the United Kingdom and the bourgeois revolution in the United States are often not considered to be social revolutions that would require major changes in society.[14] The strength of the working class (IV9) does not work particularly well, but this has been reformulated into hypotheses about the working class being in coalition with various groups (Luebbert 1991; Baldwin 1990; Esping-Andersen 1990). Nonetheless, these variables form one theoretical hypothesis that shows agreement on twelve positive and three negative cases.

Hypothesis 7.1: Precondition Explanations of Legal and Political Rights: Countries with a politically and economically strong landed upper class, a politically subordinate bourgeoisie, a strong state, and military-bureaucratic absolutism will not become liberal democracies unless they are occupied by military forces of democratic countries after World War II.

However, the Moore thesis does not differentiate well between the liberal democratic and social democratic countries. For instance, the red-green (i.e., working class and peasant) coalition works quite well in

Scandinavia, but not in industrialized Belgium or the Netherlands. The Catholic coalition with liberals or conservatives works in three of four authoritarian countries (but obviously not in Japan) but is mixed elsewhere. Coalitional theses help differentiate the Anglo-Saxon and Scandinavian democracies and help to clarify some questions about Germany and Italy. Using power resources theory's focus on working-class strength combined with working-class coalitions, the picture becomes clearer. All social democratic countries exhibit working-class strength (IV9), and they form working-class coalitions with either the peasants, small farmers, Catholics, or liberals (IV11). The liberal democracies are more reliant on a liberal-labor coalition, although Belgium and the Netherlands form a religious coalition. These coalition theories involving social and liberal democracy can be brought together with coalitions of working-class parties with either liberal (Luebbert 1991) or agrarian parties (Baldwin 1990). The only exception might be Ireland, but the mobilization of the nation against the British may well have served as a functional equivalent for mass solidarity in a grand coalition.

The fascist countries generally lack working-class strength (IV9), but the major exception is Germany. In this area, too much emphasis has been put on Germany's being a late developer relative to the United Kingdom, France, and the United States. When comparisons are made to Finland, Norway, Denmark, Canada, Australia and other countries, Germany in 1900 is hardly a backward country, and indeed, it has surpassed the United Kingdom in many industrial production categories. This leads to a strong working class in Germany and one that led the world in its radical politics. However, the strong German working class could not find an adequate coalition partner with either the liberals or peasants (Hicks, Misra, and Ng 1995, pp. 339–40; Abraham 1986). Instead, Catholics and conservatives coalesced during the Weimar Republic, and a working-class coalition did not emerge. After accounting for Italy, the combined coalition variable (IV11 in Table 7.2) shows agreement on these three hypotheses for fourteen positive cases and four negative cases. Ireland is the sole questionable country.

Hypothesis 7.2: Working-Class Coalition Explanations of Legal and Political Rights: Countries with labor movements in coalition with peasants/ farmers or liberal political parties will develop long-lasting legal and political rights. Other coalitions of liberals and conservatives or peasants and conservatives that ignore labor will lead to non-democratic interludes.

Thus, on the whole, the precondition and coalition hypotheses work well with the significant exception of Italy. This is not the time or the place for an analysis of Italy, but work needs to be done to adequately explain why a country of city-states with important phases of democracy

Table 7.2. The development of legal and political rights, 1789 to 1945

1. DATA: Variables in first column, countries in first row. Y=Yes, N=no, n=maybe no, y=maybe yes; Countries in order of presentation: United Kingdom, France, Switzerland, United States, Australia, Ireland, Canada, New Zealand, Netherlands, Belgium, Denmark, Finland, Norway, Sweden, Germany, Austria, Italy, and Japan.

	UK	FRA	SWZ	USA	AUSL	IRE	CAN	NZ	NETL	BEL	DEN	FIN	NOR	SWE	GER	AUS	ITA	JPN
IV1	N	n	N	N	n	N	N	N	N	N	N	N	N	N	Y	Y	n	Y
IV2	y	N	N	y	y	N	N	N	N	N	N	N	N	N	Y	Y	y	Y
IV3	n	N	N	y	y	n	N	N	N	N	N	N	N	N	y	Y	y	Y
IV4	N	N	N	N	n	n	N	N	N	N	N	N	N	N	y	Y	n	Y
IV5	n	N	N	N	N	N	N	N	N	N	N	N	N	N	Y	Y	y	Y
IV6	y	Y	N	N	N	y	N	N	N	N	N	N	N	N	N	N	N	N
IV7	N	N	N	N	N	n	N	N	N	N	N	n	N	N	Y	Y	Y	Y
IV8	Y	Y	Y	Y	N	N	N	N	N	N	N	N	y	Y	y	N	N	N
IV9	Y	y	N	n	n	y	n	n	Y	Y	Y	Y	N	N	N	N	N	N
IV10	N	y	N	N	N	y	N	N	y	Y	N	Y	N	N	Y	Y	Y	N
IV11	Y	y	Y	Y	Y	y	y	y	Y	Y	Y	Y	Y	Y	Y	Y	Y	N
DV	Y	Y	Y	Y	Y	Y	Y	Y	Y	Y	Y	Y	Y	Y	N	N	N	N

190

II. REDUCED EXPLANATION OF LEGAL AND POLITICAL RIGHTS: Independent variables across the top, countries down the columns. Contradictory answers are underlined.

Theses: Countries:	Downing IV1	Moore IV2 IV3 IV4 IV5				IV7	WC coalition IV11	Number of contradictions
Agree on all								
Positive	N	N	N	N	N	N	Y	0 in 12 countries
Negative	Y	Y	Y	Y	Y	Y	N	0 in 3 countries
Contradictions								
United Kingdom	N	y	n	N	N	N	Y	1 – IV2
Australia	N	y	Y	N	N	N	Y	2 – IV2 and 3
Italy	n	y	y	n	n	y	N	3 – IV1, 4, and 5

III. *VARIABLES: IV1*=country has established military bureaucratic authoritarianism (Downing); *IV2*=landed upper class has high amount of economic power (Moore); *IV3*=landed upper class has high amount of political power (Moore); *IV4*=bourgeois political power is low or bourgeois is dependent on state and landed elite (Moore); *IV5*=state is strong, interventionist, and repressive (Moore); *IV6*=revolutionary break with the past (Stephens); *IV7*=fascist coalition of landed upper class, strong state, and dependent bourgeois (Moore); *IV8*=industrialization is in advanced phase by 1860 (Lipset, Wilensky, or Flora); *IV9*= working class is organized and exerts some power (Therborn and Korpi); *IV10*=Catholic coalition with liberals or conservatives (Stephens thesis); *IV11*=working class is in some coalition with either the liberals (Luebbert), peasants or small farmers (Baldwin); *DV*=liberal or social democratic form of government from 1900-50 (versus a fascist, authoritarian, or populist-absolutist government in the same period).

and a nation-state with little military-bureaucratic authority developed a fascist regime.

The explanation of citizenship rights now moves from legal and political rights – political democracy – to social and participation rights – economic democracy. Although economic rights are similar to legal and political rights, they require separate treatment since they both were created in the twentieth century and participation rights are a new form of citizenship rights. The social rights variable is measured by social transfer payment expenditures as a percent of GNP from 1950 to 1990 (Y > 16%; y > 12% but ≤ 16%; n ≥ 10% to ≤ 12 %; and N < 10%). Table 7.3 summarizes liberal, power resources, and state-centric variables that can be used to explain social rights.[15] The liberal explanation of industrialization (variable IV1) fares rather poorly with four positive and four negative contradictions. A high percentage of the aged population (IV2) does moderately well, but worse in the more privatized welfare states of the United Kingdom and Switzerland.

Three factors – labor power, state structures, and war solidarity – have the fewest contradictions. First, working-class strength (IV3) and working-class coalitions with liberal or agrarian parties (IV4) are effective in eight countries with weak social rights and six countries with strong social rights. Finland is an exception on these and all other variables, and that is because Finland's expenditures in the 1950s were rather low. Picking a later date for Finland on social expenditures would make its social rights high, and these variables and those to follow would be a perfect fit. Australia, Italy, and France are other exceptions. Australia's working-class strength is too high for the lowest welfare state in this group of countries. Italy and France, even when collective bargaining extensions to non-union workers are included in working-class strength, are too low on labor power for it to be an effective explanation of their relatively strong social rights.[16]

Hypothesis 7.3: Coalition Theory Explaining Social Rights: Countries with strong labor movements that develop coalitions with other parties will have strong social rights programs. This process of building a strong labor movement will be greatly aided by proportional electoral systems.

Second, all three state-centric variables are effective in eight countries weak on social rights and seven countries strong on social rights. Proportional representation (variable IV6) seems to be present in most of the strong welfare states. A Roman legal system (IV7) is closely correlated to the proportional electoral systems (IV6), and the strength of the ministry of labor is quite effective (IV8), but it seems to be a consequence rather than a cause. The exceptions other than Finland (which was mentioned above) are France and Switzerland. France has a relatively weak ministry of labor, and this is clearly connected to the weaker role that trade unions play in France (intermittent political strikes being the exception). Switzerland has a Roman legal system and proportional representation, but its extreme decentralization mitigates against strong social rights.

Hypothesis 7.4: State-centric Theory: Countries with proportional election systems and a Roman law system of government develop a stronger ministry of labor and more extensive social rights.

Third, the war variable (IV10) focuses on the combined effects of being occupied or losing the war in producing solidarity and then social rights in most countries. Of the positive cases, Sweden is a major exception on the war variables because it was neutral and it has a strong welfare state. Although Sweden encountered a strong threat during World War II and was caught between the Allied and Axis powers, this is not the same as suffering war deaths. Of the negative cases, Japan does not fit, but that can be partially explained by the long way it had to travel in developing a welfare state and being occupied by a "liberal regime" after the war. Finally, Ireland was neutral during World War II like Sweden, but it has exactly what one would expect from a neutral country.

Hypothesis 7.5: Countries with extensive occupation during wartime (i.e., being occupied or losing the war) will develop status leveling and strong social rights. This process reverses when countries do all their fighting on foreign soil.

The partially reduced explanation of the social rights (part II in Table 7.3) shows that the power resources, state-centric, and war variables, although not perfect, give a reasonable explanation of social rights. Six of nine strong welfare states (positive cases) are well explained by these variables. Sweden is a minor contradiction due to its neutrality during World War II. Italy and France are important contradictions on labor power and state institutions, and they have tended to fashion alternative mechanisms (political strikes and demonstrations) to provide for social rights. Australia is high on labor power, but an argument could be made that it did not develop adequate working-class coalitions. Finally, Finland does not fit a low social rights country at all, but that is because it developed into a strong welfare state a little later than the other countries. On the whole, the table provides a plausible argument for power resources, state-centric, and external influence theories.[17]

With participation rights, the patterning is consonant with the working-class strength hypotheses (see Table 7.4). Strong participation rights

Table 7.3. The development of social rights, 1880 to 1990

I. DATA: Variables in first column, countries in first row below; Y=Yes, N=no, y=weak yes, n=weak no; *IV*=independent variables, *DV*=dependent variable. Country order is: Australia, Japan, United States, Canada, Switzerland, New Zealand, United Kingdom, Ireland, Finland, Italy, France, Belgium, Austria, Germany, Denmark, Norway, Sweden, and Netherlands

	ASL	JPN	USA	CAN	SWZ	NZ	UK	IRE	FIN	ITA	FRA	BEL	AUS	GER	DEN	NOR	SWE	NET
IV1	N	Y	Y	N	N	N	Y	N	N	N	Y	Y	N	Y	N	N	y	y
IV2	N	Y	N	Y	Y	N	Y	N	y	N	Y	Y	Y	Y	Y	Y	Y	Y
IV3	y	N	N	n	N	n	N	n	y	N	n	y	y	y	Y	Y	Y	y
IV4	N	N	N	N	Y	N	N	n	n	N	N	y	y	Y	Y	Y	Y	y
IV5	N	Y	N	N	Y	N	N	Y	Y	N	n	N	N	Y	n	y	N	N
IV6	N	N	N	Y	Y	N	N	N	Y	N	Y	Y	Y	Y	Y	Y	Y	Y
IV7	N	N	N	Y	Y	N	N	N	Y	N	Y	Y	Y	Y	Y	Y	Y	Y
IV8	n	N	N	N	N	N	n	N	y	N	n	Y	Y	Y	Y	Y	Y	Y
IV9	n	Y	y	n	N	n	Y	N	y	N	y	Y	Y	Y	n	n	y	y
IV10	N	Y	N	N	N	N	N	N	Y	N	Y	Y	Y	Y	Y	N	N	Y
DV	N 8.0	N 8.2	N 9.0	N 9.8	n 11	n 11	n 12	N 9.1	y 15	Y 19	y 15	Y 19	Y 19	y 15	y 14	y 13	y 15	Y 22

II. REDUCED EXPLANATION OF SOCIAL RIGHTS: Variables are across, and countries are down the column. Contradictory answers are underlined below.

	Labor power: IV3 IV4	State structures: IV6 IV7 IV8	War solidarity: IV10	Variables that are in contradiction:
Agree on all				
Positive cases	Y Y	Y Y Y	Y	0 in 6 countries
Negative cases	N N	N N N	N	0 in 5 countries
Contradictions				
Australia	y N	N N N	N	1 – IV3
Finland	Y y	Y Y Y	y	7 – IV3, 4, 6, 7, 8, and 10
Italy	y n	Y Y Y	Y	1 – IV4
France	n N	Y n N	Y	4 – IV3, 4, 6, and 8
Switzerland	N N	Y Y N	N	2 – IV6 and 7
Japan	N N	N N N	Y	1 – IV10
Sweden	Y Y	Y Y Y	N	1 – IV10

III. VARIABLES: IV1=strong industrialization or national wealth, 1880-1990; *IV2*=percentage of population over 65 years of age is high, 1900-1990; *IV3*=working class strength from 1950 to 1990 is measured by the average of union membership ratios and collective bargaining coverage rates from Table 7.1. Italy and Ireland bargaining extension figures are estimated from neighbors (Y > 66, y ≤ 66 & ≥ 60, n < 60 & ≥ 50, N < 50; *IV4*=working class coalition with the agrarian or liberal parties, 1918-1990; *IV5*=critical weakness of capital at points of important social legislation; *IV6*=proportional representation, 1880-1990; *IV7*=Roman legal system; *IV8*=strong ministry of labor; *IV9*=high degree of manufacturing industry; *IV10*=solidarity due to occupation or losing last world war; and *DV*=strong social rights as a whole from 1950-90 with the number indicating the averages of pensions, health, educational, and family allowance programs (Y > 16%, y > 12% & ≤ 16%, n ≥ 10% & ≤ 12%, and N < 10%).

Table 7.4. The development of participation rights, 1880 to 1990

I. DATA: Variables in first column with IV meaning independent variable, and DV meaning dependent variable. Y=Yes, N=no, y=weak yes, n=weak no. Countries in order are: United States, Switzerland, France, United Kingdom, Canada, Japan, New Zealand, Ireland, Australia, Italy, Belgium, Finland, Denmark, Norway, Austria, Netherlands, Sweden, and Germany.

	USS	SWZ	FRA	UKA	CAN	JPN	NIEZ	IREL	ITAL	BEL	FIN	DEN	NOUR	ANUST	NETH	SWED	GER
IV1	Y	N	Y	Y	Y	N	N	N	N	Y	N	N	N	N	Y	y	Y
IV2	y	Y	y	y	Y	Y	N	N	n	Y	N	N	Y	Y	Y	Y	Y
IV3	N	n	n	n	N	N	n	n	y	Y	Y	Y	Y	Y	y	Y	Y
IV4	N	N	N	N	n	N	n	n	y	y	y	Y	Y	Y	Y	Y	Y
IV5	N	N	N	N	Y	N	n	Y	n	n	y	n	y	Y	n	Y	Y
IV6	N	N	N	N	n	N	N	n	N	N	y	y	Y	Y	y	n	Y
IV7	N	Y	N	N	N	N	N	Y	Y	Y	Y	Y	Y	Y	Y	y	Y
IV8	N	Y	Y	n	N	N	N	N	Y	Y	Y	Y	Y	Y	Y	Y	Y
IV9	N	N	N	N	N	N	n	N	y	y	y	y	Y	Y	Y	Y	Y
IV10	N	N	Y	Y	N	Y	N	N	Y	Y	Y	Y	Y	Y	Y	Y	Y
DV	N	N	N	N	N	N	N	N	n	y	Y	Y	Y	Y	Y	Y	Y
	0.0	0.0	0.5	0.5	0.5	1.0	1.0	1.0	1.5	2.0	3.0	3.0	3.0	3.0	3.5	3.5	4.0

II. *REDUCED EXPLANATION OF PARTICIPATION RIGHTS*: Independent variables are across the top, and countries are down the columns. Contradictory answers are underlined.

	Labor power IV4 IV6	State structures IV7 IV8 IV9	Welfare state IV3	Variables that are in contradictions
Agree on all				
Positive	Y Y	Y Y Y	Y	0 in 7 countries
Negative	N N	N N N	N	0 in 7 countries
Contradictions				
Belgium	Y N	Y Y Y	Y	1–IV6
Switzerland	N N	Y Y N	n	2–IV7 and 8
France	N N	N Y N	n	1–IV8
Italy	y N	Y Y Y	y	4–IV3, 4, 7, 8, and 9

III. *VARIABLES*: *IV1*=strong industrialization or national wealth as measured by GNP, 1880-1990; *IV2*=high degree of manufacturing industry; IV3=strong welfare state in terms of expenditures; *IV4*=working class strength as measured by union membership ratios, 1950-90 and collective bargaining extension (OECD 1994); *IV5*=critical weakness of capital at points of important social legislation (i.e., after world wars); IV6=working class coalition with the agrarian or liberal parties, 1918-90; *IV7*=proportional representation, 1880-1990; *IV8*=Roman legal system; *IV9*=strong ministry of labor; *IV10*=solidarity due to occupation during WWII or due to having lost WWII; *DV*=strong overall participation rights form 1950-90 consisting of an average (Y=1.0 and y=0.5) for union protections, labor market intervention, works councils, and workers on corporate boards.

are measured by adding the presence of legislated protections for unions, formal works councils, widespread workers on corporate boards, and active labor market policy expenditures over 0.50 percent of GNP (the variable adds 1.0 for a strong yes and 0.50 for a weak yes).

Using the welfare state, labor power, and political structure variables, the partial reduction in part II of Table 7.4 shows a good explanation in seven of eight countries with strong participation rights (Huber-Stephens and Stephens 1982). It also explains seven of ten negative cases. Working-class strength (IV4) is the strongest factor explaining participation rights, with only Belgium seeming to fall by the wayside with weaker participation rights. Working-class coalitions with agrarian or liberal parties (IV6), which were discussed earlier, feed into legal and political rights and are close to working-class strength as the strongest predictor of the more recently appearing participation rights. And with participation rights, which do not come until the 1950s, Germany is not as much of an outlier as it was on political democracy because the SPD forms an important coalition with the liberal (FDP) party in the postwar era, and Ireland loses its "grand coalition" solidarity after independence movements are no longer necessary.

A strong welfare state (IV3) in and of itself can be a factor, but the countries that were moderately strong on the welfare state (e.g., Belgium) drop out when participation rights are considered. State-centric variables have support with proportional representation (IV7), the legal system (IV8), and ministries of labor (IV9) being effective in seven positive and seven negative countries.

Some countries should have stronger participation rights. Given Switzerland's Roman legal system and proportional representation and France's legal system, both countries should have stronger participation rights. Belgium probably should have stronger participation rights, but the dominant trade union federation opposed participation rights because they were "co-optative" (Stephens-Huber and Stephens 1982, p. 225). Finally, Italy is troublesome because of contradictions on working-class strength, strong welfare state presence, and all three state-centric variables. While these contradictions cannot be explained away as in earlier analyses, participation rights are still developing. France, Italy, and Belgium – three Latin countries – have passed recent laws which could develop into effective participation rights, but Switzerland is unlikely to do so.

Hypothesis 7.6: Working-Class Strength and Coalitions Explaining Participation Rights: Countries with strong labor movements that have already developed a welfare state through working-class coalitions will be more likely to develop strong participation rights.

Momentous Change over Centuries

Hypothesis 7.7: State-centric Explanations of Participation Rights: Countries with strong labor institutions will be more likely to develop strong participation rights.

In looking at all four citizenship rights over a period of many centuries, a group of hypotheses is added to the usual explanation of citizenship rights. The most analyzed rights in the most frequently examined period – liberal and political rights from 1789 to 1945 – support most of the usual precondition hypotheses of Moore and Stephens. Combining Luebbert, Baldwin, and to some extent Stephens, they also support a loosened working-class coalition hypothesis with a number of allies from peasants to liberals. The addition to this period and the dominant explanation in the earlier period from 1200 to 1815 is the formation or avoidance of military-bureaucratic absolutism hypothesis put forward by Downing and Tilly. In the more recent periods with social and participation rights, labor power theses flowing from the precondition hypotheses based on class-related variables and state-centric theses in many ways connected to the war hypotheses help explain those citizenship rights.

SEQUENCING RIGHTS OVER TIME

T. H. Marshall presented a developmental theory of rights from legal to political and then social rights. Giddens (1982) and Mishra (1981) severely criticized this sequencing theory. Giddens states that Marshall "writes as though the development of citizenship came about as something like a natural process of evolution, helped along where necessary by the beneficent hand of the state" (p. 171). Giddens goes on to criticize Marshall's failing to "emphasize that citizenship rights have been achieved in substantial degree only through struggle" (p. 171), but the Giddens critique cannot be substantiated because class struggle is clearly present in Marshall's conception of the development of rights. Indeed, Marshall even refers to the development of citizenship rights as a war between capital and labor, and his seminal article is called "Citizenship and Social Class," not "Citizenship and Social Evolution"! But the question of the natural sequencing of rights as a pattern for other countries remains a problem, especially since it has been linked to modernization and development theories, which have been under attack for many years now.

This section will address the question of sequencing in two ways: (1) what are the sequencing patterns of countries, especially any patterns that may emerge within regime types? and (2) what are the consequences for countries that follow different progressions of rights? Much of this involves some conceptual questions about when rights actually emerge, so each right will be examined concerning the sequencing question.

First, concerning legal rights, there are many rights that could be considered, which was a problem encountered in Chapter 2 concerning the measurement and comparison of rights in a number of countries. This chapter focuses on rights to hold property being protected in the courts for men, women, and ethnic groups, and rights to free speech and religion, which are often considered to be primary civil rights (Martin 1993, ch. 5).[18] Nine countries did not exist before 1800 when other countries were formulating their first legal rights, and they are dropped from the analysis except for Prussia and the United Provinces, which were strong states at that time. Table 7.5 compares the completion of these rights in ten countries.

Universalistic legal rights for men's claims to property are protected by courts early and well before political and social rights in the seventeenth and eighteenth centuries. Property rights for single women varied, but the critical category of legal rights to property for married women occurs much latter. In the United States, the determination of this date is quite complicated because of the primacy of state laws in many instances, but the agreed upon date tends to be around the turn of the century (Hoff 1991; Therborn 1995, p. 108). Other countries with more patriarchal systems did not confer this right until the 1930s or even after the end of World War II (Stetson 1987; Frevert 1988; van der Burght 1990; Kruse 1939). Legal rights for ethnic/racial groups fare much worse. Jews in Germany, Austria, and Italy had their property confiscated on a mass scale in the 1930s. As a result, legal rights to property were begun with the new constitutions after World War II with some property claims being held in abeyance until the fall of the East German communist state. Indigenous and former slave populations in the United States, Australia, Canada, and a few other countries did not have citizen status until well into the twentieth century, so their property rights were ignored while their lands and properties were often taken. Rights to free speech and the freedom of religion have been in existence in many of the liberal and mixed countries since the seventeenth and eighteenth centuries (with Japan being the major exception). These same freedoms were weak to begin with in many of the traditional countries (with France being a major exception). The *Kulturkampf* in Germany was a clear abridgement of religious freedom, and the rise of fascism in Germany, Italy, and Austria that erased property rights for Jews also brought a rescission of the freedoms of religion and speech.

While the data are not as precise for legal rights as they are for the following three citizenship rights, sequencing estimates can be made.[19] It appears that property rights for males were established well before other citizenship rights, and that in the liberal countries, with the exception of Japan, freedoms of speech and religion were quite early as well. Religious and speech rights came later in the social democratic and traditional countries, but they were abridged in the mid–twentieth century with the rise of fascism in many traditional countries. However, women's property rights tend to come around the turn of the century for most countries, and this overlaps male working-class political rights and many early social rights. In comparing the three regimes, the data are not robust enough to make differentiations between social democratic and liberal countries, but the averages for years of possessing legal rights in the traditional countries are clearly lower than the other two regimes: male legal rights – 180.0 for traditional regimes is less than 272.3 for social democratic and less than 250.0 for liberal regimes; religious rights – 97.3, less than 221.7 and 196.0; and married women's legal rights – 30.0, less than 60.7 and 57.5.

The data on political rights in Table 7.6 are more established (Therborn 1977; Flanz 1983). Although the average for liberal countries is brought down by the low score for Japan, liberal countries established political rights for men well before the other two regime types. The United Kingdom is also early on the elite male franchise, and according to Esping-Andersen's score this could also be legally considered a liberal country. The social democratic regimes are only slightly earlier than traditional regimes on their initial formation of elite male voting rights, but those rights were revoked for four of five traditional countries leaving a much later beginning date. The average number of years for possessing political rights in traditional regimes (64.2) is less than that in social democratic (91.4) and liberal (114.0) regimes.

Although developing a little later, political rights for all men tend to follow a similar pattern (64.2 for traditional regimes being lower than 81.2 and 98.4 for social democratic and liberal regimes). Political rights for women in the social democratic countries are moderately higher than the liberal countries, but this is mainly due to Switzerland's granting the franchise to women very late in 1971. However, social democratic (80.2) and liberal (62.0) average regime scores are much higher than the traditional regime score (46.4). Ethnic political rights are troublesome because some countries do not have clear minority groups and others have many. Nonetheless, where minority voting applies, these rights seem to appear just after World War II in traditional countries and distressingly later in liberal countries. Social democratic countries gave voting rights to the indigenous Saami much earlier.[20] In sum, political rights for men develop first in liberal regimes, and for women in social democratic regimes. But political rights for indigenous and dominated peoples develop very late for liberal countries.

Table 7.5. *Sequencing legal rights in ten countries according to regime type*

Countries by regime types	1st right implemented		2nd right implemented		3rd right implemented		4th right implemented	
Social democratic								
Denmark	LM_{1788}	217	LS_{1849}	146*	LR_{1849}	146*	LW_{1925}	70
Netherlands[a]	LM_{1581}	300*	LS_{1581}	300*	LR_{1815}	180	LW_{1957}	35
Sweden	LM_{1695}	300	LS_{1776}	219	LR_{1809}	186	LW_{1921}	74
Average:		*272.3*		*221.7*		*170.7*		*59.7*
Traditional								
Austria	LM_{1867}	128	LS_{1945} (1867)<1938>	50*	LR_{1945} (1867)<1938>	50*	LW_{1945}	50*
France	LM_{1815}	180*	LS_{1815} (1791)<1799>	180*	LR_{1815}	180*	LW_{1965}	30
Germany[a]	LM_{1815}	180	LS_{1949} (1871)<1933>	46*	LR_{1949} (1871)<1933>	46*	LW_{1977}	18
Average		*180.0*		*97.3*		*92.0*		*30.0*
Liberal								
Switzerland	LM_{1648}	300	LS_{1803}	192*	LR_{1803}	192*	LW_{1980}	15
United States	LM_{1795}	200*	LS_{1795}	200*	LR_{1795}	200*	LW_{1905}	90[b]
Average		*250.0*		*196.0*		*196.0*		*52.5*
Mixed								
Japan	LM_{1879}	116	LS_{1947}	48*	LR_{1947}	48*	LW_{1947}	48*
United Kingdom	LM_{1689}	300	LS_{1795}	200*	LR_{1795}	200*	LW_{1883}	112

ABBREVIATIONS:

LM = Men having the right to hold property is upheld in the courts.

LR = Right to freedom of religion is protected in constitution or equivalent document.

LS = Rights to free speech protected in the constitution or equivalent document.

LW = Married women having the right to hold property is upheld in the courts.

NOTES:

The abbreviated type of legal right, the year of implementation, and the cumulative years of enforcement to 1995 are listed under the headings for the 1st through 4th rights implemented. Parentheses indicate the date of previously created legal rights, and relational brackets indicate the date of an internally created reversal of rights. An asterisk refers to a tie with another score.

[a] Australia, Canada, Belgium, Finland, New Zealand, Norway, Ireland, and Italy were excluded because they did not exist in 1800. Germany as Prussia and the Netherlands as the United Provinces were included because they were important countries at the time.

[b] Wenig (1995) makes the case for 1960 in Louisiana, which has a Roman law system, and even later for Oklahoma. However, Therborn (1995) and Hoff (1991) report dates closer to the turn of the century.

SOURCES: Maddex (1995); Glendon (1989); Hoff 1991, pp. 187–91 and 377–81; Rhoodie (1989); Stetson (1987, pp. 87–94), Frevert (1988, p. 323), Van der Burght (1990, pp. 1–2), Kruse (1939, p. 259), Scannell (1985), and Therborn (1995, pp. 107–109).

Table 7.6. *Sequencing political rights in eighteen countries according to regime type*

Countries by regime types	1st right implemented	2nd right implemented	3rd right implemented	4th right implemented[a]
Social democratic				
Denmark	PE_{1901} 94	PM_{1915} 80	PW_{1915} 80*	PR_{1950} 80* / 45
Finland	PE_{1906} 89*[a]	PM_{1906} 89*[a]	PW_{1906} 89	PR_{1906} 89 / 89
Netherlands	PE_{1887} 108	PM_{1917} 78	PW_{1922}[b] 73	PR 73 / —
Norway	PE_{1898} 97	PM_{1913} 82	PW_{1913} 82	PR_{1913} 82 / 82/80
Sweden	PE_{1909} 84	PM_{1918} 77	PW_{1918} 77	PR_{1918} 77 / 77/74
Average	*94.4*	*81.2*	*80.2*	*73.3/72.0*
Traditional				
Austria	PE_{1955} (1918)<1934> 40	PM_{1955} (1918)<1934> 40*	PW_{1955} (1918)<1934> 40*	PR_{1955} 40* / 40*
Belgium	PE_{1919} 74	PM_{1919} 74*	PW_{1948} 47	PR 47 / —
France	PE_{1884} (1790)<1795> 111	PM_{1884} (1790)<1795> 111*	PW_{1944} 51	PR 51 / —
Germany	PE_{1949} (1870)<1933> 46	PM_{1949} (1919)<1933> 46*	PW_{1949} (1919)<1933> 46*	PR_{1949} (1919)<1933> 46* / 46*
Italy	PE_{1945} (1919)<1922> 50	PM_{1945} (1919)<1922> 50*	PW_{1945} (1919)<1922> 50*	PR_{1945} (1919)<1922> 50* / 50*
Average	*64.2*	*64.2*	*46.4*	*45.3*
Liberal				
Australia	PE_{1903} 92*	PM_{1903} 92*	PW_{1908} 88[c]	PR_{1962} 88[c] / 33
Canada	PE_{1920} 75	PM_{1920} 75*	PW_{1920} 75*	PR_{1960} 75* / 35
Japan	PE_{1950} 45*	PM_{1950} 45*	PW_{1950} 45*	PR 45* / —
Switzerland	PE_{1848} 147	PM_{1880} 115	PW_{1971} 24	PR 24 / —
United States	PE_{1776} 213	PM_{1830} 165	PW_{1921} 74	PR_{1970} 74 / 25

Mixed

Ireland	PE$_{1919}$	74	PM$_{1919}$	74*	PW$_{1922}$	73	PR	—
United Kingdom	PE$_{1832}$	163	PM$_{1918}$	77	PW$_{1928}$	67	PR	—
New Zealand	PE$_{1907}$	88*	PM$_{1907}$	88*	PW$_{1907}$	88*	PR$_{1907}$	88*[d]

ABBREVIATIONS:

PE = Property holding males have the right to vote in national elections. *PM* = All males have the right to vote in national elections. *PW* = Women have the right to vote in national elections.

PR = All ethnic and racial groups' have the right to vote in national elections. Ethnic groups include: Inuit – Denmark and Canada; Saami – Finland, Norway, and Sweden; Jews – Austria, Germany, Italy; Aboriginals and Torres Straits people – Australia; Maori – New Zealand; United States – African Americans; None – Belgium, France, Ireland, Netherlands, Switzerland, and United Kingdom. The 1970 date for the U.S. represents the enforcement of the Voting Rights Act in the South.

NOTES:

The abbreviated type of right, year of implementation, and years of continuous rights enforcement to 1995 are listed under the headings for the 1st through 4th rights.

( ) = the date of previously created political rights, < > = the date of an internally created reversal of political rights, * = tied with a previous category.

[a] Finland was an autonomous grand duchy of the Russian empire at this time. But it had a relatively independent parliament.

[b] Daley and Nolan (1994) report 1919 instead of 1922 for the Netherlands.

[c] Full suffrage is not gained until suffrage in Victoria is passed in 1908. Others may use 1903 as the date for full suffrage for federal elections.

[d] Four Maori seats were set up in the parliament in 1867; however, universal suffrage came later.

SOURCES: Therborn (1977), Flanz (1983), Hannum (1996), Daley and Nolan (1994), Rokkan (1970), Rueschemeyer et al (1992), Mann (1994), and the Swedish, Norwegian, and Finnish Consulates.

Citizenship and Civil Society

Social rights for pensions, workman's compensation, health insurance, unemployment insurance, and family allowance programs are also well established (Hicks et al. 1995; Abbott and Deviney 1992), but they tend to reverse the patterns just discussed (see Table 7.7). Liberal countries are the clear laggards with social rights developing last in the first four categories and barely edging into second for the last category. Social democratic nations are first in three of five categories, and traditional nations are first in two of five social rights. France and Belgium bring the traditional averages down, and without those two countries, the traditional countries would be highest on four of five measures. The social democratic and traditional regimes clearly lead the liberal countries in developing three of five social rights categories with the following averages: first – 98.4 and 91.6 for social democratic and traditional regimes are greater than 87.2 for liberal regimes, second – 83.0 and 81.6, greater than 77.2; and fourth – 67.4 and 69.0, greater than 45.4. For the most part, the social democratic regimes are first in three categories, a close second in one, and third once in a tight-knit group; traditional regimes are first in two categories, second once, third once, and tied for second once; liberal regimes are never first, second twice, tied for second once, and last three times.

Participation rights include works councils, workers on corporate boards, and active state interventions in the labor market, and their dates of initiation can be seen in Table 7.8. Traditional countries like Germany and Austria have been the highest on works councils and codetermination, but many social democratic countries have followed with works councils and even stronger active labor market policies. The result is that traditional countries and social democratic countries are similar on all three rights (26.8, 17.8, and 3.0 for social democratic regimes and 33.6, 15.8, and 7.0 for traditional regimes). Liberal and mixed countries on the other hand are very weak on participation rights with only Australia, Canada, Ireland, New Zealand, and the United Kingdom exhibiting even one participation right.

Citizenship rights are difficult to compare to each other because they are not in the same units. For instance, one cannot say that legal rights are greater than social rights in the United States because liberties enforced by the courts translate poorly into education and pension services or expenditures. This does not mean that these comparisons are impossible, but just that they cannot be empirically determined in any precise way. What researchers can do is to compare countries on a particular right, and then compare their relative ranking of various rights. For instance, one may rank countries on legal and social rights, and then say that one country ranks first on one and third on the other, and another country ranks second and fourth. Consequently, the following hypotheses compare countries on sets of particular rights, rather than directly compare different rights.

Hypothesis 7.8: On political democracy, liberal countries will rank high on legal and political rights, while traditional corporatist countries will rank low on these same rights. Social democratic countries will be moderate on political democracy

Hypothesis 7.9: With economic democracy, liberal countries will rank lowest on social and participation rights. Traditional corporatist countries will rank high and social democratic countries moderately high on social rights and participation rights.

There is a clear trade-off between political democracy and economic democracy in liberal and traditional countries, but the trade-off is somewhat moderated in the social democratic countries. Liberal countries are high on legal and political rights, while traditional countries are high on social and participation rights. Social democratic countries, such as Sweden, have shown moderately high citizenship rights but not the highest levels of political, social, and participation rights. Social democratic regimes have avoided the legal and political rights rescissions that occurred in Germany, while survival rights have been defended by a strong welfare state. Legal rights in Sweden may not be as high as in the United States, especially concerning the disposition of private property due to high regulation and what some conservatives mislabel as confiscatory taxation levels, but many unique legal protections exist (e.g., the protection of the privacy of the accused before and during trial, and the presence of ombudspersons to safeguard rights).[21] Social rights in Sweden are very high but are much lower than Germany over the last century, and participation rights have not matched the German level at any time this century.

Hypothesis 7.10: Comparing All Four Citizenship Rights: Liberal regimes will be high on legal and political rights, and low on social and participation rights; traditional regimes will be low on legal and political rights, and high on social and participation rights; and social democratic regimes will be moderately high on all four rights. None of the advanced industrialized countries will be high on all four rights or low on all four rights.

According to T. H. Marshall citizenship rights should come in the following order: legal, political, social, and participation rights. On the basis of Tables 7.5 through 7.8, a simple comparison can be made to Marshall's ordering of rights – the four legal rights first, then the three political rights, followed by the five social rights and the three participation rights.[22] Using his theory as the basis of coding, scores are computed on each right's rank. Using the following notation for rights – LR

Table 7.7. Sequencing social rights in eighteen countries according to regime type

Countries by regime type	1st right implemented		2nd right implemented		3rd right implemented		4th right implemented		5th right implemented	
Social democratic										
Denmark	SU_{1907}	88	SW_{1916}	79	SO_{1922}	73	SH_{1933}	62	SF_{1952}	43
Finland	SW_{1895}	100	SO_{1917}	82	SU_{1937}	53	SF_{1948}	52	SH_{1963}	32
Netherlands	SW_{1901}	94	SH_{1909}	86	SO_{1909}	86*	SU_{1916}	79	SF_{1939}	56
Norway	SW_{1895}	100	SH_{1909}	86	SO_{1936}	82	SU_{1938}	81	SF_{1946}	49
Sweden	SH_{1891}	104	SO_{1913}	82	SW_{1916}	85	SU_{1934}	61	SF_{1948}	43
Average	*SW*	*98.4*	*SH/SO*	*83.0*	*SO*	*74.4*	*SU*	*67.4*	*SF*	*44.6*
Traditional										
Austria	SW_{1887}	108	SH_{1912}	107	SU_{1920}	75	SO_{1927}	68	SF_{1948}	42
Belgium	SO_{1924}	71	SF_{1930}	65	SU_{1912}	83	SH_{1912}	83	SW_{1971}	24
France	SH_{1930}	65	SW_{1946}	49	SO_{1946}	49*	SF_{1952}	43	SU_{1967}	28
Germany	SH_{1883}	112	SW_{1884}	111	SO_{1889}	106	SU_{1952}	68	SF_{1963}	32
Italy	SW_{1898}	102	SU_{1919}	76	SO_{1912}	83	SF_{1912}	83*	SH_{1946}	49
Average	*SW/SH*	*91.6*	*SW*	*81.6*	*SO*	*79.2*	*SF*	*69.0*	*SF*	*35.0*
Liberal										
Australia	SW_{1902}	93	SO_{1908}	87	SF_{1941}	54	SH_{1944}	51	SU_{1944}	51*
Canada	SW_{1908}	87	SO_{1927}	68	SU_{1940}	55	SF_{1944}	51	SH_{1971}	24
Japan	SW_{1911}	94	SH_{1922}	73	SO_{1941}	54	SU_{1947}	48	SF_{1971}	24
Switzerland	SW_{1911}	83	SH_{1911}	83*	SO_{1946}	49	SF_{1960}	45	SU_{1976}	19
United States	SW_{1912}	83	SU_{1935}	60	SO_{1935}	60	none	0	none	0
Average	*SW*	*87.2*	*SH/SO*	*77.2*	*SO*	*77.2*	*—*	*45.4*	*SF/SU*	*35.4*

Mixed

Ireland	SH_{1911}	84	SO_{1920}	75	SU_{1995}	51	SF_{1945}	51*	SF_{1944}	51*
New Zealand	SO_{1898}	97	SW_{1908}	87	SF_{1956}	64	SU_{1990}	65	SH_{1938}	53
United Kingdom	SH_{1911}	83	SU_{1920}	75	SO_{1925}	70	SF_{1945}	50	SW_{1946}	19

NOTE:

The abbreviated type of social right, subscripted year of implementation, and continuous number of years that the right was enforced from 1995 are under the 1st through 5th rights. The asterisk indicates ties with other rights categories.

ABBREVIATIONS:

SW = Social rights in workman's compensation programs. SO = Social rights in old age pension programs. SH = Social rights in health and sickness programs. SU = Social rights in unemployment insurance programs. SF = Social rights in family allowance programs.

SOURCES: Hicks, Misra, and Ng (1995), Abbott and Devinney (1992), and Maguire (1988) for Ireland.

Table 7.8. *Sequencing participation rights in eighteen countries according to regime type (rights, subscripted year of implementation, and cumulative years enforced based to 1995)*

Countries by regime types	1st right implemented		2nd right implemented		3rd right implemented	
Social democratic						
Denmark	WD_{1974}	21	$ALMP_{1980}$	15	(none)	0
Finland	WC_{1980}	15[a]	$ALMP_{1980}$	15	(none)	0
Netherlands	WC_{1971}	24	$ALMP_{1980}$	15	(none)	0
Norway	WC_{1956}	39	WD_{1973}	22	$ALMP_{1980}$	15
Sweden	$ALMP_{1960}$	35	WD_{1973}	22	WC_{1946}	0[b]
Average		*26.8*		*17.8*		*3.0*
Traditional						
Austria	WC_{1952}	43	WD_{1977}	18	(none)	0
Belgium	WC_{1952}	43	WD_{1977}	18	$ALMP_{1985}$	10
France	$ALMP_{1975}$	20	(none)	0	(none)	0
Germany	WC_{1951}	44	WD_{1952}	43	$ALMP_{1970}$	25
Italy	WD_{1977}	18	(none)	0	(none)	0
Average		*33.6*		*15.8*		*7.0*

Liberal						
Australia	ALMP$_{1974}$	21	(none)	0	(none)	0
Canada	ALMP$_{1965}$	25	(none)	0	(none)	0
Japan	(none)	0	(none)	0	(none)	0
Switzerland	(none)	0	(none)	0	(none)	0
United States	(none)	0	(none)	0	(none)	0
Average		9.2		0.0		0.0
Mixed						
Ireland	ALMP$_{1980}$	15	(none)	0	(none)	0
New Zealand	ALMP$_{1980}$	15	(none)	0	(none)	0
United Kingdom	ALMP$_{1975}$	20	(none)	0	(none)	0

[a] Finnish works councils are labor protection committees that are probably only half a works council in other countries.

[b] Swedish works councils exist entirely within the unions and are totally consultative. Consequently, they were scored a zero.

ABBREVIATIONS:

WC = Works councils legislated into law. *ALMP* = The threshold for active labor market policy is when expenditures were greater than 0.50% of GNP in any five year period from 1950 to 1990. *WD* = Codetermination rights on corporate boards legislated into law.

SOURCES: Janoski, McGill, and Tinsley (1997) and Janoski (1996).

= legal, PO = political, SR = social, and PA = participation – and assigning a score based on chronology, Marshall's theoretical sequencing is scored as follows: LR (1st), LR (2d), LR (3d), LR (4th), PO (5th), PO (6th), PO (7th), SR (8th), SR (9th), SR (10th), SR (11th), SR (12th), PA (13th), PA (14th), and PA (15th). The average ranking for Marshall's sequencing of each right would then be as follows: legal rights = 2.5, political rights = 6.0, social rights = 9.0, and participation rights = 14.0.[23] This is a baseline measure for the nine countries that can be seen in the center of the first row in Table 7.9.

The last four columns show how much each country and regime averages deviate from Marshall's theoretical sequencing. The liberal countries are very close, and the average for three countries is less than 1.0 point different from Marshall's score.[24] The social democratic average is +2.77 on political rights, indicating that these rights came much later than Marshall's score while social rights tended to come a bit earlier than Marshall predicts. The biggest difference comes for the traditional countries. Legal and political rights differences from Marshall's scores are +3.40 and +3.23, indicating very late sequencing on average for these rights. Conversely, the social and participation rights scores are −2.67 and −1.23, showing that in many cases social and participation rights came early. Based on these results, one could generate the following hypothesis:

Hypothesis 7.11: The Sequencing of Legal, Political, Social, and Participation Rights differs according to regime type: (1) Liberal countries follow Marshall's progression of legal, political, and social rights, but after the early development of legal and political rights, social and participation rights tend to lag. (2) Social democratic countries develop legal rights first, and then political and social rights develop simultaneously with political rights only coming slightly earlier. Participation rights are last but not least to develop. (3) Traditional countries develop some property rights for men, but social rights come very early. Political and most legal rights for the working class and women are late in developing, and in most traditional countries they are rescinded in the 1930–45 period. Participation rights begin after World War I but are firmly established after World War II.

When the full range of citizenship rights is taken under consideration, Marshall's progression of rights with some modifications seem to bear weight. The liberal countries develop political democracy but tend to stall with social and participation rights because they become fixated on protecting bourgeois concerns for property rights and sometimes spending a great deal of money on the military (e.g., the United States and the United Kingdom if it is considered a liberal country). The traditional corporatist countries seem much more concerned with social rights and go on to develop participation rights, but due to political instabilities, legal and political rights are left unprotected or even sacrificed at important points in history (e.g., Germany and Austria in the 1930s and 1940s). And the communist countries, which I have not discussed much, provide extensive social rights, and some participation rights, but have had an extremely poor record on legal and political rights. The social democratic regime types, while not being innovative leaders in initiating any one type of right, develop a path building on legal, political, social, and finally participation rights. Despite the current changes in Scandinavian countries toward stronger markets and less government, Sweden, Norway, and Denmark remain moderately high on all four rights when compared to countries from other regime types.

In the end, Marshall's path seems to be a much more stable route to full citizenship for liberal and social democratic countries than does starting early with social or participation rights as the traditional countries did. The consequences of sequential development are also important. The liberal countries are the first to embark on full legal and political rights, and with these liberties and powers they establish strong biases against social and participation rights. In many ways, the traditional countries are reversed. The ranking procedure does not adequately reflect these differences in the strength of programs. Nonetheless, the regimes appear to be path dependent on their initial selection of rights.

Hypothesis 7.12: Countries that develop all four rights in moderation and in the order of legal, political, social, and participation rights will be more stable and develop all four citizenship rights to a greater degree than countries who do not. Social democratic countries exhibit this fuller development more than liberal or traditional corporatist countries.

CONCLUSION ON LONG-TERM DEVELOPMENT

Although legal, political, social, and participation rights have not previously been put together as a coherent category of political outputs, this chapter uses citizenship theory to put all four rights in a citizenship theory to explain their genesis and their sequencing vis-à-vis each other. Despite T. H. Marshall's pioneering work in this area and theoretical critiques of his work, analyses based on his approach simply have not been done. This chapter has put citizenship rights into the larger explanatory framework that Marshall's theory requires.

Citizenship rights and social policies in the long run are explained by processes of capital and coercion. In an analogous way, citizenship rights in the short and medium run (five to twenty years) are primarily explained through internal problems, policy deliberations, and political factors. Although some effects come from outside the nation-state (the

Table 7.9. *Regime types according to Marshall's sequencing of citizenship rights*

Country and regime type	Raw rank scores				Average rank score				Average rank scores minus Marshall's baseline score			
	L R	P O	S R	P A	L R	P O	S R	P A	L R	P O	S R	P A
Marshall's Baseline	10	18	45	42	2.5	6.0	9.0	14.0				
Social democratic												
Denmark	19	29	33	42	4.8	9.7	6.6	14.0	+2.3	+3.7	-2.4	0.0
Netherlands	11	25	42	42	2.8	8.3	8.4	14.0	+0.3	+2.3	-0.6	0.0
Sweden	10	25	43	42	2.5	8.3	8.6	14.0	0.0	+2.3	-0.4	0.0
Average									0.87	2.77	-0.38	0.00
Traditional												
Austria	22	36	23	39	5.5	12.0	4.6	13.0	+3.0	+6.0	-4.4	-1.0
France	17	16	45	42	4.3	5.3	9.0	14.0	+2.2	+0.7	0.0	0.0
Germany	32	24	27	37	8.0	8.0	5.4	12.3	+5.5	+3.0	-3.6	-2.7
Average									3.40	3.23	-2.67	-1.23

Liberal

Switzerland												
United States	18	19	41	42	4.5	6.3	8.2	14.0	+2.0	+0.3	−0.8	0.0
United Kingdom	11	17	52	39	2.8	5.7	10.4	13.0	+0.3	−0.3	+1.4	−1.0[a]
United Kingdom	11	21	46	42	2.8	7.0	9.2	14.0	+0.3	−1.3	+0.2	0.0
Average								0.87	−0.43	−0.27	−0.33	

NOTE:

LR=legal rights, PO=political rights, SR=social rights, and PA=participation rights

[a] The U.S. score on participation rights is -1.0 because the three participation rights and last two social rights scores are tied in that they do not exist. The averaging of ranks 11 through 15 produces an average rank of 13.0. An argument could be made for giving each item a 15 for the last rank or a 0 for no rank since these policies did not exist.

SOURCES AND COMPUTATIONS: Rights are as listed in tables 8.5 through 8.8. There are four legal rights and three political rights (political rights for minorities are excluded due to the difficult problem of classifying who is a minority in each country). Social rights categories are five with participation rights being three. The first right implemented is given a score of −, the second, 2, and so on. The average rank scores are divided by the number of rights in each category. The deviation from Marshall's baseline rank is the average score minus the baseline score. When ties span different groups of rights, the ranks are added together and divided by the number of categories that share the score (e.g., ranks 7, 8 and 9 are added together and divided by 3 with each category then receiving a score of 8.0). If the ranks are tied within a group of rights, then no calculation is made.

215

most notable being war, economic depressions, and oil shocks), even those effects are heavily mediated by internal political and social factors. This chapter has shown that although external effects may have played a small effect in the short-term model, national preferences for capital or coercion over centuries are much more important in the long-term development of state citizenship. The type of state leads to particular state structures that promote or impede the development of citizenship rights. Citizenship rights themselves can be developed through discrimination, public goods, naturalization, and sacrifice extensions on policies of advanced industrialized countries.

This chapter presented an analysis of citizenship rights demonstrating the plausibility of four sets of hypotheses. First, legal and political rights over the long term of nearly 400 years were shown to be greater in liberal democratic than in traditional regimes. The reverse held true for social and participation rights. Second, political and economic democracy were shown to be in a trade-off with social democratic countries showing moderately high levels on all four rights.

Third, the causes of all four rights were hypothesized. Legal rights from 1200 to 1815 emerged in countries that could avoid military-bureaucratic absolutism. Legal rights from 1789 to 1990 developed in countries that did not have strong landed upper classes, subordinate bourgeoisie, dominant state, or military-bureaucratic absolutism. Political rights appeared in regimes with a strong labor movement in coalition with either liberal or agrarian allies. Social rights develop in countries with a strong labor movement in coalitions, proportional electoral systems with Roman law, and solidaristic experiences during both world wars. Participation rights are caused by a strong welfare state already existing (so efforts will not be diverted there), labor power in coalitions, and conducive political structures with proportional elections.

Fourth, Marshall's theory of development was reasserted not as a normative prescription, but as a series of steps that countries may climb to achieve all four rights. To do so, they must not skip steps as with traditional regimes or become fixated on maximizing rights in any one step as in liberal regimes. Throughout this chapter, I have demonstrated the plausibility of four important hypotheses about citizenship development, but again, I make no claim that these hypotheses are proven. Given the framework outlined here, the next step is to test these hypotheses in more detail.

8

Conclusion and Implications

Novel, important and true ideas are rare. Such ideas which are then developed into a coherent theory are even scarcer. T. H. Marshall is one of very few to have had at least one such idea, and to develop it. That is why it is important to understand and to improve upon his theory of citizenship.

Michael Mann (1988, p. 188)

Citizenship shows renewed vitality as a "novel" idea that needs theoretical development. Nations are extending citizenship to increasing numbers and percentages of people within national boundaries, and social scientists are using citizenship theories to explain this movement. As Michael Walzer states (1983, p. 31), "the primary good that we distribute to one another is membership in some human community" and with increasing frequency that "membership" is citizenship in a country. Academic interest has increased in the area of citizenship, and much more is being written using this concept, although little effort has focused systematically on social science theory. This book has taken the confusing welter of materials burgeoning in the area of citizenship and put them into a theoretical framework that is both coherent and capable of being operationalized. In so doing, it has also provided a theoretical foundation for three regime types, which have been previously grounded in left-right distinctions, or in a political theory format of liberalism, communitarianism, and expansive democracy. Each regime type with its characteristic theory has different constraints and accomplishes different things.

This conclusion summarizes this framework, which is intended to serve future empirical analyses, and points to some of the areas of citizenship and regime theory where further clarification is needed. After the summary and discussion of research frontiers, I briefly address the social policy implications of this work for the United States.[1]

Citizenship and Civil Society

THREE DOMINANT QUESTIONS OF
CITIZENSHIP THEORY

This book has covered a great deal of ground in sociology, political science, and even philosophy. In the introduction, I defined citizenship as passive and active membership in a nation-state with universalistic rights and a specified level of equality, and I introduced civil society as dynamic and responsive discourse between state, public, and market spheres in society. The two concepts of citizenship and civil society were then brought together into a complementary relationship using political theory – liberalism, communitarianism, and expansive democracy approaches – and regime theory – liberal, traditional, and social democratic groups of countries. The introduction then formulated three crucial questions of citizenship theory that shape the rest of the book. How can theories of rights and obligations be clarified to avoid the confusion that surrounds this area? How can rights and obligations be balanced at the micro- and macro-levels of society? And how can an adequate theory of the development of rights and obligations be made to cover both decades and centuries?

On the first crucial question, I addressed the confusing welter of concepts and ideas presently inhabiting the area of citizenship. While some of this work might appear to be philosophical or taxonomic, my framework of citizenship rights clarifies various problems with rights and provides a more than adequate casement to advance citizenship theory. The basis was laid for rights in conceptions of activity (active and passive) and sphere (political and economic), which uncovered the basis for participation rights. Whether they are present or absent in different countries is a major part of social policy explanation that needs to be done. Too much research has focused on either the implementation of a socialist agenda in social and sometimes participation rights demanded by the trade unions, or a defense of legal and political liberties trumpeted by conservative libertarians. However, the passage of diverse participation rights bearing the imprint of different class and status groups has taken this aspect of social policy beyond one-dimensional ideologies. Participatory mechanisms exist to varying degrees in extensive laws in many European countries, and they are now a fact of social policy. What remains are efforts to integrate these phenomena into explanations of social policy, rather than treating them as items on an ideological wish list to be advanced or decimated. A system of rights becomes established with triumphs, faults, and deadwood, and how these systems of rights actually operate in different countries are social facts and a major object of social scientific study.

Conclusion and Implications

By outlining the range of citizenship rights from the broad consensus that exists among many countries to the particular types of rights that exist in only certain regime types, and matching them with Hohfeld's (1978) theoretical work from law on the diversity of rights themselves as a category, this book clarifies the frequent confusion over what falls into the bundle of rights to be included under the rubric of citizenship. Hohfeld classified rights into liberties, claims, powers, and immunities, which were shown to correspond to legal, political, social, and participation rights in citizenship theory. It was also shown how immunities fit with affirmative action and veterans' compensatory programs. Finally, personhood was discussed in its fundamental position in generating new social rights. In this way, citizenship rights need not be perceived as a confusing set of theoretical categories.

The clarification of citizenship then focused on an approach to obligations, which are among the neglected aspects of citizenship. This theoretical stepchild, which has just recently received increasing amounts of attention, is central to citizenship theory. Researchers and commentators began to pay attention to obligations in the mid-1980s, and this has greatly accelerated in the 1990s. A number of factors may have deterred social scientists from studying obligations. The call to focus on obligations has been increasingly ideological, and serious social scientists would rather avoid the rhetoric. However, researchers are paying more attention to how people conceptualize and fulfill their obligations. Moral positions and attitudes concerning what citizens believe they ought to do are not beyond the pale of social science research (Ossowska 1970; Jackall 1988; Rose 1955).

This has also been a difficult area because obligations do not neatly fall into categories of civil rights or social policy, but three major obligations show how our social focus myopically overlooks obligations as a matter of course and assigns them to economic/taxation, defense, or criminal justice policies. Paying taxes is not often considered to be connected to social policy and citizenship. Economists more often discuss the merits of progressive and regressive taxes as part of macro-economic and redistribution policies. The obligations to pay taxes and the comparisons of people who pay and those who evade are usually targets of technical studies on the efficiency of taxes. Studies of the causes of comparative tax evasion rates and willingness to bear a high tax burden are similarly quite rare (for some exceptions see Wilensky 1976 and Steinmo 1989).

Second, defense policy covers citizens serving in the military. But as I argued in the sections on conscription, returning veterans have a tremendous impact on legal and political rights (usually positive) and on the size and quality of the welfare state (usually negative). Further, the willingness to serve is generally lumped into conservative ideology and political power (for exceptions see Janowitz 1983; Gorham 1992; Moskos and Chambers 1993). When voluntary service within the nation is considered, social policy becomes a bit more involved. This is mainly because voluntary action takes place in welfare state organizations or voluntary associations closely linked to the welfare state. However, voluntarism and fulfilling obligations have a close but awkward relationship to rights. If some action is totally voluntary, then one could hardly be fulfilling an obligation in doing it, but if no one asks people to volunteer, especially at a younger age in schools, few people realize its benefits for themselves and others (Janoski, Wilson, and Musick in press).

Third, respecting the law and other persons' rights comes under the rubric of tolerance, but the enforcement of this area generally falls into the category of law and order, not citizenship. Citizenship tends to get involved with tolerance when its absence causes problems in social policy. But teaching and learning tolerance while avoiding value relativism is a major challenge to our schools and workplaces. Consequently, these three obligations of taxation, national service, and social tolerance need to be integrated into a comprehensive theory of citizenship even though some do not see them as inherently part of citizenship. The unrecognized breadth of inquiry is probably another reason why social policy researchers have tended to downplay obligations – it appeared to be outside their purview of interest and expertise. But the net of inquiry must be thrown much wider than previously attempted.

In contrast to this confusion or avoidance of obligations, this approach also demonstrates the range of citizenship obligations as opposed to moral obligations, delineates theories of obligations allowing the delimitation of obligations and their understanding through principles of exchange, and provides for theoretical ways to enforce obligations but at the same time protect civil rights through notching mechanisms recommended by Etzioni (1993) and Martin (1993). The discussion then focuses on how positive and lesser sanctions have been ignored and how they can be enforced through greater observability, reintegrative shaming, restorative justice, and citizenship participation in the sanctioning process. Patriotism is then reconstructed with an emphasis on responsible allegiance rather than blind obedience. Building on Selznick (1992) and Habermas (1994), responsible patriotism avoids the negative aspects of nationalism but provides a basis of constitutional patriotism to support obligations and duties as well as rights in society. Finally, this chapter shows that a rights saturation does not exist, but rather an obligations deficit is the real problem.

The second crucial question of citizenship theory concerns the balance of rights and obligations. The first part of an answer deals with the basic

Conclusion and Implications

processes of restricted and generalized exchange in open and closed groups within a Weberian theory of social action. This provides an expanded theory of citizenship demanded in the previous chapters on rights and obligations with a motivational basis in emotion, tradition, and four types of rationality. Over-reliance on either restricted or generalized exchange leads to analytic problems. Too much emphasis on norms leads to a static view of society and the over-socialized reproduction of social structures. Too much emphasis on rationality leads to an under-socialized flux and, when coupled with a simplified view of rationality, allows social scientists to make ad hoc decisions about what is rational rather than examining how people actually make decisions. Much more attention in sociological research needs to be paid to measuring different mechanisms of exchange rather than advocating one or the other. Exchange mechanisms and their normative and rational motivations must be looked upon as exhibiting variation rather than a declared constancy.

After a foundation was laid for balance through restricted and generalized exchange relying on three forces of social action – emotion, tradition, and rationality – this was implemented in a typology of citizen-selves that showed citizens allegiant with the dominant political order to be incorporated, deferential, or fatalistic loyalists, and those in opposition to be active, cynical, or fatalistic opponents. The somewhat unpredictable citizen-self – opportunistic citizens – choose to act politically or not based on benefit to themselves in an individualistic and opportunistic manner. It may very well be that citizens in different regimes types appear in different proportions of each type of citizen-self, but much cross-national research needs to be done before these citizen-selves can be verified or disproved. This theoretical approach will guide empirical inquiry based on restricted and generalized exchange through interaction ritual chains; and despite the undoubted construction of selves into an infinite variety of forms, generalizations will emerge about citizen-selves in different regime types.

Next, I addressed the issue of balancing of rights and obligations in liberal, traditional, and social democratic regimes. The macro-theory of balance ends up with a complex but consistent generalization of the tendencies in these three regimes. Social democratic regimes balance a high level of rights and obligations with high membership and volunteering in associations in a moderately open society using overlapping and open generalized exchange between groups in civil society. They exhibit low levels of social closure with high equality, high naturalization, and moderate social mobility rates. Traditional regimes balance a high level of rights and obligations with little volunteering and membership with mutually exclusive and closed types of generalized exchange between groups in civil society. These regimes have high social inequality and low social mobility with rigid social closure to avoid integrating immigrating strangers. Liberal regimes balance a low to moderate level of rights and obligations with high volunteering and membership with mutually exclusive and overlapping types of restricted exchange in civil society. They couple this with high social mobility and extensive efforts to integrate immigrants through naturalization, but social inequality remains high. It was hypothesized that traditional regimes tend to establish a more stable system of rights and obligations with social closure in the short term of decades, while liberal regimes with the state bearing less weight and civil society exhibiting more openness and flexibility are also stable in protecting their modest array of legal and political rights in the long term. These syntheses and hypotheses are the beginnings of a theory of civil society that brings in other aspects of socialization, family, the media, education, workplace organization, and stratification into a more complex and powerful theory.

The third crucial question of citizenship theory involves the development of citizenship rights over decades and centuries. The short-term model consisted of four parts: (1) social demands in power resources theory, (2) state structures in state-centric theory, (3) ideology and political parties through a subordinated cultural theory, and (4) external effects through the cross-national and increasingly global effects of war, colonization, migration, trade, and economic growth. This approach recognizes ideas but subordinates them to the ideologies in interest group strategizing and generating institutions.[2] Class *and* status group influences are given an equal possibility to have influence. In some countries status groups will prevail, in some others class groups will be most important, and in a few countries class and status groups will be in a fluctuating battle for ascendance with one or the other gaining only a temporary advantage. Within this framework citizenship is extended through four processes: discrimination extension for subordinate groups, sacrifice extension for veterans, naturalization extension for immigrants, and public good extensions by bureaucrats and experts.

The results in each regime are quite diverse. Social democratic regimes with the franchise as an organizing issue, trade union strength, left party power, strong self-administration, and proportional representation have high rights and low demonstrations in an open system. Traditional regimes are similar to social democratic regimes except that they bottle up discontent in what tends to be an elitist political system creating more riots and demonstrations. On social closure they are split into colonizers with more open naturalization and mobility who develop greater tolerance and rights, and non-colonizers with closed naturalization and little social mobility who develop more authoritarian regimes. And liberal societies who never had the franchise as a labor organizing issue, developed weak trade unions, have much less left party power, and in general have a weak state. The results are a low level of rights and obligations in a society that is open to integrating immigrants, and the highest amounts of social mobility.

The synthesis involved in this model offers the possibility of avoiding the endless controversies between power resources theory and state-centric theory in that the former focuses on pressure and the latter on form. Form and pressure are entirely different aspects of the policy process and both have their impact, although measuring them in the same model may be difficult (see Janoski 1990). Finally, this approach integrated policy domains and policy streams as ways to approach the variation between different types of policies in different nations.

The analysis of citizenship over the centuries focused on two perspectives of initial development and then historical sequencing. In a first analysis of legal and political rights from 1200 to 1815, medieval constitutionalism was shown to survive war pressures and develop into a full democracy if countries could find one of five different escapes from internal repression to pay for military expenditures and to provide conscripts. In a later analysis of legal and political rights from 1789 to 1945, many but not all of Barrington Moore's hypotheses – landed upper classes with high economic and political power, low bourgeois power, and the failure to escape a strong and repressive state generated in the earlier war pressures – were highly effective in explaining the absence of rights. The extensive presence of rights also required working-class coalitions with a variety of possible partners – peasant/farmer, Catholic, or liberal parties.[3]

In the analyses of social and participation rights from 1880 to 1990, power resources variables and state-centric variables have an important effect. Working-class strength coupled with other groups in coalition governments showed the effect of power resources on social rights. Proportional representation, a Roman legal system, and a strong ministry of labor also show the strong effects of state-centric variables. War solidarity based on losing a war and suffering military occupation also had a positive impact on social rights. In the analysis of participation rights, social rights that had previously been established provide a precondition for participation. Then labor strength and state structures have a strong impact as in the earlier analysis of social rights.

In an initial test of Marshall's theory of citizenship rights sequencing, four tables presented the sequencing of four legal, four political, five social, and three participation rights. Sequencing these rights and comparing them to Marshall's ideal sequencing showed that liberal countries tend to adhere quite closely to Marshall's sequencing of legal, political, and social rights but hardly develop any participation rights at all. Traditional countries are very early in developing social rights but seriously lag in developing legal and political rights. Social democratic countries were somewhat late in developing political rights, which allows the franchise as an organizing issue, but otherwise they follow Marshall's progression. These results show that there are real consequences for not following Marshall's sequence of rights, and that countries that leap to social rights tend to suffer great difficulties in regaining legal and political rights. The results often end in extensive rights abuses and national tragedies. To make this statement is not to claim that there is any evolutionary sequencing. It does state that countries may alter the sequence slightly as in the social democratic countries without significant problems, but traditional regimes that skip political and legal rights put their citizens' well-being in significant danger. On the other hand, the early development of legal and political rights can also cause social and participation rights to stall.

The two different approaches to the development of citizenship – the formation and sequencing of rights – show that the four-part theoretical model of citizenship development over decades largely applies to the initiation of rights, and Marshall's sequence of citizenship rights is followed in the liberal countries and partially in the social democratic countries, but not at all in traditional regimes.

Thus, the three basic questions addressed in this book have been answered or at least more adequately framed. First, the confusing welter of ideas that pass under the rubric of citizenship have been ordered under definable systems of rights and obligations that have a clear relationship to each other in restricted and generalized exchange. Second, the often alluded to but little developed concept of "balance" has been developed through restricted and generalized exchange models at the macro-social and citizen-self levels. Third, the development of four citizenship rights has been explained in different periods of history, sequenced differently according to three regime types, and synthesized in a theory of power resources, state structures, party ideology, and external forces. In each analysis, the plausibility of each claim has been established with cross-national evidence, but adequate proof of the hypotheses developed in this theoretical work will require extensive data collection and further empirical analysis.

THEORETICAL AND RESEARCH ISSUES RAISED BY CITIZENSHIP

Three political theories of liberalism, communitarianism, and social democratic theory can be seen through seven different aspects of citizenship in society (see Table 8.1). Liberal citizenship envisions autonomous individuals negotiating contracts with each other through restricted exchange. This market approach to rights and obligations sees citizens as distrustful of the state although representatives are elected and citizens sometimes manage the limited state as executives. The basis of civic virtue is personal accountability, but committed citizenship through obligations to the state or society is partial and somewhat discretionary. Obligations are minimal, and rights establish the basis for the web of mutual contracts between citizens, that is, the liberal civil society with little or no state intervention. The end result is a society resting on restricted exchange with a less ordered and secure but more flexible and creative society.

Communitarian citizenship has brethren involved in hierarchical solidarities of family, religion, labor, ethnicity, or other unions. This highly ideological or theocratic approach to citizenship involves citizens responding in a subordinate way to hierarchical solidarities with a great deal of community responsibility. State intervention is frequent, but that is not seen as troublesome because citizens exhibit deference to common values and beliefs. As a result, obligations seem to prevail over rights since higher authorities control both rights and obligations, but society tends to be orderly and work well through generalized exchange. However, in times of crisis these societies have proven inflexible and somewhat intolerant.

Citizenship in expansive or social democracy puts citizens in a midpoint between loosely coupled liberalism and tightly coupled communitarianism. Neighborhood or work networks connect individuals into social networks where common interests in local and economic interests help people participate and cooperate. Instead of horizontal or vertical powers, citizens are in a matrix organization of multiple-level negotiations in a strong civil society. Common public discourse, often with state-subsidized study groups and media representing interest groups (e.g., conservative and labor newspapers), sets the stage for understanding various positions. However, expansive democracy avoids the liberal factionalism of every person with a singular interest and the communitarian consensus of complete agreement. The end result offers high rights and obligations, but this open system combines restricted and generalized exchange and is not always stable. Tensions are often present (e.g., the predictions of the end of neo-corporatism and collapse of the traditional family).

The theory of civil society I have presented provides the basis for a structural account of civil society and the creation of civic virtue. Social scientists can develop the theses of overlap and closure at the national level with the measurement of group size and resources in the public

Table 8.1. *Three models of citizenship*

	Liberal	Communitarian	Social or expansive democracy
1. Conception of the citizen	Autonomous individuals that are passively distrustful or actively managing the state	Bonded brothers and sisters, or brethren that are deferential or submissive but will act when instructed	Neighbors and co-workers that are cooperative and involved
2. Role of citizenship	Discretionary civic virtue based on personal accountability and markets	Socially coercive civic virtue supported by fraternal responsibility	Participatory civic virtue with some social pressure based on reciprocal group responsibility
3. Type of social exchange	Restricted exchange	Generalized group exchange	Generalized group and individual exchange
4. Societal interaction and solidarity	Individually negotiated contacts through a web of mutual contracts	Hierarchical solidarities – family, religion or union with consensus on common beliefs and values	Common interests and democratic participation with common pubic discourse in civil society

5. *Political power*	Horizontal – citizen self-organizing	Vertical – citizen to authority	Matrix of vertical and horizontal negotiations
6. *Political economic regime*	Liberal regime with representative democracy	Traditional regime sometimes with elitism and/or patriarchy	Social democratic regime with considerable corporatism
7. *Private life world*	Large because public sphere is small	Moderate	Small to moderate because public sphere is so large

NOTE: This table is adapted from Barber (1984, p. 219), and similarities exist between my column headings and his thin democracy, unitary, and strong democracy models.

sphere and then go on to the explanation of group interaction to promote democracy. A specific group theory must go beyond the previous survey research data on overlapping memberships, that is, identify the actual political mechanisms and group actions rather than infer politics from individual membership statistics. If civil society protects democracy, then social scientists need to show much more specifically how this is done by various groups in different societies. Civil society theory, consequently, has a bright future beyond explaining membership and participation.

Citizenship is not just an area of interest, but, rather, it is more specifically a phenomenon that can be studied as a dependent variable and used as an explanatory independent variable. There are four important sets of dependent variables in citizenship theory. First, citizenship rights and obligation studies involve the more formal aspects of citizenship. This means examining the formation of formal laws and regulations, and how they come about. Thus, dependent variables include the passage of laws, the budgeting of expenditures, the implementation of policy, and the causes of state-linked behaviors. This formal approach could concern itself with rights at a macro-social or national level. Thus, we have studies of the rise of legal rights, and then political rights. Most recently, we have studies of the rise of social and participation rights. These studies look at the legislation, funding, and implementation of various rights programs. In a similar way, obligations can be studied. These research projects would use a citizenship perspective rather than an economic, military, or criminology view to study taxes, military service, obligations, tolerance, and legal rectitude. For examples that begin to use citizenship rights in this way see Flora and Alber (1981), Janoski (1990), Steinmo (1989), Brubaker (1992), and Gorham (1992).

Second, studies that address pressures for citizenship rights and citizenship ideologies can look at the development of legislation from a group or social movement perspective. These studies look at group formation and the development of group ideologies toward citizenship. For instance, a study of political parties can look at citizenship ideology in party platform statements (Budge and Hofferbert 1990). A history of ideas approach can look at the development of citizenship rights through prominent theorists and ideologues (Somers 1995a, b). Other examples in this tradition are evident in studies of the labor and civil rights movement. But more cross-national work needs to be done on ideologies concerning all four rights and obligations.

A third group of studies looks at attitudes and behaviors toward citizenship rights. These studies have addressed public attitudes toward rights in different countries. For example, Conover et al.'s study of attitudes (1991) demonstrates the American emphasis on legal rights and the British stress on social rights (see also Almond and Verba 1965; Verba, Nie, and Kim 1978; Verba and Pye 1978; Verba, Schlozman, and Brady 1996).[4] But more needs to be done on how citizen-selves are created in relation to the state. How do citizen-selves construct a system of rights and obligations – in particular, how do citizens balance their own rights and obligations at different points in the life cycle? What processes are involved, and how do citizen behaviors range between restricted and generalized exchange? This can also include but should not be limited to how citizens vote on citizenship rights programs.

Another major group of studies focuses on civic virtue and civil society, which lays a basis for more formal citizenship. It focuses on how voluntary associations operate in civil society on citizenship issues and is more concerned with the operation of non-state organizations. For instance, how do voluntary associations and state organizations interact to protect or threaten legal rights: (1) bar associations, the American Civil Liberties Union, police associations, political parties, etc., and (2) political executives, legislatures, the Department of Justice, the FBI, local prosecutors, and local police? Examples again would include the civil rights movement and the behavior of voluntary associations. Thus, the focus is on organizational networks, organizational processes, and organizational membership in their impact on citizenship rights and duties. This work, which has yet to be done or integrated into theories of citizenship and civil society, would be the next step.

Related studies focus on the organizational structures of civil society. How do individual civil associations function to provide for citizenship? This involves their organization and how they recruit members, and how they construct networks of civil associations. On a more social psychological level, these studies look at how citizens volunteer and participate in civil society institutions, and how citizens view the state and voluntary associations. This could include the study of both the attitudes and behaviors of individuals (Janoski and Wilson 1995, Janoski, Wilson, and Musick in press). Examples include Arlene Kaplan Daniels on women's club volunteering behavior (1988), Bellah et al.'s "habits" of volunteering (1985), Wuthnow's compassionate volunteering (1991a), Chambré's study of "volunteering in old age" (1987), and Piliavin and Callero's (1988) "giving blood." These studies of "civic virtue," however, tend to drift into an indirect relationship to citizenship.

This differentiation between civic virtue and citizenship is often difficult. The main principle is that if the voluntary behavior is involved with the universalistic provision of citizenship rights, then it is of concern to citizenship theory. Consequently, participation in politics, workers councils, or the running of society-wide social programs involves citizenship. However, participation in voluntary social programs that resemble charity or leisure programs does not. The basic principle does not involve whether the state or private agencies provide services, but whether the services tend to fit universal rights, or a particularistic charity that may be provided by volunteers or paid helping hands. To be universalistic, the state usually stamps the programs with specific legal status, but this is not always the case.

Finally, a group of studies remains to be done that use citizenship as an independent variable to explain social outcomes, such as crime, divorce, unemployment, incarceration, and health. Thus, citizenship can be a dependent variable in many ways, and an independent variable with ideology or services predicting social outcomes.

RESEARCH IMPLICATIONS FOR REGIME THEORY

The three regime types proposed by Esping-Anderson (1990) were used to illustrate basic differences in citizenship processes and outcomes in eighteen different countries. Regime theory does not attempt to discover all similarities within and differences between regime types because many are irrelevant. Similarly, it does not deny the near infinite number of similarities between and differences within regime types. Regime theory provides useful generalizations for variables in this book that are important for theorizing about citizenship. Others find it useful for theorizing about the welfare state and labor markets (Esping-Anderson 1990; Kolberg 1992). In addressing citizenship, social inequality, and naturalization in eighteen countries, regime theory has been advanced, especially in providing a basis for each regime type in political theory.

However, regime theory still has a number of weaknesses that need theoretical and empirical support. First, the theoretical and ideological development of regime types – from macro-sociological studies of institutional development to the attitude formation of citizens – need further work. Much of the previous discussion has focused on this research, but it would need to be disciplined to regime theory.

Second, on the issue of where regimes come from, Esping-Anderson concludes that industrialization, economic growth, capitalism, and working-class political power had little effect on regimes (1992, pp. 114–18). To explain "clusters" of regime development, "the hope to find one single powerful causal motor must be abandoned; the task is to identify salient interaction effects" (p. 114), of which he identifies three – the nature of class mobilization, political and class coalition structure, and the history of regime institutionalization. While Esping-Anderson focuses mainly on a "theory of welfare state developments," the focus here has been on the development of citizenship, which overlaps but is broader than the welfare state. As Chapter 7 indicates, these forces begin much earlier than the welfare state and are rooted first in legal rights and then in political rights. If one wants to find the beginnings of regime types, the Tilly and Downing theory of military-bureaucratic absolutism comes much before industrialization or working-class formation. The traditional regime types in particular are subject to intense military absolutism, and most of them (Austria, France, Germany, and Italy) suffer legal and political rights rescissions at an early point. While the variables Esping-Anderson lists are certainly important for the development of welfare states, the regimes themselves have a longer history and basis in legal and political rights. Perhaps Esping-Anderson has already anticipated this when he refers to "the historical legacy of regime institutionalization" (1992, p. 114).

Third, regime theory needs to pay more attention to mixed cases. In this book, the United Kingdom is high on liberalism but not in the top category with the other liberal countries. Similarly, Ireland is high on traditionalism and New Zealand on social democracy. But each of these regimes also scores moderately high on other regime variables. Esping-Anderson has been careful to write about "regime variables" and for the most part has avoided saying that any one country is this or that regime type. This is certainly safe, but it leaves many people dissatisfied about the mixed cases. This needs to be handled more squarely by admitting that there are mixed cases that fit the regime typology less well than other countries. Related to this are "regime transformations" that need to be elaborated, perhaps in the Campbell et al. (1991) approach of "governance transformations." The most obvious example is Japan, which certainly was not a liberal country before 1945. However, other countries have also gone through regime transformations, and Mann addresses this on his elite strategy approach (1988, pp. 192–5); however, for the most part, regime theory has been excessively static.

Fourth, further research needs to be done to provide a solid basis for what could be called "citizenship regimes," which are closely related to "welfare state regimes" but cover all four citizenship rights rather than just one. This book has relied on a regime typology based on welfare state characteristics measured in the second half of the twentieth century. While these measures have proved to be a powerful explanatory factor and some evidence presented here has reached back into the eleventh through the nineteenth centuries, a regime typology to support legal and political rights must be established for empirical indicators based on those in earlier centuries. This work remains to be done, as does continuation of more current work on regimes of legal rights, political rights, and participation rights. Nonetheless, the regime approach as advanced by Esping-Anderson has proved to be an enormously powerful tool, and that is exactly what social scientists should ask of theory.

Citizenship and Civil Society

The theory of citizenship outlined in this book would lead one to focus on five different trends that would enhance citizenship and the social fabric of the United States and possibly other countries.[5] First, with regards to rights, many groups who seek to establish rights still remain, and they will continue to pursue these rights despite the critiques of rights being out of control. Many different groups from alternative genders to the mentally and physically disabled will press for rights. They will be successful if they or their representatives can mobilize resources and convince politicians and the public of their claims. New social movements for the inclusion of the mentally and physically disabled will continue, and they will be consistent with the thrust of citizenship. New movements may emerge for both the incarcerated and victims of crimes, who suffer decisive rights deprivations. But each of these movements will require effort (i.e., power resources) and responsibility, with the recognition that no right can be implemented when obligations are not fulfilled to back up these rights.

The necessary effort is clear, but responsibility as a second point requires some explanation. Responsibility through generalized exchange using a longer time horizon concerning the relationship of rights and responsibilities is necessary for building a society that works together rather than one of greedy citizens who act like hungry and wide-eyed children in a candy store. The short-term perspective of rational choice theory or utility maximization itself is a destructive ideology from academia that has persuaded many citizens that pure, short-term, self-interests are legitimate. Hence, we have developed single-issue interest groups that stay narrowly focused as a tenet of strategy. With this view come assumptions that we are all atoms interacting independently between each other with no particular responsibilities except what might be concluded for a short-term and bounded legal contract, which we will then take to court to enforce for actual losses and subjective damages. Unfortunately, the U.S. Constitution was written when the web of affiliations was stronger and more clear-cut in small communities of farmers and merchants. The rise of industrialization and urbanization after the Constitution was written created a liberal model bereft of its base assumptions – the strong bonds of family, neighborhood, community, region, and nation, not to mention humanity.

What is the way back to the reasonable creation of these connections in an increasingly bureaucratized and suburban society where people in different offices, on the freeway, and in far-off subdivisions can reconnect, especially to people in depressed areas with fewer material resources and social capital? It is through participation at work and in the community, from the small group level, to the organizational level, to the national level. Participation rights are a way to carry societies toward reconnection. Participation at work could successfully emulate workers councils and unions or employee association participation in production and planning as exemplified in Germany and Sweden. Participation at school should include parent, student, and community involvement in school policy and teacher empowerment. Student participation in school also involves the movement toward cooperative learning whereby students work with one another to solve problems, rather than individualistic learning where students get an unrealistic picture of the world as meritocratic and totally separable into projects. Participation in the community would involve clients and their representatives setting policies in hospitals, welfare bureaucracies, and employment offices with the consultation of experts from government and elsewhere. The self-administration systems of Germany and Sweden are good examples of efficient systems that already embody some of these principles.

Participation in politics would involve making it easier for citizens to vote through registration reform, and opening up access to decision making, which has occurred through sunshine laws. An area of politics that is frequently ignored concerns making political party conventions more democratic and frequent. Germany has yearly political conventions where representatives express their opinions on a wide range of issues. The parties publish the proceedings and make them available in libraries to all citizens. American conventions have nearly become a media show in which even the media is losing interest. Participation in the media is also a growing movement. Efforts by citizens to control violence and sexuality in advertising and regular programming on television are increasing in a society that has the highest homicide rate in the advanced industrialized world. Citizens are also making efforts to control agenda-setting by the media, prevent sound-bite news broadcasts, and promote debates on real issues (e.g., Fishkin's "deliberative poll"; 1993, 1994).[6]

The third point is that participation takes time and requires a moderate amount of days off from work. Currently, citizens in the United States have the least time off for holidays and vacations in the Western world. Only the Japanese work more. Because their levels of voluntary participation would consequently suffer, political observers do not recommend that the United States emulate Japan as a model of democratic procedures. Rather than extending vacations to four or five weeks, Americans might be given moderately extended floating holidays that would allow access to participation, since holidays when everyone is off are less useful. Finally, overtime and holding multiple jobs need some control. Of course, expecting extensive citizen participation may be unrealistic in that not everyone can or will want to participate. Nonetheless, increased leisure time in the United States along with opened venues would allow a major increase in participation levels. Business and public employers will object that time off work will drain productivity and efficiency, and to some extent this is true. Nonetheless, consider the amount of productivity and efficiency that is lost through crime, ignorance, and irresponsibility, not to mention unemployment through disadvantages or downsizing. Businesses spend tremendous amounts of money on security measures, employ workers who have not learned or do not care enough to do a decent job, and supply buy-out programs for people cut in downsizing actions. The general citizenry and those same businesses support others through welfare and unemployment programs.

Time off work certainly corresponds to trends pointing toward a postemployment society. Whether this trend is significant or not is unclear. What is clear is that robotics in manufacturing will lead to high productivity and profits with fewer and fewer employees. These trends point toward greater service employment or shorter working hours.

Returning to obligations for the fourth point, states and societies need a renewed emphasis on notched and low-level sanctions. States need to find a middle ground on the questions of sanctions. This requires the enforcement of obligations on many levels. The state must consistently enforce heavily sanctioned obligations. Failure to pay legitimately charged taxes and work in legally required service will continue to be heavily sanctioned in the legal system backed up with threats and jail terms. These obligations cover much more than is usually covered under citizenship rights. For instance, parents who abuse their children may have their right to keep their children in their home revoked and may be convicted of crimes and sent to jail. Similar actions can be taken for spouse, companion, or elder abusers. Surveillance and action in this area have increased tremendously in the last few decades to reinforce obligations to raise a loving family, despite criticisms of other groups who want to preserve a right to privacy.[7] On the other hand, Americans must recognize that the heavy sanctions of death and imprisonment are not enough (or are too extreme) to build a strong society.

Consequently, moderately sanctioned obligations are much more necessary. This is perhaps the weakest area of social control in modern society. Nonetheless, sanctions on misdemeanors, characterized by fines, injunctions, and symbolic judgments, are applied for failures to provide for self, family, and community. These include injunctions against parents who neglect or care poorly for their children, but whose actions do not constitute child abuse. In these cases, the state invokes not only negative sanctions of the usual criminal justice system, but also process sanctions that include various sorts of supervision of child-rearing, support payments, and so forth. Also, reintegrative shaming and restorative punishments are alternatives that bring norm violators back into the community and even their families.

Governments and communities also need to enforce mildly sanctioned activities through a number of venues. The state can publicize the responsibilities of citizens in their various roles as parents, students, workers, voters, and so forth. Governments can also provide the means to enforce sanctions through adequate but limited surveillance mechanisms. These may be very small, such as putting the social security number of the father on a birth certificate, which may allow the state to deduct support payments from wages or income tax refunds when fathers (or sometimes mothers) fail to provide for their children. Sobriety checkpoints are a further application of sanctions to obligations.

Industrialized societies must develop more positive sanctions through renewed emphasis on rituals. Although the cynical forces of society see these rituals as blatant attempts at social control, these rituals can provide clear and positive sanctions. Recognition of exemplary citizens with some sort of reward, although already done to some extent even at the national level in the United States, should be accentuated at other levels. A reasonable way of keeping track of each person's citizenship activities might not be out of the question.

However, to prevent abuses of privacy and rights and to avoid a backlash from the anti-obligation groups, the use of sanctions must be carefully monitored. In a sense, citizenship is unstable, and it is difficult to maintain a balance of rights and obligations. Liberal societies easily gravitate toward total emphasis on radical liberalism and unrestricted rights, while communitarian or traditional societies overwhelmingly stress obligations. Whether or not one uses the notching principles espoused by Etzioni's or Martin's approaches, sanctions must be monitored so that rights and a civil society are not destroyed in the process of making society better. No society should ever try to eliminate all forms of deviance for this is impossible and destructive, and ultimately removes a major creative element from society.

The fifth major point concerns the controversial issue of closure, and the inevitably associated issue of world citizenship. Citizenship depends on social closure, because membership means little if there are no boundaries for a group to belong to in the first place. Citizenship will not flourish with civic virtue in a society of strangers (Brubaker 1992).[8] Closure tells citizens who belongs, whom to care for, and from whom to expect responsible action. Without closure, rights and obligations will descend to atomistic levels of individualistic rights with the near complete shedding of responsibilities (Fishkin 1982; Murphy 1988). With closure, communities can be built with a social fabric of rights and obligations at high levels. The policies needed to reinforce this closure are not policies of intolerance and expulsion. Rather they begin with the building of communities, the caring for people where they exist or the rebuilding of new communities, and the protection of groups' and citizens' cultural capital. This would begin by protecting and revitalizing present-day communities. It would continue by avoiding aimless geographical and social mobility – people moving or fleeing simply because jobs and neighborhoods are not satisfactory.[9] On the other hand, too much social closure reinforces intolerance, misunderstanding, and an impetus to avoid helping those who really need it. Many traditional countries would benefit by opening up their naturalization policies to include alien "denizens" and reducing their hierarchical closure. Many liberal countries could reduce geographical mobility and spend more time building community.

This requires a different approach on the international level. Rather than practice exclusionary immigration policies, industrialized nations need to share money and expertise with poorer nations so that people will not be forced to become economic and political refugees. To some degree, tighter communities in the industrialized countries will forestall some migration, but these countries must also deal with the push factors of immigration. North-South sharing of resources is necessary for equitable citizenship policies to be developed on a worldwide scale.

Consequently, with greater social but not draconic closure, social groups and communities in liberal regimes could emphasize increased participation and social responsibilities through generalized exchange in their communities. From this beginning, American citizens could construct their own value-laden communities through citizenship rights and obligations.

Notes

1 Since World War II, sociological interest in citizenship rights has come in three waves. In the 1960s and 1970s, sociologists most influenced by Marshall included Dahrendorf (1959 and 1974), Bendix (1964), Lipset (1964), Lenski (1966), Parsons (1971), and Grønbjerg (1977). In the later 1970s and early 1980s, the use of citizenship stagnated; the *Cumulative Index of Sociology Journals 1971–1985* only lists four entries under citizenship. Nevertheless, Janowitz (1980), Friedman (1981), and Lash (1984) published important work. In the later 1980s and early 1990s, citizenship regained importance with many sociologists using the concept – Zald (1985), Korpi (1985 and 1989), Esping-Andersen (1985 a and b, and 1990), Giddens (1982 and 1987), Turner (1986a, 1990, 1993a and b), Roche (1987 and 1992), Dore (1987), Barbalet (1988 and 1993), Mann (1988), Janoski (1990 and 1992), Brubaker (1992), Culpitt (1992), Kalberg (1993), Somers (1993, 1995a, and 1995b), Bottomore (1992 and 1993), Steenbergen (1994), and Soysal (1994).

Political scientists have used citizenship in diverse ways from studies of Aristotle to Locke and Hobbes. Some recent work with Marshall's focus on legal, political, and social rights includes Alejandro (1993), Dagger (1985), Flora and Alber (1981), Held (1987 and 1989), Pateman (1988), King and Waldron (1988), Rokkan (1974 a and b, 1970), Conover, Crewe, and Searing (1991), Weale (1983), Keane (1988 a and b), Fierlbeck (1991), Peled (1992 a and b), Blackburn (1993), Meehan (1993) and Spinner (1994). Studies of citizenship participation are important, but they usually do not mention Marshall and his progression of three rights (Almond and Verba 1965, Verba and Pye 1978, and Parry, Moyser, and Day 1992). Numerous other studies in political science cover citizenship, but from a more philosophical level including Bridges (1994) and Martin (1993).

Two other theoretical approaches have had a more tenuous relationship with citizenship. Bowles and Gintis (1986) are among the few economists who use a citizenship rights perspective. Feminist research has had great interest in rights, but a more strained relationship with universality and the division between public and private spheres (e.g., see Dietz 1985; Fraser 1987, 1989, 1990; Lister 1990a, b, 1991; Mouffe 1993a; Radin 1993; Rohde 1993; Smith 1993; Vogel 1991).

2 What a theory of citizenship might be requires clarification. First, a theory of citizenship focuses on and attempts to explain citizenship as its major dependent variable. Second, citizenship theory may use citizenship as an independent variable explaining other phenomena like inequality, social order, or social conflict. Although related, these two types of theory are very different. This work will be primarily a theory of citizenship, although a more complete theory explaining other outcomes could also be made. For instance, Marxian theory is a capitalist theory using capitalism to explain inequality, and a theory of capitalism explaining how capitalism came about.

3 On reversals see Etzioni's concept of "reverse symbiosis" in his 1995 presidential address at the American Sociological Association convention.

4 Such theoristsb and their recent works include Bridges (1994), Beiner (1995), Etzioni (1993), Kymlicka (1995), Steenbergen (1993), Spinner (1994), Turner (1993), and others.

5 For these earlier works, see Brinkmann (1928), Maxson (1930), and even the prominent political scientist Charles Merriam (1931 and 1934).

6 In later work, Turner (1990) has also provided for state mobilization for the development of rights (i.e., "top-down" pressures along with "bottom-up" social movements), and similarly Mann (1994) has provided for social movements to complement state mobilization in his citizenship theory.

7 There is a danger in going too far afield on civic virtue. Writers on the left or right, religious or secular, practitioner or theorist easily appropriate civic virtue. It expands into a theory of society and culture, and into a critique of individualism within capitalist materialism. This unwieldiness has directly contributed to much of the confusion about identifying and theorizing about citizenship rights and obligations. While civic virtue is an important topic that I will incorporate within civil society, it is not the same as citizenship. Consequently, my approach is primarily a work of political sociology relating citizens to each other and to the state, and not a general work about the social and moral web of society.

8 Despite its extensive critique of rights, I will not deal with the critical legal studies movement because I do not as yet believe that this movement has developed a positive counter-theory. On this movement, see Tushnet (1984), Kairys (1990), and Minow (1990, pp. 164–72).

9 However, one may still differentiate between *patriotism* as fulfilling national obligations, and nationalism as pushing an ideology of national superiority to subjugate other peoples. Thus, nationalism is not a necessary but rather a variable part of citizenship. In chapter 3, I will develop the concept of "responsible patriotism" in distinction to "blind patriotism" that has been directly connected to nationalism.

10 See Borgatta and Borgatta (1992), Boudon and Bourricaud (1982), Smelser (1988), Mitchel (1968), Theodorson and Theodorson (1969), and Sills (1968).

11 The three approaches can be defined as follows. *Social scientific definitions* of citizenship tend to emphasize the aggregate construction of rights and duties in a nation-state, and the individual and group relationship between citizens and the state. Galston states it simply, that citizenship is "a package of benefits and burdens shared, and accepted by all" (1991, p. 250). It refers to what rights and obligations each nation enacts for its citizens. Who is eligible to become a citizen of the nation as a whole, and how can people or groups win or lose this citizenship? Havens goes a little further in defining

citizenship as follows: "Other persons may be subject to the authority of the state and may even owe it allegiance, but the citizen has duties, rights, responsibility and privileges that the non-citizen shares to a lesser degree or not at all" (1991, p. 742). This definition of citizenship applies to all countries if they have rights and obligations, and presumably to most kinds of democracy. While Havens makes it clear that some people are not citizens even though they live in the nation, he shows that "the status of citizen is official recognition of the individual's integration into the political system" (1991, p. 742). This social definition provides a basis for theory development in the social sciences, and it will be the focus on this book. *Legal definitions* focus on the person being subject to laws and leaders. Judges and juries then determine individual citizenship rights and obligations in the courtroom, since these concepts are established by legislation or executive action. Legal scholars and others may sometimes espouse an aggregate definition, but in practice they regard citizenship as reflected in case law, a narrowly legal context. A typical legal definition sees a citizen as: "An individual who is a native or naturalized member of a state, owes allegiance to that state, and is entitled to the protection and privileges of its laws" (Plano 1979). Legal definitions of citizenship seem to short-circuit citizenship because they remain the realm of passive rights and do not extend into active rights of political and social democracy. Indeed, their reference to allegiance and protection is almost feudal. Most legal analyses also tend to focus on immigration and naturalization law, and how a foreigner becomes a citizen. While the definition does mention the "privileges of its law," it does not specifically mention rights. Svarlien (1964, p. 88) points out that political science and sociology use citizenship in a somewhat wider sense. *Normative definitions* of citizenship focus more on what behaviors and attitudes of individuals should be, not so much on the variations in how citizens match their own rights and obligations. At the aggregate level, normative theories seem to critique cultural values such as individualism, rather than to look at the state, the legal system, or interest group pressure. Although I label these theories as normative because of the frequency of their prescriptive accounts of how people become or should become "good citizens," they do provide empirical examinations of how people view rights and obligations. This definition focuses on the role individuals take in primary groups through the creation of good citizenship and is often used in studies of political participation in government, and membership and service in voluntary associations.

The turn-of-the-century literature on citizenship and even 1950s schoolbooks focused on this prescriptive aspect of citizenship. In discussing American citizenship, Yazawa states that one of the four key elements of American citizenship involves citizens having a " 'patriotic' education to the republic and its principles" (1984, p. 200). The most compelling question during the great waves of immigration was How can these newcomers be made into good citizens? Efforts were directed at getting immigrants to adopt the customs (sometimes including religion) and language of the new nation. As Roelofs states, the "shelves of any public library, even if it is one of only moderate size, will confirm that the literature on 'good' citizenship is extensive" (1957, p. 2).

Since the mid-1960s, the more normative writings on citizenship have focused more on the empirical examination of individual citizenship (Almond and Verba 1963; Conover, Crewe, and Searing 1991). In *Habits of the*

Heart, Bellah and colleagues (1991) are exemplary in combining their ideological and normative foci on "civil religion" with empirical interviews explaining participation and individualism. In a similar tradition of political
theory, Walzer (1989) differentiates a citizen as a member of a political community, entitled to rights and responsibilities, from "the ideology of citizenship," which he sees as an early-modern interpretation of ancient
republicanism from the later Roman empire. This ideology can be an essential part of a normative definition, but it can also be part of a social definition
of competing forces.

12 Mouffe reminds us that the Romans extended citizenship first to plebeians,
then to conquered peoples, and finally to the vast majority of male imperial
subjects with the edict of Caracalla. Only women and the underclass were
excluded (Mouffe 1993, p. 138; see also Nicolet 1988 and 1993, and Sherwin-White 1939).

13 In chapter 2, I will discuss the one exception to this statement – immunities
to specific laws as compensation for systematic violations of citizenship rights
in the past. These range from affirmative action for women and African
Americans to compensation benefits for war veterans.

14 The state is not the only and ultimate source of rights. Different groups in
civil society press their own claims of rights and obligations onto the state.
But the state must certify and enforce these claims before they can be considered citizenship rights. Groups in civil society are the ultimate source of
rights claims, but citizenship rights only officially exist when the state pro-
claims and enforces their universality.

15 For succinct definitions of citizenship see Brinkmann (1930), Havens (1991),
Plano (1979), Roelofs (1957), Svarlien (1964), Thompson (1970), Simpson
and Weiner (1989), Walzer (1989), Wasserman (1991), and Yazawa (1984).

16 Three different arguments – competence, interest, and potential – can be used
to establish personhood within citizenship. First, "competence" can be used
to delineate the boundaries of citizenship, and political rights are most important in making these boundaries. I have just discussed Turner's views on
competence. Wellman (1995 p. 110) makes a similar argument when he
refers to "agency." Second, arguments are often based on "interests," that
is, if a being can express an interest in one thing or another they can hold
rights even though they cannot operate as an agent to express a claim for
that interest. Third, "potential" for human action in citizenship activities is
also used, and potential can go as far back as the fetus. Potential establishes
a basic human identity which cannot be surrendered once it is established.
Given present modes of communication and levels of science, an animal or
a lake does not possess that potential to become a citizen. Mentally and/or
physically disabled persons have potential because they were in the process
of becoming a competent human being. In my position, potential for competence has more force than immediate competence, which we can all lose.
As a result, I rule out "competence" and use both "interest" and "potential"
to include the disabled but exclude non-humans as citizens. This issue
may go in either of two ways concerning the fetus. First, if a fetus develops
into a born human being, that human being has rights as a fetus to sue for
wrongs done to them as a fetus (Wellman 1995, p. 142). However, an un-
born fetus cannot sue for not having been born because it does not exist as
a separate being. As a result, miscarriages and aborted fetuses could not
be citizens. This is not that strong an argument since the "potential"

principle would apply when the developing embryo passes into the fetus stage that has the potential to be a human being. Second, if the fetus has the potential to be a human being, then a relatively unique being is created – the pregnant mother – who has dual interests and rights, many of which conflict with one another. This would engender major difficulties with the mother's legal rights to control her own body and the fetus's right to live. From the competence position, the mother's rights would prevail without argument. However, from the combined interest and potential position, the mother's rights would have to pass a test of the conflict of rights.

17 The two common approaches to civil society are not adequate for social science. The bourgeois definition is clearly too narrow for theory construction. It includes everything that is not directly in the state, and thus leaves an undifferentiated mass of groups and networks that are needed for any social theory. Second, the normative definition of civil society is frequently used in describing the bad outcomes of state-communist behaviors. Most of the work from this perspective focuses on the analysis of the political behaviors and attitudes of groups. It looks at how parties, unions, and religions struggle against the state, but it fails to come up with a comparative theory about why some civil societies are stronger than others. For further detail on civil society, see Cohen and Arato (1992), Keane (1988a and 1988b), Taylor (1989 and 1990).

18 Somers (1995b, p. 256) divides society into four spheres resulting from a cross-classification of location (private and public) versus time (tradition and modernity, beginning and middle, or space 1 and space 2). This results in four spheres: community, civil society, de-institutionalized state, and institutional state. Civil society itself is divided between political culture and the market. Although her analysis is about the conceptual development of the metanarrative of Anglo-American citizenship, this division has affinities to the Parsonian AGIL scheme. Donati (1995) explicitly uses the AGIL scheme to delineate identity and solidarity in modern-day citizenship. Both authors claim to take a "relational approach" to citizenship, which appears to mean among other things that concepts must be embedded in a context. In their analysis, Somers puts these four spheres in a causal sequence from community through civil society and the de-institutionalized state, to the institutional state (AGIL), which Parsonians would avoid doing. Donati posits two axes of "goal attainment and value commitment" (GL) and "adaptation and integration" (AI). These analyses are quite interesting especially for ideology or *weltanschauungen*, but for framing a concrete theory of institutions in civil society I find them less useful. Although Marxists often put both the market and public sphere in civil society, I find conflating these two often oppositional institutions causes a severe loss of explanatory power.

19 The overlap between the state and private spheres is not shown in Figure 1.1 because it is less central to the argument of this chapter, and also due to limitations of constructing a two-dimensional diagram.

20 Of course, zoning, licensing, and eminent domain requirements of the state heavily impact on the use of private property.

21 The essentially public nature of the media has led to greater calls for democratic control (Keane 1991, Entman 1989).

22 This is not the place to develop a full theory of civil society. However, in Chapter 5 I will elaborate on the structures of the public sphere and potential regimes.

23 Another way to look at this is to say that civil society and citizenship can both constitute dependent variables with their own theories of causation. A theory explaining one is not the same as a theory explaining the other.

24 This tripartite approach to political theory is somewhat comparable to Habermas's (1996, pp. 296–302) discussion of models of democracy incorporated in liberal, republican, and discourse theories. Habermas, of course, invests much more time and energy into theories of public deliberation (see also Bohman 1996; Fishkin 1993). My approach also has some similarities to Gunsteren's "four concepts of citizenship" (1994, pp. 38–48) in that his "calculating bearer of rights and preferences" resembles liberal theory, and "citizen as member of a community" focuses on communitarianism. However, his third and fourth categories – republican and neo-republican citizenship – are neither adequately explained nor differentiated. He lists six elements of neo-republican citizenship and claims that they can be found in the works of three prominent persons (see Dahrendorf 1974; Oldfield 1990; Barber 1984, 1990).

25 This is probably more true in the English-speaking countries. Germanic countries have a much greater orientation toward communitarianism and expansive democracy. Further, the institution-building approach of *Volkswirtschaft* is much more evident in economics and politics.

26 See Shapiro 1986 for an extended discussion on rights in liberal theory.

27 In Chapter 4 I will extensively define and discuss restricted and generalized exchange. Until then, restricted exchange refers to reciprocal exchange where immediate paybacks are expected. Market exchanges are the best example. Generalized exchange consists of one-way exchange with a person who then has another one-way exchange with a third person. Exchange essentially goes around in a circle of giving. Families, closely knit work groups, and tight communities use generalized exchange.

28 There is much wider variation in each one of these theoretical groupings, and Etzioni in contrast to MacIntyre and Sandel definitely emphasizes reforms to make politics more accessible. However, there are no new participation rights on Etzioni's agenda (1993, pp. 233–45).

29 Liberalism can be addressed as emphasizing negative rights, and expansive democracy, positive rights. However, I have chosen not to use this terminology because of its dual meanings (Waldron 1993, pp. 213–24, Nozick 1974).

30 Esping-Andersen uses three different terms for one regime – the conservative, traditional, or corporatist regime type. This book will use the "traditional regime type" designation. To some degree this confusion appears to be due to collecting diverse papers in a book without editing for consistent terminology.

31 The one exception is on naturalization rates where the United Kingdom is clearly imperial, Ireland traditional, and New Zealand a settler country (see Chapter 5).

32 Welfare state regime theory has been attacked on other grounds. Cnaan (1992) sees the "greatest weakness" of the theory to be a "failure to provide sound empirical support for his very interesting theoretical formulations" (p. 69), and Stephens (1994, p. 209) and others would like to see cluster analysis methods used for constructing the regime measures. O'Connor (1996) finds that gender must be brought into regime theory, especially concerning labor market measures. However, Esping-Andersen does show how

women do not have the managerial careers in Sweden that they find in the United States (1990, p. 208–14). Klein (1991) finds that health, housing, and education are excluded, and that the high level of analysis sometimes leads to dangers of over-simplification. In another analysis, I find that liberal regimes tend toward horizontal education systems, traditional regimes toward vertical, and social democratic toward a mix; but this will be a topic for further work. Cnaan (1992) finds that Esping-Anderson ignores voluntary associations, which are very important to the liberal regime type. Chapter 5 will go into some detail on this issue concerning voluntary associations in civil society. Analysts from Australia and New Zealand have pointed to a fourth regime type (Castles and Mitchell, 1991), and Stephens (1994) even discusses nine regime types. But these proliferating specificities are typical criticisms. Counter-theories must come up with solid empirical and theoretical foundations.

33 Although Wexler's (1990) complaints about the loss of discourse and identity processes due to the capitalist commodification and the communications media are laudable, the solution can come through citizenship by means of rights to control media, production, and consumption processes (see Chapters 3 and 4 concerning participation rights in the media).

CHAPTER 2

1 Informal rights may exist within subcultures that enforce them with social pressure or group rules, but they often conflict with the norms in other subcultures. Enacting citizenship rights is an attempt to form a consensus through rights about these informal norms. These informal rights, whether labeled natural or human rights, provide the basis for citizenship claims, but again, they are not citizenship rights unless they are enforced and universally applied by the state.

2 Others also have difficulties with social and "industrial rights." Barbalet (1988, pp. 22–7, 40) develops "industrial rights" and notes that they are analogous to political rights (p. 25). But he simply accepts Marshall's description of them and concludes that "their incorporation in citizenship may appear problematic" because of their class bias. Held refers to economic rights as control over the workplace (1989, p. 169), but then describes these same rights as including a guaranteed minimum income, which clearly confuses these rights with social rights (1991, p. 171). Social rights in the first source refer to economic maintenance of the population and then to universal and free education. All of this could be fit together, but Held does not go much beyond Giddens in doing so. Taking Goldthorpe's (1978, p. 203) advice on the "working out of the logic of citizenship," I recast much but not all of "industrial citizenship" or "economic civil rights" as an enlarged fourth right called participation rights.

3 Bendix's logic (1964, pp. 77–8) comes from the legal distinction between status and capacity in Graveson (1953, pp. 55–6). However, Graveson can be interpreted in two ways: (a) status is a position in society to which rights, duties, and capacities can be attached, or (b) status is a static position in society and capacities are dynamic possibilities for change. The problem is that status and capacity can be on the same level of abstraction, or capacity can be subordinated to status. Whatever Graveson's intent, Bendix considers "status" as a "state of being" and "capacity" as a "power of doing," and both concepts are at the same level of abstraction.

Stronger support for the active/passive distinction can be found in Manville's discussion of Athenian citizenship where "passive rights" have a "juridical sense of status" and the more active conception of rights "depends upon action within, and with regard to, the community to which one belongs" (1990, pp. 5–6). The essential distinction between active and passive rights can be conveyed by two examples of Greek citizenship: one passive right was to be protected from torture involved in judicial ceremonies (Manville 1990, p. 11), while one active right was to participate with critical judgment in the direction of the *polis* (Held 1987, p. 36–7). Turner (1990, pp. 200 and 207–10) also uses the active/passive distinction when he distinguishes between top-down state action (passive) and bottom-up social movement demands (active) to create or extend rights. Vernon's description of citizenship in industry and guild socialist conceptions of active rights is very much on the mark, although the radical syndicalist aspects of the theory are not at all what is being discussed here (1986, pp. 146–7, and 166). Bowles and Gintis distinguish between active and passive rights (1986, p. 215), as does Held (1987, pp. 36–41, 47–8, 161–2). In the philosophical literature, Raphael's distinction between "rights of recipience" and "rights of action" is helpful (1965, p. 207). Others refer to a distinction between active and passive, but link active rights with liberties (see Gewirth 1982; Tuck 1979). This leads to the distinction between negative and positive rights – "freedom from" and "freedom to" (White 1984, pp. 134–42). See Gewirth (1996) for a discussion of positive and negative rights that overcomes many previous biases toward liberties and encompasses detailed arguments for rights to economic democracy. Narveson mentions "action rights" and "welfare rights," which imply political and participation rights, but then goes on to discuss negative and positive rights (1984, p. 97). On the whole, active rights need a conception of citizens encountering private ownership or control of property or office, and some philosophical notions seem so enamored with contractual liberalism that they are not usually very helpful in getting beyond restricted exchange.

4 This book uses civil rights as being synonymous with legal rights; consequently, political rights are excluded from this category.

5 See Dan-Cohen (1986) for an extensive analysis of how organizational rights are derivative from and subordinate to individual rights.

6 "Private" also includes public organizations that essentially operate toward workers and clients as if those organizations were indeed private. For instance, a public hospital operates largely like a private hospital with most decisions made behind closed doors. Although a public hospital may be more open to political intervention, workers and patients could still claim participation rights over operations through worker or patient community councils. Consequently, public managerial authority is similar to private management as far as workers and even many clients are concerned. Another example would be citizen review councils of the public police force.

7 Participation rights are more commonly discussed in the European discourse on the welfare state. Hernes (1987, pp. 145–7) mentions participatory rights applying to firms, bureaucracies, and elsewhere. Napthali (1929), Dahl (1986, pp. 101–13), Unger (1987, pp. 508–39), and Nickel (1987, pp. 147–70) all contain discussions of participation or economic rights.

8 Participation through self-administration includes the power to make policy

decisions, unlike U.S. advisory bodies that only make recommendations or trade unions in the former Soviet Union that usually just seconded state production goals.

9 A liberal theorist could argue that liberal societies have more liberties than other societies; however, these supposed liberties are often contradicted by the widespread violations of legal rights in homicide and incarceration rates. For instance, American claims to be the "land of the free" does not sit well with being the world leader in putting its citizens in jail! Further, one could hardly speak of legal and political rights for African Americans in the U.S. South before 1964. Actual voting participation was probably a more accurate indicator of rights than saying the Constitution guaranteed voting rights to African Americans. On the other hand, social democracy seems to provide a large range of legal rights, some of which are not offered in liberal countries (e.g., ombudspersons, legal aid for civil cases, and protection of the identities of defendants). But at the same time its obligations to pay taxes and to participate in national service (i.e., a curtailments of the right to private property and personal liberty) are much higher than liberal societies. In the end, speaking of absolute freedom through high levels of liberties or rights leads to many contradictions.

10 Lane and Ersson (1991, p. 204) compile an index of rights based on political rights, civil rights, discrimination, and Humana's 1983 human rights scale. Although they consider only European countries, averaging scores for regime types show that social democratic regimes (average = 9.07) are clearly higher than traditional (7.97) or liberal regimes (8.15). However, their liberal regimes only include Switzerland. When the United Kingdom is considered a liberal country the average score is 8.35. Looking at all eighteen countries for Humana's 1983 scores, social democratic regimes have the highest average (95.4), followed by the liberal regime (93.4) and the traditional regime (90.2). The mixed countries are New Zealand 96, Ireland 94, and the United Kingdom 93 (Humana 1984). Sums from the Freedom House scores were calculated for these same countries from 1973 to 1995 (Freedom House 1981–95). The results were generally inconclusive except that traditional countries tended to have much lower civil rights scores due to restrictions on freedom of the press in France, Germany, and Italy. However, there was very little variation between these 18 countries probably because Freedom House did not report their raw scores.

11 One could push the right to bear arms even further in the libertarian direction so that most everyone would agree that absolute liberty in this area is not desirable. For instance, one might maintain that we have the right to nuclear weapons. If a citizen has sufficient resources, they could claim the right to have missiles with nuclear warheads. This would make governments very cautious in attempting to abridge the rights of those citizens. However, most governments constrain citizens' rights to possess such destructive weapons, and few citizens object to this.

12 This paragraph takes a position against natural rights as a basis for citizenship theory. My position toward citizenship takes a social science perspective embracing an empirical position, which leaves it closer to the legal realist or positive law perspective. Nonetheless, any group in claiming rights can invoke natural rights claims or rhetoric, and this would be part of an appropriate ideological analysis.

13 This was recognized early in the United States because trade unions could

form organizations on the basis of civil rights, but strikes and boycotts were prevented due to the absence of participation rights (Rayback 1966, pp. 54–74).

14 Considerable confusion exists in Giddens's work on social and economic rights. In earlier articles (1982), Giddens appears to refer to a fourth right, and Held (1989, p. 169) even puts a fourth right – "economic civil rights" – into a citizenship rights table. However, in Giddens's 1982 piece, it is not clear that he actually targets a universal citizenship right or is simply describing Marshall's "industrial citizenship" in the private sector. In Giddens's latter writings (1987, pp. 200–1), he clearly labels (mislabels in my view) Marshall's "social rights" as his concept of "economic citizenship rights." In a similar manner, Preuss mixes social rights and participation rights under "distributive rights," which interfere with markets when they protect "the employees; the consumers; the clients; the tenants etc. against the power of the employers; the producers; the landlords" (1986, pp. 163–9).

15 Hohfeld has been widely used in sophisticated discussions of rights, and Sumner states that "the beginning of wisdom . . . [on rights] . . . lies in Wesley Hohfeld's celebrated classification of 'fundamental legal conceptions' " (1987, p. 18). John Commons used Hohfeld in his book *The Legal Foundations of Capitalism* (1968). More recent rights theorists like Melden (1985, pp. 7–60) and Sumner (1987, pp. 18–53) also use Hohfeld's categories. Moderate critiques and modifications of Hohfeld can be found in Kanger and Kanger (1966), Fitch (1967), Ross (1962), Lindahl (1977), Stoljar (1984), and White (1984).

16 Liberties are where some theorists tend to stop on rights. For instance, Rawls (1971), Benn and Peters (1959, pp. 72 and 93), Dworkin (1977), and Nozick (1974) cannot seem to get beyond liberties. And in telling fashion, they largely ignore Hohfeld's clarification of rights. Liberties are assumed to be open to the extent that they can be achieved unilaterally, while Hohfeld's claims, powers, and immunities cannot. However, no right is totally unilateral because even liberties are limited when they conflict with other people's liberties *and* where they require societal enforcement and group support mechanisms.

17 Immunities must be handled carefully because they are exceptions to universality, which can be seen in the problems with present-day affirmative action programs. First, eligibility must be determined. Membership in a group that has suffered at the hands of unjust government policy must be verified. For instance, African Americans who lived under Jim Crow laws in the South would be entitled to affirmative action, but not immigrants from the West Indies who did not suffer under these government injustices. Second, immunities must be delimited. Employment preference for veterans and education benefits apply for a specific period of time to specific veterans. Leaving affirmative action programs indefinite or unlimited was a serious problem for immunities, which are not intended to be permanent. Eligibility must be allowed to run out. And third, the benefit must be formally legislated and specified. Federal affirmative action programs in the United States were brought about by executive order of the president, which does not have the legitimacy of a legislated law. Benefits and requirements were often vague and subject to common law interpretations of the more general charge of discrimination. As a result, affirmative action programs for African Americans never passed the verification, delimitation, and formality

tests. The same problems for affirmative action applied to women, but the solution is different. Given the presence of laws on direct discrimination against women, the unfair distribution of child and elder care is the main problem. An agency much like the Veterans Administration – HOMECCA (the Home, Caring, and Community Administration) – could administer universalistic programs that would award delimited benefits to any citizen who can be verified as a legitimate and unpaid provider of child or elder care. While most citizens who forgo employment to help the needy would be women, a few would be men, and they would also be eligible for educational, employment, or pension benefits. The agency would provide advice and support for caring and socialization, along with verifying eligibility and benefit levels. In either case, immunities need to be formally legislated with eligibility verified and benefits delimited.

18 Liberal legal theorists like Nozick (1974), Dworkin (1977), and Mead (1986) often ignore, downplay, or subordinate Hohfeld's multilateral rights. Hart summarizes two liberal positions: "For Nozick the supreme value is freedom – the unimpeded individual will; for Dworkin it is equality of concern and respect" (Hart 1983, p. 217). Though their theories may differ on many counts, the atomistic individual is the focal point of rights (Wolgast 1987, pp. 12–8). This concern with basing rights on the individual without much concern with social interaction partially biases their analysis of rights in the direction of liberties, as opposed to claims and powers.

19 Mishra (1981, p. 33) further states that social rights are not finite, while civil and political rights are. But civil and political rights are not as limited as Mishra indicates. Civil rights can be expanded into legal assistance for the whole population in order to make access to law available for all citizens, i.e., "Judicare" (Pratte 1988, p. 69). Capitalist societies have far to go in making legal institutions blind to class and status. Of course, stating that social rights are not finite implies that they could be infinite, which of course is hardly the case for social rights given budgetary constraints.

20 Held's contribution to this debate seem to center around a critique of Giddens, which is itself a critique of Marshall. He criticizes Giddens for misinterpreting Marshall as having misclassified rights, presenting an evolutionary view of development, and ignoring conflict. He further accuses Giddens of using key terms in an inconsistent way (economic civil rights versus social rights, versus economic rights) and putting too much emphasis on class conflict. Held goes on to emphasize international civil society, but he does not develop his position on rights much beyond this critique of Giddens.

21 For instance, the following statement by Thomas Hobbes from *Leviathan* makes little sense in citizenship theory: "To have received from one, to whom we think our selves equall, greater benefits than there is hope to Requite, disposeth to counterfeit love; but really secret hatred; and puts a man into the estate of a desperate debtor, than in declining the sight of his creditor, tacitely wishes him there, where he might never see him more. For benefits oblige; and obligation is thraldome; and unrequitable obligation, perpetuall thraldome, which is to one equall, hatefull" (Miller 1993, p. 15). However, this statement makes perfect sense in Richard Emerson's social exchange theory of power.

22 Coleman (1990) spends much time discussing economic, psychological, and some sociological exchange theory. In 949 pages of theoretical text, he does not mention T. H. Marshall or citizenship rights.

23 This chapter does not consider the personhood of nature or the environment because they do not have a direct connection to human beings (Etzioni 1993, pp. 8–9; Turner 1986b, p. 9). For such objects to have citizenship, they would have to be capable of exercising responsibilities and have a self. In-animate objects presumably and conveniently exercise their rights by being left alone; however, they would have to do something in order to assume responsibilities (unless of course they fulfill responsibilities by remaining in-animate) and feel something in order to have a self. Corporations as a group of humans can do this in a somewhat contorted way, and totally disabled persons have a self with impaired abilities to fulfill responsibilities. But rocks and the sky have no self and can fulfill no responsibilities other than what human imagination can impart to them.

24 Within this category, however, there is a complication, which is somewhat analogous to the deserving and nondeserving poor. This is between the people with natural, unnatural, and self-inflicted impairments. In societies that grant the disabled rights, persons born with naturally occurring or accidental disabilities are afforded the full range of rights and benefits with little question. Persons born with conditions that appear to be of volitional causation on their parents part – drug-induced or careless action – have a more difficult time. Some citizens will fault the parent, but not the offspring. However, persons who are the cause of their own impairments, whether it be through chronic drug use or extraordinarily reckless behavior, have the least successful claims for benefits. Or if they are successful, backlash results. The question is not new, and Tocqueville comments that "nothing is so difficult to distinguish as the nuances which separate unmerited misfortune from an adversity produced by vice" (1968, p. 15). Many citizens will see the reckless person as violating obligations to prudent behavior, and although these impaired persons may be afforded rights, they will be given at a minimum and grudgingly.

25 This statement clearly relies on liberal theory. Communitarian theory would reject this statement and would probably reverse it. Nonetheless, it is a more defensible position to build from individual civil rights than from group rights (see Martin 1993).

26 See the hostile conflict between English-speaking groups in French-speaking Quebec over the use of English signs.

27 My position does not argue for all separatist movements and civil wars being unjust. Rather it is arguing that given the existence of a nation-state, group rights will lead to separatism and segregation rather than national integration.

28 The exception to this is an ethnic group that is dispersed throughout a nation, which would be swamped in any one regional or local council.

29 For instance, states could establish reproduction councils to cover troublesome issues for hospitals including genetic testing and abortion, and environmental councils for communities affected by large plants, landfills, and other problems (Hernes 1987; Foster 1980).

CHAPTER 3

1 The government organizations represented by acronyms in this quote are as follows: GI Bill refers to Veterans Administration programs, the FHA is the Federal Housing Administration, the SBA is the Small Business Admin-

istration, the TVA is the Tennessee Valley Authority, the EPA is the Environmental Protection Agency, the REA is the Rural Electrification Administration, the USDA is the U.S. Department of Agriculture, and the NIH is the National Institutes of Health.

2 Initial criticisms have come from Dahrendorf (1974 and 1986), Mead (1986), and Janowitz (1983). This has been followed by the communitarian critique of Etzioni (1993), MacIntyre (1981 and 1990), Sandel (1982 and 1984), and Selznick (1993). More recently, the greedy citizen has been approached through questions of values and virtues in education and society (Sandin 1992; Bennett 1993; Carter 1993; Nussbaum 1996; and Wilson 1995 and 1997).

3 Even in Turner's most recent *Citizenship and Social Theory*, citizenship duties and obligations, while mentioned (Turner 1993b, p. 164–5, and Kalberg 1993, pp. 98–102), hardly play an important role in theory building.

4 We may talk about rights existing as we can talk about freedom or spirituality, but for rights to behaviorally exist, they need enforcement through action. For instance, my behavioral silence enables you to exercise your right to freely speak about your religious or political beliefs.

5 Social and direct service obligations refer to responsibilities connected to the state. These are not private virtues. This will become clear when I discuss items two and four in the section on obligations controversies.

6 We should not be troubled by conflicts between rights and obligations since these phenomena belong to major social institutions, which themselves are often in conflict (Alford and Friedland 1985, pp. 256–8 and 427–43). These conflicts may exist at the individual, group and societal levels.

7 The framework of consent approach seeks to delineate the ways that people consent to be governed. Three important contributors to this approach are Pateman, Tussman, and Simmons. Pateman (1979) believes that citizens should be more active in a participatory democracy because in that way citizens influence the content of democracy. Only in this way can consent theory operate. Tussman (1960) sees consent being necessary for obligation, but also notes that many citizens have not agreed to a government at all. Tussman tries to resolve this difficulty by folding in those who have not consented as if they are minors who were obligated during childhood to whatever obligations that their parents have consented. Those adults who do consent are like parents who decide to be role models by making sure that the state is worthy of its citizens' obedience. Simmons (1979) accepts the requirement of consent, but does not fold it into childhood's original sin. Instead he examines the process of consent in more detail, delineating a number of requirements of an obligation being in place – accepting a right. Thus, to have an obligation means to have accepted a right, and that process requires a person to exert some effort (i.e., make a decision) to obtain a benefit that he or she wants from a source that he or she can countenance. One does not incur an obligation when one is forced to accept it, does not want the benefit, or totally objects to the provider. The citizen need not consent to state power *in toto*, but rather consents piecemeal to each enjoyed right and borne obligation.

8 The second group of theories focuses on other foundations for obligations. John Rawls (1971 and 1964) uses the notion of fair play where benefits are voluntarily accepted. Passive receipt does not entail obligation. However, he differentiates "duty" from "obligation" in that a just society requires the

natural duty to obey arising from initial consent behind the veil, which seems difficult to separate from the state's artificial obligation to obey. Nonetheless, he claims that the natural duty to obey is "more fundamental" (Rawls 1971, p. 116, Hirschman 1992, pp. 89–94). Richard Flathman (1972, 1980 and 1987) distinguishes constitutive and instruction rules. Constitutive rules should be obeyed because they make sense by definition (e.g., promises should be kept, otherwise they are not promises). An instruction rule involves normative reasons to obey. For instance, people follow the rules so that everyone benefits from the outcome (e.g., obeying traffic signals). However, self-interest is not always a good reason to follow a rule (e.g., one may obey traffic signals to avoid a ticket). Walzer (1970, 1983) sees consent not as present or absent, but rather as an organic creation of numerous participative acts in local communities and voluntary groups outside of the state. However, he tends to avoid the hierarchical relationship of citizen to the state, while emphasizing the horizontal relationship between citizens with little connection to the state.

9 The third group of theories looks for alternative frameworks outside liberal consent. Fishkin (1982) seeks the limits of obligations and states that citizens are obligated to help those in need when they can do so at minimal cost to themselves. Hence, people are not morally compelled to fulfill obligations of a heroic nature (this position will be discussed in this chapter).

10 Obligations can also be viewed from Gewirth's perspective: (1) "tentative obligations" state that rules should be followed but the specific application is in doubt, while "determinative obligations" state that the rule should always be followed; (2) "institutional obligations" apply to organizations and are determined by special membership rules; (3) "political obligations" consist of ruler and citizen obligations; and (4) "civil obligations" depend on agents, defendants, and peers (Gewirth 1970, 1978; Phillips 1986).

11 Minority groups in middle or higher classes often respect these obligations, but for different reasons. Political tactics for advancing rights or survival strategies may cause people to obey obligations that the acceptance of rights would not otherwise entail. However, minority groups in lower social classes may see these violations of rights as license to engage in crime.

12 The communitarian platform (Etzioni 1993, pp. 251–67) in emphasizing obligations over rights in order to correct the present imbalance creates problems of balancing rights and obligations, but it also needs to provide room for social protest, inequality, and civil disobedience. This does not mean that an extreme civil libertarian position need be embraced, but simply that obligations cannot callously be demanded of groups whose rights were denied in the past. There are situations where obligations are diminished due to rights being violated (see the previous example on African American obligations in view of being denied true education and welfare rights).

13 One may put Fishkin's argument into two sets of hypotheses. Consider the following abbreviations: A = scale of action or the number of persons who could help perform an obligation; O = scale of obligation or number of situations; and R = scale of recipience which would be the number of persons who would be affected. Under civic virtue, closure is essential and $>A$ implies $< (O+R)$, which means that the person helping another wants closure to help more (they want credit and targeting on the people whom they know). But under citizenship obligations, closure is not necessary for taxa-

tion to fund a program and the opposite conditions result: >A implies > (O+R). This means that the helping person wants the state to be solving many serious problems affecting a large number of persons before he or she will fund government action with taxes.

14 Alternatively, a utilitarian logic could be used to justify one right over another due to the intensity of feeling or self-interest connected with that right. However, majority rule that aggregates societal happiness can lead to serious civil rights violations for individuals. For instance, the Nazis' depriving German Jews of their property might be justified under utilitarian principles if it made Germany better off as a whole (Waldron 1993, p. 209–11). Martin attacks the utilitarian position as incapable of defending against serious threats to civil rights (1993, pp. 324–9).

15 This may be seen by some as leading to a utilitarian solution – the greatest good for the greatest number – that might undergird authoritarian rule. However, it only applies to situations where rights are in conflict, and numerous other safeguards protect the person or group who suffers as a result of the decision.

16 Wellman (1995, p. 241) finds that legal and moral rights can be weighed on their moral grounds, but in most instances this weighing must be "qualified by the special circumstances of the case in question" (p. 233). This makes weighing rights a very complex process.

17 These principles are too complicated to go into in this chapter. See chapters 5 and 7 in Martin's book for examples of (1) national security and freedom of speech, which is a conflict between different rights, and (2) the Mormon father and Jewish mother arguing about the religious instruction of their minor son, which is a conflict within the freedom of religion. See also Waldron's discussion of a conflict over free speech rights between a Nazi and a Communist in direct conflict (1993, p. 222).

18 Martin does not use the phrase "citizenship rights" but uses "civil rights" instead. However, he defines "civil rights" in a manner very close to my usage. He states that civil rights include two basic forms that an injury should not be done, and that a benefit should be provided. Since he goes beyond liberties to include "service-providing conduct," his concept includes legal, political, and social rights in the Marshallian tradition (1993, p. 100–1). Consequently, I regard "citizenship rights" and "civil rights" to be more or less synonymous in Martin's usage.

19 However, it totally avoids the quantity of citizens' implications of society present in Etzioni's societal benefits breaking all ties.

20 The level of sanctions has probably fallen too low in U.S. schools. For instance, truant officers in the United States seem to have fallen into disuse, and attendance problems in the schools have increased accordingly. Students may just as well hang out at the mall as go to school. Some communities are reinstituting the truant officer, which then requires the school to be able to enforce sanctions within the school. One community has jailed parents, but this involves serious problems of giving children leverage over their parents and clear-cut violations of the parents' rights. See Etzioni (1993, pp. 89–115) for a critique of the lack of responsibility and sanctions in present-day American schools.

21 The United States has the highest incarceration rate in the industrialized world. Ten years ago, it had been third to the Soviet Union and South Africa (data taken from national sources and Mauer 1994).

22 See Brown (1995, pp. 186–88) for references to eight specific examples reported in the *New York Times* concerning neighborhood actions against crime and vandalism.

23 Dissident communities and disadvantaged minorities in ghettos and elsewhere are well known for refusing to give information to the police, even when lawbreakers are harming the community. While this is a problem, the reasons for withholding this information is often tied to the previous denials of rights to these groups in the first place. See the earlier discussion of "recipience."

24 There are a number of reasons why Japanese police are very effective in keeping crime to a very low rate: police training for fifty weeks rather than eight weeks, strict supervision by senior officers, and accountability to civilian Public Safety Commissions (Bayley 1976, pp. 53–83). However, my main concern here is the effective sanctioning of obligations, not overall police effectiveness.

25 The German police have apprenticeship training lasting three years and on-the-job training of thirty to fifty weeks (Thomaneck 1985, p. 1976). The Swedish police also have extensive training with forty-one weeks.

26 In 1987, Swedes paid 56.7% of GDP on total taxes (21.1% personal income taxes, 13.7% social security taxes, 13.7 VAT taxes, and 8.2% other taxes); Germans paid 37.6% (10.9% income taxes, 14.0% social security taxes, 9.6% VAT taxes, and 3.1% other taxes); and U.S. citizens paid 30.0% (10.9 income taxes, 8.6% social security taxes, 5.0 sales taxes, and 5.5% other taxes) (OECD 1990 p. 22 and 1987a). U.S. taxes as a percentage of GDP were the lowest in the Western world.

27 Obligations play a particularly tenuous role in academic discourse, and obligations to the state are probably most problematic. Much academic discourse has led the fight against obligations, especially against the over-obligated Nazi and Imperial Japanese soldiers blindly following the horrible orders of a brutal state. Anti-war protesters during the Vietnam War made conscription an obligation to disparage. Some feminists have severely criticized marriage obligations to love, honor, and obey embedded in patriarchal bondage, and often see divorce as a right to escape the tyrannies of marriage. Each of these critiques has legitimate arguments and an evidentiary base. In a more subtle way, academia has bemoaned the stifling life of small towns, class communities, and sexual prudery as contrary to more socially mobile and cosmopolitan lifestyles. For the social sciences, advocating "cosmopolitan rights" may be a hidden value position, while supporting obligations has become evidence of subservience to the state or outmoded thought.

28 Responsible patriotism could even allow one to be a revolutionary patriot trying to drastically change the nation-state's policies, while still maintaining respect for citizens and their basic rights. See Greenfeld (1992) for a historical discussion of patriotism and Brubaker (1996) for a process view.

29 Multiculturalism can be handled within this framework by having citizens be a hyphenated citizen of a nation. Hence an "A-, B-, C-, . . . , Z-Xian" of any particular country would be a mix of particularistic characteristics of ethnic, religious, gender, or other groups and the positive or negative support of the nation-state in question. However, when an A-Xian comes to the position of secession or ethnic nationalism, patriotism breaks down.

30 Although world citizenship is impossible at the moment, European, North

American, and other geographically bounded citizenships are possible since they do provide closure and large numbers of human beings outside the category. See Soysal 1994 and Nussbaum 1996 for opposing views.

31 Ideologies of nationalism for seceding groups in social movements would develop a different conditional view of patriotism toward the existing state, and a new view of patriotism toward the counterfactual state they are trying to erect.

CHAPTER 4

1 Philosophers and legal scholars in jurisprudence have examined the relationship of rights and obligations in much more detail. These works can be divided into three areas: (1) in Austin's approach, rights are grounded in obligations or vice versa (Salmond 1924, Allen 1977, Cranston 1973, and Kelsen 1941; (2) in Bentham's work, rights are defined by obligations or vice versa (Raphael 1967, Dworkin 1977); or (3) rights and obligations are opposite sides of the same coin (Lamont 1946, Benn and Peters 1959, Radin 1938, Bradley 1962, Kocourek 1927, and Pollock 1929). See White (1984, pp. 56–73) for a review of these positions.

2 The Christmas Eve Theorem is "if a Swede must choose between improved hospital standards and a trip to Mallorca, he will take both" (Andersen 1987, p. 180).

3 In making this distinction, we are following a distinction made by Sears and Funk (1991).

4 See Dimaggio (1994) on "relational contracting" in the economy.

5 After being backed into a corner by interest determinism, one could only find altruistic behavior under extreme conditions: for example, an earthling who out of the goodness of his or her heart helps Martian invaders destroy the earth and all its inhabitants (including the earthling who helped in the process). Thus, helping the Martian was clearly not in his or her self-interest and consequently was altruistic behavior.

6 The next few paragraphs rely heavily on Peter Ekeh's (1974) *Social Exchange Theory*.

7 In place of Ekeh's terminology, I am using "singular exchange" instead of "exclusive restricted exchange" and "multiple exchange" instead of "inclusive restricted exchange."

8 Yamagishi and Cook (1993) identify this as "group-generalized exchange"; however, I see their definition of this process as lacking in a generalized exchange procedure. Resource pooling in a corporation is superseded by restricted exchanges of wages for work. Their concept needs to be differentiated by internal group processes (either restricted or generalized).

9 The supermarket state also leads to vulnerabilities to privatization.

10 Although related to "multilateral exchange," generalized exchange implies a more cooperative relationship (see Campbell, Hollingsworth, and Lindberg 1991, pp. 23–8).

11 These mechanisms are adapted from Axelrod's discussion of support norms. He refers to these eight mechanisms as internalization, metanorms, dominance, social proof, reputation, membership, deterrence, and law (1986, pp. 1108–9).

12 This emphasis on emotion does not deny the rational components of resource

mobilization theory, but instead it provides a complement for planned actions. Thus, I am not supporting the spontaneous emergence of social movements through emotion, but rather am putting together planning and the radicalization that takes place in actual protest and demonstration processes.

13 For instance, Coleman presents an equation that predicts when trust occurs: when the probability of gain divided by the probability of loss is greater than the value of the loss divided by the value of the gain, then trust will occur (1990, pp. 99–106). In another cross-classification, Andaleeb (1992) uses motives and ability to produce outcomes, which is similar to positive concern and predictability.

14 When the self is less involved, people recognize that relationships are based on selfish motives (i.e., Freudian sexual interests becoming brutishly erotic or rational choice becoming boringly selfish).

15 See Coleman (1990, pp. 199) on subjective and objective interests.

16 Readers may search in vain for references to the "self" in Cook (1987, 1991), Gergen, Greenberg, and Willis (1980), Heath (1976), and Laver (1980). Economists, of course, treat value as an externality that is exogenous to their calculations. However, this is like constructing a theory of color based on black and white (England and Kilbourne 1990, pp. 164–6).

17 Surveys of recent social exchange literature reveal the same conclusion (Coleman 1990; Axelrod 1984).

18 Coleman eschews sociological for economic terminology. In many cases they mean the same thing: "individual's constitution" refers to the self and its identity, "picoeconomics" refers to micro-interaction, the "evolutionary feedback process that results in learning and a self" is simply socialization. But Coleman also avoids standard sociological theorists when he discusses their concepts. When discussing "framing" he does not reference Erving Goffman (but he instead refers to Tversky and Kahneman 1981); when dealing with rights he does not mention T. H. Marshall; when dwelling on exchange he ignores Richard Emerson, mentions Karen Cook only in passing (pp. 315 and 673), recommends the reader to see the literature in economics (p. 673, n. 5); and when touching on the self, does not mention social psychologists or symbolic interactionists. While he is free to choose his terms, most of them refer to restricted exchange and interaction theories that avoid the self or national identity.

19 A more challenging example would be to take Henry Ford and his grandson as examples of self-development and the complex interplay of rationality, emotion, and tradition as both hung onto irrational and unprofitable ideas as they grew older.

20 Coleman probably drops the self because this concept would terribly complicate the mathematical developments in chapter 34 that require a more simplistic and totally rational view of the self (and where the explanation must again be the corporate self of Ford Motor Company).

21 This typology is based on Almond and Verba (1965), Bulmer (1975), Devine (1992), Dufty et al. (1969), Lane and O'Dell (1978), and Lockwood (1975). There are other typologies. Leca (1990, pp. 159–61) develops a different typology consisting of activist (military), civil, participative and private citizenship. Verba and Nie's (1972) typology includes inactives, voting specialists, parochial participants, communalists, campaigners, and complete activists. However, their typology focuses only on political rights and mixes dimensions (i.e., political activity in voting, contacting and campaigning with

level of activity of cosmopolitans and locals). Parry, Moyser, and Day's typology is based on almost inactives, just voters, collective activists, contacting activists, direct activists, party campaign activists, and complete activists (1990, pp. 227–37). Verba et al. (1993, p. 307) is somewhat similar, but includes social participation as well in their typology: voters, canvassers, protestors, community activists, board members, campaign workers, and campaign givers. Sabel presents a typology with craftsmen, would-be craftsmen, peasants, and ghetto workers (1982). His classification of peasants and ghetto workers would correspond to two types of marginal citizens.

22 See Sears and Funk (1991) concerning differentiating the rational behavior of restricted exchange from more long-term (non-rational) interests in generalized exchange.

23 The "discovery" of the opportunistic citizen as the "privatized worker" was predicated on the upwardly mobile workers moving as individuals to suburban homes leaving their closely knit, working-class communities in the United Kingdom (Goldthorpe et al. 1969).

24 This approach has a number of important differences from Almond and Verba (1965). They carry the baggage of functionalist and modernization theory that I avoid. They also use "parochial" in a way I would probably reserve for apathy, and then construct a mixed typology – parochial subject, subject-participant, and participant-parochial – that I find problematic (1965, pp. 16–26). In a related work, Thompson, Ellis, and Wildavsky (1990) range from full activity to inactive fatalism.

25 A critical aspect of the typology concerns how it approaches exchange. Although I have included this in the description, the typology would be an independent variable that would predict types of exchange. Consequently, the relationship of the typology to exchange is a hypothesized relationship (being part of the definition of each citizen type would create a tautology). In principle, the more active a citizen, the more generalized exchange they exhibit concerning citizenship.

26 The debate is considerably more complex than can be reviewed here. First, efficacy is often divided into internal efficacy (personal ability to understand) and external efficacy (ability to influence others). Each produces some different results with participation. Second, participation can range from pure political participation (as in Parry et al. 1992), neighborhood participation (Berry et al. 1993), and voluntary association participation (Wuthnow 1991a and 1991b).

CHAPTER 5

1 This paragraph is based on liberal democracies that developed early, and many other countries in this study developed differently. In the late industrializing countries in the later nineteenth century, the market was often controlled to some degree, and socialization for war inculcated many institutions and persons with obligations. But countries such as Germany lacked political democracy at this time. The imbalance of rights and obligations was not quite as great on economic and social rights but was troubled due to the lack of political rights. Although Marshall says there has been a "marked shift of emphasis from duties to rights" in the last century, this movement was highly diverse in the early and late developing countries of Europe (1964, p. 77).

2 At different historical periods this can occur in reverse. For instance, the nobles pushed for the Magna Carta against the king, and the bourgeoisie did much the same against the aristocracy. In each case, the mode of production is exerting pressure against the state, rather than the state correcting for the mode of production (Sandoz 1993; Holt 1993).

3 Dagger (1981, pp. 721–6) also mentions size and fragmentation. These two arguments are excellent discussions of the destruction of citizenship, but they do not apply well to the early Industrial Revolution. Size is an argument that applies well to twentieth-century America and Europe, but size was not a major factor in the 17th and 18th centuries. Fragmentation – the multiplicity of school districts, police and fire districts, sewer districts, cultural districts, transit districts, port authorities, metropolitan councils, welfare offices, etc. – is not evident in the early industrial revolution due to the limited role of the state.

4 The old institutionalism consists of works by Selznick (1949 and 1957), Gouldner (1954), and the early Homans (1950).

5 Much of the impetus for this approach comes from the organizational culture and the new "organizational" institutionalism in sociology (natural systems and organized anarchy theory with (DiMaggio and Powell 199), and the new "political" institutionalism (March and Olsen 1984, 1989; Skocpol 1992; Steinmo, Thelen, and Longstreth 1992; Weaver and Rockman 1993a). Although some influence comes from the new "economic institutionalism" of Piore and Sabel (1984), the transaction cost approach does not fit this paradigm since it is actually very close to the neoclassical theory with individualistic and rational assumptions.

6 This approach is so buried in sociology that it is somewhat hard to reference. Nonetheless, upon opening almost any introductory sociological textbook, one can find chapters on each of these more macro-institutions, which could also come under the rubric of policy domain with reference to the state's role.

7 Although political structure certainly plays a role, these institutions or regimes are not political structures. These regimes consist of considerable informal structuring of interest groups outside of the state into a network of organizations with specific and necessary norms of behavior. Thus, I refer to a political institution and not to a political structure.

8 Japan is a good example of a liberal regime based on elite principles.

9 Belgium is highly consociationalist, and Germany does not exhibit peak corporatist tendencies, but Germany has many aspects of societal corporatism in its institutions. However, both countries are traditional regimes.

10 Peak corporatism is often referred to as the bargaining between labor, management, and the state concerning national wage agreements. However, societal corporatism refers to the more decentralized bargaining in self-administered institutions where labor, management, and the state also bargain.

11 It is also subject to its own fragmentation due to technological changes such as electronic mail, cable TV, personal communication systems (PCs), and other forms of more specialized communication (Ganley 1992).

12 Figure 7.2 is an approximation of the size and influence of state, public, market, and private spheres. It consequently leaves room for dispute about the relative size of each sphere. Its intent is to make a theoretical point of overlap or non-overlap.

13 The state church in the United Kingdom violates this pluralist proviso.

14 Traditional regimes tend to be elite-dominated, but the elites differ. In France, the elites are an technocratic elite mostly connected to the state and educated in elite universities. In Japan, the elite is a corporate elite, and consensus is based in ethnic and to some extent class homogeneity (e.g., class differences exist but are mitigated by more equal salaries and the protection of jobs).

15 One might argue that Canada hardly fits this picture with its language and political policies; however, I would argue that its basic cleavages do not basically structure class politics in Canada. As a result, Canada is more similar to the United States than consociationalist Belgium or the Netherlands. If Quebec attains greater autonomy, a consociational structure could develop.

16 Primary socialization includes going to the UAW toy store at Christmas time or reading the union comic books available from the LO in Sweden.

17 Discussions at this point sometimes degenerate into questions of coercion based on conceptions of absolute freedom (Hayek 1979). A sociological position based on Durkheimian social control keeps these absolute freedoms or liberties in check.

18 In a similar way, Rothschild-Whitt and Whitt's "collective organizations" (1986) tend to denigrate careerist and instrumental behavior in favor of ideologically supportive behavior.

19 However, the more the United States uses a voucher system to promote private schools, the more it creates a functional equivalent of the European vertical school systems.

20 This statement must remain somewhat tentative because all but one of the pluralist countries (the United Kingdom) have fought world wars overseas, while all but one of the corporatist countries (Sweden) have fought world wars on home soil (Janoski 1992).

21 Verba, Schlozman, and Brady (1996, p. 70) provide comparative political activity rates for Austria, Germany, the Netherlands, the United Kingdom, and the United States; however, their countries remain too few to make any generalizations.

22 The Freedom House scores discussed in Chapter 2 are not as useful as the scores reported here. Freedom House reduces their scores from 0 to 28 for political rights and 0 to 45 for civil rights to 1 to 7 final scores. For countries in this study, the scores are mostly ones with an occasional two, and the main differences are freedom of the press. Their masking of important variation makes these advanced industrialized countries appear nearly the same.

23 One might even speak of equilibrium positions, but this often leads to numerous troubles since conflict theories are hostile to the concept of equilibrium because many groups within society may have many more obligations than rights.

24 This meshes with Olsen's study of voluntary association activities in the Swedish city of Gävle and Indianapolis in the United States, in which Swedish voluntary association activities were only slightly higher (1982, p. 128).

25 There is some controversy over the independence of voluntary associations in neo-corporatist nations, but this tends to refer to indirect control (e.g., through tax interpretations) rather than direct manipulation by the state (see Gjems-Onstad 1990; Nordhaug 1990; Yishai 1990).

CHAPTER 6

1 Citizenship rights theory has been criticized for excluding conflict (Mishra 1981, p. 29), but both Marshall and Bendix place conflict in a central position in their theories. Marshall saw conflict as the motor of citizenship rights development and referred to three levels of conflict: non-system conflict – areas of free choice or random noise; pro-system conflict – group conflict within a competitive political system that strengthens its unity; and anti-system conflict – destabilizing conflict that can lead to the destruction of the social system (1964, pp. 29–32; 1981, p. 156). In other writings, Marshall also focuses on conflict (1964, pp. 104, 123; 1977, p. 123, pp. 29–32; 1981, p. 156). Bendix sees citizenship rights developing with regard to class and status group struggles along with forces external to society (1964, pp. 43–5, 72–3). Others clearly recognize the role of conflict in Marshall's work (Lipset 1964, p. xxii; Halsey 1984, p. 13; Pinker 1981, p. 7; Turner 1986, pp. 59–64, 92; Lockwood 1974).

2 Whether the causes of homosexuality are achieved though personal action or ascribed by the genetic code is highly debated.

3 Citizenship rights theory clearly rests on Weberian social theory of class, status, and state. However, it does not resolve social policy debates between Domhoff (1986/87, 1987), Skocpol and Orloff (1986), Quadagno (1987), and Stinchcombe (1985) on the relative strengths of worker demands, elite manipulation, state autonomy, and societal needs. These factors can vary considerably from country to country, and comparative work using this theory has been rare.

4 Marshall's theory of the development of citizenship rights has also been criticized by Mishra for its necessary character (1981, p. 31), and by Giddens for its irreversible trend of development (1981, pp. 227–8; 1982, p. 172). Giddens and Mishra see an evolutionary theory that fits poorly with the facts. For instance, the social rights of pensions and health insurance in Germany came well before political rights were initially established in Weimar and reestablished in 1952 (Rimlinger 1971, p. 339; Mishra 1981, p. 32). But Marshall, Bendix, and Turner do not have an evolutionary theory. Marshall had little reason to discuss the reversibility of citizenship in two centuries of English history because few major regressions had occurred from that time perspective. In other essays, Marshall shows that citizenship rights need not progress in a particular order (1981, pp. 138–215). Marshall recognized that welfare states can regress to fewer rights or vault over other rights. Bendix simply claims that the rights can be "distinguished and analyzed" (1964, pp. 3, 76–9). Turner does not present an evolutionary theory. He sees Giddens's criticism of Marshall as a plausible deduction given the tone of Marshall's original essay, but Marshall "did not adhere to an immanent, evolutionary perspective" in practice (1986, pp. 46–7).

5 Williamson and Pampel (1993) would dispute this statement, but they take a far narrower view of social demands restricting them to class and labor union groups alone.

6 The cause of this alliance goes back to the differing modes of production in Prussia and Sweden. Sweden had few large estates like Prussia. Swedish farmers tended to own their own land, supplied a reasonable number of military conscripts, and were not overly taxed. German peasants in Prussia worked

on estates, were widely conscripted, and were heavily taxed in times of war (Downing 1992, pp. 84–112, 187–211).

7 In considering both political and economic democracy, liberalism's record is not particularly impressive in the post–World War II period, even with legal and political rights. Recall previous discussions of protections of confidentiality for the accused in Sweden, and failures to secure voting rights for blacks in the American South. Also, the correlations in chapter 5 show that liberalism is not associated with a wide variety of citizenship rights, even legal rights (see Table 5.2 on four rights). On the other hand, some might consider the high regulation and taxation in social democratic and some traditional countries to lessen democracy. However, I believe that this approach unduly privileges property rights over the other three types of rights, and non-property related legal rights..

8 If this seems unreasonable, consider the problems with democracy that the United States has: (1) lack of third parties and inability to get African Americans represented in the national government (Guinier 1991 a, b); (2) meaningless and infrequent political party conventions compared to the yearly conventions in Germany with published results; and (3) its being the last of the Western industrialized countries (along with Switzerland) to enact full political democracy (Therborn 1977).

9 The state is present in the earlier long-term model in two ways: (1) an "arena" where parties and ideologies play out their efforts, and (2) the effects of bureaucratic structures and interests. In this more short-term model, however, the state emerges as an actor apart from the bureaucracy. As such, it is portrayed as a separate entity composed of elite, party, and other interests that now control the executive and considerable parts of the legislature (Hicks et al. 1989, pp. 404–5). These leaders may foment a mobilization somewhat like a social movement from above (Turner 1990a, pp. 200–1). In the long term, the state is an arena filled by parties and ideologies, but in the short run, the state is a specific and active entity with autonomy in foreign affairs.

10 Self-administration emerged with the *Knappschaftskassen* – mutual aid funds formed by miners and encouraged by Frederick the Great. Workers and employers had an equal say in electing the fund executives and controlled fifty-three funds (Tenfelde 1977, pp. 90–8). To forestall social demands from workers, Bismarck sought a pension and health system run by executive bureaucracies, but funded by employers and unions. Ignoring employer and union traditions in the 1870s, Bismarck introduced laws that replaced self-administration with state management, but employers and workers opposed them. After the Reichstag rejected two such laws in 1881 and 1982, Bismarck abandoned the idea of total state administration. Self-administration won out and was formally introduced in the German welfare state in 1883 along with courts of arbitration with tripartite control in health insurance. In this way, union and employer demands for self-administration triumphed over Bismarck's opposition (Heidenheimer 1981; Tennstedt 1977; Hentschel 1983; Huber 1981; Dawson 1912, p. 72).

11 One should be careful about unilateral arguments concerning state movements. As I argue here concerning Bismarck's pensions and as Aldon Morris (1984, pp. 31 and 281–2) argues about the civil rights movement, the assumption that the state acted without extensive social pressure overlooks extensive social demands.

12 The sweeping changes in Swedish and New Zealand politics during the 1990s are not addressed in this book.

13 Policy domains may be referred to by other terminologies such as "dimensions" (Budge and Hofferbert 1990), "issue domains" (McDonagh 1989), "policy areas" (Amenta and Carruthers 1988), "policy styles" (Richardson, Gustafsson, and Jordan 1981), "programs" (Rose 1985), "sectors" (Scott and Meyer 1983), or "subsystems" (Freeman 1985). Each of these terms may have some slightly different meanings, but they tend to converge on the meaning of policy domain as I am using it here.

14 This approach has been put forth in as an explanation of agenda setting, but its logic is more broadly applicable to policy formation and implementation.

15 For instance, many classic studies of a substantive policy begin with the real world problem and how it came to public consciousness (e.g., Bailey 1950). Those same studies then go to policy domains and examine the proposals of various experts, and then end up in the halls and corridors of political power. The result of these case studies is that successful cases of policy formation are selected so that the three streams always converge, which tends to result in a pluralist explanation that requires the participation of all groups to work. Policy failures where the streams do not converge are much less frequently studied, and as a result, the opening and closing of policy windows are overlooked.

16 Hypotheses in policy streams theory are somewhat speculative in quantitative research. Case studies have more evidence. Most of the problem comes with the first two variables since political power is easy to measure. What constitutes problem recognition? Perhaps newspaper and TV attention could be such a measure. What constitutes effective organization of the policy domain? Convergence in theories is probably impossible, but convergence around the recognition of a problem would be a possibility. This would have to be measured by a content analysis (see Burstein 1985).

17 These two terms are similar to Hicks and Misra's (1993, pp. 672–3) use of instrumental and infra-resources. Instrumental resources primarily refer to party action, interest group press, electoral leverage, and strike and social protests. These are clearly power resources that exert pressure for change. Infra-resources are more oriented to state constraints that would affect the form of legislation, fiscal capacity, and internal state relations to the rest of society. "Sub-governmental administrative authority" is the one area that does not fit. However, I also agree with Amenta (1993, p. 759) that quantitative method will have difficulty explaining many aspects of state-centric theories, especially those that apply to cross-national constants and policy domains (see Janoski 1991).

18 The elite approach sometimes confuses compromise with working-class defeat and elite victory. In any social conflict, success is better measured by incremental movement toward a goal rather than complete victory. Further, switching the goal is not fair (when the working class obtains pensions, elite analysts sometimes say that the working class has only strengthened the capitalist system in the long run).

19 In this section, dominant ideologies or meta-narratives of citizenship could be developed in terms of political theory for each regime type. Following Somer's analysis (1995b, p. 256–59), the liberal regimes' ideology is motivated by a community ("state of nature") distrust of government that op-

erates through the market and political culture to influence the institutional state (Locke's vision triumphing over Hobbes's). Communitarian ideology operates in the opposite way with the institutional state operating to control the market and political culture and eventually to control strong but particularistic communities (Hegel's and perhaps Hobbes's vision overcoming Locke's). Social democratic ideology evidences a balance of the two with strong grassroots socialist ideology matched by an equally strong state with competence in the public sphere (Locke, Napthali, and Hegel in equal struggle). However, a cross-national comparision of regime ideologies needs much more evidence and analysis than this simple sketch.

20 The Union of South Africa is an exception to this statement.

21 This is a very unpopular idea in a country of immigration. The disadvantages of immigration to native workers are vulnerable to arguments of selfishness (e.g., there is abundance for all, but natives workers want to keep it for themselves) and contribution (e.g., immigrants make tremendous contributions to host countries). There are powerful arguments to the contrary in economics (e.g., increasing the supply of labor will decrease its price) and sociology (e.g., opening class boundaries to diverse ethnic groups will reduce labor solidarity).

22 Finland fits this scenario least well. Although it has high rates of naturalization, these do not really reflect the large numbers of naturalizations because this is due to an extremely low population of foreign aliens, which is not the case for other Nordic countries. Finland has also pursued a very cautious policy of immigration (note that it has the lowest 1975–84 immigration rate of the non-colonizers) because of its Finlandization policy and possibility of receiving large amounts of migrants from the former Soviet Union and the new Russia.

23 Non-colonizers may have less naturalization for cultural or national identity reasons. As emigration increases, remaining natives have a crisis of identity unlike the citizens of colonizing countries. When former citizens appear to reject their homeland and the state does not develop colonies for the praise and glory of the nation, citizens staying at home rationalize that rejection and lament their weak state and economy. Elites push for and masses generally accept greater state control to promote growth. Being blocked from colonization and watching fellow citizens abandon your country causes citizens to have a crisis of national identity and become susceptible to nationalism. This may or may not lead to war, but it most certainly leads to closure on national identity and an intensification of solidarity through cultural and ethnic purity. Weakened by emigration, a significant segment of society looks at immigrants as the final insult to national identity. Naturalization means the disappearance of their nation and *ethnie*.

CHAPTER 7

1 There are other explanations that are incorporated in various ways into this analysis, but they are not the primary focus. For these works, see Berg-Schlosser and de Meur (1994), Dahl (1989), Hermens (1941), Linz (1978, 1980), Sani and Sartori (1985), and Vanhanen (1984).

2 One problem with Flora and Alber's approach is that the "monarchist/reformist" countries are a mixed group that take two entirely different paths of citizenship rights development.

3 One excellent aspect of Therborn's theory is his emphasis on European connections to ancient Greek and Roman citizenship. Even though these democracies lapsed during the Middle Ages, the connection to them is important in differentiating Europe from other countries. In my interpretation, the main causal point here is individualism, which was greatly aided by the Reformation (Wuthnow 1989). This would help explain why the colonization of the Ottoman Empire did not produce citizenship, while the colonization of the English and French empires did.

4 Social movements have clearly played a role in the limiting of military mobilization by social revolutions (the limitations of French military expeditions in the late 1700s) or threats to withdraw support (the constraints on military mobilization over the Swedish crown). Thus, this approach should not be seen as more elite than social. It clearly combines both forces.

5 The United States is an exception to this process of subordination.

6 This "progression of biological interests" in war could certainly be extended further back in time to interests of the state based on knights and horses. Titmus actually starts in the 1800s.

7 This process is more complicated than can be portrayed here. For instance, although African Americans served in the U.S. military during in World War I and World War II, their numbers were too few to gain many rights. After Truman's desegregation order, African Americans first served in great numbers during the Vietnam War. However, they reaped few citizenship benefits from this participation because the war was very unpopular. Many blacks served in the war against Iraq, but the war was comparatively short. Consequently, war context can provide a crucial intervening variable to gaining citizenship rights through military service.

8 See the discussions on citizenship in the medieval Italian city states in Reisenberg (1992, pp. 87–102) and Pocock (1975).

9 For details on the Boolean method and the further reduction of tables in comparative and historical research, see Ragin (1989).

10 These data come largely from Stephens (1989) and Rueschemeyer, Huber-Stephens, and Stephens (1992). Where my data differ significantly, the reasons are indicated in an endnote to the discussion.

11 The independent variables in the text are matched with the variable numbers in the tables by indicating "IV" with the appropriate number.

12 This is why my scores differ on this point from Stephens's analysis (Rueschemeyer et al. 1992, p. 144). In sum, the United States is not a "yes" on both the political and economic power of a landed upper class. These scores cannot be reconciled with the Paige (1975) description of the United States being dominated by small and independent land-holding farmers.

13 The power of the bourgeois in Germany is an intriguing puzzle when compared to the United Kingdom. Both countries had landed upper classes with considerable political power and declining economic power, which declined earlier in the United Kingdom. Two factors differentiate the countries. First, Germany had no escape from military pressure through foreign resource mobilization, alliances, or geopolitical isolation. Although economic resources became high by the end of the nineteenth century, it was weak beforehand. As a result, the United Kingdom escaped military absolutism due in no way to the declining power of its landed upper class. Germany did not. Second, the military played different roles within each country. The United Kingdom concentrated its mobilization outside the British Isles, es-

pecially since it was an imperial and naval power, while the German army was mobilized within the German borders, making its military presence threatening and prestigious. Consequently, landed upper-class power was reinforced.

14 The revolutionary break with the past is the weakest variable in this model not so much because of its mixed behavior but more because of its hazy meaning. Stephens (1989, p. 1023) states that peasant revolutionary potential must be low for fascism, yet he says British peasants have a high revolutionary potential (see table on p. 1067). This directly contradicts Skocpol's (1979) work on revolutions which indicates that British peasants were not likely to revolt.

15 This form of tabular analysis is rather simplistic compared to more sophisticated studies (see Janoski and Hicks 1994), but I want to use one method for each right to keep explanatory coherence.

16 Two variables that go along with working-class strength are a conjunctural weaknesses of capital (IV5) and a high proportion of workers in the manufacturing sector (IV9). But the employment in manufacturing argument presents a very mixed picture, while capital weakness seems to be a good explanation for some countries but not for Japan, the United Kingdom, Denmark, and Norway.

17 This tabular analysis may seem odd to readers familiar with the welfare state literature because it is certainly not as sophisticated as many current analyses of social rights. I use the tabular format for two reasons. First, it is presented here not to prove but to make plausible three hypotheses. Second, the other three rights have not had sophisticated quantitative analysis. Consequently, the method is kept consistent for all four rights. Again, the intent throughout this book is to show plausibility and not proof.

18 Legal rights for major ethnic and racial groups in each country are certainly important, but data collection problems made equivalent data impossible to collect.

19 The beginning date for men's property rights is somewhat tenuous, but few would disagree that their property rights came before those of others. And in the sequencing methodology to follow, it does not really matter precisely when a right was introduced but rather its ranking vis-à-vis the other rights.

20 These comparisons are hazardous. While the Saami did have the vote, they had little to vote on since they were woefully outnumbered. A more meaningful measure of Saami voting rights could focus on the establishment of the special parliaments and cultural rights to preserve their way of life. Further, comparing the rights of Jews and Gypsies to the rights of Aboriginals, Maori, and Saami is stretching categories considerably. Finally, seven countries do not have indigenous populations, and although guestworkers could be counted, they are short-term residents compared to indigenous peoples.

21 For instance, after the assassination of Prime Minister Olof Palme, the accused man had rights to keep his name out of the media. The newspapers and TV could not mention his or any other accused person's name in public. Americans and Britons accused of such crimes would have no such rights.

22 One could also follow the same procedures as above but instead of using ranks use the cumulative years of continuous existence of each type of program (cumulative numbers are in the following tables). Abbott and Deviney (1992) have devised a more complicated method: (1) take all the possible sequences and assign them a probability, and then compare the probability

of their happening to their actual probability occurrences; and (2) take a score for each decade according to the number of programs that each country has (see also Abbott and Hrycak 1990).

23 The computations are made as follows: LR: $2.5 = (1+2+3+4)/4$; PO: $6.0 = (5+6+7)/3$; SR: $9.0 = (8+9+10+11+12)/5$, and PA: $14.0 = (13+14+15)/3$.

24 The United Kingdom is included in the liberal total because it represents Marshall's theory of sequencing and since the liberal category was short on countries because too many were colonies. The United Kingdom was the closest longstanding regime to a liberal country.

CHAPTER 8

1 Some may object that values have been infused throughout the text of this book. At a very deep epistemological level this is true of this work as it is true of just about any work. Nonetheless, I have not pushed a normative paradigm in this book, but rather a framework that can be used to explain existing forms of rights and obligations in a number of countries. American readers especially should not view the examination of participation rights as being normative because the United States has few participation rights. Other countries have extensive participation rights, and a theory that purports to be comparative must have the scope to explain the emergence and functioning of these rights too.

2 A cultural theorist would probably come up with exactly the opposite approach, but this is somewhat of a chicken and egg problem depending upon where one chooses to stop in time to identify independent and dependent variables. If one stops earlier, ideas seem to generate the proposals, but if one stops later, interests seem to prevail.

3 Citizenship develops in industrialized countries by requiring the cultural idea of individualism, which was begun with the ancient Greeks and the Romans and then reborn in the Reformation and the resurgence of the city. But within this cultural context, the long-term development of citizenship depends on external forces pressuring for tolerance, understanding, and overall understanding of diverse social forces and cultural formations in the world system.

4 Ichilov provides an excellent division of individual dimensions of the citizenship role that are also useful at more aggregate levels (1990, pp. 18–21). At the small group level, citizenship ideas consist of attitudes including motivations from inside (voluntary) and outside (obligatory), actions (inactive, passive, and active), and means/ends orientations (particularistic versus universalistic). Much of this helps people form self-identities concerning their relationship to the state and other citizens. At the national level, social attitudes or cultural beliefs focus on ideas about citizenship that have a strong grounding in the country and that are also produced by elites in the media, politics, and intellectual circles. National identity is a parallel formation concerning rights and obligations. At a social psychological level, citizenship behaviors concern participation in politics, voluntary associations, and taking part in and fulfilling rights and obligations of citizenship. At the national level, citizenship behaviors include the political ideologies and power, and participatory actions of formal or informal politics (political party politics versus social movements).

5 A number of groups in the United States are recommending citizenship pro-

grams: the Alliance for National Renewal/National Civic League, the New Citizenship Project, the American Civic Forum, the Center for Civic Education, and the Society for the Advancement of Socio-Economics.

6 Societies in the industrialized world have moved in the last half century from the heroes of production to the heroes of consumption (Lowenthal), and hence it is not surprising that the consumption of rights along with other material goods has dominated much of our cultural life in the post–World War II period. While the government cannot necessarily control the media and this overwhelming change that affects movie stars, superstar athletes, and the values of teenagers in schools, some steps can be taken by states and communities. Participation rights to control of the media are one major step. Societies produce and consume culture. Culture is not a deterministic freight train that charges through history independent of human will. Societies make and control culture, and if societies want to stop movies or rock lyrics advocating teenage suicide and violent rape, or television programs and commercials advocating blind but ever escalating consumption of luxury status symbols, it can be done.

7 Feminism is clearly on the side of pushing many of these private questions into the public sphere. As such, privacy is not among feminists' top priorities.

8 Soysal (1994) states that she "contests the foundational logic of national citizenship" (p. 2) in bounded populations and closure. However, I would contend that although boundaries have changed, they are still important. For instance, Europe has moved to a United States of Europe model, but boundaries still exist. Just as the United States of America admits neighbors more easily (Canada and Mexico), Europe will admit persons from the fringe more easily (e.g., Turkey and Morocco) while excluding immigrants from more distant countries (Rwanda and Afghanistan).

9 Finding the position between German closure and American openness is not an easy task. The Germans are often able to protect the integrity of neighborhoods through regulation and keeping foreigners and "Germanic flight" at bay. Americans accept large numbers of foreigners but are constantly fleeing to new and improved suburbs or segregated enclaves in order to avoid the great unwashed. Both approaches have their disadvantages in terms of citizenship.

References

Abbott, Andrew and Stanley Deviney. 1992. "The Welfare State as Transnational Event: Evidence from Sequences of Policy Evaluation." *Social Science History* 16:245–74.

Abbott, Andrew and Alexandra Hrycak. 1990. "Measuring Resemblance in Sequence Data." *American Journal of Sociology* 96(1):144–85.

Abraham, David. 1986. *The Collapse of the Weimar Republic.* New York: Holmes Meier.

Adler, Stephen and Wade Lambert. 1993. "Just about Everyone Violates Some Laws, Even Model Citizens." *Wall Street Journal,* March 12, p. 1.

Alber, Jens. 1987. *Vom Armenhaus zum Wohlfahrtsstaat.* Frankfurt: Campus Verlag.

Albertini, Rudolf von. 1971. *Decolonization: The Administration and Future of the Colonies, 1919–1969.* Garden City, N.Y.: Doubleday.

Alderfer, C. P. 1972. *Existence, Relatedness, and Growth.* New York: Free Press.

Alejandro, Roberto. 1993. *Hermeneutics, Citizenship and the Public Sphere.* Albany. State University of New York Press.

Alexy, Robert. 1992. "Rights, Legal Reasoning and Rational Discourse." *Ratio Juris* 5(2):143–52.

Alford, Robert and Roger Friedland. 1985. *The Powers of Theory.* Cambridge: Cambridge University Press.

Allen, C. K. 1931. *Legal Duties.* Aalen: Scientia Verlag.

Almond, Gabriel and Sidney Verba. 1965. *The Civic Culture: Political Attitudes and Democracy in Five Nations.* Boston: Little Brown.

——— 1980. *The Civic Culture Revisited.* Boston: Little Brown.

Alpsten, B. 1974. "Methods of Evaluation and Planning of Police Work." Pp. 9–52 in *Methods of Evaluation and Planning in the Field of Crime.* European Committee on Crime Problems. Vol. 16. Strasbourg: Council of Europe.

Amenta, Edwin. 1993. "The State of the Art in Welfare State Research on Social Spending Efforts in Capitalist Democracies since 1960." *American Journal of Sociology* 99(3):750–63.

Amenta, Edwin and Bruce Carruthers. 1988. "The Formative Years of U.S. Social Spending Policies." *American Sociological Review* 53(5):661–78.

Ames, Walter L. 1981. *Police and Community in Japan.* Berkeley: University of California Press.

References

Andaleeb, Syed Saad. 1992. "The Trust Concept: Research Issues for Channels of Distribution" *Research in Marketing* 11:1–34.

Andersen, Bent Rold. 1987. "The Quest for Ties between Rights and Duties." Pp. 166–83 in Adalbert Evers and Helga Nowotny, *The Changing Face of Welfare*. Aldershot: Gower.

Anderson, James. 1982. "The Historical Development of Black Vocational Education." Pp. 180–222 in H. Kantor and D. Tyack, *Work, Youth and Schooling*. Stanford: Stanford University Press.

Andrain, Charles. 1985. *Social Policies in Western Industrial Nations*. Berkeley: Institute of International Studies.

Andrews, Molly. 1993. *Lifetimes of Commitment*. Cambridge: Cambridge University Press.

Arato, Andrew and Jean Cohen. 1984. "Social Movements, Civil Society and the Problem of Sovereignty." *Praxis International* 4(3):266–83.

Archer, Clive. 1985. "The Police in Sweden." Pp. 255–72 in J. Roach and J. Thomaneck, *Police and the Public Order in Europe*. London: Croom-Helm.

Aron, Raymond. 1974. "Is Multinational Citizenship Possible?" *Social Research* 41:638–56.

Ascher, Carol. 1994. "Essay Review: Retravelling the Choice Road." *Harvard Educational Review* 64(2):209–21.

Axelrod, Robert. 1984. *The Evolution of Cooperation*. New York: Basic Books.
  1986. "An Evolutionary Approach to Norms." *American Political Science Review* 80(4):1095–1112.

Bacharach, Samuel and Edward Lawler. 1981. *Bargaining: Power, Tactics and Outcomes*. San Francisco: Jossey-Bass.

Bade, Klaus J. 1983. *Vom Auswanderungsland zum Einwanderungsland? Deutschland 1880–1980*. Berlin: Colloquium Verlag.
  1990. *Auslander-Aussiedler-Asyl in der Bundesrepublik Deutschland*. Hannover: Niedersächische Landeszentrale für politische Bildung.

Bader, Veit. 1995. "Citizenship and Exclusion: Radical Democracy, Community, and Justice." *Political Theory* 23(2):211–46.

Bailey, Stephen. 1950. *Contress Makes a Law*. New York: Columbia University Press.

Balabkins, Nicholas. 1971. *West German Reparations to Israel*. New Brunswick, N.J.: Rutgers University Press.

Baldwin, Peter. 1990. *The Politics of Social Solidarity: Class Bases of the European Welfare State 1875–1975*. Cambridge: Cambridge University Press.

Banfield, Edward. 1958. *The Moral Basis of a Backward Society*. New York: Free Press.

Barbelet, J. M. 1988. *Citizenship: Rights, Struggle, and Class Inequality*. Minneapolis: University of Minnesota Press.
  1993. "Citizenship, Class Inequality and Resentment." Pp. 36–56 in Bryan Turner, *Citizenship and Social Theory*. Newbury Park, Calif.: Sage.

Barber, Benjamin. 1984. *Strong Democracy*. Berkeley: University of California Press.
  1990. "Service, Citizenship, and Democracy: Civil Duty as an Entailment of Civil Rights." Pp. 27–43 in Williamson Evers, *National Service: Pro & Con*. Stanford: Hoover Institution Press.

Barber, Bernard. 1983. *The Logic and Limits of Trust*. New Brunswick, N.J.: Rutgers University Press.

References

Barclay, David. 1974. "Social Politics and Social Reform in Germany, 1890–1933." Ph.D. dissertation, Stanford University.

Bauman, Zygmunt. 1992. *Intimations of Postmodernity*. London: Routledge.

Bayley, David. 1976. *Forces or Order: Police Behavior in Japan and the United States*. Berkeley: University of California Press.

Bean, R. 1989. *International Labour Statistics*. Routledge: London.

Becker, Harold. 1973. *Police Systems of Europe*. Springfield, Ill.: Thomas.

Beiner, Ronald. 1995. *Theorizing Citizenship*. Albany: State University of New York Press.

Bellah, Robert. 1975. *The Broken Covenant: American Civil Religion in Time of Trial*. New York: Seabury.

Bellah, Robert, Richard Madsen, William Sullivan, Ann Swidler, and Stephen Tipton. 1985. *Habits of the Heart: Individualism and Commitment in American Life*. Berkeley: University of California Press.

1991. *The Good Society*. New York: Knopf.

Bendix, Reinhard. 1964. *Nation-Building and Citizenship*. New York: John Wiley and Sons.

1978. *Kings or People*. Berkeley: University of California Press.

Benn, S. and R. S. Peters. 1959. *Social Principles and the Democratic State*. London: Allen Unwin.

Bennett, William. 1993. *Book of Virtues*. New York: Simon and Schuster.

Bergmann, Joachim and Walther Müller-Jentsch. 1983. "The Federal Republic of Germany: Cooperative Unionism and Dual Bargaining System Challenged." Pp. 229–78 in Solomon Barkin, *Worker Militancy and Its Consequences*. 2d ed. New York: Praeger.

Bergmann, Jorg. 1991. *Discrete Indiscretions: The Social Organization of Gossip*. New York: Aldine de Gruyter.

Berg-Schlosser, Dirk and Gisèle de Meur. 1994. "Conditions of Democracy in Interwar Europe." *Comparative Politics* 26(3) (April):253–79.

Berry, Jeffrey, Kent Portney, and Ken Thomson. 1993. *The Rebirth of Urban Democracy*. Washington, D.C.: Brookings Institution.

Billis, David. 1993. "A Theory of the Voluntary Sector." Pp. 156–71 in David Billis, *Organizing Public and Voluntary Agencies*. London: Routledge.

Blackburn, Robert. 1993. *Rights of Citizenship*. London: Mansell.

Bobbio, Norberto. 1988. "Gramsci and the Conception of Civil Society." Pp. 73–99 in John Keane, *Civil Society and the State: New European Perspectives*. London: Verso.

Bohman, James. 1996. *Public Deliberation: Pluralism, Complexity, and Democracy*. Cambridge, Mass.: MIT Press.

Boli, John. 1991. "Sweden: Is There a Viable Third Sector?" Pp. 94–124 in Robert Wuthnow, *Between States and Markets*. Princeton: Princeton University Press.

Borgatta, Edgar and Marie Borgatta. 1992. *Encyclopedia of Sociology*. New York: Macmillan.

Borjas, George and Richard B. Freeman. 1992. *Immigration and the Work Force*. Chicago: University of Chicago Press.

Boswell, Jonathan. 1991. *Community and the Economy*. London: Routledge.

Bottomore, Tom. 1992. "Citizenship and Social Class, Forty Years On." Pp. 55–93 in T. H. Marshall and Tom Bottomore, *Citizenship and Social Class*. London: Pluto Press.

1993. "Citizenship." P. 75 in William Outhwaite and Tom Bottomore, *The*

References

Blackwell Dictionary of Twentieth-Century Social Thought. Oxford: Basil Blackwell.

Boudon, Raymond, and François Bourricaud. 1982. *Critical Dictionary of Sociology*. Chicago: University of Chicago Press.

Boulding, Elise. 1988. *Building a Global Civil Culture: Education for an Interdependent World*. New York: Teachers College Press.

Bowles, Samuel and Herbert Gintis. 1986. *Democracy and Capitalism*. New York: Basic Books.

Bradley, F. H. 1962. *Ethical Studies*. Oxford: Oxford University Press.

Braithwaite, John. 1989. *Crime, Shame and Reintegration*. Cambridge: Cambridge University Press.

Braithwaite, John, and Stephen Mugford. 1991. "Conditions of Successful Reintegration Ceremonies." *British Journal of Criminology* 34(2):139–71.

Brewer, John, Adrian Guelke, Ian Hume, Edward Moxon-Browne, and Rick Wilford. 1988. *The Police, Public Order and the State*. New York: St. Martin's Press.

Bridges, Thomas. 1994. *The Culture of Citizenship*. Albany: State University of New York Press.

Briggs, Vernon. 1992. *Mass Immigration and National Interest*. Armonk, N.Y.: M. E. Sharpe.

Brissot, Jacques-Pierre. 1789. *Le Patriote français* (Girondist newspaper). No. 35, September 5.

Brody, David. 1983. "On the Failure of U.S. Radical Politics." *Industrial Relations* 22:141–63.

Brogan, Denis W. 1960. *Citizenship Today: England–France–the United States*. Chapel Hill: University of North Carolina Press.

Brown, David W. 1995. *When Strangers Cooperate*. New York: Free Press.

Brinkmann, Carl. 1928. *Recent Theories of Citizenship in Its Relation to Government*. New Haven: Yale University Press.

———— 1930. "Citizenship." Pp. 471–74 in David Sills, *The International Encyclopedia for the Social Sciences*. New York: Macmillan.

Brubaker, William Rogers. 1992. *Citizenship and Nationhood in France and Germany*. Cambridge, Mass.: Harvard University Press.

———— 1996. *Nationalism Reframed*. Cambridge: Cambridge University Press.

Budge, Ian, and R. Hofferbert. 1990. "Mandates and Policy Outputs." *American Political Science Review* 84:111–31.

Bulkeley, William. 1991. "As Schools Crumble, Holyoke, Mass., Voters Reject Tax Increases." *Wall Street Journal*, November 25, p. 1.

Bulmer, Martin. 1975. *Working Class Images of Society*. London: Routledge and Kegan Paul.

Burger, Julian. 1987. *Report from the Frontier*. London: ZED Press.

Burstein, Paul. 1991. "Policy Domains: Organization, Culture, and Policy Outcomes." *Annual Review of Sociology* 17:327–50.

Byrne, James, Arthur Lurigio, and Joan Petersilia (eds.). 1992. *Smart Sentencing: The Emergence of Intermediate Sanctions*. Newbury Park, Calif.: Sage.

Calhoun, Craig. 1991. "Morality, Identity and Historical Explanation: Charles Taylor on the Sources of the Self." *Sociological Theory* 9(2):232–63.

———— 1992. "Why Nationalism: Sovereignty, Self-determination and Identity in a World System of States." Paper presented at the Citizenship and Civil Society Thematic Working Group, Duke University.

References

Campbell, John C., J. Rogers Hollingsworth, and Leon Lindberg. 1991. *Governance of the American Economy*. Cambridge: Cambridge University Press.

Carens, Joseph. 1986. "Rights and Duties in an Egalitarian Society." *Political Theory* 14:31–49.

1988. "Immigration and the Welfare State." Pp. 207–30 in Amy Gutmann, *Democracy and the Welfare State*. Princeton: Princeton University Press.

Carter, Stephen. 1993. *The Culture of Disbelief*. New York: Basic Books.

Castles, Francis and Deborah Mitchell. 1991. "Three Worlds of Welfare Capitalism or Four?" Australian National Unversity Graduate Program in Public Policy, Discussion Paper 21–90.

Castles, Stephen and Mark J. Miller. 1993. *The Age of Migration*. New York: Guilford.

Chambré, Susan Maizel. 1987. *Good Deeds in Old Age: Volunteering by the New Leisure Class*. Lexington: D. C. Heath.

Cnaan, Ram. 1992. "Review of Three Worlds of Welfare Capitalism." *Acta Sociologica* 35:69–78.

Cohen, Jean. 1982. *Class and Civil Society: The Limits of Marxian Critical Theory*. Amherst: University of Massachusetts Press.

Cohen, Jean and Andrew Arato. 1992. *Civil Society and Social Theory*. Cambridge, Mass.: MIT Press.

Cohen, Michael D. and James G. March. 1974. *Leadership and Ambiguity*. Boston: Harvard Business School Press.

Coleman, James. 1990. *The Foundations of Social Theory*. Cambridge, Mass.: Harvard University Press.

Collins, Randall. 1981. "On the Micro-foundations of Macro-sociology." *American Journal of Sociology* 86:984–1014.

1987. "Interaction Ritual Chains, Power and Property." Pp. 193–206 in Jeffrey Alexander, Bernhard Giesen, Richard Münch, and Neil Smelser, *The Micro-Macro Link*. Berkeley. University of California Press.

1988. "Social Exchange and Related Theories." Pp. 337–70 in Randall Collins, *Theoretical Sociology*. New York: Harcourt Brace Jovanovich.

1993. "Emotional Energy as the Common Denominator of Rational Action." *Rationality and Society* 5(2):203–30.

Commons, John. 1968. *The Legal Foundations of Capitalism*. Madison: University of Wisconsin Press.

Connor, W. 1972. "Nation-Building or Nation-Destroying?" *World Politics* 24(10):319–55.

Conover, Pamela Johnston, Ivor Crewe, and Donald Searing. 1991. "The Nature of Citizenship in the United States and Great Britain: Empirical Comments on Theoretical Themes." *Journal of Politics* 53(3):800–32.

Conover, Pamela Johnston, Stephen T. Leonard, and Donald Searing. 1993. "Duty is a Four-Letter Word: Democratic Citizenship in a Liberal Republic." Pp. 147–172 in George Marcus and Russell Hanson, *Reconsidering the Democratic Republic*. University Park: Pennsylvania State University Press.

Conover, Pamela and Donald Searing. 1994. "Democracy, Citizenship and the Study of Political Socialzation." Pp. 24–55 in Ian Budge and David McKay, *Developing Democracy*. Thousand Oaks, Calif.: Sage.

Cook, Rebecca. 1994. *The Human Rights of Women*. Philadelphia: University of Pennsylvania Press.

Cook, Chris and John Paxton. 1992. *European Political Facts 1918–90*. New York: Facts on File.

References

Cook, Karen. 1987. *Social Exchange Theory*. Newbury Park, Calif.: Sage.

    1991. "The Microfoundations of Social Structure: An Exchange Perspective." Pp. 29–45 in Joan Huber, *Macro-Micro Linkages in Sociology*. Newbury Park: Sage.

Cook, Karen and Margaret Levi. 1990. *The Limits of Rationality*. Chicago: University of Chicago Press.

Cook, Karen, Jodi O'Brien, and Peter Kollock. 1990. "Exchange Theory: A Blueprint for Structure and Process." Pp. 158–84 in George Ritzer, *Frontiers of Social Theory*. New York: Columbia University Press.

Cook, Karen, and Toshio Yamagishi. 1988. "Generalized Exchange, Networks, and the Problem of Collective Action." Paper presented at the International Social Networks Conference.

Cranston, Maurice. 1973. *What Are Human Rights?* New York: Basic Books.

Crouch, Colin. 1990. "Generalized Political Exchange in Industrial Relations in Europe during the Twentieth Century." Pp. 69–116 in Bernd Marin, *Governance and Generalized Exchange*. Frankfurt: Campus Verlag.

    1992a. "Citizenship and Community in British Political Debate." Pp. 69–95 in Colin Crouch and Anthony Heath, *Social Research and Social Reform*. Oxford: Clarendon Press.

    1992b. *Industrial Relations and European State Traditions*. Oxford: Clarendon Press.

Culpitt, Ian. 1992. *Welfare and Citizenship: Beyond the Crisis of the Welfare State?* Thousand Oaks, Calif.: Sage.

Curtis, James, Edwin Grabb, and Douglas Baer. 1992. "Voluntary Association Membership in Fifteen Countries." *American Sociological Review* 52(2): 139–52.

Dagger, Richard. 1981. "Metropolis, Memory, and Citizenship." *American Journal of Political Science* 24(4):715–37.

    1985. "Rights, Boundaries and the Bonds of Community." *American Political Science Review* 79(2):436–47.

Dahl, Robert. 1985. *A Preface to Economic Democracy*. Berkeley: University of California Press.

    1986. *Democracy, Liberty, and Equality*. Oslo: Norwegian University Press.

    1989. *Democracy and Its Critics*. New Haven: Yale University Press.

Dahl, Robert, and Charles Lindblom. 1976. *Politics, Economics and Welfare*. Chicago: University of Chicago Press.

Dahrendorf, Ralf. 1959. *Class and Class Conflict in Industrial Society*. Stanford: Stanford University Press.

    1974. "Citizenship and Beyond: The Social Dynamics of an Idea." *Social Research* 41:673–701.

    1986. "Economic Growth, Governability, and Entitlements." *Washington Quarterly* 9:61–5.

    1987. "Rights of Citizenship." *Reporting from the Russell Sage Foundation* 10:6–7.

    1994. "The Changing Quality of Citizenship." Pp. 10–19 in Bart van Steenbergen, *The Condition of Citizenship*. Newbury Park, Calif.: Sage.

Daley, Caroline and Melanie Nolan. 1994. *Suffrage and Beyond*. New York: New York University Press.

Damon, Frederick. 1980. "The Kula and Generalized Exchange." *Man* 2:267–92.

Dan-Cohen, Meir. 1986. *Rights, Persons and Organizations*. Berkeley: University of California Press.

References

Daniels, Arlene Kaplan. 1988. *Invisible Careers: Women Civic Leaders and the Voluntary World*. Chicago: University of Chicago Press.

Davies, D. G. 1979. *International Comparisons of Tax Structures in Federal and Unitary Countries*. Canberra: Centre for Research on Federal Financial Relations at the Australian National University.

Davis, John. 1992. *Exchange*. Minneapolis: University of Minnesota Press.

Dawson, William. 1912. *Social Insurance in Germany 1833–1911*. London: Fischer-Unwin.

DeMaria, William. 1989. "Combat and Concern: The Warfare-Welfare Nexus." *War and Society* 7(1):71–87.

Demo, David. 1992. "The Self-Concept over Time: Research Issues and Directions." *Annual Review of Sociology* 18:303–26.

Devine, Fiona. 1992. "Social Identities, Class Identity and Political Perspectives." *Sociological Review* 40(2):229–52.

Dickinson, James. 1986. "Spiking Socialist Guns." *Comparative Social Research* 9:69–108.

Dietz, Mary. 1985. "Citizenship with a Feminist Face." *Political Theory* 13(1): 19–37.

　　1992. "Context Is All: Feminism and Theories of Citizenship." Pp. 63–85 in Chantal Mouffe, *Dimensions of Radical Democracy*. London: Verso.

DiMaggio, Paul. 1994. "Culture and Economy." Pp. 27–57 in Neil Smelser, *Handbook of Economic Sociology*. New York: Russell Sage Foundation.

DiMaggio, Paul and Walter Powell. 1991. *The New Institutionalism in Organizational Analysis*. Chicago: University of Chicago Press.

Domhoff, G. William. 1986/87. "Corporate Liberal Theory and the Social Security Act." *Politics and Society* 15(3):297–330.

　　1987. "The Wagner Act and Theories of the State." *Political Power and Social Theory* 6:159–85.

Donati, Pierpaolo. 1995. "Identity and Solidarity in the Complex of Citizenship." *International Sociology* 10(3):299–314.

Donohue, William. 1994. *The Twilight of Liberty: The Legacy of the ACLU*. New Brunswick: Transaction Press.

Dore, Ronald. 1987. "Citizenship and Employment in an Age of High Technology." *British Journal of Industrial Relations* 25:202–25.

Downing, Brian. 1992. *The Military Revolution and Political Change*. Princeton: Princeton University Press.

Driedger, Diane. 1989. *The Last Civil Rights Movement: Disabled Peoples' International*. New York: St. Martin's Press.

Droz, Jacques. 1983. "In Search of Prussia." *Journal of Modern History* 55:71–7.

Dryzek, John and Robert Goodin. 1985. "Risk-Sharing and Social Justice." *British Journal of Political Science* 16:1–34.

Dufty, N. F. (ed.). 1969. *The Sociology of the Blue Collar Worker*. Leiden: E. J. Brill.

Durkheim, Emile. 1933. *The Division of Labor*. New York: Free Press.

Dworkin, Ronald. 1977. *Taking Rights Seriously*. Cambridge, Mass.: Harvard University Press.

　　1981. "Is There a Right to Pornography?" *Oxford Journal of Legal Studies* 1:177–212.

Ekeh, Peter. 1974. *Social Exchange Theory: The Two Traditions*. Cambridge, Mass.: Harvard University Press.

References

Elias, Norbert. 1978. *The History of Manners*. New York: Pantheon.

Eliasoph, Nina. 1990. "Political Culture and the Presentation of a Political Self." *Theory and Society* 19(4):465–94.

Elster, Jon. 1989. *Solomonic Judgement: Studies in the Limitations of Rationality*. Cambridge: Cambridge University Press.

Emerson, Richard. 1972. "Exchange Theory, Part II: Exchange Relations, Exchange Networks and Groups as Exchange Systems." Pp. 58–87 in Joseph Berger, Morris Zelditch, and Bo Anderson, *Sociological Theories in Progress*. Boston: Houghton Mifflin.

——— 1976. "Social Exchange Theory." *Annual Review of Sociology* 2:335–62.

——— 1987. "Toward a Theory of Value in Social Exchange." Pp. 11–46 in Karen Cook, *Social Exchange Theory*. Newbury Park, Calif.: Sage.

England, Paula. 1993. "The Separative Self: Androcentric Bias in Neoclassical Assumptions." Pp. 37–53 in Marianne Ferber and Julie Nelson, *Beyond Economic Man: Feminist Theory and Economics*. Chicago: University of Chicago Press.

England, Paula and Barbara Kilbourne. 1990. "Feminist Critiques of the Separative Model of Self." *Rationality and Society* 2(2):156–71.

Entman, Robert. 1989. *Democracy without Citizens: Media and the Decay of American Politics*. New York: Oxford University Press.

Erickson, Robert and John Goldthorpe. 1992. *The Constant Flux*. Oxford: Clarendon Press.

Esping-Andersen, Gøsta. 1985. *Politics against Markets*. Princeton: Princeton University Press.

——— 1990. *Three Worlds of Welfare Capitalism*. Princeton: Princeton University Press.

——— 1992. "The Three Political Economies of Welfare Capitalism." Pp. 92–123 in Jon Eivind Kolberg, *The Study of Welfare State Regimes*. New York: M. E. Sharpe.

Etzioni, Amitai. 1991. *A Responsive Society*. San Francisco: Jossey-Bass.

——— 1993. *The Spirit of Community*. New York: Crown.

Eyerman, Ron and Andrew Jamison. 1991. "Research on Social Movements in Sweden." Pp. 247–61 in Dieter Rucht, *Research on Social Movements*. Frankfurt: Campus Verlag.

Federal Republic of Germany (FRG). 1993. "The White Ring: Crime Prevention and Assistance for Crime Victims." *Focus on Germany* 4(93):12–13.

Feiler, Bruce S. 1991. *Learning to Bow: An American Teacher in a Japanese School*. New York: Ticknor and Fields.

Feinberg, J. 1966. "Duties, Rights and Claims." *American Philosophy Quarterly* 3:137–44.

——— 1970. "The Nature and Value of Rights." *Journal of Value Inquiry* 4(4): 243–57.

Fierlbeck, Katherine. 1991. "Redefining Responsibility: The Politics of Citizenship in the United Kingdom." *Canadian Journal of Political Science* 24(3): 575–93.

Finkel, S. 1985. "Reciprocal Effects of Participation and Political Efficacy: A Panel Analysis." *American Journal of Political Science* 29:891–913.

——— 1987. "The Effects of Participation on Political Efficacy and Political Support." *Journal of Politics* 49:441–64.

Fischer, Claude. 1982. *To Dwell among Friends*. Chicago: University of Chicago Press.

References

Fishkin, James. 1982. *The Limits of Obligation*. New Haven: Yale University Press.

1993. *Democracy and Deliberation*. New Haven: Yale University Press.

1994. "The Televised Deliberative Poll: The British Experiement." Paper presented at the American Sociological Association Convention, Los Angeles.

Fitch, Frederic. 1967. "A Revision of Hohfeld's Theory of Legal Concepts." *Logic et Analyse* 39/40:269–76.

Flanz, Gisbert. 1983. *Comparative Women's Rights and Political Participation in Europe*. Dobb's Ferry, N.Y.: Transnational.

Flathman, Richard E. 1972. *Political Obligation*. New York: Atheneum.

1976. *The Practice of Rights*. Cambridge: Cambridge University Press.

1980. *The Practice of Political Authority*. Chicago: University of Chicago Press.

1987. *The Philosophy and Politics of Freedom*. Chicago: University of Chicago Press.

Flora, Peter. 1988. *Growth to Limits*. 4 vols. New York: De Gruyter.

Flora, Peter and Jens Alber. 1981. "Modernization, Democratization, and the Development of Welfare States in Western Europe." Pp. 64–80 in Peter Flora and Arnold Heidenheimer, *The Development of Welfare States in Europe and America*. New York: Transaction.

Flora, Peter and Arnold Heidenheimer. 1981. *The Development of Welfare States in Europe and America*. New York: Transaction.

Fogelman, Ken. 1990. "Citizenship in Secondary Schools: A National Survey." Appendix E in Commission on Citizenship *Encouraging Citizenship*. London: HMSO.

1991. *Citizenship in the Schools*. London: David Fulton.

Foster, C. 1980. *Comparative Public Policy and Citizen Participation*. New York: Pergamon.

Franz, Wolfgang and David Soskice. 1994. "The German Apprenticeship System." Wissenschaftszentrum für Sozialforschung Discussion Paper FS I 94–302.

Fraser, Nancy. 1987. "Women, Welfare and the Politics of Need Interpretation." *Hypatia* 2(1):103–21.

1989. "Talking about Needs: Interpreative Contests as Political Conflicts in Welfare-State Societies." *Ethics* 99:291–313.

1990. "Struggle over Needs: Outline of a Socialist-Feminist Critical Theory of Late-Capitalist Political Culture." Pp. 199–225 in Linda Gordon, *Women, the State, and Welfare*. Madison: University of Wisconsin Press.

Fraser, Nancy and Linda Gordon. 1994. "Civil Citizenship against Social Citizenship." Pp. 90–107 in Bart van Steenbergen, *The Condition of Citizenship*. Thousand Oaks, Calif.: Sage.

Freeden, Michael. 1978. *The New Liberalism: An Ideology of Social Reform*. Oxford: Oxford University Press.

1986. *Liberalism Divided: A Study in British Political Theory, 1914–1939*. Oxford: Oxford University Press.

1990. "Human Needs and Welfare: A Communitarian View." *Ethics* 100(3): 489–502.

1991. *Rights*. Minneapolis: University of Minnesota Press.

Freeman, Gary. 1979. *Immigrant Labor and Racial Conflict in Industrialized Societies*. Princeton: Princeton University Press.

References

1985. "National Styles and Policy Sectors: Explaining Structured Variation." *Journal of Public Policy* 5:467–96.

1994. "Can Liberal States Control Unwanted Migration?" *Annals of the American Academy* 534 (July):17–30.

Frevert, Ute. 1988. *Women in German History*. Oxford: Berg.

Frey, Bruno and W. W. Pommerhene. 1982. "Measuring the Hidden Economy: Though This Be Madness, There Is Method in It." Pp. 3–27 in V. Tanzi, *The Underground Economy in the United States and Abroad*. Lexington, Mass.: D. C. Heath.

Friedman, Debra. 1987. "Notes on 'Toward a Theory of Value in Social Exchange.'" Pp. 47–58 in Karen Cook, *Social Exchange* Newbury Park, Calif.: Sage.

Friedman, Kathi. 1981. *Legitimation of Social Rights and the Western Welfare State*. Chapel Hill: University of North Carolina Press.

Friedman, Milton. 1980. *Free to Choose*. New York: Harcourt Brace Jovanovich.

Friedman, Lawrence. 1990. *The Republic of Choice*. Cambridge, Mass.: Harvard University Press.

Fromkin, Howard and C. R. Snyder. 1980. "The Search for Uniqueness and Valuation of Scarcity: Neglected Dimensions of Value in Exchange Theory." Pp. 57–75 in K. Gergen, M. Greenberg, and R. Willis, *Social Exchange: Advances in Theory and Research*. New York: Plenum Press.

Fullinwider, Robert. 1988. "Citizenship and Welfare." Pp. 261–78 in Amy Gutmann, *Democracy and the Welfare State*. Princeton: Princeton University Press.

Galie, Peter. 1988. "State Courts and Economic Rights." *Annals of the American Academy of Political and Social Science* 496:76–87.

Galston, William. 1991. *Liberal Purposes: Goods, Virtues, and Diversity in the Liberal State*. Cambridge: Cambridge University Press.

Gambetta, Diego. 1988a. *Trust: Making and Breaking Cooperative Relations*. London: Basil Blackwell.

1988b. "Mafia: the Price of Distrust." Pp. 158–75 in Diego Gambetta, *Trust: Making and Breaking Cooperative Relations*. London: Basil Blackwell.

Ganley, Gladys. 1992. *The Exploding Political Power of Personal Media*. Norwood, N.J.: Ablex.

Gergen, Kenneth, Martin Greenberg, and Richard Willis. 1980. *Social Exchange: Advances in Theory and Research*. New York: Plenum Press.

Gewirth, Alan. 1970. "Obligation: Political, Legal, Moral." Pp. 55–88 in J. Pennock and J. Chapman, *Political and Legal Obligation*. New York: Atherton Press.

1978. *Reason and Morality*. Chicago: University of Chicago Press.

1982. *Human Rights: Essays on Justification and Application*. Chicago: University of Chicago Press.

1996. *The Community of Rights*. Chicago: University of Chicago Press.

Giddens, Anthony. 1981. *Contemporary Critique of Historical Materialism*. Berkeley: University of California Press.

1982. "Class Division, Class Conflict and Citizenship Rights." Pp. 164–80 in Anthony Giddens, *Profiles and Critiques in Social Theory*. Berkeley: University of California Press.

1987. *The Nation-State and Violence*. Berkeley: University of California Press.

1989. "A Reply to My Critics." Pp. 249–301 in David Held and John B.

References

Thompson, *Social Theory of Modern Societies*. Cambridge: Cambridge University Press.

Gjems-Onstad, Ole. 1990. "The Independence of Voluntary Organizations in a Social Democracy." *Non-profit and Voluntary Sector Quarterly* 19(4): 393–407.

Glendon, Mary Ann. 1977. *State Law and Family*. Amsterdam: North-Holland.
  1987. *Abortion and Divorce in Western Law*. Cambridge, Mass.: Harvard University Press.
  1989. *The Transformation of Family Law: State, Law and Family in the U.S. and Western Europe*. Chicago: University of Chicago Press.
  1991. *Rights Talk: The Impoverishment of Political Discourse*. New York: Free Press.

Goldthorpe, John. 1978. "The Current Inflation: Toward a Sociological Account." Pp. 186–214 in Fred Hirsch and John Goldthorpe, *The Political Economy of Inflation*. Cambridge, Mass.: Harvard University Press.

Goldthorpe, John, David Lockwood, Frank Bechhofer, and Jennifer Platt. 1969. *The Affluent Worker*. Cambridge: Cambridge University Press.

Gorham, Eric. 1992. *National Service, Citizenship, and Political Education*. Albany: State University of New York Press.

Gostin, Larry. 1995. "Towards Resolving the Conflict." Pp. 7–20 in Larry Gostin, *Civil Liberties in Conflict*. London: Routledge.

Gouldner, Alvin. 1954. *Patterns of Industrial Bureaucracy*. Glencoe: Free Press.

Gourevitch, Peter. 1986. *Politics in Hard Times*. Ithaca: Cornell University Press.

Gransow, Volker. 1989. "Bocksprung in die Zivilgesellschaft." *Blätter für deutsche und internationale Politik*, Heft 12.

Grasmick, Harold, Robert Bursik, and Bruce Arneklev. 1993. "Reduction in Drunk Driving as a Responce to Increased Threats of Shame, Embarrassment, and Legal Sanctions." *Criminology* 31(1):41–67.

Graveson, R. H. 1953. *Status in the Common Law*. London: Athlone.

Gray, John. 1989. *Liberalisms*. London: Routledge.

Grebennikov, V. V. (ed.). 1987. *Rights of Soviet Citizens: Collective Normative Acts*. Moscow: Progress.

Greenfeld, Liah. 1992. *Nationalism: Five Roads to Modernity*. Cambridge: Harvard University Press.

Grønbjerg, Kirsten. 1977. *Mass Society and the Extension of Welfare: 1960–1970*. Chicago: University of Chicago Press.

Grossman, Jonathan. 1967. *The Department of Labor*. New York: Praeger.

Guinier, Lani. 1991a. "The Triumph of Tokenism." *Michigan Law Review* 89(5):1077–154.
  1991b. "No Two Seats: the Elusive Quest for Political Equality." *Virginia Law Review* 77(8):1414–1514.

Gunsteren, H. van. 1978. "Notes on a Theory of Citizenship." Pp. 9–35 in P. Birnbaum, J. Lively, and G. Parry, *Democracy, Consensus and Social Contract*. London: Sage.
  1994. "Four Conceptions of Citizenship." Pp. 36–48 in Bart van Steenbergen, *The Condition of Citizenship*. Newbury Park, Calif.: Sage.

Gutmann, Amy. 1988. *Democracy and the Welfare State*. Princeton: Princeton University Press.

Habermas, Jürgen. 1989. *The Structural Transformation of the Public Sphere: An Inquiry into a Category of Bourgeois Society*. Cambridge, Mass.: MIT Press.

References

1994. "Citizenship and National Identity." Pp. 20–35 in Bart van Steenbergen, *The Condition of Citizenship*. Newbury Park, Calif.: Sage.

1996. *Between Facts and Norms*. Cambridge: Polity Press.

Hadow, W. H. 1923. *Citizenship*. Oxford: Oxford University Press.

Hall, John H. 1995. *Civil Society: Theory, History, Comparisons*. Cambridge: Polity Press.

Halsey, A. H. 1984. "T. H. Marshall: Past and Present 1893–1981." *Sociology* 18:1–18.

Haltern, Utz. 1985. *Bürgerliche Gesellschaft: Sozialtheoretische und sozialhistorische Aspekte*. Darmstadt: Wissenschaftliche Buchgesellschaft.

Hamilton, V. Lee and Joseph Sanders. 1992. *Everyday Justice: Responsibility and the Individual in Japan and the United States*. New Haven: Yale University Press.

Hammar. Tomas. 1985. *European Immigration Policy*. Cambridge: Cambridge University Press.

1990. *Democracy and the Nation-State: Aliens, Denizens, and Citizens in a World of International Migration*. Aldershot: Avebury.

Hannum, Hurst. 1996. *Autonomy, Sovereignty, and Self-Determination: The Accommodation of Conflicting Rights*. Philadelphia: University of Pennsylvania Press.

Hardacre, Helen. 1991. "Japan: The Public Sphere in a Non-Western Setting." Pp. 217–42 in Robert Wuthnow, *Between States and Markets*. Princeton: Princeton University Press.

Harrison, M. L. 1991. "Citizenship, Consumption and Rights: A Comment on B. S. Turner's Theory of Citizenship." *Sociology* 25(2):209–14.

Hart, H. L. A. 1949. "The Ascription of Responsibility and Rights." *Proceedings of the Aristotelian Society* 49:171–94.

1958. "Legal and Moral Obligation." Pp. 82–107 in A. I. Melden, *Essays in Moral Philosophy*. Seattle: University of Washington Press.

1961. *The Concept of Law*. Oxford: Clarendon Press.

1983. "Between Utility and Rights." Pp. 214–26 in Marshall Cohen, *Ronald Dworkin and Contemporary Jurisprudence*. Totowa, N.J.: Rowman and Allanheld.

Havens, Murray. 1991. "Citizenship." Pp. 742–45 in *The American Intellectual Encyclopedia*. New York: Grolier.

Hayek, Friedrich. 1979. *The Road to Serfdom*. London: Routledge and Kegan Paul.

Headrick, Rita. 1978. "African Soldiers in World War II." *Armed Forces and Society* 4(3):501–26.

Heath, Anthony. 1976. *Rational Choice and Social Exchange: A Critique of Exchange Theory*. Cambridge: Cambridge University Press.

Hechter, Michael and S. Kanazawa. 1993. "Group Solidarity and Social Order in Japan." *Journal of Theoretical Politics* 5(4):455–93.

Heidenheimer, Arnold. 1981. "Unions and Welfare State Development in Britain and Germany." West Berlin: International Institute for Comparative Social Research, Wissenschaftszentrum Discussion Paper.

Heinemann, Eduard. 1929. *Sozial Theorie des Kapitalismus*. Frankfurt: Suhrkamp Verlag.

Held, David. 1987. *Models of Democracy*. Stanford: Stanford University Press.

1989. "Citizenship and Autonomy." Pp. 162–84 in David Held and John Thompson, *Social Theory of Modern Societies*. Cambridge: Cambridge University Press.

References

1991. "Democracy, the Nation State and the Global System." *Economy and Society* 20(2):138–72.

Hentschel, Richard. 1983. *Sozialpolitik*. Frankfurt: Suhrkamp Verlag.

Hermens, Ferdinand. 1941. *Democracy or Anarchy?* Notre Dame, Ind.: University of Notre Dame Press.

Hermet, Guy. 1990. "The Citizen-Individual in Western Christianity." Pp. 116–40 in Pierre Birnbaum and Jean Leca, *Individualism: Theories and Methods*. Oxford: Oxford University Press.

Hernes, Helga Maria. 1987. *Welfare State and Woman Power*. Oslo: Norwegian University Press.

Hicks, Alexander and Joya Misra. 1993. "Political Resources and the Growth of Welfare in Affluent Captialist Democracies, 1960–1982." *American Journal of Sociology* 99(3):668–710.

Hicks, Alexander, Joya Misra, and Tang Nah Ng. 1995. "The Programmatic Emergence of the Social Security State." *American Sociological Review* 60(3):329–49.

Hirschmann, Nancy. 1992. *Rethinking Obligation*. Ithaca: Cornell University Press.

Hoffman, Daniel. 1986. "Personhood and Rights." *Polity* 19:74–96.

Hoff Wilson, Joan. 1991. *Law, Gender, and Justice*. New York: New York University Press.

Hohfeld, Wesley. 1978. *Fundamental Legal Conceptions*. Westport, Conn.: Greenwood Press.

Hollifield, James. 1992. *Immigrants, Markets and States*. Cambridge, Mass.: Harvard University Press.

Holt, J. C. 1993. "The Ancient Constitution in Medieval England." Pp. 22–56 in Ellis Sandoz, *The Roots of Liberty*. Columbia: University of Missouri Press.

Homans, George. 1950. *The Human Group*. New York: Harcourt, Brace and World.

Howard, Rhoda. 1992. "Dignity, Community, and Human Rights." Pp. 81–102 in A. An-Na'im, *Human Rights in Cross-Cultural Perspectives*. Philadelphia: University of Pennsylvania Press.

Huber, Ernst. 1981. *Deutsche Verfassungsgeschichte seit 1789*. Vols. 4–6. Stuttgart: Kohlhammer Verlag.

Huber, Evelyne, Charles Ragin, and John Stephens. 1993. "Social Democracy, Christian Democracy, Constitutional Structure, and the Welfare State." *American Journal of Sociology* 99(3):711–99.

Hudson, S. D. and D. N. Husak. 1980. "Legal Rights: How Useful is Hohfeldian Analysis?" *Philosophical Studies* 37:45–53.

Humana, Charles. 1983. *World Human Rights Guide*. New York: PICA Press.
1993. *World Human Rights Guide*. 3d ed. New York: Oxford University Press.

Hunt, G. 1986. "Gramsci, Civil Society and Bureaucracy." *Praxis International* 6(2):206–219.

Ichilov, Orit. 1990. "Dimensions and Role Patterns of Citizenship in Democracy." Pp. 11–24 in Orit Ichilov, *Political Socialization, Citizenship Education, and Democracy*. New York: Teachers College of Columbia University.

Ignatieff, Michael. 1984. *Citizenship and the Needs of Strangers*. London: Chatto and Windus.
1989. "Citizenship and Moral Narcissism." *Political Quarterly* 60(1):63–74.

References

International Institute for Strategic Studies. 1966/67–92/93. *The Military Balance*. London: International Institute for Strategic Studies.

Iyengar, Shanto. 1991. *Is Anyone Responsible?* Chicago: University of Chicago Press.

Jackall, Robert. 1988. *Moral Mazes*. Oxford: Oxford University Press.

Jacobi, Otto, Berndt Keller, and Walther Müller-Jentsch. 1992. "Germany: Codetermining the Future." Pp. 218–69 in Anthony Ferner and Richard Hyman, *Industrial Relations in the New Europe*. London: Basil Blackwell.

Jacobs, Jane. 1960. *The Death and Life of Great American Cities*. New York: Random House.

Janoski, Thomas. 1990. *The Political Economy of Unemployment*. Berkeley: University of California Press.

——— 1991. "Synthetic Strategies in Comparative Sociological Research." *International Journal of Comparative Sociology* 1/2:59–81.

——— 1992. "The Reformulation of Citizenship Rights Theory: Participation, Obligation, and Development" Center for International Studies, Duke University, Working Paper.

——— 1996. "Explaining State Intervention to Prevent Unemployment: The Impact of Institutions on Active Labour Market Policy Expenditures in 18 Countries." Pp. 697–724 in Günther Schmid, Jacqueline O'Reilly and Klaus Schöman, *International Handbook of Labour Market Policy and Evaluation*. Cheltenham: Edward Elgar.

Janoski, Thomas and Elizabeth Glennie. 1995a. "The Roots of Citizenship: Explaining Naturalization in Advanced Industrialized Nations." Pp. 11–39 in Marco Martinello, *Citizenship in the Economic Community*. Aldershot: Avebury.

——— 1995b. "The Double Irony of Granting Citizenship: Colonialism and Indigenous Decline as Causes of Naturalization Rates." Paper presented at the American Sociological Association Convention, Washington, D.C.

Janoski, Thomas, Christa McGill, and Vanessa Tinsley. 1997. "Making Institutions Dynamic in Cross-National Research: Time-Space Distancing in Explaining Unemployment." *Comparative Social Research* 16:227–68.

Janoski, Thomas and John Wilson. 1995. "Pathways to Voluntarism: Family Socialization and Status Transmission Models." *Social Forces* 74(1):271–92.

Janoski, Thomas, John Wilson, and Mark Musick. In press. "Being Volunteered: A LISREL Analysis of Citizenship Attitudes and Behaviors as Causes of Volunteering." *Sociological Forum*.

Janowitz, Morris. 1976. "Military Institutions and Citizenship in Western Societies." *Armed Forces and Society* 2(2):185–204.

——— 1978. *The Last Half-Century*. Chicago: University of Chicago Press.

——— 1980. "Observations on the Sociology of Citizenship: Obligations and Rights." *Social Forces* 59(1):1–24.

——— 1983. *The Reconstruction of Patriotism: Education for Civic Consciousness*. Chicago: University of Chicago Press.

Jary, David. 1991. "'Society as Time-Traveller: Giddens on Historical Change, Historical Materialism and the Nation-State in World Society." Pp. 116–59 in Christopher Bryant and David Jary, *Giddens' Theory of Structuration: A Critical Appreciation*. London: Routledge.

References

Johnson, Chalmers. 1982. *MITI and the Japanese Miracle*. Stanford: Stanford University Press.

Jones, Gill and Claire Wallace. 1992. *Youth, Family and Citizenship*. Buckingham: Open University Press.

Kairys, David. 1990. *The Politics of Law*. New York: Pantheon.

Kalberg, Stephen. 1980. "Max Weber's Types of Rationality." *American Journal of Sociology* 85:1145–79.

　　1993. "Cultural Foundations of Modern Citizenship." Pp. 91–114 in Bryan Turner, *Citizenship and Social Theory*. Newbury Park, Calif.: Sage.

Kanger, Stig and Helle Kanger. 1966. "Rights and Parliamentarism." *Theoria* 32: 85–115.

Karst, Kenneth. 1989. *Belonging to America: Equal Citizenship and the Constitution*. New Haven: Yale University Press.

Katzenstein, Peter. 1984. *Corporatism and Change*. Ithaca: Cornell University Press.

　　1985. *Small States in World Markets*. Ithaca: Cornell University Press.

Keane, John. (ed.) 1987a. *Re-discovering Civil Society*. London: Verso.

　　1987. *Socialism and Civil Society*. London: Verso.

　　1988a. *Democracy and Civil Society*. London: Verso.

　　1991. *The Media and Democracy*. London: Polity Press.

　　(ed.) 1988b. *Civil Society and the State*. London: Verso.

Kelsen, Hans. 1941. "The Pure Theory of Law and Analytical Jurisprudence." *Harvard Law Review* 55:44–70.

Kemper, Theodore. 1989. *Research Agendas in the Sociology of Emotions*. Albany: State University of New York Press.

Kennedy, Paul. 1987. *The Rise and Fall of the Great Powers*. New York: Vintage.

Kettner, James. H. 1978. *The Development of American Citizenship, 1608–1870*. Chapel Hill: University of North Carolina Press.

King, Desmond. 1991. "Citizenship as Obligation in the United States: Title II of the Family Support Act of 1988." Pp. 1–31 in Ursula Vogel and Michael Moran, *The Frontiers of Citizenship*. New York: St. Martin's Press

King, Desmond and Jeremy Waldron. 1988. "Citizenship, Social Citizenship and the Defense of Welfare Provision." *British Journal of Political Science* 18(1):415–45.

Kingdom, John. 1992. *No Such Thing as Society? Individualism and Community*. Buckingham: Open University Press.

Kingdon, John. 1984. *Agendas, Alternatives, and Public Policies*. Boston: Little, Brown.

Kitschelt, Herbert. 1985. "Materiale Politisierung der Produktion." *Zeitschrift für Soziologier* 14(3):188–208.

Kjellberg, Anders. 1992. "Sweden: Can the Model Survive?" pp. 88–142 in Anthony Ferner and Richard Hyman, *Industrial Relations in the New Europe*. Oxford: Blackwell.

Klein, Rudolf. 1991. "Review of Three Worlds of Welfare Capitalism." *Journal of Public Policy* 11(2)233–5.

Knoke, David and Edward O. Laumann. 1982. "The Social Organization of National Policy Domains." Pp. 255–70 in Peter Marsden and Nan Lin, *Social Structure and Network Analysis*. Newbury Park, Calif.: Sage.

Knoke, David, Franz Pappi, Jeffrey Broadbent, and Yutaka Tsujinaka. 1996. *Comparing Policy Networks*. Cambridge: Cambridge University Press.

References

Kocourek, A. 1927. *Jural Relations*. Indianapolis: Bobbs-Merrill.

Kolberg, Jon E. 1992. *The Study of Welfare State Regimes*. New York: M.E. Sharpe.

Kornblum, William. 1978. *Blue-Collar Community*. Chicago: University of Chicago Press.

Kornhauser, William. 1959. *The Politics of Mass Society*. Glencoe, Ill.: Free Press.

Korpi, Walter. 1983. *The Democratic Class Struggle*. London: Routledge Kegan Paul.

    1985. "Power Resources Approach vs. Action and Conflict." *Sociological Theory* 3:31–55.

    1989. "Power, Politics, and State Autonomy in the Development of Social Citizenship." *American Sociological Review* 54:309–28.

    1994. "Class, Gender and Power in the Development of Social Citizenship." Paper presented at the International Sociological Association Meetings, Bielefeld.

Kramer, Eric. 1993. "Mass Media and Democracy." Pp. 77–98 in John Murphy and Dennis Peck, *Open Institutions*. Westport, Conn.: Praeger.

Kritz, Mary, Lin Lean Lim, and Hania Zlotnik. 1992. *International Migration Systems: A Global Approach*. Oxford: Clarendon Press.

Kruse, Vinding. 1939. *The Right of Property*. Vol. 1. London: Oxford University Press.

Kukathas, Chandran. 1992. "Are There Any Cultural Rights?" *Political Theory* 20(1):105–39.

Kumar, Krishnan. 1993. "Civil Society: An Inquiry into the Usefulness of an Historical Term." *British Journal of Sociology* 44(3):375–95.

Kymlicka, Will. 1990. *Contemporary Political Philosophy*. Oxford: Clarendon Press.

    1992. "The Rights of Minority Cultures." *Political Theory* 20(1):140–46.

Kymlicka, Will. 1995. *Multicultural Citizenship*. Oxford: Clarendon Press.

Laband, David, and Deborah Heinbuch. 1987. *Blue Laws: The History, Economics, and Politics of Sunday-Closing Laws*. Lexington, Mass.: D.C. Heath.

Lamont, William D. 1946. *The Principles of Moral Judgement*. Oxford: Clarendon Press.

Lampert, Nick. 1986. "Job Security and the Law in the USSR." Pp. 256–77 in David Lane, *Labor and Employment in the USSR*. Brighton: Harvester Press.

Lane, David, and Felicity O'Dell. 1978. *The Soviet Industrial Worker*. New York: St. Martin's Press.

Lane, Jan-Erik. 1991. *Political Data Handbook OECD Countries*. Oxford: Oxford University Press.

Lane, Jan-Erik, and Svante O. Ersson. 1991. *Politics and Society in Western Europe*. 2d ed. Newbury Park, Calif.: Sage.

Lash, Scott. 1984. *The Militant Worker*. Rutherford: Fairleigh Dickinson University Press.

Laver, Michael. 1981. *The Politics of Private Desires*. Harmondsworth: Penguin.

Lawson, Edward. 1992. *Encyclopedia of Human Rights*. New York: Taylor and Francis.

Layton-Henry, Zig. 1985. "Great Britain." Pp. 89–126 in Tomas Hammar, *European Immigration Policy*. Cambridge: Cambridge University Press.

References

Leach, Jerry. 1983. "Introduction" Pp. 1–26 in Jerry Leach and Edmund Leach. *The Kula: New Perspectives on Massim Exchange.* Cambridge: Cambridge University Press.

Leca, Jean. 1990. "Individualism and Citizenship." Pp. 141–89 in Pierre Birnbaum and Jean Leca, *Individualism: Theories and Methods.* Oxford: Oxford University Press.

Lehmbruch, Gerhard and Philippe Schmitter. 1982. *Patterns of Corporatist Policy-making.* Newbury Park, Calif.: Sage.

Lenski, Gerhard. 1966. *Power and Privilege.* New York: McGraw-Hill.

Leonard, Peter. 1983. "Marxism, the Individual and the Welfare State." Pp. 64–82 in Philip Bean and Stewart MacPherson, *Approaches to Welfare.* London: Routledge and Kegan Paul.

Levi-Strauss, Claude. 1969. *The Elementary Structures of Kinship.* Boston: Beacon.

Lewin, Leif. 1988. *Ideology and Strategy.* Cambridge: Cambridge University Press.

Lichtenberg, Judith. 1990. *Democracy and the Mass Media.* Cambridge: Cambridge University Press.

Lidtke, Vernon. 1985. *The Alternative Culture.* New York: Oxford University Press.

Lijphart, Arend. 1968. *The Politics of Accommodation.* Berkeley: University of California Press.

    1984. *Democracies: Patterns of Majoritan and Consensus Government in 21 Countries.* New Haven: Yale University Press.

Lindahl, Lars. 1977. *Position and Change.* Dordrecht: Reidel.

Linz, Juan. 1978. *Crisis, Breakdown and Reequilibration.* Baltimore: Johns Hopkins University Press.

    1980. "Political Space and Fascism as a Late-Comer." Pp. 153–89 in Stein Larsen, Bernt Hagtvet, and J. P. Myklebust, *Who Were the Fascists?* Bergen: Universitets Forlaget.

Lipset, Seymour Martin. 1964. "Introduction." Pp. v–xxii in T. H. Marshall, *Class, Citizenship and Social Development.* Chicago: University of Chicago Press.

    1977. "Why No Socialism in the United States?" Pp. 31–149 in S. Bialer and S. Sluzar, *Radicalism in the Contemporary Age.* Boulder: Westview Press.

    1981. *Political Man.* Expanded and updated edition. Baltimore: Johns Hopkins University Press.

    1983. "Radicalism or Reformism: The Sources of Working Class Politics." *American Political Science Review* 77(1):1–18.

Lister, R. 1990a. *The Exclusive Society, Citizenship and the Poor.* London: CPAG.

    1990b. "Women, Economic Dependency and Citizenship." *Journal of Social Policy* 19(4):445–67.

    1991. "Citizenship Engendered." *Critical Social Policy* 32:65–71.

Locke, John. 1967. *Two Treatises of Government.* New York: Mentor Books.

Lockwood, David. 1974. "For T. H. Marshall." *Sociology* 8:363–67.

    1975. "Sources of Variation in Working Class Images of Society." Pp. 239–50 in Martin Bulmer, *Working Class Images of Society.* London: Routledge and Kegan Paul.

Lombardi, John. 1942. *Labor's Voice in the Cabinet.* New York: Columbia University Press.

Lorenz, Edward. 1992. "Trust and the Flexible Firm." *Industrial Relations* 31(3):445–92.

References

Lowenthal, Leo. 1987. *False Prophets*. New Brunswick, N.J.: Transaction.

Lowi, Theodore. 1979. *The End of Liberalism*. New York: Norton.

    1984. "Why Is There No Socialism in the United States? A Federal Analysis." Pp. 37–53 in R. Golembiewski and A. Wildavsky, *The Costs of Federalism*. New Brunswick, N.J.: Transaction.

Luebbert, Gregory. 1991. *Liberalism, Fascism, or Social Democracy: Social Classes and the Political Origins of Regimes in Interwar Europe*. Oxford: Oxford University Press.

Luhmann, Niklas. 1979. *Trust and Power*. New York: John Wiley and Sons.

    1988. "Familiarity, Confidence, Trust: Problems and Alternatives." Pp. 94–107 in Diego Gambetta, *Trust*. London: Basil Blackwell.

Lyons, David. 1969. "Rights, Claimants and Beneficiaries." *American Philosophical Quarterly*. 6:173–85.

    1970. "The Correlativity of Rights and Duties." *Nous* 4(1):45–55.

    1977. "Human Rights and General Welfare." *Philosophy and Public Affairs* 6(2):113–29.

MacIntyre, Alasdair. 1981. *After Virtue*. South Bend, Ind: University of Notre Dame Press.

    1983. "Moral Philosophy: What Next?" Pp. 1–15 in Stanley Hauerwas and Alasdair MacIntyre, *Revisions: Changing Perspectives in Moral Philosophy*. Notre Dame, Ind.: University of Notre Dame Press.

Macpherson, C. B. 1962. *The Political Theory of Possessive Individualism*. Oxford: Oxford University Press.

Maddex, Robert. 1995. *Constitutions of the World*. Washington, D.C.: Congressional Quarterly Press.

Maguire, Maria. 1988. "Ireland." Pp. 241–384 in Peter Flora, *Growth to Limits, Volume 2*. Berlin: Walter de Gruyter.

Mann, Michael. 1986. *The Sources of Social Power*. Vol. 1. Cambridge: Cambridge University Press.

    1988. "Ruling Class Strategies and Citizenship." Pp. 188–209 in Michael Mann, *States, War and Capitalism*. London: Basil Blackwell.

    1994. *The Sources of Social Power*. Vol. 2. Cambridge: Cambridge University Press.

Manville, Philip. 1990. *The Origins of Citizenship in Ancient Athens*. Princeton: Princeton University Press.

March, James and Johan Olsen. 1984. "The New Institutionalism: Organizational Factors in Political Life." *American Political Science Review* 78(3): 734–49.

    1989. *Rediscovering Institutions*. New York: Free Press.

Marin, Bernd. 1990. "Introduction." Pp. 13–35 in Bernd Marin, *Governance and Generalized Exchange*. Frankfurt: Campus Verlag.

Markus, Hazel and Elissa Wurf. 1987. "The Dynamic Self-Concept: A Social-Psychological Perspective." *Annual Review of Psychology* 38:299–337.

Marshall, T. H. 1964. *Class, Citizenship and Social Development*. Chicago: University of Chicago Press.

    1981. *The Right to Welfare and Other Essays*. London: Heinemann.

Martin, Cathy Jo. 1992. *Shifting the Burden: The Struggle over Growth and Corporate Taxation*. Chicago: University of Chicago Press.

Martin, Rex. 1980. "Human Rights and Civil Rights." *Philosophical Studies* 37: 391–403.

References

1982. "On the Justification of Rights." Pp. 153–86 in G. Fløstad, *Contemporary Philosophy*. The Hague: Martinus Nijhoff.

1993. *A System of Rights*. Oxford: Clarendon Press.

Maslow, Abraham. 1970. *Motivation and Personality*. 2d ed. New York: Harper and Row.

Mauer, Marc. 1994. *Americans Behind Bars: The International Use of Incarceration, 1992–1993*. Washington, D.C.: The Sentencing Project.

Maxson, Charles. 1930. *Citizenship*. New York: Oxford University Press.

McAuley, Alastair. 1979. *Economic Welfare in the Soviet Union*. Madison: University of Wisconsin Press.

McAuley, Mary. 1969. *Labour Disputes in Soviet Russia*. Oxford: Clarendon Press.

McDonagh, E. L. 1989. "Issues and Constituencies in the Progressive Era." *Journal of Politics* 51:119–36.

Mead, Lawrence. 1986. *Beyond Entitlement: The Social Obligations of Citizenship*. New York: Free Press.

Meehan, Elizabeth. 1993. *Citizenship and the European Community*. Newbury Park, Calif.: Sage.

Melden, Abraham I. 1959. *Rights and Right Conduct*. Oxford: Clarendon Press.

1985. *A Theory of Rights*. Totowa, N.J.: Rowman and Allanheld.

Mellors, Colin and John McKean. 1984. "The Politics of Conscription in Western Europe." *West European Politics* 7(3):25–42.

Melucci, Alberto. 1981. "Ten Hypotheses for the Analysis of New Social Movements." Pp. Xx–xx in Diana Pinto, *Contemporary Italian Sociology*. Cambridge: Cambridge University Press.

Merriam, Charles. 1931. *The Making of Citizens*. Chicago: University of Chicago Press.

1934. *Civic Education in the U.S.* New York: American Historical Association.

Miller, William Ian. 1993. *Humiliation*. Ithaca: Cornell University Press.

Minow, Martha. 1990. *Making all the Difference: Inclusion, Exclusion and American Law*. Ithaca: Cornell University Press.

Mishra, Ramesh. 1981. *Society and Social Policy*. Atlantic Highlands, N.J.: Humanities Press.

1986. "Social Analysis and the Welfare State: Retrospect and Prospect." Pp. 20–32 in Else Øyen, *Comparing Welfare States and Their Futures*. Aldershot: Gower.

Mitchel, G. D. 1968. *Dictionary of Sociology*. Chicago: Aldine.

Moore, Barrington. 1965. *The Social Origins of Dictatorship and Democracy*. Boston: Beacon.

Morgan, Robert. 1984. *Disabling America: The "Rights Industry" in Our Time*. New York: Basic Books.

Morris, Aldon. 1984. *The Origins of the Civil Rights Movement*. New York: Free Press.

Morrison, Mary Jane. 1989. "Constitutional Reasoning for Rights." *Missouri Law Review* 54(1):29–73.

Moskos, Charles C. 1988. *A Call to Civic Service: National Service for Country and Community*. New York: Free Press.

1990. "National Service and Its Enemies." Pp. 191–208 in Williamson Evers, *National Service: Pro & Con*. Stanford: Hoover Institution Press.

References

Moskos, Charles and John W. Chambers. 1993. *The New Conscientious Objection*. Oxford: Oxford University Press.

Mouffe, Chantal. 1993a. "Citizenship." Pp. 138–9 in Joel Krieger et al., *The Oxford Companion to Politics of the World*. New York: Oxford University Press.

———. 1993b. "Feminism, Citizenship and Radical Democratic Poliics." Pp. 367–84 in Judith Butler and Joan Scott, *Feminists Theorize the Political*. New York: Routledge.

Mouritzen, Poul. 1987. "The Demanding Citizen: Driven by Policy, Self-Interest, or Ideology?" *European Journal of Political Research* 15(4):417–35.

Murphy, Raymond. 1988. *Social Closure*. Oxford: Clarendon Press.

Murray, Charles. 1984. *Losing Ground*. New York: Basic Books.

Nagel, Jack. 1987. *Participation*. Englewood Cliffs, N.J.: Prentice Hall.

Napthali, Fritz. 1929. *Wirtschaftsdemokratie*. Berlin: ADGB.

Narveson, Jan. 1984. "Negative and Positive Rights in Gewirth's *Reason and Morality*." Pp. 96–107 in Edward Regis, Jr., *Gerwirth's Ethical Rationalism*. Chicago: University of Chicago Press.

Neuman, W. Russell. 1986. *The Paradox of Mass Politics*. Cambridge, Mass.: Harvard University Press.

Nickel, James, 1987. *Making Sense of Human Rights*. Berkeley: University of California Press.

Nicolet, Claude. 1988. *The World of the Citizen in Republican Rome*. Berkeley: University of California Press.

Nordhaug, Odd. 1990. "Voluntary Organizations and Public Incentive Systems." *Non-profit and Voluntary Sector Quarterly* 19(3):237–50.

Norregaard, John. 1990. "Progressivity of Income Tax Systems." *OECD Economic Studies* 15:83–110.

North Carolina Department of Transportation. 1993. "The Adopt-A-Highway Program." Raleigh, N.C.: Department of Transportation Memorandum.

Nozick, Robert. 1974. *Anarchy, State, and Utopia*. New York: Basic Books.

Nussbaum, Martha. 1996. *For Love of Country: Debating the Limits of Patriotism*. Boston: Beacon.

Oakeshott, M. 1975. "On the Civil Condition." Pp. 108–84 in M. Oakeshott, *On Human Conduct*. Oxford: Oxford University Press.

O'Connor, Julia. 1996. "From Women in the Welfare State to Gendering Welfare State Regimes." *Current Sociology*. 44(2):1–124.

OECD. 1987a. *Taxation in Developed Countries*. Paris: OECD.

———. 1987b. *International Tax Avoidance and Evasion*. Paris: OECD.

———. 1987c. *The Future of Migration*. Paris: OECD.

———. 1990. *Taxpayers' Rights and Obligations*. Paris: OECD.

———. 1991. *Historical Statistics, 1960 to 1989*. Paris: OECD.

———. 1992. *National Accounts Statistics*. Paris: OECD.

———. 1994. *Employment Outlook*. Paris: OECD.

Oldfield, Brian. 1990. *Citizenship and Community*. London: Routledge.

Olsen, Marvin E. 1982. *Participatory Pluralism*. Chicago: Nelson-Hall.

Olson, Sven. 1988. "Sweden." Pp. 1–116 in Peter Flora, *Growth to Limits*. Berlin: De Gruyter.

Oosterwegel, Annerieke and Louis Oppenheimer. 1993. *The Self-System: Developmental Changes between and within Self-Concepts*. Hillsdale, N.J.: Lawrence Erlbaum.

References

Orloff, Ann Shola. 1988. "The Political Origins of America's Belated Welfare State." Pp. 37–80 in Margaret Weir, Ann Shola Orloff, and Theda Skocpol, *The Politics of Social Policy in the United States*. Princeton: Princeton University Press.

Ossowska, Maria. 1970. *Social Determinants of Moral Ideas*. Philadelphia: University of Pennsylvania Press.

Otter, Casten von. 1983. "Sweden: Labor Reformism Reshapes the System." Pp. 187–228 in Solomon Barkin, *Worker Militancy and Its Consequences*. 2d ed. New York: Praeger.

Pagen, Anthony. 1988. "The Destruction of Trust and Its Economic Consequences in the Case of Eighteenth-Century Naples." Pp. 127–41 in Diego Gambetta, *Trust*. London: Basil Blackwell.

Paige, Jeffrey. 1975. *Agrarian Revolution*. New York: Free Press.

Parkin, Frank. 1982. *Max Weber*. Chinchester: Ellis Horwood.

Parry, Geraint. 1991. "Conclusion: Paths to Citizenship." Pp. 166–201 in Ursula Vogel and Michael Moran, *The Frontiers of Citizenship*. New York: St. Martin's Press.

Parry, Geraint, George Moyser, and Neil Day. 1992. *Political Participation and Democracy in Britain*. Cambridge: Cambridge University Press.

Parsons, Talcott. 1969. "Full Citizenship for the Negro American." Pp. 252–301 in Talcott Parsons, *Politics and Social Structure*. New York: Free Press.

——— 1971. *The System of Modern Societies*. Englewood Cliffs, N.J.: Prentice Hall.

Pateman, Carole. 1979. *Participation and Democratic Theory*. Cambridge: Cambridge University Press.

——— 1983. "Feminist Critiques of the Public/Private Dichotomy." Pp. 281–303 in S. Benn and G. Gaus, *Public and Private in Social Life*. London: Croom Helm.

——— 1988. "The Patriarchal Welfare State." Pp. 231–60 in Amy Gutmann, *Democracy and the Welfare State*. Princeton: Princeton University Press.

Paton, George Whitecross. 1972. *A Text-book of Jurisprudence*. 4th ed. Oxford: Clarendon Press.

Pekkarinen, Jukka, Matti Pohjola, and Robert Rowthorn. 1992. *Societal Corporatism*. Oxford: Oxford University Press.

Peled, Yoav. 1992a. "Ethnic Democracy and the Legal Construction of Citizenship." *American Political Science Review* 86(2):432–43.

——— 1992b. "Religion and Citizenship in the Liberal State." Paper presented at the American Political Science Association Convention, Chicago.

Pencak, William. 1984. "Veterans' Movements." Pp. 1332–47 in *the Encyclopedia of American Political History*. Vol. 3. New York: Scribners.

Percy, Stephen. 1989. *Disability, Civil Rights, and Public Policy*. Tuscaloosa: University of Alabama Press.

Perlman, Selig. 1928. *A Theory of the Labor Movement*. New York: Augustus Kelley.

Perry, T. D. 1977. "A Paradigm of Philosophy: Hohfeld on Legal Rights." *American Philosophical Quarterly* 14:41–50.

——— 1980. "Reply in Defence of Hohfeld." *Philosophical Studies* 37:203–9.

Pestoff, Victor. 1977. *Voluntary Associations and Nordic Party Systems*. Stockholm: Stockholms Universitet.

Peters, B. Guy. 1991. *The Politics of Taxation*. Cambridge, Mass.: Blackwell.

Petersen, R. A. 1979. "Revitalizing the Culture Concept." *Annual Review of Sociology* 5:137–66.

References

Phillips, Derik. 1986. *Toward a Just Social Order*. Princeton: Princeton University Press.

Pierson, Christopher. 1984. "New Theories of State and Civil Society." *Sociology* 18(4):563–71.

1991. *Beyond the Welfare State*. University Park: Pennsylvania State University Press.

Piliavin, Jane and Peter Callero. 1991. *Giving Blood*. Baltimore: Johns Hopkins University Press.

Pinker, Robert. 1981. "Introduction." Pp. 1–28 in T. H. Marshall, *The Right to Welfare and Other Essays*. New York: Free Press.

Piore, Michael and Charles Sabel. 1984. *The Second Industrial Divide*. New York: Basic Books.

Pitkin, Hannah. 1965. "Obligation and Consent. I." *American Political Science Review* 59(4):990–9.

1966. "Obligation and Consent. II." *American Political Science Review* 60(1):39–52.

Piven, Frances Fox and Richard Cloward. 1979. *Poor Peoples Movements*. New York: Random House.

1988. *Why Americans Don't Vote*. New York: Pantheon.

Plano, Jack. 1979. "Immigration and Citizenship." In *The American Political Dictionary*. New York: Holt, Rinehart and Winston.

Pocock, J. G. A. 1975. *The Machiavellian Moment: Florentine Political Thought and the Atlantic Republican Tradition*. Princeton: Princeton University Press.

Pollock, F. H. 1929. *First Book of Jurisprudence*. 6th ed. London: Macmillan.

Portis, Edward. 1985. "Citizenship and Personal Identity." *Polity* 18:457–72.

Pratte, R. 1988. *The Civic Imperative: Examining the Need for Civic Education*. New York: Teachers College Press of Columbia University.

Preuss, Ulrich. 1986. "The Concept of Rights and the Welfare State." Pp. 151–72 in G. Teubner, *Dilemmas of Law in the Welfare State*. Berlin: De Gruyter.

Putnam, Robert D. 1993. *Making Democracy Work: Civic Traditions in Modern Italy*. Princeton: Princeton University Press.

Quadagno, Jill. 1987. "Theories of the Welfare State." *Annual Review of Sociology* 13:109–28.

Radin, M. 1938. "A Restatement of Hohfeld." *Harvard Law Review* 51:1141–64.

Radin, Margaret Jane. 1993. "The Pragmatist and the Feminist." Pp. 559–74 in Patricia Smith, *Feminist Jurisprudence*. New York: Oxford University Press.

Ragin, Charles. 1989. *The Comparative Method*. Berkeley: University of California Press.

Raphael, David D. 1967. "Human Rights, Old and New." Pp. 54–67 in David D. Raphael, *Political Theory and the Rights of Man*. Bloomington: Indiana University Press.

Rawls, John. 1971. *A Theory of Justice*. Cambridge, Mass.: Harvard University Press.

1982. "The Basic Liberties and Their Priority." Pp. 1–87 in Sterling McMurrin, *The Tanner Lectures on Human Values*. Salt Lake City: University of Utah Press.

1993. *Political Liberalism*. New York: Columbia University Press.

Rayback, Joseph. 1966. *A History of American Labor*. New York: Free Press.

References

Raz, Joseph. 1984. "Legal Rights." *Oxford Journal of Legal Studies* 4:1–21.
   1986. *The Morality of Freedom*. Oxford: Clarendon Press.
Regini, Marino. 1995. *Uncertain Boundaries: The Sociological and Political Construction of European Economies*. Cambridge: Cambridge University Press.
Reisenberg, Peter. 1992. *Citizenship in the Western Tradition*. Chapel Hill: University of North Carolina Press.
Rhoodie, Eschel. 1989. *Discrimination against Women*. Jefferson, N.C.: McFarland.
Richardson, A. 1990. *Talking about Commitment*. London: Prince's Trust.
Richardson, Jeremy, Gunnel Gustafsson, and Grant Jordan. 1981. "The Concept of Policy Style." Pp. 1–16 in Jeremy Richardson, *Policy Styles in Western Europe*. Boston: Allen Unwin.
Rimlinger, Gaston. 1971. *Welfare Policy and Industrializaton in Europe, America and Russia*. New York: John Wiley and Sons.
Ritter, Gerhard and Klaus Tenfelde. 1975. "Der Durchbruch der freien Gewerkschaften Deutschlands zur Massenbewegung im letzten Viertel des 19. Jahrhunderts." Pp. 61–121 in Heinz Vetter, *Vom Sozialistengesetz zur Mitbestimmung*. Cologne: Bund Verlag.
Robertson, David. 1981. "Politics and Labor Markets." Ph.D. dissertation, Indiana University.
Roche, John. P. 1949. *The Early Development of United States Citizenship*. Ithaca: Cornell University Press.
Roche, Maurice. 1987. "Citizenship, Social Theory, and Social Change." *Theory and Society* 16:363–99.
   1992. *Rethinking Citizenship*. London: Polity Press.
Roelofs, H. Mark. 1957. *The Tension of Citizenship*. New York: Holt, Rinehart and Winston.
Rohde, Deborah. 1993. "Feminist Critical Theories." Pp. 594–609 in Patricia Smith, *Feminist Jurisprudence*. Oxford: Oxford University Press.
Rohlen, Thomas. 1983. *Japan's High Schools*. Berkeley: University of California Press.
Rokkan, Stein. 1966. "Mass Suffrage, Secret Voting and Political Participation." Pp. 101–31 in Lewis Coser, *Political Sociology*. New York: Harper and Row.
   1970. *Citizens, Elections, Parties*. New York: David McKay.
   1974a. "Cities, States and Nations." Pp. 73–97 in Shmuel Eisenstadt and Stein Rokkan, *Building States and Nations*. Beverly Hills, Calif.: Sage.
   1974b. "Dimensions of State Formation and Nation-Building." Pp. 562–600 in Charles Tilly, *The Formation of Nation States in Western Europe*. Princeton: Princeton University Press.
Rose, Arnold. 1955. "Sociology and the Study of Values." *British Journal of Sociology* 6(4):1–17.
Rose, Richard. 1985. "The Programme Approach to the Growth of Government." *British Journal of Political Science* 15(1):1–28.
Ross, Alan Anderson. 1962. "Logic, Norms and Roles." *Ratio* 4:36–49.
Ross, Davis. 1969. *Preparing for Ulysses: Politics and Veterans during World War II*. New York: Columbia University Press.
Rothman, David. 1982. "Who Speaks for the Retarded? The Rights and Needs of Devalued Persons." Pp. 8–27 in Stanley Hauerwas, *Responsibility for Devalued Persons*. Springfield, Ill.: Thomas.

289

References

Rothschild, Joseph. 1981. *Ethnopolitics, A Conceptual Framwork*. New York: Columbia Univeristy Press.

Rothschild-Whitt, Joyce and Allan Whitt. 1986. *Work without Bosses*. Cambridge: Cambridge University Press.

Rothstein, Bo. 1992. "Labor-Market Institutions and Working-Class Strength." Pp. 33–56 in Sven Steinmo, Kathleen Thelen, and Frank Longstreth, *Structuring Politics*. Cambridge: Cambridge University Press.

—— 1996. *The Social Democratic State*. Pittsburgh: University of Pittsburgh Press.

Rucht, Dieter. 1991. "The Study of Social Movements in Western Germany: Between Activism and Social Science." Pp. 175–202 in Dieter Rucht, *Research on Social Movements*. Frankfurt: Campus Verlag.

Rueschemeyer, Dietrich, Evelyne Huber Stephens, and John D. Stephens. 1992. *Capitalist Development and Democracy*. Chicago: University of Chicago Press.

Ruggie, Mary. 1984. *The State and Working Women*. Princeton: Princeton University Press.

Sabatier, Paul. 1991. "Toward Better Theories of the Policy Process." *PS: Political Science and Politics* 24(2):147–56.

Sabel, Charles. 1982. *Work and Politics*. Cambridge: Cambridge University Press.

Sadurski, Wojciech. 1986. "Economic Rights and Basic Needs." Pp. 49–66 in C. J. G. Sampford and D. J. Galligan, *Law, Rights and the Welfare State*. London: Croom-Helm.

Sailor, Wayne, Jacki Anderson, Ann Halvorsen, Kathy Doering, John Filler, and Lori Goetz. 1989. *The Comprehensive Local School*. Baltimore: Paul H. Brookes.

Sales, Arnaud. 1991. "The Private, the Public and Civil Society: Social Realms and Power Structures." *International Political Science Review* 12(4):295–312.

Salmond, John William. 1957. *Jurisprudence*. 11th ed. London: Sweet and Maxwell.

Sandel, Michael. 1982. *Liberalism and the Limits of Justice*. Cambridge: Cambridge University Press.

—— 1984. "The Procedural Republic and the Unencumbered Self." *Political Theory* 12:85–93.

—— 1996. *Democracy's Discontent*. Cambridge, Mass.: Harvard University Press.

Sanders, Heywood. 1980. "Paying for the Bloody Shirt: The Politics of Civil War Pensions." Pp. 137–60 in Barry Rundquist, *Political Benefits*. Lexington, Mass.: D. C. Heath.

Sandin, Robert. 1992. *The Rehabilitation of Virtue*. New York: Praeger.

Sandoz, Ellis. 1993. *The Roots of Liberty: Magna Carta, Ancient Constitution and the Anglo-American Tradition of Rule of Law*. Columbia: University of Missouri Press.

Sani, Giacomo and Giovanni Sartori. 1985. "Polarization, Fragmentation and Competition in Western Democracies." *Acta Politica* 12:346–77.

Sapon-Shevin, Mara. 1990. "Student Support through Cooperative Learning." Pp. 65–79 in William Stainback and Susan Stainback, *Support Networks for Inclusive Schooling*. Baltimore: Paul H. Brookes.

Saunders Peter. 1993. "Citizenship in a Liberal Society." Pp. 57–90 in Bryan Turner, *Citizenship and Social Theory*. Newbury Park, Calif.: Sage.

Sawyer, Malcolm C. 1976. *Income Distribution in OECD Countries*. Paris: OECD.

References

Sawyer, P. H. 1982. *Kings and Vikings: Scandinavia and Europe A.D. 700–1100*. London: Methuen.

Sawyer, P. H. and Birgit Sawyer. 1993. *Medieval Scandinavia*. Minneapolis: University of Minnesota.

Scannell, Yvonne. 1985. "Changing Times for Women's Rights" Pp. 61–72 in Eiléan Ní Chuilleanáin *Irish Women: Image and Achievement*. Dublin: Arlen House.

Schefter, Martin. 1977. "Party and Patronage: Germany, England, and Italy." *Politics and Society* 7:403–55.

Schmid, Günther, Bernd Reissert, and Gert Bruche. 1992. *Unemployment Insurance and Active Labor Market Policy*. Detroit: Wayne State University Press.

Schumacher, Bruno. 1958. *Geschichte Ost- und Westpreussens*. Würtzburg: Holzner Verlag.

Schumpeter, Joseph. 1950. *Capitalism, Socialism and Democracy*. 3d ed. New York: Harper.

Scott, W. R. and J. Meyer. 1983. "The Organization of Societal Sectors." Pp. 129–53 in J. W. Meyer and W. R. Scott, *Organizational Environments*. Newbury Park, Calif.: Sage.

Sears, David and Carolyn Funk. 1991. "The Role of Self-Interest in Social and Political Studies." *Advances in Experimental Social Psychology* 24:1–91.

Selbourne, D. 1991. "Who Would Be a Socialist Citizen?" Pp. 91–104 in Geoff Andrews, *Citizenship*. London: Lawrence and Wishart.

Seligman, Adam. 1992. *The Idea of a Civil Society*. New York: Free Press.

Selznick, Philip. 1949. *TVA and the Grass Roots*. Berkeley: University of California Press.

——— 1957. *Leadership and Administration*. New York: Harper and Row.

——— 1992. *The Moral Commonwealth*. Berkeley: University of California Press.

Sewell, William. 1985. "Ideologies and Social Revolutions: Reflections on the French Case." *Journal of Modern History* 57:57–85.

Shalev, Michael. 1983. "The Social Democratic Model and Beyond." *Comparative Social Research* 6:315–52.

Shapiro, Ian. 1986. *The Evolution of Rights in Liberal Theory*. Cambridge: Cambridge University Press.

Shapiro, Joseph P. 1993. *No Pity: People with Disabilities Forging a New Civil Rights Movement*. New York: Random House.

Shatter, Alan. 1986. *Family Law in the Republic of Ireland*. 3rd Ed. Dublin: Wolfhound Press.

Shelley, Mack. 1983. *The Permanent Majority*. University: University of Alabama Press.

Shelton, Dinah. 1992. "Subsidarity, Democracy and Human Rights." Pp. 43–54 in D. Gomian, *Broadening the Frontiers of Human Rights*. Stockholm: Scandinavian University Press.

Sheehan, Bernard. 1973. *Seeds of Extinction: Jeffersonian Philanthropy and the American Indian*. Chapel Hill, N.C.: University of North Carolina Press.

Sherwin-White, A. N. 1939. *Roman Citizenship*. Oxford: Clarendon Press.

Shklar, Judith. 1991. *American Citizenship: The Quest for Inclusion*. Cambridge, Mass.: Harvard University Press.

Shotter, John. 1993. "Psychology and Citizenship: Identity and Belonging." Pp.

References

115–38 in Bryan Turner, *Citizenship and Social Theory*. Newbury Park, Calif.: Sage.

Showstack-Sassoon, A. 1983. "Civil Society." Pp. 72–4 in Tom Bottomore, *Dictionary of Marxist Thought*. Cambridge, Mass.: Harvard University Press.

Sigel, Roberta and Marilyn Hoskin. 1991. *Education for Democratic Citizenship: A Challenge for Multi-Ethnic Societies*. Hillsdale, N.J.: Lawrence Erlbaum.

Sills, David. 1968. *International Encyclopedia of the Social Sciences*. New York: Macmillan, Free Press.

Simmel, Georg. 1956. *Conflict and the Web Group of Affiliations*. Glencoe, Ill.: Free Press.

Simmons, A. John. 1979. *Moral Principles and Political Obligation*. Princeton: Princeton University Press.

Simpson, J. A. and E. S. C. Wiener. 1989. "Citizen" and "Citizenship." In *The Oxford English Dictionary*. Oxford: Clarendon Press.

Singer, Beth. 1993. *Operative Rights*. Albany: State University of New York Press.

Skocpol, Theda. 1979. *States and Social Revolutions*. Cambridge: Cambridge University Press.

    1985. "Cultural Idioms and Political Ideologies in the Revolutionary Reconstruction of State Power." *Journal of Modern History* 57:86–96.

    1992. *Protecting Soldiers and Mothers*. Cambridge, Mass.: Harvard University Press.

Skocpol, Theda and Ann Orloff. 1986. "Explaining the Origins of Welfare States." Pp. 229–54 in S. Lindenberg, J. Coleman, and S. Nowak, *Approaches to Social Theory*. New York: Russell Sage Foundation.

Smelser, Neil. 1988. *Handbook of the Social Sciences*. Newbury Park, Calif.: Sage.

Smith, Anthony. 1991. *National Identity*. Reno: University of Nevada Press.

Smith, Patricia. 1993. "On Law and Jurisprudence: Feminism and Legal Theory." Pp. 483–91 in Patricia Smith, *Feminist Jurisprudence*. New York: Oxford University Press.

Smith-Lovin, Lynn. 1993. "Can Emotionality and Rationality Be Reconciled?" *Rationality and Society* 5(2):283–93.

Soltwedel, Rüdiger. 1984. *Mehr Markt am Arbeitsmarkt*. Munich: Philosophia Verlag.

Somers, Margaret. 1993. "Citizenship and the Place of the Public Sphere." *American Sociological Review* 58:587–620.

    1995a. "What's Political or Cultural about Political Culture and the Public Sphere?" *Sociological Theory* 13(2):113–44.

    1995b. "Narrating and Naturalizing Civil Society and Citizenship Theory." *Sociological Theory* 13(3):229–74.

Sowell, Thomas. 1984. *Civil Rights: Rhetoric or Reality?* New York: Quill/Morrow.

Soysal, Jasmine. 1994. *The Limits of Citizenship*. Chicago: University of Chicago Press.

Spinner, Jeff. 1994. *The Boundaries of Citizenship*. Baltimore: Johns Hopkins University Press.

Stainback, William, Susan Stainback, and Marsha Forest. 1989. *Educating All Students in the Mainstream of Regular Education*. Baltimore: Paul H. Brookes.

References

Steenbergen, Bart van. 1994. *The Condition of Citizenship*. Thousand Oaks, Calif.: Sage.

Steinmo, Sven. 1989. "Political Institutions and Tax Policy in the United States, Sweden, and Britain." *World Politics* 61:500–35.

Steinmo, Sven, Kathleen Thelen, and Frank Longstreth. 1992. *Structuring Politics*. Cambridge: Cambridge University Press.

Stephens, John D. 1989. "Democratic Transition and Breakdown in Europe, 1870–1939: A Test of the Moore Thesis." *American Journal of Sociology* 94(5):1019–77.

———. 1994. "Review Essay: Welfare State and Employment Regimes." *Acta Sociologica* 37(2); 207–11.

Stephens Huber, Evelyn and John D. Stephens. 1982. "The Labor Movement, Political Power and Workers Participation in Western Europe." *Political Power and Social Theory* 3:215–49.

Stern, Frederick. 1957. *The Citizen Army*. New York: St. Martin's Press.

Stetson, D. 1987. *Womens' Rights in France*. New York: Greenwood Press.

Stinchcombe, Arthur. 1983. *Economic Sociology*. New York: Academic Press.

———. 1985. "The Functional Theory of Social Insurance." *Politics and Society* 14(4):411–30.

Stoecker, Helmuth. 1985. "The Position of Africans in the German Colonies." Pp. 119–30 in Arthur Knoll and Lewis Gann, *Germans in the Tropics*. New York: Greenwood Press.

Stoljar, Samuel. 1984. *An Analysis of Rights*. London: Macmillan.

Strang, David. 1991. "The Inner Incompatibility of Empire and Nation: Popular Sovereignty and Decolonization." *Sociological Perspectives* 35:367–84.

Stråth, Bo and Ralf Torstendahl. 1992. "State Theory and State Development." Pp. 12–37 in Ralf Torstendahl, *State Theory and State Development*. London: Sage.

Streeck, Wolfgang. 1992. *Social Institutions and Economic Performance*. Newbury Park, Calif.: Sage.

Stumpp, Karl. 1973. *The Emigration from Germany to Russia in the Years 1763 to 1862*. Lincoln, Neb.: American Historical Society of Germans from Russia.

Sullivan, William. 1982. *Reconstructing Public Philosophy*. Berkeley: University of California Press.

Sumner, L. W. 1987. *The Moral Foundation of Rights*. Oxford: Clarendon Press.

Suret-Canale, Jean. 1971. *French Colonialism in Tropical Africa, 1900–1945*. London: C. Hurst.

Svarlien, Oscar. 1964. "Citizenship." Pp. 88–89 in Julius Gould and William Kolb, *A Dictionary of the Social Sciences*. New York: Free Press.

Swidler, Anne. 1986. "Culture in Action: Symbols and Strategies." *American Sociological Review* 51(2):273–86.

Taylor, Charles. 1986. "Human Rights: The Legal Culture." In UNESCO, *Philosophical Foundations of Human Rights*. Paris: UNESCO.

———. 1989. *Sources of the Self: The Making of the Modern Identity*. Cambridge: Cambridge University Press.

———. 1990. "Modes of Civil Society." *Public Culture* 3(1):95–118.

Taylor, Charles and Michael Hudson. 1972. *World Handbook of Political and Social Indicators*. 2d ed. New Haven: Yale University Press.

References

Taylor, Charles and David Jodice. 1983. *World Handbook of Political and Social Indicators.* 3d ed. New Haven: Yale University Press.

Tenfelde, Klaus. 1977. *Sozialgeschichte der Bergarbeiterschaft an der Ruhr im 19. Jahrhundert.* Bonn–Bad Godesberg: Verlag Neue Gesellschaft.

Tennstedt, Florian. 1977. *Geschichte der Selbsverwaltung in der Krankenversicherung.* Bonn: Verlag der Ortskrankenkassen.

Thränhardt, Anna M. 1990. "Traditional Neighborhood Associations in Industrial Society: The Case of Japan." Pp. 347–60 in Helmut K. Anheier and Wolfgang Seibel, *The Third Sector.* Berlin: De Gruyter.

——— 1992. "Changing Concepts of Voluntarism in Japan." Pp. 278–89 in K. McCarthy, V. Hodgkinson, Russy Sumariwalla, et al., *The Nonprofit Sector in the Global Community.* San Francisco: Jossey-Bass.

Theodore, George and Achiles Theodorson. 1969. *A Modern Dictionary of Sociology.* New York: Cromwell.

Therborn, Göran. 1977. "The Rule of Capital and the Rise of Democracy." *New Left Review* 103(May/June):3–41.

——— 1992a. "The Right to Vote and the Four World Routes to/through Modernity." Pp. 62–91 in Rolf Torstendahl, *State Theory and State History.* Newbury Park, Calif.: Sage.

——— 1992b. "Lessons from 'Corporatist' Theorizations." Pp. 24–43 in Jukka Pekkarinen, Matti Pohjola, and Bob Rowthorn, *Social Corporatism.* Oxford: Clarendon Press.

——— 1995. *European Modernity and Beyond.* Thousand Oaks, Calif.: Sage.

Thomaneck, Jürgen. 1985. "Police and Public Order in the Federal Republic of Germany." Pp. 143–84 in J. Roach and J. Thomaneck, *Police and the Public Order in Europe.* London: Croom-Helm.

Thompson, Dennis. 1970. *The Democratic Citizen.* Cambridge: Cambridge University Press.

Thompson, Michael, Richard Ellis, and Aaron Wildavsky. 1990. *Cultural Theory.* Boulder: Westview Press.

Thomson, Dennis. 1992. "Comparative Politic toward Cultural Isolationists in Canada and Norway." *International Political Science Review* 13(4):433–49.

Thornton, Russell. 1986. *American Indian Holocaust and Survival.* Norman: University of Oklahoma Press.

Tilly, Charles. 1990. "Where Do Rights come From?" Center for Studies of Social Change, New School for Social Research, Working Paper Series no. 98, July.

——— 1991. *Coercion, Capital, and European States, AD 990–1990.* London: Basil Blackwell.

Titmuss, Richard. 1963. "The Social Division of Welfare." Pp. 34–55 in Richard Titmuss, *Essays on the Welfare State.* London: Allen Unwin.

Tocqueville, Alexis de. 1968. "Memoir on Pauperism." Pp. 1–27 in Seymour Drescher, *Tocqueville and Beaumont on Social Reform.* New York: Harper and Row.

——— 1969. *Democracy in America.* New York: Doubleday.

Torney, Judith, A. Oppenheim, and Russell Farnen. 1975. *Civic Education in Ten Countries: An Empirical Study.* New York: Halsted Press.

Traxler, Franz. 1990. "Political Exchange, Collective Action and Interest Governance." Pp. 37–67 in Bernd Marin, *Governance and Generalized Exchange.* Frankfurt: Campus Verlag.

References

Treu, Tiziano. 1992. *Participation in Public Policy-Making*. Berlin: De Gruyter.

Tuck, Richard. 1979. *Natural Rights Theories: Their Origin and Development*. Cambridge: Cambridge University Press.

Turner, Bryan. 1986a. *Citizenship and Capitalism*. London: Allen Unwin.

⸻ 1986b. "Personhood and Citizenship." *Theory, Culture and Society* 3(1):1–16.

⸻ 1988. *Status*. Minneapolis: University of Minnesota Press.

⸻ 1990. "Outline of a Theory of Citizenship." *Sociology* 24:189–217.

⸻ 1991. "Further Specification of the Citizenship Concept: A Reply to M. L. Harrison." *Sociology* 25(2):215–18.

⸻ 1992. "Citizenship, Social Change and the Neofunctionalist Paradigm." Pp. 214–37 in Paul Colomy, *The Dynamics of Social Systems*. Newbury Park, Calif.: Sage.

⸻ 1993a. "Contemporary Problems in the Theory of Citizenship." Pp. 1–18 in Bryan Turner, *Citizenship and Social Theory*. Newbury Park, Calif.: Sage.

⸻ 1993b. "Outline of a Theory of Human Rights." Pp. 162–90 in Bryan Turner, *Citizenship and Social Theory*. Newbury Park, Calif.: Sage.

⸻ 1993c. *Citizenship and Social Theory*. Newbury Park, Calif.: Sage.

⸻ 1994. "Postmodern Culture/Modern Citizens." Pp. 155–68 in Bart van Steenbergen, *The Condition of Citizenship*. Newbury Park, Calif.: Sage.

Turner, Jonathan, and Randall Collins. 1989. "Toward a Microtheory of Structuring." Pp. 118–30 in Jonathan Turner, *Theory Building in Sociology*. Newbury Park, Calif.: Sage.

Tushnet, Mark. 1984. "An Essay on Rights." *Texas Law Review* 62(8):1363–1403.

Tussman, Joseph. 1960. *Obligation and the Body Politic*. Oxford: Oxford University Press.

Tversky, A. and D. Kahneman. 1981. "The Framing of Decisions and the Rationality of Choice." *Science* 211:453–8.

Tyler, Tom R. 1990. *Why People Obey the Law*. New Haven: Yale University Press.

Unger, Roberto. 1987. *False Necessity*. Cambridge: Cambridge University Press.

United Nations. 1993. *Human Development Report – 1993*. New York: United Nations.

Van der Burght, G. 1990. *Dutch Matrimonial Property and Inheritance Law and Its Fiscal Implications*. Deventer: Kluwer.

Van der Wal, Koo. 1990. "Collective Human Rights." Pp. 83–98 in Jan Berting et al., *Human Rights in a Pluralist World*. Westport, Conn.: Meckler.

Vanhanen, Tatu. 1984. *The Emergence of Democracy*. Helsinki: Societas Scientiarum Fennica.

Verba, Sidney and Norman Nie. 1972. *Participation in America: Social Equality and Political Democracy*. New York: Harper and Row.

Verba, Sidney, Norman Nie, and Jae-On Kim. 1978. *Participation and Political Equality*. Cambridge: Cambridge University Press.

Verba, Sidney and Lucien Pye. 1978. *The Citizen and Politics: A Comparative Perspective*. Stamford, Conn.: Greylock.

Verba, Sidney, Kay Lehman Schlozman, and Henry Brady. 1996. *Voice and Equality: Civic Voluntarism in American Politics*. Cambridge, Mass.: Harvard University Press.

Vernon, Richard. 1986. *Citizenship and Order*. Toronto: University of Toronto Press.

References

Visser, Jelle. 1989. *European Trade Unions in Figures*. Deventer: Kluwer Law.

Vogel, Ursula. 1991. "Is Citizenship Gender-Specific?" Pp. 58–85 in Ursual Vogel and Michael Moran, *The Frontiers of Citizenship*. New York: St. Martin's Press.

Vogel, Ursula and Michael Moran. 1991. *The Frontiers of Citizenship*. New York: St. Martin's Press.

Waldron, Jeremy. 1981. "A Right to Do Wrong." *Ethics* 92(1):21–39.

——— 1984. *Theories of Rights*. Oxford: Oxford University Press.

——— 1987. *Nonsense upon Stilts: Bentham, Burke and Marx on the Rights of Man*. London: Methuen.

——— 1993. *Liberal Rights*. Cambridge: Cambridge University Press.

Wallerstein, Immanuel. 1989. *The Modern World System III*. New York: Academic Press.

Walzer, Michael. 1970. *Obligations: Essays on Disobedience, War and Citizenship*. Cambridge, Mass.: Harvard University Press.

——— 1983. *Spheres of Justice*. New York: Basic Books.

——— 1989. "Citizenship." Pp. 211–19 in Terence Ball, James Farrand, and Russell Hanson, *Political Innovation and Conceptual Change*. Cambridge: Cambridge University Press.

——— 1990. "The Communitarian Critique of Liberalism." *Political Theory* 18(1): 6–23.

Warren, Mark. 1992. "Democratic Theory and Self-Transformation." *American Political Science Review* 86(1):8–23.

Wasserman, Jack. 1991. "Citizenship." In *Americana Encyclopedia*. New York: Grolier.

Weale, Albert. 1983. *Political Theory and Social Policy*. New York: St. Martin's Press.

——— 1991. "Citizenship beyond Borders." Pp. 155–64 in Ursula Vogel and Michael Moran, *The Frontiers of Citizenship*. New York: St. Martin's Press.

Weaver, R. Kent and Bert Rockman. 1993a. "When and How Do Institutions Matter?" Pp. 445–61 in R. K. Weaver and B. Rockman, *Do Institutions Matter?* Washington, D.C.: Brookings Institution.

——— 1993b. "Institutional Reform and Constitutional Design." Pp. 462–82 in R. K. Weaver and B. Rockman, *Do Institutions Matter?* Washington, D.C.: Brookings Institution.

Weber, Max. 1978. *Economy and Society*. Berkeley: University of California Press.

Weir, Margaret and Theda Skocpol. 1985. "State Structures and the Possibilities for 'Keynesian' Responses to the Great Depression in Sweden, Britain and the United States." Pp. 107–68 in Peter Evans, Dietrich Rueschmeyer, and Theda Skocpol, *Bringing the State Back in*. Cambridge: Cambridge University Press.

Wellman, Carl. 1982. *Welfare Rights*. Totowa, N.J.: Rowman and Allanheld.

——— 1985. *A Theory of Rights: Persons under Laws, Institutions, and Morals*. Totowa, N.J.: Rowman and Allanheld.

——— 1995. *Real Rights*. New York: Oxford University Press.

——— 1997. *An Approach to Rights*. Dordrecht: Kluwer Academic.

Wenig, Mary M. 1995. "Marital Property and Community Property." Pp. 442–48 in David Levinson, *Encyclopedia of Marriage and the Family*. New York: Macmillan.

References

Wexler, Philip. 1990. "Citizenship in the Semiotic Society." Pp. 164–75 in Bryan Turner, *Theories of Modernity and Post-modernity*. Newbury Park, Calif.: Sage.

White, Alan. 1984. *Rights*. Oxford: Clarendon Press.

1987. *Methods of Metaphysics*. London: Croom-Helm.

Wilensky, Harold. 1975. *The Welfare State and Equality*. Berkeley: University of California Press.

1976. *The New Corporatism, Centralization and the Welfare State*. Beverly Hills, Calif.: Sage.

Williamson, John and Fred Pampel. 1993. *Old-Age Security in Comparative Perspective*. New York: Oxford University Press.

Willis, Paul. 1977. *Learning to Labor*. Farnborough: Saxon House.

Wilmer, Franke. 1993. *The Indigenous Voice in World Politics*. Newbury Park: Sage.

Wilson, Frank L. 1990. "Neo-corporatism and the Rise of New Social Movements." Pp. 67–83 in Russell Dalton and Manfred Keuchler, *Challenging the Political Order*. Oxford: Oxford University Press.

Wilson, James Q. 1995. *On Character*. Washington, D.C.: American Enterprise Institute.

1997. *Moral Judgement*. New York: Basic Books.

Wolgast, Elizabeth. 1987. *The Grammar of Justice*. Ithaca: Cornell University Press.

Wright, Martin. 1991. *Justice for Victims and Offenders*. Milton Keynes: Open University Press.

Wuthnow, Robert. 1989. *Communities of Discourse*. Cambridge, Mass.: Harvard University Press.

1991a. *Acts of Compassion: Caring for Others and Helping Ourselves*. Princeton: Princeton University Press.

1991b. *Between States and Markets*. Princeton: Princeton University Press.

Wyzan, Michael. 1990. *The Political Economy of Ethnic Discrimination and Affirmative Action*. New York: Praeger.

Xie, Yu. 1992. "The Log-Multiplicative Layer Effect Model for Comparing Mobility Tables." *American Sociological Review*. 57(3):380–95.

Yamagishi, Toshio and Karen Cook. 1993. "Generalized Exchange and Social Dilemmas." *Social Psychology Quarterly* 56(4):235–48.

Yates, Jonathan. 1988. " 'Reality' on Capitol Hill." *Newsweek*, November 26, p. 12.

Yazawa, Melvin. 1984. "Citizenship." Pp. 199–209 in Jack Greene, *Encyclopedia of American Political History*. New York: Scribners.

Yishai, Yael. 1990. "State and Welfare Groups: Competition or Cooperation?" *Nonprofit and Voluntary Sector Quarterly* 19(3):215–35.

Zald, Mayer. 1985. "Political Change, Citizenship Rights and the Welfare State." *Annals of American Politics* 479:48–66.

Subject Index

Subject Index

Subject Index

Development over decades (*cont.*)
naturalization extension, 144, 145*t*, 146–7, 171; patronage, 154–5, 162*f*; policy domain, 157–8; policy streams, 157–8, 159, 172; policy outcomes, 162*f*; problem stream, 159; professionals, 146; public goods extension, 145*f*, 146, 171; riots, 150–1*t*, 153; root causes, 162*t*; sacrifice extension, 145*f*, 146, 171; settling countries, 144, 168; social demands, 148, 149–54, 168, 170*f*, 171, 173, 175, 222, 258n5, 259n11; social movements, 143, 150–1*t*, 152–4, 160; stability, 153–4; state formation, 8, 148, 156–8, 162*f*; state structures, 143, 148, 171, 222; trade unions, 149, 150–1*t*, 152–4, 163; war, 143, 164–7
Development over centuries, 25–7, 105, 173–216, 261–4; bourgeoise, 105, 185, 188; power, 190–1*t*, 216, 223, 262n13; capital, 173–4, 177–8, 180, 216; economic coercion, 182, 216; weaknesses, 194–5*t*, 196–7*t*, 263n16; cities, 173, 178, 180, 181*f*, 185, 186–7*t*, 189; coalition formation, 185, 188–9, 190–1*t*, 194–5*t*, 196–7*t*, 198, 199, 216, 258–9n6; coercion, 178, 180, 182; colonialization, 184; deterministic aspects, 216, 258n4 (*see also* Development . . . , rescissions); escapes from taxes, 178, 179*f*, 184–5, 186–7*t*; escapes from conscription, 179*f*, 183, 185, 186–7*t*; excluding conflict, 258n1; factories, 173; formation of rights, 174–99, 216; french revolution, 184; geo-political isolation, 179*f*, 184; Glorious revolution 188; industrial revolution, 180, 184, 185, 188, 190–1*t*; industrialization, 194–5*t*, 196–7*t*; manufacturing, 194–5*t*, 196–7*t*; landed upper class, 185–6, 190–1*t*, 216, 223, 262n13; medieval constitutionalism, 27, 178, 179*f*, 180, 183; independentparliaments, 186–7*t*; military-bureaucratic absolutism, 179*t*, 180, 182, 184, 185, 186–7*t*, 190–1*t*, 199, 216, 231; military revolution, 173; ministry of labor, 192–3, 194–5*t*, 196–7*t*, 223; neutrality, 193; parliaments, 185, 186–7*t*; proportional representation, 49, 194–5*t*, 196–7*t*, 216; population of aged, 194–5*t*; populist absolutism, 184, 186–7*t*; power resources, 223–4; proto-democratic base, 184; proto - states, 184; rescissions, 5, 149, 154, 174, 176, 200, 216 (*see also* Sequencing citizenship rights, rescissions) revolutionary break, 188, 190–1*t*, 263n14; Roman legal system, 192–3, 194–5*t*, 196–7*t*, 198, 216, 223; sequencing of rights, 4, 173, 176, 199–213, 214–15*t*, 216, 223–4; social movements, 4, 173–5, 180, 181*f*, 182; organized working class, 190–1*t*, 194–5*t*, 196–7*t*, 198, 216, 223; state structures, 174, 198, 216, 223–4; strong state, 190–1*t*; welfare systems, 181*f*; strong welfare state, 196–7*t*, 198, 216; working class, 5, 24, 148, 147, 162*f*, 163, 231, 263n16; war, 173–5, 177–8, 179*f*, 180, 181*f*, 182–3, 186–7*t*; war solidarity, 192–3, 194–5*t*, 196–7*t*, 198–9, 216, 222
Development, theories of, over decades, 144–8, 148–71; elite theory, 27, 171, 173–4, 176–7, 231; coalitions, 160–3; modernization, 176, 255n24; power resources theory, 27, 142–3, 146–7, 148–54, 160, 172, 175–7, 189, 193, 222–4; state centric theory, 27, 142–3, 146–8, 154–60, 172, 222, 224; theoretical synthesis, 160, 172, 222–4; trade-off theories, 157, 158–9, 164; over centuries, 173–216, 261nn1&2, 262n3; developmental perspective; Flora, 174, 176; dictatorship and democracy trajectories, Moore, 174–5, 223; elite strategy, Mann, 4, 173–4; inside-out approach, Therborn, 174, 176–7; power resources theory, Korpi, 173, 174, 175–6, 193; sequencing theory, Marshall, 4, 27, 174–6, 199–213; state-centric theory, 193, 199; state structure, 194–95*t*, 196–7*t*, 223; theoretical synthesis, 222–4; war and citizenship, Tilly and Downing, 173–4, 177–8, 179*f*, 180, 181*f*, 182–3, 223; war, Titmus, 182–5
Deviance, 235
Disability, 32, 46–7, 121, 143, 153, 232, 240–1n16, 248n24
Disappearances 36–7*t*
Discourse, 132–3, 225
Dissent, 60–1, 72
Doing, 29–30, 30*t*, 243n3
Double voting, 50
Downs Syndrome parents groups, 14
Draft, 60
Duty, 249n8 (*see also* Obligation)

Economic democracy, 33, 50
Economic rights or economic civil rights, 29, 42, 45, 243n2, 246n14, 247n20

Subject Index

Subject Index

Separatism, 48, 248n27

Sequencing citizenship rights, 4, 27, 172, 173, 199–201, 202–3t, 204–7, 208–9t, 210–11t, 212–13, 214–15t, 216, 223–4, 263n22; criticisms of sequencing, 199–200, 224, 258n4; legal rights (mens property, religion speech, women's property), 200–1, 202–3t, 207, 212–13; participation rights (works councils, active labor market policy, codetermination), 206, 210–11t, 207, 212–13; political rights (voting for propertied males, all males, women, ethnic/racial groups), 201, 204–5t, 20, 212–13; rescissions, 174, 200, 202–3t, 204–5t, 207, 212, 216 (*see also* Development over centuries, recissions), social rights (workmen's compensation, old age pensions, health and sickness, unemployment insurance, family allowances); 206, 207, 208–9t, 212–13; skipping steps, 213, 216, 224

Settler countries, 143–4, 167, 168

Sexual preference, 143 (*see also* Gays)

Sicily, 116

Slavery, 144, 149, 188, 200

Social action, (Weberian), 85–7, 86t, 88t, 103, 221; active, 29–30; conventions, 86t; affectual action, *see* Social action, emotional action; emotional action, 85, 86t, 103, 221, 253–4n12; informal sanctions, 86t; legal norms, 86t; passive 29–30; rational action, 85, 86t, 87, 88t, 221; formal rationality, 86t, 87, 88t; practical rationality, 86t, 87, 88t; substantive rationality, 86t, 87, 88t; theoretical rationality, 86t, 87, 88t; rational action, 85, 86t, 221

Social closure, 82, 84, 104, 123–4, 137t, 138t, 139, 141, 165–6, 222, 225, 235–6, 265nn8&9

Social contract, 133

Social democratic parties, 122, 149, 153, 156, 149, 161; SPD in Germany, 149, 161, SAP in Sweden, 122, 156, 161

Social democracy, 105, 153

Social inequality, 123–4, 126–7t, 137t, 138f, 222, 230, 250n12, 255n23; Gini index, 126–7t, 170f

Socialization, 59, 92, 99, 103, 107, 119, 222, 257n16; anthems, 101; status transmission, 99; parental socialization, 99, 119; pledges, 101; primary, 92, 103; schooling, 101–2

Social mobility, 20, 49, 100, 102, 118, 119, 123–4, 137t, 138t, 140, 149,

163, 168, 222, 236; social fluidity (β), 127t; social immobility (ø–Q_x), 127t; total mobility (TMR), 127t, 152, 163

Social movements, 1, 4, 7, 14–15, 24, 46–7, 85, 97, 107, 121–2, 123, 140, 142–3, 146, 150–1t, 152–4, 160, 173, 264n4

Social norms, 84

Social partners, 115

Social policy implications, 232–6

Social transfer payments, 130–1t

Soldiers, 170f, 177, 182

Solidarity, 79–80, 81, 85, 124, 140, 165, 216

Solidarity movement in Poland, 114

South Africa (Union of), 251n21, 261n20

South America, 177

Spain, 184, 186–7t

State, models of, *see* Regime theory

State centric theory, 142, 154, 199, 146–7, 154

State capacities, 143, 152, 154; strong state, 155, 171, 173

State formation, 154

State mobilization, 142–3, 146–7, 164–71, 173, 181f; total mobilization for war, 182

State structures, 143, 171, 174, 181f, 198, 223

Status, 6, 11, 19, 25, 48, 107, 114, 118, 122, 138f, 140, 147, 148–9, 154, 163, 168, 171, 180, 182, 222, 243–4n3, 258n3

Stigmatized groups, 9

Strikes, 115, 119, 245n13

Structured polity approach, *see* State centric theory

Subjects, 9, 101, 142, 182

Supererogation, 62–3

Supermarket state, 81, 253n9

Sweden, 22, 23t, 24, 33, 34t, 36–7t, 40–1t, 57t, 58t, 68, 70, 112, 113f, 114, 119, 122, 123, 126–7t, 128, 130–1t, 132, 134–5t, 146, 149, 150–1t, 155–7, 161–3, 166–7t, 176, 184, 186–7t, 190–1t, 193, 194–5t, 196–7t, 202–3t, 204–5t, 207, 208–9t, 210–11t, 213, 214–15t, 233, 243n32, 252n26, 253n2, 257n20, 258n6, 259n7, 260n15, 262n4

Switzerland, 23t, 34t, 36–7t, 40–1t, 57t, 58t, 126–7t, 130–1t, 134–5t, 150–1t, 166–7t, 176, 177, 186–7t, 188, 190–1t, 192, 193, 194–5t, 196–7t, 198, 201, 202–3t, 204–5t, 208–9t, 210–11t, 214–15t, 245n10, 259n8

System of rights, 54, 73, 218

Tasmanian people (Australia), 167
Taxes, 6, 26, 44, 53, 57t, 63, 70, 74,
80–1, 91, 95, 112, 120, 125, 128, 129,
130–1t, 137t, 141, 147, 168, 177,
181f, 183, 207, 219, 220, 228, 234,
252n26; domestic extraction, 179t;
taxpayer, 83
Tolerance, 141, 169, 220, 228
Torture, 36–7t, 179, 180
Tory politics, 87
Tracks of history, 164; tracklaying
vehicles, 164
Trade associations, 125
Trade unions, 7, 12, 39, 114, 117–19,
120, 132, 134–5t, 136t, 147, 149, 150–
1t, 152, 154, 163–4, 218, 222, 245–
6n13; craft, 149; strength of working
class, 152, 154, 188–9, 196–7t, 223;
economistic and job control unionism,
164
Trickledown economics, 133, 136
Turkey, 265n8
Turkish workers, 111
Trust, 26, 76, 79, 81–2, 87–92, 101–3,
116, 120, 140, 254n13; community,
89–90; predictability, 87; social
concern, 82, 87; time, 89–90

Ungovernability, 117
Unions, see Trade unions
Union of Soviet Socialist Republics
(USSR), 48, 60, 245n8, 251n21
United Autoworkers (UAW), 117
United Kingdom, 3, 4, 6, 7, 22, 23t, 34t,
36–7t, 40–1t, 50, 57t, 58t, 105, 113f,
126–7t, 130–1t, 133, 134–5t, 146, 150–
1t, 166–7t, 169, 172, 174–6, 183–5,
186–7t, 189, 190–1t, 192, 194–5t, 196–
7t, 202–3t, 201, 204–5t, 206, 208–9t,
210–11t, 214–15t, 231, 242n31,
245n10, 255n23, 257n13,
257nn20&21, 262n12, 263nn14&16,
264n24; Glorius Revolution 188;
Magna Carta 256n2
United States, 2, 17, 22, 23t, 24, 32, 34t,
36–7t, 40–1t, 48, 50, 53, 56, 57t, 58t,
67–8, 109, 111–12, 113f, 114, 120,
122, 126–7t, 128, 130–1t, 132–3, 134–
5t, 149, 150–1t, 152, 156, 158–9, 161–
4, 166–7t, 168, 174–6, 183, 188, 190–
1t, 194–5t, 196–7t, 200, 202–3t, 204–
5t, 206, 208–9t, 210–11t, 212, 214–
15t, 217, 232–6, 245nn8&9, 245n13,
251n21, 257nn19,21,&24, 262n17,
262n12, 264–5n5; American South,
164, 188, 245n9, 246n17, 259n7,
265nn8&9

United States of Europe, 265n8
United Way, 14, 117
Universalism, 8–9, 25, 28, 35–6, 38, 49,
110, 140, 142, 143–4, 146–7, 156,
162f, 164, 168–9, 171, 182, 200, 230,
247n17
Urbanization, 103

Vacations, 233–4
Values, 264n1
Veterans, 32, 128, 144, 145f, 146–9,
164–5, 222
Veterans Administration, 156, 157, 164,
248n1, 247n17
Veto group, 115
Vietnam War, 252n27
Vinland (short-lived Viking settlement in
America), 169
Violence, 173
Voluntary associations, 14, 17, 26, 80, 82,
84, 107, 112–14, 122–3, 129, 132–3,
134–5t, 136t, 137t, 139, 157, 158,
163, 229, 239n11, 257nn24&25,
264n4; three views of, 107
Volunteering, 7, 10, 67, 79, 101, 128, 220,
229; national service, 220, 221, 229
Voting, 7, 31t, 35, 35t, 34t, 128, 130–1t,
149, 150–1t, 229, 257n7 (see also
Franchise)

Wage depression, 168
Wage restraint, 120, 120f, 125, 153
Wagner–Peyser Act, 155
Walloons, 48, 118
War, 3, 105, 128, 142, 143–4, 146, 162f,
164–5, 172–3, 178–83, 216, 219–20,
223, 255n1, 257n20, 262–3n13;
American Civil War, 164, 182;
military occupation, 108, 193, 194–5t,
223; neutrality, 164–5, 193; Northern
War, 184; pressures, 178–9; Thirty
Years War, 184; war variable, 193,
195; Vietnam War, 252n27
Wasps, 173, 178
Weise Ring, 69–70
Welfare state, 43, 50, 109, 112, 120, 129,
136, 140, 148–9, 154–6, 181f, 192–3,
194–5t, 259n10; financing by
insurance, 129; financing by general
revenue, 129; social transfer payments,
130–1t
Welfare state regimes, see entries under
Regime
World systems theory, 7, 154, 164–71
Women, 41t, 42, 46, 49 121, 147–8,
162f, 175, 180, 182, 200–1,
240nn12&13, 247n17, 265n7

Subject Index

Working class, 5, 24, 148, 147, 162*f*, 163 (*see also* Class)
Work organization, 225
Works councils, 24, 28, 43, 50, 114, 130–1*t*, 189, 190–1*t*, 192–3, 196–7*t*, 198–9, 211
World War I, 164, 262n7
World War II, 32, 51, 106, 144, 149, 164–
5, 169, 188, 193, 194–5*t*, 200–1, 237n1, 262n7, 265n6

Yugoslavia, 49

Zone of indifference, 62–4
Zoning, 241n20

Name Index

Abbott, Andrew, 174, 206, 209, 263–4n22
Abraham, David, 163, 189
Adler, Stephen, 53
Alber, Jens, 154, 174, 176, 228, 237n1, 261n2
Albertini, Rudolf von, 171
Alejandro, Roberto, 237n1
Alford, Robert, 249n6
Allen, C. K., 253n1
Almond, Gabriel, 9, 95, 98, 229, 237n1, 239n11, 254n21, 255n24
Alpsten, B, 70
Amenta, Edwin, 260n13, 260n17
Ames, Walter, 70
Andaleeb, Syed Saad, 254n13
Andersen, Bent Rold, 76, 253n2
Anderson, James, 60
Andrain, Charles, 42
Arato, Andrew, xi, 7, 8, 12, 241n17
Archer, Clive, 70
Aristotle, 237n1
Aron, Raymond, 72
Austin, John, 253n1
Axelrod, Robert, 84–5, 119, 253n11, 254n17

Bacharach, Samuel, 93
Baer, Douglas, 132, 135, 136
Bailey, Stephen, 260n15
Baldwin, Peter, 163, 185, 188, 191, 199
Banfield, Edward, 116
Barbalet, J. M., 3, 6, 7, 85, 148, 237n1, 243n2
Barber, Benjamin, 28, 227, 242n24
Barber, Bernard, 87–8, 93
Barclay, David, 156
Bayley, David, 68, 70, 252n24
Bean, R., 151
Becker, Harold, 70
Beiner, Ronald, 238n4

Bellah, Robert, 7, 108, 229, 240n11
Bendix, Reinhard, xi, 4, 7, 28, 29, 42, 237n1, 243n3, 258n1, 258n4
Benn, S., 246n16, 253n1
Bennett, William, 249n2
Bentham, Jeremy, 253n1
Bergmann, Joachim, 153
Bergmann, Jorg, 69
Berg-Schlosser, Dirk, 261n1
Berry, Jeffrey, 100, 255n26
Billis, David, 12
Bismarck, Otto von, 259nn10&11
Blackburn, Robert, 237n1
Bobbio, Norberto, 7
Bohman, James, 242n24
Boli, John, 21, 123, 133
Borgatta, Edgar, 238n10
Borgatta, Marie, 238n10
Boswell, Jonathan, 118
Bottomore, Tom, 9, 237n1
Boudon, Raymond, 238n10
Bourricaud, Franois, 238n10
Bowles, Samuel, 237n1, 244n3
Bradley, F. H., 253n1
Brady, Henry, 98, 229, 257n21
Braithwaite, John, 69
Brewer, John, 70
Bridges, Thomas, 25, 237n1, 238n4
Bridges, William, 3
Briggs, Vernon, 168
Brinkmann, Carl, 238n5, 240n15
Brissot, Jacques-Pierre, 52
Brody, David, 161
Brown, David W., 66–7, 70, 73, 252n22
Brubaker, W. Rodgers, 8, 10, 72, 165, 228, 235, 237n1, 252n28
Bruche, Gert, 115, 129
Budge, Ian, 228, 260n13
Bulkeley, William, 81
Bulmer, Martin, 95, 254n21

311

Name Index

Burger, Julian, 168
Burstein, Paul, 146, 157, 260n16
Byrne, James, 69

Calhoun, Craig, xi
Callero, Peter, 229
Campbell, John C., 121, 231, 253n10
Caracalla, 240n12
Carruthers, Bruce, 260n13
Carter, Stephen, 249n2
Castles, Francis G., 243n32
Chambers, John W., 128, 220
Chambré, Susan Maisel, 93, 229
Cloward, Richard, 131, 160
Cnaan, Ram, 242n32
Cohen, Jean, 7, 8, 12, 241n17
Cohen, Michael, 159
Coleman, James, 45, 94–5, 247n22,
    254n13, n15, n17–20
Collins, Randall, 85, 90
Commons, John, 246n15
Connor, W, 168
Conover, Pamela, xi, 228, 237n1, 239n11
Cook, Chris, 151
Cook, Karen, 84, 93, 253n8,
    254nn16&18
Cook, Rebecca, 41
Cranston, Maurice, 253n1
Crouch, Colin, 75–6, 115, 118, 125
Culpitt, Ian, 42, 237n1
Curtis, James, 132, 135, 136

Dagger, Richard, 102–3, 105, 237n1,
    256n3
Dahl, Robert, 109, 244n7, 261n1
Dahrendorf, Ralf, 1, 48, 90, 104, 237n1,
    242n24, 249n2
Daley, Caroline, 205
Damon, Frederick, 76
Dan-Cohen, Meir, 47, 48, 244n5
Daniels, Arlene Kaplan, 229
Dawson, William, 259n10
Day, Neil, 75, 237n1, 255n21
de Meur, Gisèle, 261n1
Demo, David, 92–3
Devine, Fiona, 254n21
Deviney, Stanley, 174, 206, 209, 263n22
Dewey, John, 20
Dietz, Mary, 237n1
Dimaggio, Paul, 158, 253n4, 256n5
Domhoff, G. William, 160, 258n3
Donati, Pierpaolo, 241n18
Dore, Ronald, 237n1
Downing, Brian, 106, 163, 173, 174, 177,
    178–87, 191, 199, 231, 259n6
Dryzek, John, 164
Dufty, N. F., 254n21

Durkheim, Emile, 8, 81, 85
Dworkin, Ronald, 45, 246n16, 247n18,
    253n1

Ekeh, Peter, 24, 61, 76–9, 82–5,
    253nn6&7
Ellis, Richard, 98, 255n24
Elster, Jon, 95
Emerson, Richard, 94, 247n21
England, Paula, 103, 254n16
Entman, Robert, 241n21
Erickson, Robert, 127
Errson, Svante O., 245n10
Esping-Andersen, Gøsta, 18, 21, 22, 105,
    108, 115, 125, 148, 149, 163, 174–6,
    188, 230, 231, 237n1, 242–3n32
Etzioni, Amitai, 2, 7, 20, 53–4, 61, 63–5,
    220, 235, 238n4, 242n28, 248n23,
    249n2, 250n12, 251n19
Eyerman, Ron, 153

Fierlbeck, Katherine, 237n1
Finkel, S., 100
Fishkin, James, 62–3, 233, 236, 242n24,
    250n9, 250–1n13
Fitch, Frederic, 246n15
Flanz, Gisbert, 201, 205
Flathman, Richard, 250n8
Flora, Peter, 174, 176, 191, 228, 237n1,
    261n2
Fogelman, Ken, xi, 101
Ford, Henry, 254n19
Foster, C., 42, 248n29
Franz, Wolfgang, 120
Fraser, Nancy, 148, 237n1
Frederick the Great, 259n10
Freeden, Michael, 1
Freeman, Gary, 165, 168, 260n13
Frevert, Ute, 200, 203
Friedland, Roger, 249n6
Friedman, Debra, 94
Friedman, Kathi, 237n1
Friedman, Lawrence, 28
Fromkin, Howard, 93
Funk, Carolyn, 77, 253n3, 255n22

Galie, Peter, 42
Galston, William, 7, 20, 53, 63, 104,
    238n11
Gambetta, Diego, 87, 116
Ganley, Gladys, 256n11
Gergen, Kenneth, 254n16
Gewirth, Alan, 244n3, 250n10
Giddens, Anthony, 10, 29, 42, 44–5, 199,
    237n1, 243n2, 246n14, 247n20,
    258n4
Gintis, Herbert, 237n1, 244n3

312

Name Index

Name Index

Name Index

Name Index